Conquest and Empire

The reign of Alexander the Great

# CONQUEST AND EMPIRE

## The reign of Alexander the Great

### A. B. BOSWORTH

*Professor of Classics and Ancient History,*
The University of Western Australia

The right of the
University of Cambridge
to print and sell
all manner of books
was granted by
Henry VIII in 1534.
The University has printed
and published continuously
since 1584.

**Cambridge University Press**

Cambridge

New York   Port Chester

Melbourne   Sydney

Published by the Press Syndicate of the University of Cambridge
The Pitt Building, Trumpington Street, Cambridge CB2 1RP
40 West 20th Street, New York, NY 10011, USA
10 Stamford Road, Oakleigh, Melbourne 3166, Australia

First published 1988
Reprinted 1989

Printed in Great Britain by Bath Press, Bath, Avon

*British Library cataloguing in publication data*

Bosworth, A. B.
Conquest and empire: the reign of Alexander the Great
1. Alexander, III, King of Macedonia
2. Macedonia – Kings and rulers – Biography
I. Title
938'.07'0924    DF234

*Library of Congress cataloguing in publication data*

Bosworth, A. B.
Conquest and empire: the reign of Alexander the Great/A.B. Bosworth
    p.   cm.
Bibliography.
Includes index.
1. Alexander, the Great, 356–323 BC.
I. Title
DF234.B66   1988
938'.07'0924–dc19
[B]    87-35499 CIP

ISBN 0 521 34320 8 hard covers
ISBN 0 521 34823 4 paperback

DIS MANIBUS
S.F.J.B.

# Contents

# Maps

# Preface

The reign of Alexander the Great has always engrossed the interest of countless readers, and, not surprisingly, the interest has stimulated a flood of biographies. In 1976 it could be said that books on Alexander were appearing at the rate of more than one a year, and the last decade has not witnessed any slackening of publication. A new monograph therefore requires apology and justification. That may in part be provided by the circumstances of writing. Originally this work was conceived as a contribution to Volume VI of the *Cambridge Ancient History*, designed to give a survey of the period for the informed reader, with reference to the most recent literature. What emerged exceeded all reasonable bounds for a general history, and the Cambridge University Press generously undertook to publish a revised version as a book in its own right. My work is a synthesis of recent research and at the same time represents a distillation of my own thinking. It forms part of a tetralogy. My two-volume *Commentary on Arrian's History of Alexander* (part II not yet published) provides the detailed exposition of evidence and technical discussion of historical and textual cruces. The general historiographical principles of research on Alexander are expounded in my new monograph, *From Arrian to Alexander: Studies in Historical Interpretation* (Oxford, 1988). In the present work I draw explicitly on my more specialist studies to provide a composite narrative history of the period. Its justification is primarily comprehensiveness and its basis in recent research. I do not claim exhaustive bibliographical coverage (that would be a herculean and unproductive endeavour), but it is my hope that the reader will be directed immediately to what is new or pertinent.

This book is in no sense intended as a biography of Alexander, which I consider undesirable to attempt and impossible to achieve. Instead I focus on the impact of Alexander in its widest sense, the effect of his conquests upon Macedon, the Greek world and what was formerly the Persian Empire. It is impossible, even if one wished to do so, to avoid the person of Alexander. For better or worse the evidence of the sources is stubbornly centred upon him and he is the ineluctable reference point. The nucleus of the book is necessarily the

campaign narrative, the large chapter entitled 'The gaining of empire'. This
charts the progress of Alexander, the process of conquest, and deals in passing
with events elsewhere. The rest of the book is more synoptic, drawing
together general themes: the history of mainland Greece under Macedonian
suzerainty, the organisation and control of the newly acquired territory, the
evolution of the instrument of conquest, the Macedonian army, and finally the
origins of ruler worship. The narrative chapters cover the theme of conquest,
the thematic ones that of empire. Both parts of the book are connected by a
large number of cross-references, and I hope that my work will be not only
read sequentially but also, as it were, horizontally. The two parts are intended
to be complementary and the effect should be a cumulative picture, the details
expounded in the campaign narrative being recapitulated in the general
synthesis of the thematic studies. That, I hope, does some justice to the
richness and complexity of the period.

My obligations are few and many. Like Sir William Tarn before me (*si
parva licet componere magnis*) I have been forced to work in geographical
isolation, and my physical contacts with other scholars have been confined to
brief periods of leave. That means that my writing is perhaps more personally
oriented than it might have been, and I cannot make acknowledgements of
direct assistance. On the other hand, I am deeply indebted to all scholars
working in the field, who have kept my interest alive and, by and large, treated
my heresies with courtesy and understanding. I am glad yet again to pay
tribute to the teaching and example of Peter Brunt, whose methodological
principles I hope I have not violated too grossly, and to the stimulus of the
published writings and personal friendship of Ernst Badian, who has had the
greatest impact (for good) on Alexander studies throughout the last three
decades. I should also acknowledge the influence of Fritz Schachermeyr, who
has created the most galvanic and evocative Alexander of all time. These are
the masters. *Nobis in arto et inglorius labor.*

This book could not have been written without the support of my university
and in particular its library facilities. I am particularly grateful for a CTEC
Special Research Grant which gave me a term's teaching relief for my writing.
Once more I must express my gratitude to Carol Freele, Kay Sanders and
Susan O'Connor for their efficiency and cheerfulness in the face of a
burdensome manuscript. Finally my especial thanks to my wife who has read
much of the book and put up with it all.

The maps were drawn by David Cox of Cox Cartographic Ltd.

*July 1987*                                                                    A.B.B.

# Abbreviations

Listed below are the most frequently used abbreviations. Otherwise references to literary and epigraphical evidence follow standard conventions, and the citations of journal titles in general conform to the format of *L'Année Philologique*.

| | |
|---|---|
| *FGrH* | F. Jacoby, *Die Fragmente der griechischen Historiker*. Berlin and Leiden, 1923– (see below, p. 296). The ancient authors are there listed by number (i.e. *FGrH* 124 F 7 refers to fragment 7 of the author (Callisthenes) who is numbered 124 by Jacoby) |
| Head, *HN*² | B. V. Head, *Historia Numorum*. 2nd ed. Oxford, 1911 |
| *IG* | *Inscriptiones graecae*. 1st ed. Berlin, 1873– ; 2nd ed. Berlin, 1913– |
| Moretti, *ISE* | L. Moretti, *Iscrizioni Storiche Ellenistiche*. Florence, 1967, 1976 |
| *OGIS* | *Orientis graecae inscriptiones selectae*, ed. W. Dittenberger. 2 vols. Leipzig, 1903–5 |
| *SEG* | *Supplementum epigraphicum graecum*. Leiden, 1923– |
| *SIG*³ | *Sylloge inscriptionum graecarum*, ed. W. Dittenberger. 3rd ed. Leipzig, 1915–24 |
| Tod, *GHI* | M. N. Tod, *A Selection of Greek Historical Inscriptions*. 2: *From 403 to 323 B.C.* Oxford, 1948 |

# I

# GENERAL NARRATIVE

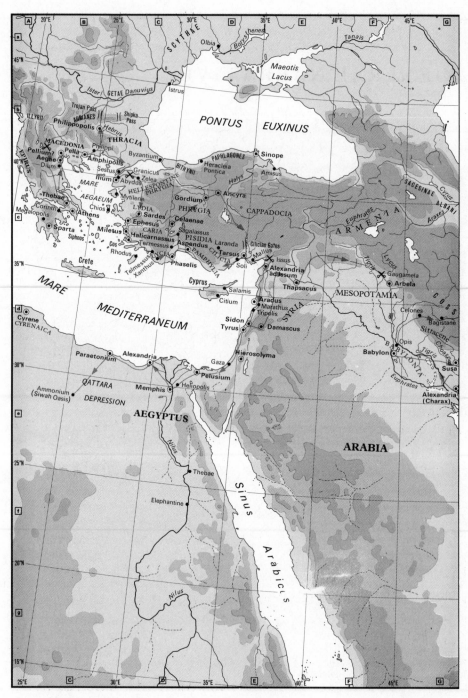

1. *Alexander's empire.*

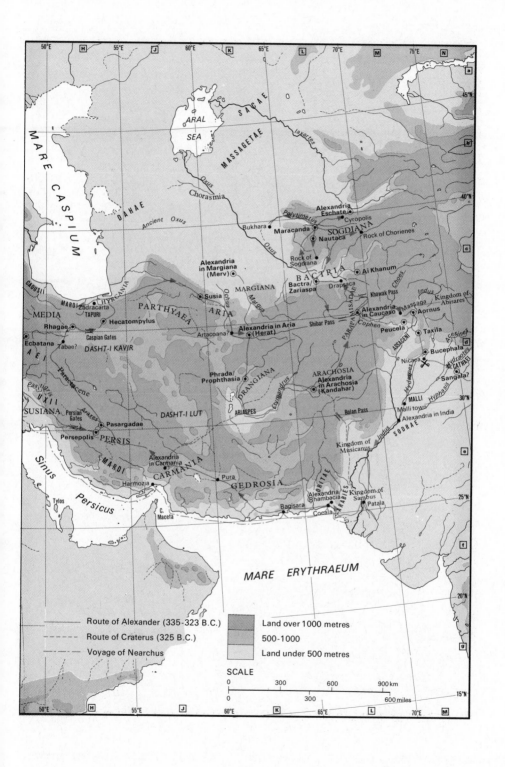

Route of Alexander (335-323 B.C.)
Route of Craterus (325 B.C.)
Voyage of Nearchus

Land over 1000 metres
500-1000
Land under 500 metres

SCALE

| 0 | 300 | 600 | 900 km |

| 0 | 300 | 600 miles |

I

# Prologue

## 1. The legacy of Philip

The period 336–323 B.C. is inevitably designated the age of Alexander. It marked a huge expansion of the imperial boundaries of Macedon, a virtually unparalleled outpouring of resources, material and human. *Imperium terris, animos aequabit Olympo.* The prophecy made for Romulus' foundation applies even more appositely to the milieu of Alexander. His empire was in any sense world-wide, his concept of his person and achievements super-human. From the time of his death his name has been an evocative symbol of worldly glory, alternately eulogised and excoriated as the type of the magnanimous conqueror or the intemperate tyrant; and the history of his reign has all too often been a thinly disguised biography, distorted by the personality and values of its author.[1] This book is an attempt to analyse Alexander's impact on his world without any preconceived model of his personality or motives. *Sine ira et studio* is perhaps an impossible ideal, given the controversial and highly emotive nature of some of the subject matter, but one should at least attempt to base one's interpretation upon the extant sources.[2] Even there we may find prejudice enough, but we have some prospect of identifying and discounting bias, both apologetic and vituperative. Our history of the period can only be fragmentary, based on episodes randomly highlighted in the literary tradition or the scattering of documentary evidence preserved by chance. We may not go beyond the material at our disposal. Alexander the man will always elude us, thanks to the distorting filter of ancient (and modern) judgements and our grossly inefficient documentation, but the events of his reign can be discussed in context and the focus is occasionally clear. That is a sufficiently important theme. The face of the world was changed within a decade, and the events and the forces at work are worth exposition and discussion, even if the personalities of the main actors are irretrievable.

With equal justice the period might be termed the age of Philip. The

[1] Interesting digests of modern views of Alexander are given by Schachermeyr 1973, 609–57 and Badian 1976a. See also (on the German scene) Demandt 1972.
[2] See the Bibliography (pp. 295ff.) for a brief review of the source tradition.

Macedon that Alexander inherited was the creation of his father. The army he led was forged by Philip. The material resources of the Macedonian throne were acquired by Philip. The system of alliances which turned the Balkans into a virtual annexe of Macedon was Philip's development, and the war against Persia was launched at the end of Philip's reign. In his first years, at least, Alexander was continuing a process begun by his father, and his reign cannot be understood without constant reference to his predecessor. What follows is in no sense a history of Philip, rather a contextual stage setting to introduce the accession of Alexander.

As is well known, Philip came to power in 359 B.C., when Macedon was threatened with dissolution, debilitated by a decade of dynastic feuding and crippled by military defeat at the hands of the Illyrians. During the next twenty-three years he made a world power out of that ruined inheritance, creating a political, military and financial basis for empire. On the political front Macedon was welded into a unity, focused on the person of the king. That came about partly by coercion. After his decisive early victory over the Illyrians (358) Philip was able to dominate the turbulent principalities of Upper Macedonia (Lyncestis, Orestis, Elimiotis and Tymphaea) which straddled the Pindus range between the upper Haliacmon and Epirus and had traditionally maintained their independence of the monarchy of Macedon proper, based on the lower plains. For the first time they became integral parts of the greater kingdom. Their nobility was absorbed into the court at Pella and achieved distinction under both Philip and Alexander.[3] At the same time they offered a fertile recruiting ground for both infantry and cavalry; no less than three of the original six phalanx battalions of Alexander came from the upper principalities.[4]

The political union was cemented by marriage. Unashamedly polygamous, Philip contracted a sequence of unions, particularly in the early years of his reign. One of his first wives came from Elimiotis (Phila, the sister of Derdas and Machatus), and there is little doubt that the marriage was designed to help the process of annexation. Other wives came from peripheral non-Macedonian areas: Audata from Illyria, Philinna and Nicesipolis from Thessaly and Meda from the Getic North.[5] The most important was the formidable Olympias who came from the royal house of Molossia and was taken to Philip's bed by 357 at latest. This marriage linked together the two dynasties on either side of the Pindus and gave Philip direct influence on the Molossian throne. When he ultimately intervened in Epirus, the reigning king Arybbas was deposed in favour of his nephew, Alexander, the brother of Olympias.[6] These marriages were the linchpins of the great nexus of guest-friends which was to support

---

[3] Note the list of trierarchs in Arr. *Ind.* 18.5–6 and the list of domiciles in Berve 1926, 2.445. The most brilliant, Perdiccas and Craterus, were from Orestis.

[4] See below, p. 259, with the literature there cited.

[5] On Philip's marriages the prime evidence is a famous fragment of Satyrus the Peripatetic (Athen. 557B–E). On the many problems it presents see Martin 1982, 66–70 and Tronson 1984.

[6] Cf. Hammond and Griffith 1979, 2.504–9; *contra* Errington 1975b.

Philip's interests through the Balkans. At the same time the risk of dynastic conflict which they posed was obviated by the clear superiority that Olympias enjoyed over her fellow consorts.

As the king's network of alliances expanded, the influence of his nobility contracted. Philip increased the élite body of royal Companions (*hetairoi*), attracting immigrants from the wider Greek world. Men who would accept his patronage were given lavish donations of land and status at court. Of Alexander's close circle of boyhood friends three (Nearchus of Crete; Erigyius and Laomedon of Mytilene) were non-Macedonian. Other prominent figures, notably the chief secretary, Eumenes of Cardia, came from abroad. Their loyalty was to the king alone. However intimate and important their functions, they stood apart from the rest of the Macedonian hierarchy, never fully accepted and often resented.[7] Even after Alexander's death Eumenes' foreign extraction was a liability when he commanded troops, and his own Macedonians were finally to turn against him with the bitter gibe, 'plague from the Chersonese' (Plut. *Eum*. 18.1).

Philip's lavishness to his new men was matched by benefactions to the old nobility. The new acquisitions of land in Chalcidice and Thrace were parcelled out to new and old alike. Polemocrates, father of the great marshal Coenus, obtained estates in the hinterland of Olynthus.[8] His primary holdings were in Elimiotis, in Upper Macedonia, and he now had interests, directly conferred by the king, in the new territories. Philip was sharing the advantages of conquest while diversifying the power base of his nobility. He also, it seems, founded the institution of the Pages:[9] the sons of prominent nobles received an education at court in the immediate entourage of the king, developing a personal attachment to him while necessarily serving as hostages for the good behaviour of their families. As a result the nobility was simultaneously coerced and rewarded, diluted and diversified. As the frontiers of the kingdom expanded, loyalty to the crown brought tangible rewards, and those rewards involved financial interests and military obligations outside the old baronial centres of power. In the climate of success and expansion there was less incentive to challenge the supremacy of the king at Pella, and even the influx of favoured Companions from beyond the borders was tolerable.

Philip reigned as an autocrat. The political institutions of Macedon were informal and rudimentary, and there were few practical constraints on a strong king. Like his son, Philip presumably consulted an inner council of intimates on major issues of state,[10] but nothing suggests that the council was anything other than advisory. Again, it might be prudential to consult the

---

[7] On the general antipathy between Greeks and Macedonians see Badian 1982, particularly 39–43.

[8] *SIG*³ 332. On the location see Hammond and Griffith 1979, 2.338.

[9] Arr. IV.13.1: cf. Hammond and Griffith 1979, 2.401; cf. 167–8 (though there is no evidence of the institution before Philip; nothing indicates that the assassins of Archelaus were Pages).

[10] Cf. Arr. I.25.4; Curt. VI.8.1–15, 11.9–10. See further Berve 1926, 1.33–4; Bosworth 1980a, 161–2.

opinions of the army on various occasions but there was nothing incumbent on the king to hold regular assemblies and he was in no sense bound by popular opinion.[11] It is suggested that by tradition the army exercised capital jurisdiction,[12] but that is a strictly limited area. Even there procedure was apparently fluid and informal, and there was certainly no body of Macedonian statute law. The king operated in a framework of precedent and tradition but, provided that he had the resources and the personality to assert his will, he could do what he liked with the minimum of consultation. That is the constant lament of Demosthenes, that the Greek *poleis* which had public processes of decision-making could not compete with an immensely shrewd autocrat who concealed his actions and policies.[13] For most effective purposes Philip *was* Macedon. He concluded treaties in his own name with sovereign states, sent his own ambassadors to the Amphictyonic Council, and (like his predecessors) struck coins in his own name. Perhaps the best illustration of the advantages of his position is the fate of the hapless Athenian embassy which travelled to Macedon in the summer of 346 to ratify the Peace of Philocrates. Ratification meant the physical presence of Philip, and the ambassadors were forced to wait impatiently at Pella while the king completed his campaigns in Thrace, increasing the territorial possessions which would be confirmed by the peace. The peace was finally accepted at Pherae, on the eve of his attack on Thermopylae, when it was too late for the Athenians to take effective counter-action.[14] Given that he was the only contractual party on the Macedonian side, his initiative was unlimited.

This considerable freedom of action was underpinned by the huge financial resources of Macedon. The mineral reserves of the kingdom, previously centred in the territory east of the River Axios,[15] were vastly expanded when Philip occupied the site of Crenides in 356 and exploited the rich veins of gold and silver in the neighbouring mines of Mt Pangaeum. According to Diodorus (xvi.8.6) this area alone supplied revenues of more than 1,000 talents and Philip extended his mining operations to Chalcidice, exploiting the deposits in the mountainous terrain north of Olynthus. What is more, as the boundaries of the kingdom expanded, so did its fiscal basis: dues upon landed property and extraordinary levies (*eisphorae*).[16] Philip's financial power was comparatively unmatched, except by the Great King, and it gave him invaluable advantages. Diodorus mentions his capacity to keep a formidable mercenary force and to bribe collaborators in the Greek world. Though emotively expressed, the statement is true and important. Philip did attract a large and

---

[11] See now Lock 1977a; Errington 1978.

[12] Curt. vi.8.25; cf. Errington 1978, 86–90. On the most famous instance, the capital trial of Philotas (330 B.C.), see below, pp. 101ff.

[13] Dem. xviii.235; cf. i.4, viii.11.

[14] Note the classic description of Demosthenes xix.155–61 (cf. xviii.32). On the details see Hammond and Griffith 1979, 2.341–5.

[15] See Borza 1982, 8–12; Hammond and Griffith 1979, 2.69–73.

[16] Arr. 1.16.5, on which see Bosworth 1980a, 126.

versatile body of mercenaries which he could use in the most remote theatres of operation and deploy independently of the Macedonian native levy. In 342/1, when the main army was fully engaged in the Thracian hinterland, he was able to send out two separate mercenary forces, under Eurylochus and Parmenion, to intervene in the affairs of Eretria far to the south.[17] His financial reserves ensured that he never suffered the embarrassment of Athenian generals serving in the north Aegean, who were often forced to maintain their mercenaries by subsidiary campaigning for other paymasters or by simple extortion, euphemistically termed 'good will' payments (Dem.VIII.25). His men could be guaranteed continuity of employment and regular payment.

The diplomatic intrigue Diodorus speaks of is equally important. Philip attracted the most prominent figures of the Greek world to Pella, where he entertained lavishly and dispersed huge sums as gifts, in traditional Homeric hospitality. Bribery or guest-friendship, it depended on one's perspective. Philip could buy good-will, encourage political co-operation or even finance dissidents to seize power in their home city. At its starkest the power of money was seen in the Olynthian campaign of 349/8, when Torone, Mecyberna and perhaps Olynthus itself fell through internal treachery and (if we may believe Demosthenes) the Olynthian cavalry was betrayed by its commanders.[18] Not everyone who received Philip's money was disloyal,[19] but few can have been unaffected. Every individual and every community which had the money to do so used it for diplomatic advantage; and the system of *proxenia* ensured that nationals of one city were in honour obliged to promote the interests of another. In this sense Philip's activity was almost orthodox. What was unusual was its scale and complexity. Few Greek cities can have been without citizens who had benefited directly from his largesse, and far more than Greeks were affected. Philip had inaugurated his reign with diplomatic payments to his neighbour, the Paeonian king (Diod. XVI.3.4), and he will have acquired allies in the north by payment as much as by conquest. Even relations with Persia might be affected. Refugees from the court of the Great King, men like Amminapes or even Artabazus, were entertained at Pella,[20] incurring obligations which might be repaid after their rehabilitation. The advantages were great, the expenses colossal. Philip did not merely spend money, alleges the contemporary critic, Theopompus (*FGrH* 115 F 224): he threw it away. His treasury was never flush with excess funds, and Alexander himself is alleged to have been severely embarrassed for ready money on the eve of his invasion of Asia.[21] That is a measure of the expendi-

---

[17] Dem. IX.58 (somewhat earlier a force of 1,000 mercenaries had dismantled the fortifications at Porthmus). For other evidence of Philip's use of mercenaries see Parke 1933, 162–4.

[18] Dem. XIX.265–7; cf. Diod. XVI.53.2 with Hammond and Griffith 1979, 2.322–4.

[19] For the situation at Athens see below, pp. 211–13.

[20] For Amminapes (Berve 1926, 2 no. 55) see Curt. VI.4.25; for Artabazus (Berve 1926, 2 no. 152) see Diod. XVI.52.3; Curt. V.9.1, VI.5.2.

[21] Plut. *Al.* 15.2; cf. Arr. VII.9.6; Curt. X.2.24 with Hamilton 1969, 36–7 *contra* Bellinger 1963, 36ff.

ture. What is not in doubt is the magnitude of the royal revenues and the financial power of Macedon.

The greatest resource of Macedonia was probably its population. After his incorporation of Upper Macedonia Philip was master of a territory some 20,000 square kilometres in area, comprising some of the richest agricultural land in the Balkans.[22] Its population was necessarily large and was certainly augmented by the internal peace that prevailed in his reign. As always, there are no statistics and no basis for quantification. But for the male population of military age there are some interesting figures. The Macedonian infantry under arms in 334 B.C. numbered 27,000, and there were ample reserves that could be mustered in subsequent years.[23] The cavalry also was numerous and of high calibre – something over 3,000 at the time of Philip's death. These numbers are formidable, and they comprise only the nucleus of Philip's military resources: his native Macedonian forces. With the allied contingents that would normally take the field with him they amounted to an army without parallel in Greek history. Indeed it can be argued that Philip never needed to mobilise more than a fraction of the forces at his disposal. At the climactic battle of Chaeronea his army is estimated at 30,000 foot and 2,000 horse – and that was an army augmented by numerous allies (Diod. xvi.85.5). His campaigns, numerous though they were, never fully exploited his reserves of manpower, and his military strength, it is safe to say, rose steadily throughout his reign.

Mere numbers are only part of the story. Macedon was populous before Philip, but its infantry was a primitive rabble.[24] The mobilisation of the foot soldiers as a political as well as a military force may predate his reign,[25] but it is highly probable that the introduction of the 12-cubit *sarisa* as the fundamental offensive weapon was his innovation.[26] From the beginning of the reign he imposed systematic training, to produce a cohesive and immensely strong formation that could surpass the depth and compactness of the Theban phalanx. This primary striking force was supplemented by light-armed auxiliaries, archers and, in due course, a siege train manned by the finest contemporary military engineers (retained by Philip's gold). The Macedonian cavalry was, as always, superb, and its discipline was sharpened by regular training which evolved the classic tactic of attack in wedge formation. For most of the reign the national army was used on the marches of the kingdom, in relatively brief campaigns against Illyrian or Thracian adversaries. It made few forays into the Greek world proper – to crush the Phocian mercenaries at

---

[22] See Borza 1982, esp. 12–20, suggesting that the coastal lowlands were malarial (cf. Borza 1979).

[23] See below pp. 266ff. and, for more documentation, Bosworth 1986.

[24] Thuc. iv.124.1; see also (an illuminating passage) ii.100.5.

[25] This depends on the very vexed interpretation of Anaximenes, *FGrH* 72 F 4; for recent and different approaches to the problem see Brunt 1976, Hammond and Griffith 1979, 2.705–9, Develin 1985.

[26] Implied by Diod. xvi.3.1–2. See Hammond and Griffith 1979, 2.421 and, for a different view, Markle 1978.

the Crocus Field (352) and perhaps to finish off the Olynthian campaign. By and large the military profile was as Demosthenes describes it in his *Third Philippic* (IX.49–50): brief opportunistic raids with flexible composite forces of mercenaries, cavalry and light-armed, rather than any large body of heavy infantry. It was generally considered, he says, that Philip could not be compared with Sparta at her prime. Those delusions were rudely shattered by Chaeronea, and even Chaeronea gave an imperfect picture of the true strength of Macedon.

We should also consider the outlying territories, particularly Thessaly and Thrace, which Philip turned into virtual annexes of Macedon. From the beginning of his reign he was involved in the affairs of Thessaly, taking one of his first wives (Philinna) from Larisa, the city traditionally most involved in Macedonian politics.[27] Later, in 353, he intervened in the internecine struggle between the tyrant house of Pherae and the Thessalian League, centred around the old capitals of Pharsalus and Larisa. After his crushing defeat of Pherae in 352 he was elected *archon* of an expanded league which now included all Thessaly. What exactly was meant by this is uncertain, but it did apparently give Philip some revenue from imposts on Thessalian trade and control of the joint military forces of Thessaly.[28] He could and did intervene in conflict between cities; garrisons were imposed, notably at Pherae, and, more drastically, there were mass exiles from the north-western cities of Pharcadon and Tricca (Diod. XVIII.56.5). Inevitably his partisans acquired key positions and he re-established the tetrarchies, the old regional divisions of Thessaly, imposing one of his own men upon each of them as controller.[29] Two of those tetrarchs (Daochus and Thrasydaeus) came from Pharsalus and are named by Demosthenes (XVIII.295) as quislings. Indeed Pharsalus occupied a dominant position in Philip's Thessaly. It provided the representatives to the Amphictyonic Council as well as a cavalry élite which formed a counterpart to the Macedonian royal squadron (see below, p. 264). The other cities were relatively depressed, but the relatives of Philip's two wives must have exercised power and influence in and beyond Larisa and Pherae. It proved a stable settlement. Both Philip and Alexander worked with the existing aristocracy of Thessaly (Medeius of Larisa enjoyed high favour as a Companion)[30] and used the traditional cavalry strength of the territory. There was no attempt to mobilise the depressed peasantry into an effective infantry on the Macedonian model. Thessaly remained comparatively weak under its traditional governing circle, now absorbed to some degree in the Macedonian

---

27 The chronology is vexed, but the marriage must be early. Cf. Hammond and Griffith 1979, 2.225; Martin 1982.

28 For the complex evidence see Hammond and Griffith 1979, 2.285–95.

29 Theopompus, *FGrH* 115 F 208–9; *SIG*³ 274 VIII. Cf. Hammond and Griffith 1979, 2.533–8; Martin 1985, 104–10; Errington 1986, 55–7. It has often been argued that Philip also organised a coup at Larisa, exiled his former supporters there and imposed a garrison. This theory rests on highly questionable evidence and should be discarded (Martin 1985, 102–4; 255–60).

30 Berve 1926, 2 no. 521 (see below, p. 171). He was presumably a grandson of Medeius, dynast of Pharsalus in 395 (Diod. XIV.82.5).

court. It could be mobilised with Macedon but never deployed against the monarchy – as long as Philip's partisans remained stable in power.

His policy in Thrace was not dissimilar. A potential threat if united under a single king, the Thracian lands were renowned in the fifth century for their large population and financial strength.[31] From Philip's accession what had been a single kingdom under the redoubtable Odrysian Cotys was divided among his three sons, who were unable or disinclined to form a common front against him. The two western kingdoms were forced into vassal status, probably by 352, and in his great Thracian campaign of 342/1 he attacked and conquered the Odrysian heartland in the Hebrus valley, deep in modern Bulgaria. As a result the reigning kings, Teres and Cersebleptes, were deposed,[32] and Thrace as a whole came under the control of a Macedonian general. Regional control points were established in the form of new cities, the most important Philippopolis (Plovdiv) and Cabyle, where the motley collection of new settlers formed alien enclaves, necessarily dependent on the favour of the Macedonian king (see below, p. 246). But it was more than mere military occupation. Native princes continued to exercise power locally, and by the end of Alexander's reign the Odrysian Seuthes (Berve 1926, 2 no. 702) had virtually re-established a kingdom – under Macedonian suzerainty. Other princes were attracted to the Macedonian court and later led contingents of their nationals in Alexander's army (the most notorious was Sitalces, who led a unit of javelin-men at Issus and Gaugamela).[33] Like Thessaly, Thrace was neutralised as a potential danger, its peoples ruled by compliant natives under Macedonian patronage and providing auxiliary forces, both cavalry and light infantry. Other peoples in the north enjoyed similar relations with the Macedonian throne. From early in the reign the Paeonians and Agrianians of the upper Strymon valley were subjects of the Macedonian king, their rulers holding power by grace of Philip and their troops swelling the army of Macedon.

By the end of the 340s B.C. Macedon had become a superpower. Few realised it, certainly not the citizens of the Greek city states which might have been considered Philip's chief rivals. But in fact there was no real challenge. As early as 346 the Athenian orator Isocrates wrote an open letter to the Macedonian king, urging him to unite the four principal powers of Greece (Athens, Argos, Sparta and Thebes) and lead them in a crusade against Persia. These cities, he said in a memorable phrase, were reduced to a common level of disaster (Isocr. v.40). The statement is overstressed for rhetorical purposes, but there is an element of truth in it. No single city state (or even coalition) was a match for Philip. Indeed two of Isocrates' four major powers could be considered anachronisms even in his own day. Argos can never have been considered a significant military power since its catastrophic

---

[31] Hdt. v.3; Thuc. ii.97.5.
[32] [Dem.] xii.8; Diod. xvi.71.2. See in general Hammond and Griffith 1979, 2.554–9.
[33] Justin xi.5.1; Frontin. *Strat.* ii.11.3. On Sitalces see Berve 1926, 2 no. 712.

defeat at the hands of Cleomenes of Sparta in 494 B.C., and in more recent
years (370) it had been visited by one of the most atrocious examples of Greek
political violence, in which a purge of property owners had been followed by
reprisals against the democratic leaders (Diod. xv.57.3–58.4). Argos was
relatively impotent, of little value for or against Philip.

Much the same could be said of Sparta. The defeat at Leuctra (371) and still
more the liberation of Messenia (370/69) had contracted Spartan ambitions
and Spartan resources. The male citizen population now dipped below 1,000,
and there was no thought of rectifying the situation by enfranchising the
subject classes. Spartan society remained in its rigid hierarchical straitjacket,
but its territories were confined to old Laconia and Cythera. The erstwhile
helots of Messenia now formed a separate and antipathetic state, its capital on
Mt Ithome a formidable fortress. Another fortress, Megalopolis, blocked
access to Messenia by the north. It had been founded on Theban initiative in
the 360s B.C. and united the scattered populations of south-west Arcadia into a
single great defensive complex. The Spartan leadership was totally recalcitrant,
totally incapable of renouncing its traditional claims to hegemony over the
Greek world. That hegemony could only be achieved by first destroying and
resettling Megalopolis and then attacking Messenia. Only the first step in the
programme was ever attempted; Megalopolis was attacked (abortively) in
353/2 and 331/0. Given the scanty military population of Sparta, her political
ambitions could only be supported by mercenaries, and the mercenaries could
only be retained by campaigning outside Laconia. Spartan kings by necessity
became glorified *condottieri*, the great Agesilaus ending his life in the service
of Egypt and his son, Archidamus, dying in battle against the Lucanians of
southern Italy. That meant that in practice Spartan forces could rarely be
deployed in the field, and Sparta was neutral in the great crisis of 338,
reserving her forces for the higher end of the conquest of Messenia.

For Philip this attitude was a godsend. It allowed him to befriend and
support the leading families of Argos and Messenia, not to mention Megalopolis. His sympathisers were stigmatised as traitors by Demosthenes, but
two centuries later the Megalopolitan historian, Polybius, gave a spirited
defence: their wooing of Philip ensured local autonomy and security from
Sparta.[34] That was justified. Sparta's intentions were naked and threatening,
Philip's less so. The Macedonian king supported his partisans financially,
militarily and morally, and in 338 the final reward was the partitioning of
Spartan borderland to his allies in Messenia, Arcadia and Argos (see below,
p. 198). Spartan ambitions were a considerable asset for Philip, who could
expand his sphere of influence by espousing the cause of the states directly
threatened.

The Thebans were in a similar position. Their period of glory in the 360s
was short-lived, abruptly terminated by the unpleasant and ruinously expensive Sacred War with Phocis. Theban hegemonial ambitions had driven the

---

[34] Polyb. xviii.14.2–15, *contra* Dem. xviii.295.

Phocian leaders to occupy the sanctuary at Delphi (356), and the financial resources of the city and its confederation were simply insufficient to match the mercenary armies which Phocis paid from the treasures of Apollo. Like the Spartans, the Thebans sent their hoplite forces to fight for causes overseas. In 353, at the height of the Sacred War, they sent the cream of their army under their premier general, Pammenes, to support the revolt of the Persian satrap Artabazus. A decade later Lacrates with a thousand hoplites formed the spearhead of the Persian invasion of Egypt.[35] The Theban hoplite army still had the greatest military reputation in the Greek world, but numbers were relatively small. Field armies serving outside Boeotia contained no more than 8,000 hoplites from the confederation. At the same time there were bitter international hostilities. The Spartans, the Phocians and the tyrants of Pherae had been inveterate enemies. At Athens the attitude towards Thebes was rarely anything other than chilly; and the drastic fate meted out to dissidents within the confederacy (Plataea, Thespiae and Orchomenus, all destroyed) ensured a plentiful supply of exiles to whom the name of Thebes was anathema. After the Sacred War Thebes was in no position to dominate. Indeed her interests had been eminently served by Philip, who in 346 crushed the power of Phocis in central Greece and confirmed Thebes as mistress of the Boeotian confederacy.

Athens was the most complex of the states of Greece. Firmly democratic since 403 B.C., the city had to some degree recovered the power it had lost in the Peloponnesian War. The Athenian navy, on paper at least, was supreme in the contemporary world. Many of the ships in the dockyards were unseaworthy, but navies of over a hundred ships could put out to sea in a crisis.[36] The Second Athenian Confederacy, it is true, had been all but destroyed by the calamitous Social War (357–355). Only a rump of militarily insignificant allies stayed loyal to the city. Fortunately during the naval ascendancy of the 360s the Athenians were able to establish a number of cleruchies (settlements of Athenian citizens overseas). Samos had been occupied in 365; the Chersonese was ceded to Athens in its entirety in 353/2 by the Thracian king Cersebleptes. In the northern Aegean the islands of Imbros, Lemnos and Scyros had become annexes of the Athenian state and (like Samos) received regular officials from the capital. The Athenians were fiercely retentive of these exclaves, which guaranteed a modest competence to citizens who would otherwise have been indigent. Poteidaea, which harboured Athenian cleruchs for a mere five years (361–356), was stubbornly claimed as an Athenian possession, its occupation by Philip denounced as an outrage a decade and more after the event ([Dem.] VII.9–10).

At the same time the domestic revenues of the city increased, from a nadir of

---

[35] Cf. Diod. XVI.34.1; Dem. XXIII.138, with Hammond and Griffith 1979, 2.264–7 (Pammenes); Diod. XVI.44.2, 47.1, 49.1–6.

[36] In 357/6 the number of ships in the dockyards is listed as 283 (*IG* II².1611, line 9); the ships effectively in action at that time are estimated at 120 (Diod. XVI.21.1).

130 talents to some 400 talents by the mid-340s B.C.[37] This development went hand in hand with a fundamental change in economic administration. The theoric fund, once responsible only for occasional disbursements at festival time, became the receptacle of all public monies remaining after basic administrative expenses were met. Except in time of war, when Attica was directly threatened, the commissioners of the fund disbursed the proceeds as they thought fit, on public works and direct cash grants to the people.[38] As Demosthenes repeatedly complains, the existence of the fund was a disincentive to rash declarations of war. The *demos*, which profited as a whole from the theoric administration, was generally reluctant to vote for elaborate military adventures. When Athenian interests were conceived as threatened, as in 352/1 when Philip attempted to force Themopylae and then made a push to the shores of the Propontis, the *demos* might respond vigorously and promptly, but by and large there was little that could be called offensive initiative. Generals (at this period professional generals like Chares and Phocion, who were elected year after year) were assigned to areas of special importance, the Hellespont and Samos, and were expected to retain and maintain mercenaries from local resources.

It did not make for effective military resistance to Philip. Indeed it was only at critical moments, such as the fall of Olynthus, that Philip was conceived as a serious threat to Athenian interests. Even Demosthenes was far from consistent in his crusading fervour and was prepared to countenance peace and alliance between 348 and early 346. There was little sympathy for the Macedonian king. Few Athenians will have forgotten his opportunistic annexation of Amphipolis, Pydna and Methone, not to mention Poteidaea; and the end of the Sacred War in 346 was widely – and rightly – seen as a diplomatic humiliation not to be tolerated. Philip, to his intense annoyance, suffered intense diplomatic pressure from Athens to restore what the *demos* saw as its proper possessions, and his settlement of Phocis was only accepted grudgingly and under coercion. On the other hand the warnings of Demosthenes in the late 340s fell on deaf ears. Few Athenians seriously believed that they would see a Macedonian army in Attica. They would vote for limited campaigns against Macedonian-backed regimes in Euboea or even military assistance to the threatened area of Acarnania, but full-scale war against Macedon was not seriously envisaged.

Philip's intentions towards Athens are more difficult to assess, given the systematic ambiguity of his actions. It seems unlikely that he would ever have countenanced an ultimate settlement that left the city free of constraints. Athens had played a mischievous role in Macedonian politics at the time of his accession. It had continuously supported the Phocian regime against him. The demands for territory once allegedly Athenian but now his were unremitting and outrageous. If he needed proof of Athenian intransigence, it

---

[37] Dem. x.37–80; Theopompus, *FGrH* 115 F 166.
[38] For a convenient digest of the evidence and recent literature see Rhodes 1981, 514–17.

was amply given in 341, when he was fully engaged in Thrace. Then the Athenian general Diopeithes took advantage of his absence to attack one of his allies, Cardia, and carried hostilities into his Thracian territories. When he complained, his ambassador was arrested by Diopeithes and at Athens Demosthenes successfully argued against the recall of the delinquent general.[39] Ultimately there was little alternative to a military confrontation. It came late in 340 when Philip attacked Byzantium and in the course of the siege captured the entire grain fleet on its way to Athens. This was an intensely hostile act, striking at the very lifeline of Athens, which was notoriously dependent on imported grain. The declaration of war that followed reflected the gravity of the action. Faced with a threat to the grain supply, the *demos* unhesitatingly diverted the administrative surplus from the theoric fund to finance the hostilities.

The final campaign was a little delayed but, once launched, was rapid and decisive. Philip did not seriously contemplate tackling the Athenian fleets in the Propontis, for his own fleet was vestigial and inexperienced. Instead he spent the campaigning year of 339 securing his northern frontiers. Late in the year he moved south, leading yet another Amphictyonic force, in theory to attack Locris. This immediately brought him into conflict with the Thebans, who had come to resent his domination of Central Greece and took advantage of his absence in the north to expel a Macedonian garrison from the mouth of Thermopylae. In the face of the common threat, Athens and Thebes allied themselves and, despite overtures by Philip and his allies, the alliance remained firm. In August 338 came the dénouement. Philip's army, a fraction of his total strength, faced a coalition of roughly equivalent numbers: the Theban and Athenian levies together with a few allied contingents, the most notable from Achaea. It was not an impressive array. The two principals had precious little support from the other Greek states, which were content to wait upon (and profit from) the result.

It was catastrophic. In the plain of Chaeronea the Macedonian phalanx proved its superiority over traditional hoplite forces. The Athenians alone lost 1,000 dead and 2,000 prisoners, and the Boeotians suffered heavy casualties, including the entire Sacred Band. The end of the day saw Philip supreme in Greece. For Thebes it meant the end of her hegemony in Boeotia and the replacement of her moderate democracy by a strictly limited oligarchic junta, comprised mainly of returned exiles.[40] Athens by contrast suffered only the loss of her remaining allies (but not her cleruchies, with the possible exception of the Chersonese) and was compensated by the acquisition of Oropus, territory which since 366 had been part of Boeotia. The price was formal alliance with Macedon. The same applied to the other states of southern Greece which, if they had not done so before, concluded treaties of alliance.

[39] In his speech *On the Chersonese* (Dem. VIII). On the background see Hammond and Griffith 1979, 2.563–6.
[40] See now the detailed survey by Gullath 1982, 7–19.

The Spartans stood alone. They refused submission in any form, suffered invasion and lost border territories to their embittered neighbours (see below, p. 198). Elsewhere Macedonian garrisons occupied key citadels. They are attested at Thebes, Corinth and Ambracia, and there may have been others. There was also a degree of political subversion, as Philip ensured that his partisans were established in government. In 337 a constitutive meeting of allies was convened at Corinth, and the political system Philip had created was confirmed by a common peace.[41] Its pillars were the freedom and autonomy of all parties (under Macedonian hegemony) and the interdiction of political change and social revolution. It was administered by a *synedrion* of delegates from all allied states and the executive officer was Philip himself. The propaganda was abolition of war and *stasis* under the benign presidency of Macedon; the reality all too often was the preservation of sycophantic and oppressive regimes by the threat of military action. Whatever ideological perspective one takes, the result of the common peace is the same. It entrenched a network of governments largely sympathetic to Philip and guaranteed them stability.

The forum of allies at Corinth also declared war on Persia. This was the climactic act of the reign and was carefully prepared. From the early years of the century the Persian empire had been ripe for attack. Plagued by succession disputes in the royal house and endemic revolts in the satrapies, its whole fabric had been at times threatened with dissolution. In the late 360s practically the entire empire west of the Euphrates was alienated from the Great King at Susa. The Egyptians had asserted their independence as early as 404 and under a series of native pharaohs repelled successive Persian invasions. More seriously, since the impressive display given by Cyrus' mercenaries at Cunaxa, the nucleus of royal armies had regularly been recruited from Greece, and the Great King's interventions in the politics of the Balkans had often been designed to secure a supply of prime troops for his campaigns or to deny them to his antagonists. The most aggressive and successful monarch during the fourth century was Artaxerxes III Ochus (358–338). He was able to crush revolt in Asia Minor after his accession. In Phoenicia he forced Sidon to submission with fire and slaughter and finally (in 343 or 342) he reconquered Egypt and placed the land under a native satrap. This record of achievement is illusory. Sidon had long maintained its independence and only fell through treachery (by the Greek mercenary commander, Mentor of Rhodes). Similarly the conquest of Egypt had been preceded by disastrous failure a decade earlier.[42] The successful invasion was spearheaded by Greek troops with Greek commanders, and on both sides it was the mercenaries who did the effective fighting. They apparently made private treaties with each other and on one occasion Lacrates of Thebes turned

[41] For the details see below, pp. 187ff.
[42] Cf. Diod. XVI.48.1, attributing the Egyptian success to their Greek generals, the Athenian Diophantus and the Spartiate Lamius.

against his Persian allies in the interests of the Greek defenders of Pelusium (Diod. XVI.49.4–6). The Persian success depended on the Great King's ability to pay and keep mercenaries. That had long been evident, and the military weakness of the Persian empire was a commonplace by Philip's accession. Isocrates had repeatedly urged a crusade against Persia and the settlement of Greek refugees in the King's lands. On a more practical level the Spartan king, Agesilaus, apparently envisaged the annexation of Asia Minor east of Cilicia, and the Thessalian dynast, Iason of Pherae, also had designs on Persian possessions.[43] The satrapies of Asia Minor were undeniably a natural and lucrative target for aggression.

We cannot date the origins of Philip's ambitions against Persia. There is no literary evidence for them until the latter part of his reign. As late as his *Fourth Philippic* (341) Demosthenes can only argue on circumstantial evidence that Philip planned to attack the Persian king (Dem. x.31–3).[44] In fact Artaxerxes Ochus rejected Athenian overtures at that juncture and refused subsidies to support operations against Philip (Aesch. III.238). The only Persian involvement against Philip was when Ochus felt his territory threatened by the siege of Perinthus (340) and instructed his generals to co-operate with the defenders (Diod. XVI.75.1). Once the presumed threat to the Propontis receded, his interest in containing Philip also ebbed. Philip, as always, had kept his ultimate intentions secret, deferring them (as was inevitable) until he had imposed a stable and permanent settlement on southern Greece. After Chaeronea the time for a declaration of hostilities was propitious. Shortly before the battle Ochus was assassinated by his vizier, the sinister Bagoas, who then eliminated the immediate family of the deceased king, leaving his youngest son, Arses, to reign as his puppet. The dynastic convulsion provoked revolution in Egypt and Babylon (see below, p. 34), and the weakness of the empire was patent to all observers. Accordingly Philip had his allies declare war on Persia, with the avowed intention of avenging the sacrilege of Xerxes and liberating the Greek cities of Asia Minor (see below, p. 189). It was an explicit renewal of the aims of the Delian League, and the Macedonian king was assuming the mantle of Aristeides. He would expand his realm by retaliating for past offences against the Hellenes, and, far from promoting his private interests, he was acting for the entire Greek world. His

---

[43] *Hell. Ox.* 22.4; Xen. *Hell.* IV.1.41 (Agesilaus); Isocr. V.119–20; Xen. *Hell.* VI.1.12 (Iason).

[44] Much has been made of the supposed connection between Philip and Hermeias, the dynast of Atarneus in Asia Minor, who died in Persian custody in 341 (for a conservative exposition of the problem see Hammond and Griffith 1979, 2.518–22). The theory is based on modern speculation and the conviction of the ancient commentators that Hermeias was the agent of Philip obliquely mentioned by Demosthenes (x.32). Even if the identification is correct, Demosthenes is dealing in rumour and innuendo, without knowledge of Philip's intentions. Indeed the tradition on Hermeias has only one explicit statement that he collaborated. Callisthenes (cited by Didymus *in Dem.* col. 6, lines 55–7) says that he died without revealing anything of his agreements with Philip. The context is problematic. Hermeias' death was reported in very different ways and the circumstances were obviously not widely known. Callisthenes at all events spoke of collusion between him and Philip, but what that collusion can have been is a complete mystery.

allies endorsed the declaration of war, fixed the military contributions of each state and passed resolutions forbidding any Hellene to fight on the Persian side. The supreme commander of the combined forces was Philip, at once *hegemon* of the common peace and general in the war of revenge. In the spring of 336 campaigning began in earnest, when a Macedonian expeditionary force 10,000 strong crossed the Hellespont and began the work of liberation (and subjugation) on the coast of Asia Minor. Philip was never able to assume leadership. He was cut down by assassination in the autumn of that same year, and command devolved upon his successor – with fatal results.

II **The young Alexander**

That successor was Alexander. Perhaps the eldest of Philip's sons, he was born in the summer of 356.[45] Only one other son, the mentally afflicted Arrhidaeus, is reliably attested in the ancient tradition, and from the beginning, it seems, Alexander was marked out as crown prince.[46] As the son of Olympias, the blood of the royal house of Epirus flowed in his veins, and he referred his lineage to Andromache and Achilles on his mother's side, to Heracles on his father's. His pedigree for him was no genealogical fiction, and in later years he behaved explicitly as the lineal descendant of both Heracles and Achilles and consciously fostered character traits appropriate to both (see below, pp. 281ff.). From the outset heroic emulation was an abiding spur to action.

His physical appearance is elusive. In later years the court sculptor, Lysippus, was thought to have given the best plastic representation, catching the characteristic leftward inclination of the neck and the peculiar expression of the eyes – an inner brilliance overlaid by a film of moisture.[47] These soft, almost erotic, features were offset by a general fierceness of expression (illustrated in some of the early coin portraits) and a harsh, loud voice.[48] So far the characteristics are well attested, and they were imitated *ad nauseam* by Alexander's successors. Other traits are less clear. Plutarch (*Al.* 4.3) reports that his complexion was fair, with a tendency to redness around the chest and face – the Alexander sarcophagus of Sidon depicts him with a perceptible flush.[49] His hair, clustered in ringlets, was thrown back from the forehead in a

---

[45] Plut. *Al.* 3.5, giving the precise date 6 Hecatombaeon (*c.* 20 July); cf. Badian 1982, 48. Aristobulus (*ap.* Arr. vii.28.1) suggests that he was born in October.

[46] Justin xi.2.1 mentions another half-brother, Caranus, who was killed after Alexander's accession. The statement has been accepted at face value (Berve 1926, 2 no. 411; Unz 1985), but the absence of any other attestation is most suspicious (the *fratres* mentioned by Justin xii.6.14 are probably brothers of Cleopatra). Given Justin's record elsewhere, it is highly likely that he has distorted his original. Cf. Heckel 1979.

[47] See particularly Plut. *Al.* 4.1–3; *de Al.f.* ii.2 (335B). For commentary on the ὑγρότης of Alexander's eyes see the physiognomist Polemon (in J. Cramer, *Anecdota Graeca* iv.255, lines 16–17). See also Schwarzenberg 1967, 70–1.

[48] For the eroticism see particularly Dio Chrys. iv.112; Luc. xliii(*Im.*).6. For the harshness of voice (and its later vogue) see Plut. *Pyrrh.* 8.2; *Mor.* 53c.

[49] Schefold 1968, plates 52 and 58.

central parting (the famous *ánastole*). The nose rose straight to the forehead which, judging from the coin portraits, bulged slightly above the eyes.[50]

How these features combined in the life it is perhaps impossible to say. All the extant portraits are to some degree idealised, based on originals which emphasised the majesty and godlike attributes of their subject, whether it was Lysippus evoking the parallel with Achilles or Apelles unashamedly assimilating the king to Zeus.[51] But the portraits must have been based upon recognisable features and their likeness was reasonably close. This is clearly implied by the famous story of Cassander's trembling fit at the very sight of a statue of Alexander at Olympia (Plut. *Al.* 74.6). At all events the early portrait on the Alexander sarcophagus (perhaps contemporary) strongly resembles the coins from the Babylon mint which were issued in the last years of the reign.[52] Both have the rounded chin, the straight nose and the slight bulge of the forehead. They may well reflect a common model which assimilated the king to Heracles, but the peculiarities of feature (which recur in the commemorative issues of Ptolemy I and Lysimachus) appear authentic.

Alexander was by no means imposing in stature but extraordinarily well co-ordinated physically, blessed with speed and outstanding stamina. By all accounts his emotional disposition was passionate in the extreme, ranging from outbursts of spontaneous affection and generosity to paroxysms of uncontrollable anger. From the early years the sources stress the awe and respect he inspired in his entourage (cf. Arr. 1.14.4). There is little doubt that from the outset he considered it his royal prerogative to impose his will on others, and the worst sin was to flout his authority or to reject his benefactions. Not surprisingly he became a stereotype of inflated arrogance for philosophers and rhetoricians of later ages. This temperament was reinforced and encouraged in the autocracy of Philip's court. It was, it seems, subjected to a fairly rigorous physical discipline by his chief tutor, his mother's kinsman Leonidas, which must have contributed to his capacity for hardship and physical exertion, so amply attested in the later campaigns.

His intellect was sharp. From his earliest years he was enthused by poetry, particularly (and predictably) the Homeric epics but also a wide span of lyric and drama. He is said to have known Euripides by heart (Nicobule, *FGrH* 127 F 2) and (fatefully for Cleitus) he was well aware of the context of quotations. If we may believe Plutarch (*Al.* 8.3), his range of reading included the historian Philistus and the dithyrambs of Telestus and Philoxenus. At the age of fourteen his education was expanded when Philip invited Aristotle to court as his academic supervisor. A miniature Academy was established in the precinct of the Nymphs near Mieza (on the slopes of Mt Vermion, near modern Naoussa). The classic meeting of minds has always been the inspiration for speculation and myth, and it is difficult even to outline what

---

[50] Plut. *Pomp.* 2.1; Aelian, *VH* XII.14. Cf. Bieber 1964, 50–5 with plates XXI–XXII.
[51] Schwarzenberg 1967, 1976.
[52] Bieber 1964, 50–1. For the Babylon issues see Dürr, in Schwarzenberg 1976, 274.

Aristotle might have taught. But two decades earlier the Academician philosopher, Euphraeus of Oreus, had apparently treated the court of Perdiccas III to the full rigours of geometry and dialectic (Athen. 508E). Alexander probably experienced Aristotle's regular curriculum.[53] Plutarch speaks of ethical and political instruction, and it is extremely likely that he received a basic training in eristics. It cannot be said that it left him with a deep and lasting sympathy for philosophy, but he encouraged formal debate and kept a retinue of intellectuals who included the philosopher Anaxarchus of Abdera. His enormous curiosity about the geographical limits of the world, already apparent in his boyhood (Plut. Al. 5.1), may well have been encouraged by Aristotle, but there is no evidence that he was profoundly affected by any detailed instruction in that field.

The period at Mieza probably ended in 340. In that year Alexander acted as regent in Macedonia while his father was active in the Propontis. He had disposal of the royal seal and clearly transacted the day-to-day business of the monarchy. His energies were further occupied in a successful campaign against the Maedi of the upper Strymon (see below, pp. 245–6). His military career continued with his father, first in the northern campaigns of 339 (cf. Justin IX.1.8) and then at the battle of Chaeronea, where he commanded the Macedonian left and allegedly broke the Theban line. Subsequently he served with Antipater, Philip's senior diplomat, in conducting peace negotiations with Athens. He maintained a high public profile and his position as crown prince was apparently unchallenged.

That situation changed abruptly in 337, when Philip decided on another dynastic marriage, this time to a lady of Macedon proper: Cleopatra, the sister of Hippostratus and niece of Attalus. Cleopatra's origins are unknown, but there is no doubt that she belonged to the traditional nobility of Macedon. She was also (it is alleged) married for love, not for political reasons (as was the Elimiote princess Phila, the only other wife of Philip who could be said to be of Macedonian extraction). That alienated Olympias, and a deep rift developed in the royal house.[54] The new queen's uncle, Attalus, was hostile and abrasive, and at the marriage feast he openly prayed for the advent of legitimate sons for Philip (Athen. 557D; Plut. Al. 9.7). It was an insult direct, aimed at Olympias' marital fidelity and also her non-Macedonian origins. A celebrated brawl resulted, Philip drawing his sword against his son, and in the aftermath Olympias took residence in her native Epirus. Alexander more ominously went to one of the Illyrian peoples (which, we cannot say). This marked the climax of the alienation. There had probably been an earlier quarrel in the

[53] Plut. Al. 7.5. The training in eristics is postulated (on the basis of Isocr. Ep. 5) by Merlan 1954. See further Hamilton 1969, 17–20; Schachermeyr 1973, 81–93 (visionary); Badian 1982, 38–9 (sceptical).
[54] Explicit in Satyrus (Athen. 557D); Plut. Al. 9.6; Justin IX.7.2.3; Arr. III.6.5. The crisis cannot be minimised.

prelude to the marriage,[55] when Alexander had allegedly been worried by the request of the Carian satrap, Pixodarus, to marry his daughter to Arrhidaeus, Alexander's mentally deficient half-brother. Alexander made overtures to the Carian on his own account and effectively sabotaged the marriage. His action provoked a violent response from Philip, who upbraided him in the strongest terms and exiled at least five of his friends, including Harpalus, Ptolemy and Nearchus. This is an obscure episode and some of the details recorded by Plutarch may be unhistorical. But the exile of Alexander's friends is fact, confirmed by Arrian (III.6.5), who dates the incident around the time of Philip's marriage to Cleopatra. It suggests an atmosphere of distrust and insecurity, in which Alexander increasingly felt his position undermined by the rising faction of Attalus.

The rift had to be closed, ostensibly at least. While Alexander was alienated from his father and supported by the Illyrians, there was a real danger of his being promoted as a pretender to the Macedonian throne, as had happened many times in the past with disaffected members of the Argead house. Accordingly he was persuaded to return to court through the good offices of a respected guest-friend, Demaratus of Corinth (Plut. Al. 9.12–14). By the time he reappeared at Pella, Attalus had probably left for Asia Minor as one of the three commanders of the expeditionary force (spring 336). One source of friction was obviated. A second diplomatic offensive was aimed at Epirus. The Molossian king, Alexander (the brother of Olympias), was invited to marry his own niece, Cleopatra. Even though Olympias remained intransigent, there was now no threat of a rupture between the two monarchies. The year passed in preparations for what was to be a brilliant state wedding. The venue was the old capital of Aegae, where a prodigious number of guests were assembled from the whole of the Greek world. The marriage was duly contracted and celebrated by a formal symposium. For the following day games were scheduled at the theatre. Philip made his entrance between the two Alexanders, his son and son-in-law. The new concord was on full display, and to mark his confidence Philip walked at a distance from his bodyguard. At that moment he was fatally stabbed by a disgruntled young noble, Pausanias of Orestis, who had a personal grievance against Attalus and indirectly against Philip, who had refused to give him redress. The truth must be more complicated, for others are explicitly stated to have been involved in the

[55] Plutarch (Al. 10.1–4) is the only source. He records the incident *after* Alexander's return from his sojourn with the Illyrians. There is hardly time in 336 for the negotiations described, and the veracity of the entire story has been challenged (Ellis 1981, 135–6; Hatzopoulos 1982b). But Plutarch gives no positive indication of chronology (αὖθις at 10.1 (cf.9.5) I take to be a thematic connective without temporal force), and his *Life of Alexander* often distorts the sequence of events for narrative convenience. I note that Plutarch's story presupposes Olympias' presence at court (10.1), before her withdrawal to Epirus. Pixodarus' overtures could have come in the spring or summer of 337, when Philip's invasion plans were declared and the Persian empire was in chaos. The fact that he dated an official document by the first regnal year of Arses (below, p. 230) means nothing. If he was planning defection, he would not advertise the fact.

conspiracy (see below, pp. 25–6), and there were clearly complex political forces at work. It is probably too simple to argue that because Olympias and Alexander benefited from the assassination either or both instigated it. There must have been many political sub-currents at the Macedonian court, particularly in the turbulent finale of Philip's reign, and we cannot hope to reconstruct them. All that can be said is that the murder on that October day of 336[56] precipitated a crisis. Alexander's position was strong but far from unassailable. The events of the last year had guaranteed a lively opposition to his accession and there were others who had some claim to the throne. Dynastic competition had been the bane of the monarchy in the past and there was every chance that it would be renewed. At worst the very integrity of the kingdom was in question.

[56] For the date see Bosworth 1980a, 45–6; Hatzopoulos 1982a.

## 2

# The gaining of empire (336–323 B.C.)

## I      The accession

The first few days of Alexander's reign must have been among the most critical of his career. Unfortunately no connected account survives of them. There are scraps of epitome and random flashbacks from later history, but most of the crucial details are irretrievably lost. There is infinite scope for speculation and imaginative reconstruction,[1] but the sources themselves allow very little to be said. We must be prepared to admit our ignorance, however galling that may be.

At first there was turmoil. Alexander's friends gathered round him and occupied the palace, already armed for battle (Arr. 1.25.2). There was every reason to expect trouble, given the dynastic troubles of Philip's last year. The family and supporters of Attalus will certainly not have welcomed his accession, and there were other figures who might oppose him or form a focus for opposition. Amyntas (who had ephemerally succeeded his father Perdiccas in 359)[2] and the sons of Aeropus from the princely house of Lyncestis are said to have commanded general attention (Plut. *Mor.* 327c). Only one of these groups is mentioned in the context of the assassination, the Lyncestian brothers. The sources strongly indicate that they were involved in the actual murder.[3] That may be a *post eventum* fabrication to justify their subsequent execution, but there is no reason to believe so. The brothers may well have helped Pausanias plan the assassination. They had personal motives as strong as his own (their father, it seems, had been exiled by Philip),[4] and they probably intended to be king-makers, giving their support to the ultimate

---

[1] The principal discussions, dominated by the question of the responsibility for Philip's murder, are Badian 1963, Bosworth 1971a, Ellis 1971, 1981, Kraft 1971, 11–42, Fears 1975, Hammond 1978b, Develin 1981.

[2] Justin VII.5.9–10; cf. Errington 1974, 25–8, Prestiannini Giallombardo 1973/4; *contra* Ellis 1971, 15ff., Hammond and Griffith 1979, 2.208–9, 702–4.

[3] Arr. 1.25.2; Curt. VII.1.6; Justin XI.2.1–2. Arist. *Pol.* 1311b1–3 states that Pausanias acted out of personal motives, not that he acted alone. It is only Diodorus (XVI.94.2–3) who implies that he had no accomplices.

[4] Polyaenus IV.2.3; cf. Bosworth 1982, 79.

victor in the power struggle. One of them was in fact successful. Alexander son of Aeropus was married to a daughter of Antipater, the senior diplomat of Philip's reign. Together with his father-in-law he attached himself to his royal namesake and was one of the first to acclaim him king. There followed a more general acclamation, probably engineered by Antipater, whose support was one of the key factors in the succession crisis.[5] In the absence of Parmenion he was the senior statesman surviving from the previous reign, and he was able to rally a majority of the court around Alexander. His advice certainly helped the twenty-year-old king manœuvre himself to security. The Lyncestian brothers were the first victims. Two of them, Arrhabaeus and Heromenes, were arrested and reserved for execution. How and why is uncertain. They may have been denounced by others or revealed their involvement by premature action. At all events they were not close to Alexander or to Antipater. Only the king's namesake obtained pardon and promotion. He may not have been as directly inculpated as his brothers, but the sources stress his involvement, and as the brother of convicted regicides he should have shared their fate even if technically innocent.[6] The fact that Antipater could procure his safety is very strong evidence that he had the dominant role at Aegae.

Alexander came to the throne immediately after the death of his father, but the details of his investiture are a mystery. It is totally unknown what acts and ceremonies conferred legitimacy upon a Macedonian king.[7] Acclamation was certainly important. In the immediate aftermath of Philip's death he was proclaimed by members of the nobility in the palace, and there is every reason to think that he was also acknowledged by the commons in an assembly at Aegae. Whether or not such a meeting had constitutional significance, it was advisable to have public endorsement of his regime. A formal assembly is attested some days later, in which Alexander addressed the people as king, promising to continue his father's policies (Diod. XVII.2.2; Justin XI.1.7–10). He was enlisting popular favour by emphasising continuity of government, appealing to the commons as his father's son. There could be no compromise with the assassins. At Philip's funeral, some days after the murder, a number of culprits were executed, including the sons of Aeropus.[8] That as much as anything clears Alexander of involvement in the murder. Otherwise his accomplices, if they were punished at all, would have been secretly done to death, not exposed to the dangers of public execution where they might denounce him. However grateful he might have been for Philip's death, Alexander personally had no part in it and could assume the duties of filial piety. The act of vengeance complete, Philip's body was cremated and his

---

5  Cf. Berve 1926, 2.46, no. 94, Badian 1963, 248. His active intervention is only recorded in the highly suspect Alexander-Romance (Ps.-Call. 1.26), but he was close enough to the young king to intercede successfully for his son-in-law.

6  Curt. VI.11.20; VIII.6.28.

7  See now Errington 1978, esp. 94–6.

8  Diod. XVII.2.1; Plut. Al. 10.7. The scene is apparently described in the fragmentary papyrus epitome P. Oxy. 1798 (for a conservative text with a new join see Parsons 1979).

ashes were interred in state in the royal cemetery.[9] Their relationship had been troubled in the past, but for the moment death cancelled all. The son gave his father a royal burial, publicly attesting the direct succession. The ruler had changed but the rule was the same.

Behind the public façade the struggle for power was intense and ruthless. Alexander's rivals and enemies were gradually destroyed. Amyntas son of Perdiccas was accused of conspiring against Alexander, and killed.[10] He was dead by the summer of 335, when his wife Cynane was available for remarriage (Arr. 1.5.4; cf. *Succ.* F 1.22 Roos), and he cannot have long survived his uncle. An Argead, married to a daughter of Philip, he was too important a figure to be left at large and was probably dead by the time Alexander moved south to deal with the unrest in Greece. The family of Attalus was a slightly less pressing problem, since Attalus was in Asia Minor with the expeditionary force there. Alexander sent one of his friends, Hecataeus, to arrest or assassinate him, a task which proved relatively simple. Parmenion, Philip's senior general, shared the command with Attalus and refused to co-operate in any move against the new king. Accordingly Attalus shelved his plans for joint action with Athens and tried to ingratiate himself with Alexander. He was too late. Hecataeus engineered his death before the king could respond to his overtures.[11] Attalus was gone, within a few months of the king's death, and his relatives were also eliminated (Justin XI.5.1). His niece Cleopatra with her infant daughter fell victim to the implacable Olympias. Alexander's mother had returned from her self-imposed exile in Epirus at the news of Philip's death[12] and was less inhibited in showing her satisfaction at the event. While Alexander was temporarily away from the capital she barbarously did to death both infant and mother. Alexander expressed horror at the deed, but he had apparently done nothing to protect the victims, and their deaths cannot have been unwelcome to him. The relicts of Philip's last marriage and its beneficiaries were now gone, and Alexander

---

[9] There is a distinct possibility that Philip's last resting-place was the magnificent Tomb II of the Great Tumulus at Vergina, recently excavated by Manolis Andronikos. Its splendid accoutrements are certainly compatible with a royal burial, and the majority of scholars have cautiously accepted that it does contain the mortal remains of Philip II (Andronikos 1979, 1980, Hammond 1982, Green 1982, Borza 1981-2. See, for a forensic analysis of the bones, Prag et al. 1984). Unfortunately problems subsist. It remains to be explained why the main chamber containing the male remains should have been hastily closed, its walls roughly stuccoed, when Alexander had all the time and incentive to give his father a perfect burial. Even if the Greek crisis had called him away, the tomb could have been closed at any time subsequently, when its decoration was complete. It is equally puzzling why the antechamber with the female burial should have been added later. If the remains are those of Cleopatra, it is most curious that Alexander allowed the usurper (whose family he had extirpated) to share his father's tomb for all eternity.

[10] Curt. VI.9.17, 10.24; cf. Justin XII.6.14. There is also a report that Alexander disposed of a half-brother named Caranus (Justin XI.2.3, cf. XII.6.14; Berve 1926, 2 no. 411), but it is unique to Justin and cannot be accepted in the absence of corroborative evidence.

[11] Diod. XVII.2.4-6, 5.1-2; Curt. VII.1.3.

[12] Berve 1926, 2 no. 581; Hammond and Griffith 1979, 2.685-6; Borza 1981, 76; *contra* Develin 1981, 97-8.

was left the sole male representative of the Argead house. The only other surviving son of Philip, Arrhidaeus, was mentally incapacitated and no threat to him.

Alexander was greatly indebted to the senior statesmen of the previous reign. Antipater, as we have seen, was instrumental in his securing the capital after the assassination, and without Parmenion's support Attalus would have been a far greater threat in Asia. In fact Parmenion had a double loyalty. He had married one of his daughters to Attalus (Curt. vi.9.18) and might have been expected to stand with him. Instead he helped Hecataeus to contrive his death (Curt. vii.1.3). Such support necessarily had its price, and it is not surprising that Parmenion and his sons were at the top of the military hierarchy during the first years of the reign. Others will have made similar choices and obtained similar rewards. Those who did not compromise faced death or exile, men like Amyntas son of Antiochus, who left Macedonia out of hostility to Alexander and became a mercenary commander in Persian service.[13] The wounds of the accession would take years to heal, but one simple result had been achieved. Alexander was secure on the throne and there was no credible challenger; the fortunes of the Argead house rested on him alone. To that extent the murders were necessary, as was their quick execution. The new king could not leave Macedonia to deal with Greek unrest, still less fight an extended campaign in the north, if there were still unsatisfied contenders for power at home.

## II     Consolidation in Europe

Alexander needed to assert his authority outside the kingdom almost as much as he did within it. The assassination of his father had encouraged widespread unrest and dissidence in southern Greece (see below, p. 188). This he suppressed in the winter after his accession in a virtually bloodless campaign. The only military action was at the very beginning, when the Thessalians attempted to block the main route through the vale of Tempe. The young king promptly circumvented their position, driving south along the coast and cutting steps in the face of Mt Ossa to bring his army into Thessaly to the rear of the enemy.[14] That was the end of armed resistance. Alexander was successively acknowledged in Thessaly, Thermopylae and Corinth and returned to Macedonia before the spring as *hegemon* of the Corinthian League and supreme commander of the war of revenge against Persia. He next turned to the north, to complete some of the unfinished business from his father's reign. His main target was the Triballian kingdom, centred in the valley of the Danube near its confluence with the Oescus. Philip had probably campaigned against the Triballians during his conquest of Thrace, but he was not able to impose a lasting peace and actually suffered humiliating losses at their hands

---

[13] Arr. 1.17.9; Curt. iii.11.8; cf. Errington 1974, 26–7.
[14] Polyaenus iv.3.23 (the sole source, but universally accepted).

(as well as a crippling wound) when he returned from his Scythian campaign in 339.[15] There were also Thracian tribes which had managed to preserve their independence. The Tetrachoritae of the Haemus range had been subjected to a campaign at Antipater's hands around 340,[16] and, if they were forced to submission then, it was no more than a temporary expedient. A demonstration of Macedonian military power in the north was justified and desirable, and it began with the spring in 335 B.C.

Alexander set out from Amphipolis with a moderate-sized army. It was by no means the complete levy of Macedon, but it contained a number of units later used in Asia, the phalanx battalions of Upper Macedonia and the cavalry squadrons from Bottiaea and Amphipolis. There was also cavalry from Upper Macedonia (Arr. 1.2.5), never to be used in Asia, as well as light troops, slingers and archers. We can only guess at the total. It is unlikely to have exceeded 15,000, but, unlike the army Alexander led into Asia, it was a predominantly Macedonian force, at a peak of morale and expertise. From Amphipolis he went west across the river Nestos and then northwards through the Rhodope range toward Philippopolis in the Hebrus valley.[17] This was territory already pacified by Philip and presented no military problem; but after nine days' march he reached the passes of the central Haemus, which were held against him by the autonomous Thracians. The pass actually taken was probably the Trojan, on the later Roman road between Philippopolis and Oescus, but the more easterly Shipka pass cannot be ruled out. At all events the resistance was perfunctory. A preliminary barrage of loaded waggons passed harmlessly through the Macedonian lines, and the wretchedly armed mountaineers could not withstand the frontal assault of the Agrianians and hypaspists with the phalanx following. There was carnage for a few minutes, and Alexander was master of the pass and of the considerable number of women and children left behind by the enemy. This booty was carefully conveyed to the coast and to Macedonia (Arr. 1.1.11–2.1).

Alexander pressed on north to deal with the Triballian king, who had taken the precaution of evacuating the countryside of non-combatants. The Triballian warriors met the enemy a few days' march from the Danube, circling the Macedonian army as it approached and occupying a position to the south, backed by the river Lyginus. Alexander retraced his steps to meet them and once more there was a brief and crushing victory. The Triballians could hold their own when it was a matter of skirmishing with the advance screen of archers and slingers, but the combination of the cavalry and the solid wall of the phalanx was irresistible. They broke, and the survivors melted away into the woodland behind them. It was an awesome display of Macedonian efficiency, and the Triballians made no further attempt to challenge their

[15] Justin IX.3.1–3; Didymus, in Dem. col. 13.1–7; cf. Hammond and Griffith 1979, 2.559, 583; Bosworth 1980a, 52–3; Gerov 1981.

[16] Theopompus, FGrH 115 F 217–18; Polyaenus IV.4.1.

[17] Arr. 1.1.5. For the route see Neubert 1934; Bosworth 1980a, 54; Gerov 1981, 488; contra Papazoglou 1977, 29–30.

passage. The bulk of their population had taken refuge on Peuce, one of the many islands formed by the divergence of the main stream of the Danube. It was protected by rising banks and, more importantly, by the rapid current of the river. Alexander made an attempt at a landing, using warships which had sailed from Byzantium to effect a liaison with the army, but the current was too violent and the landing places too densely defended for the few vessels available. But a direct assault would have been an expensive luxury. Alexander could overrun and devastate the Triballian hinterland at his leisure. It was not far from harvest-time, and the defenders ran the risk of starvation if his depredations were not checked. He needed only to wait for the capitulation.

Meanwhile there was a brief interlude. The Getic peoples of the northern Danubian plain had gathered by the riverside, hoping to deter the invader from crossing. That was a mistake. Alexander took their appearance as a challenge – and an opportunity to display the versatility of his army. Using ships, log canoes and hides stuffed with chaff, he transported a substantial part of his forces across the Danube in a single night. They had crossed into rich cornland, and the king proceeded to ravage it; the *sarisa* blades of the phalanx, held horizontally and diagonally, made havoc of the fresh harvest (Arr. 1.4.1). The unfortunate Getae kept their distance, first retreating to a lightly fortified town and then withdrawing their entire population beyond the cultivated area. They preserved themselves, but their town was looted and then destroyed. Alexander withdrew to the river, piously sacrificed to Zeus, Heracles and the Danube itself, and transported his army unscathed back to camp. It was a gratuitous act of terrorism on a helpless people, but it demonstrated yet again the efficiency and ruthlessness of the invaders and proved that the Danube was no defence against them.

The immediate consequence of these actions was a spate of embassies from the surrounding peoples, notably from Syrmus the Triballian king. Submission was offered and accepted, and the Triballians became friends and allies of Macedon on much the same level as the Thracians. True to the treaty they sent a contingent to the invasion army of 334,[18] depleting their forces at home and supplying hostages for their good behaviour. Alexander's presence had been widely felt and embassies came from surprisingly far afield. The Celtic peoples, who were pressing into the Balkans and causing difficulties for Macedon's Illyrian neighbours,[19] sent a delegation and received the same terms as the Triballians. The area technically subject to Macedon now covered the central Danubian plain, and Alexander's demonstration of military prowess ensured that it remained quiet during his absence.

Alexander now retraced his steps, taking the direct route south to Macedon, along the valleys of the Oescus and the Strymon, and he received the hospitality of his staunch ally, Langarus king of the Agrianians. Here, in the upper reaches of the Strymon, the news came of a serious threat by the Illyrian

[18] Diod. XVII.17.4; cf. L. Robert in *Fouilles d'Aï Khanoum* 1.208–10.
[19] Theopompus, *FGrH* 115 F 40; Polyaenus VII.42.

peoples of the north and west. Cleitus, probably king of the Dardani and son of the formidable Bardylis who had terrorised Macedon in the days of Perdiccas III, had made common cause with the king of the Taulantii (domiciled in the hinterland of Epidamnus) and was embarking on an invasion of Macedonia (Arr. 1.5.1). This was a challenge which could not be ignored. The north-western provinces of the kingdom could not be left undefended against their traditional enemies, especially when there was the risk of disaffection in the wake of the execution of the Lyncestian brothers. Their home territory was directly in the path of the invaders, and there might even be sympathisers to welcome them. The king moved with the rapidity that was becoming his hallmark. While Langarus invaded the lands of the Autariatae to the west and prevented any attack on the Macedonian column (Arr. 1.5.3), Alexander himself drove through Paeonia, crossing the Axios at Stobi and continuing west towards the upper reaches of the Erigon (Crna). He then moved south towards the plain of modern Florina, the heart of ancient Lyncestis. There Cleitus had already occupied a fortress. Arrian (1.5.5) names it Pellium and states that it was sited on the river Eordaicus, but his topographical details are too vague to support an identification.[20] It was certainly on the Macedonian border, close to Eordaea and the western city of Edessa, and its occupation was a threat to the whole of western Macedonia. Fortunately Alexander came on the scene before Cleitus could join forces with his Taulantian allies, and he began by laying siege to Pellium. He was soon diverted by the arrival of the Taulantian king with a large levy of tribesmen. It was impossible to continue the siege under harassment from the surrounding mountains, and foraging parties could not operate in the face of attack from the more mobile Illyrians (Arr. 1.5.9–11). Alexander carried out a tactical withdrawal, which involved a river crossing under the threat of attack from the Taulantians on the mountainside. Once again the phalanx showed its calibre, drilling in full view of the enemy in the plain by the city, and its performance was impressive enough to drive the enemy from the foothills into the fortress. He was then able to manage the river crossing in relative comfort; the rearguard of light infantry, which the king commanded personally, kept at bay the Illyrians remaining in the mountains while the army crossed file by file. A missile barrage protected the rearguard itself during its crossing. There were no casualties, and the superiority of the Macedonian military technique was fully evident.

For the moment Alexander was on the defensive, standing between the Illyrians and the Macedonian lowlands, but he did not need to wait long. His reconnaissance had revealed that the invaders were camping without defences or sentries, their morale high after the Macedonian retreat. He promptly launched a night attack, only two days after his withdrawal, and, falling on the enemy with an advance force of archers, Agrianians and phalanx infantry, he made havoc. The survivors either fled into Pellium or made their way to the

[20] See further Bosworth 1982; *contra* Hammond, 1980a, 49–57.

western mountains under hot pursuit. It was a decisive victory which removed any Illyrian threat to the northern provinces, and, although it was hardly effortless, it was achieved without significant losses. A vast gulf in terms of military effectiveness had opened between Macedon and her neighbours to the north. Alexander could not continue the campaign because of the news of the Theban revolt and the danger of general warfare in southern Greece. There was no time to force the Illyrian kings into formal submission. Instead Cleitus was left in Pellium to burn the fortress and retreat with the remnant of his army (Arr. 1.6.11). But the defeat was too complete for there to be any renewal of hostilities. No further trouble with the Illyrians is attested during Alexander's reign, and there was an Illyrian contingent in his army in 334. The only choice was to keep the peace with Macedon.

The Theban crisis (see below, p. 194) was a more pressing concern, and Alexander tackled it with frightening speed and ruthlessness. He led his army through the passes into Eordaea and forged south through Upper Macedonia, to the middle reaches of the Haliacmon via modern Kozani and the Siatista gap and south again to Thessaly by way of the Peneus valley and Tricca.[21] On the seventh day's march he had reached Pelinna, where he briefly broke his journey. Five days later he entered Boeotia, probably taking the inland route through Heracleia, Doris and the Cephisus valley rather than forcing the passes at Thermopylae. His speed was such that he arrived at Onchestus, barely three hours' march from Thebes, before the rebels were aware of his approach, and he was able to pre-empt any additional forces being sent by the city's numerous sympathisers. The Thebans stood by themselves, but they were at bay and still formidable. In the past they had fielded armies up to 7,000 strong, and in this crisis they enlisted slaves and metics to man the walls (Diod. XVII.11.2). The nodal point of their defence was the Cadmeia, the citadel where the Macedonian garrison was besieged. Its south side formed part of the city defences, and it was vital to keep the attacking army well away from the sector. If the invaders effected a junction with the garrison and entered the Cadmeia, the city was vulnerable from all sides. Accordingly a double palisade was set up outside the south wall of the Cadmeia and the Thebans prepared for their last defence. They were outnumbered by the Macedonians (Diod. XVII.11.2), but they were not so outmatched in technique as the northern tribesmen and were fighting from a prepared position.

The battle itself is variously reported and difficult to reconstruct. It began with an attack on the palisades by two phalanx battalions backed by archers and light infantry. For the moment the king kept his hypaspists and the royal *agema* in reserve[22] and there is no record of his using cavalry. The Thebans were defending a relatively small front in the vicinity of the Cadmeia and there

---

[21] Bosworth 1982, 78, 81; Hammond 1980d.

[22] Arr. 1.8.1–3; cf. Diod. XVII.11.1–12.2. According to Arrian (citing Ptolemy) the initial attack was premeditated, launched by Perdiccas without authorisation. If so, it was an unparalleled piece of insubordination by a senior officer. It is more likely that the narrative is biased, to taint Perdiccas with the stigma of failure (Bosworth 1980a, 80–1; but see Roisman 1984, 374–6).

was no space for a general engagement. The first attack was unsuccessful and the defenders were able to repel the attacking line, whose cohesion was disrupted by the palisades. Alexander himself now entered the action, and his *corps d'élite* met the Theban hoplites. At this critical stage the accounts differ. Arrian states that the Thebans were by this time in disorder and unable to resist the shock of the phalanx, while Diodorus claims that they held their ground despite heavy losses, until the Macedonians effected an entry over an unguarded stretch of the walls.[23] Arrian's account is suspiciously contracted at this point, and it is possible that his source Ptolemy did not wish to underscore the heroic resistance of the Thebans. In any case Arrian himself (1.8.5) confirms that the walls were largely stripped of defenders, and it would have been relatively easy for the larger Macedonian army to have spared a detachment to attack a vulnerable sector of the fortifications. Ptolemy apparently placed the focus on Alexander, implying that it was his intervention that forced the Thebans back into the city and allowed the walls to be occupied. It is certainly not impossible that the Theban defences were breached elsewhere and that the news of it caused panic among the army defending the Cadmeia. Once the attackers achieved an entry the Thebans were lost. The final assault came from all directions, one group of the army joining with the garrison on the citadel while the rest swarmed over the undefended walls. The Theban cavalry managed to outrun pursuit and escaped through the northern gate, but the rest were enveloped and cut down. A brief stand at the Ampheion was soon broken, and general carnage ensued, as Alexander's Boeotian and Phocian allies glutted their hatred of Thebes and enthusiastically abetted the Macedonians in the slaughter. The tragedy was inevitable once the Thebans decided on resistance. Outnumbered as they were, they could not prevent a liaison between the attackers and the garrison of the Cadmeia, and their fortifications were woefully inadequate. At least their defence was stubborn and costly. Five hundred Macedonians are said to have fallen (Diod. XVII.14.1), and it had been a far cry from the bloodless victories in the north. The Thebans, however, suffered 6,000 casualties and 30,000 survivors were enslaved. Their city ceased to exist. The massacre and its aftermath effectively suppressed the unrest in southern Greece (see below, p. 196), and Alexander could justly congratulate himself on a brilliantly successful year. He had reinforced Macedonian control in all directions and given several object lessons illustrating the futility of challenging his awesome military machine.

Thebes had fallen late in September. Shortly afterwards Alexander was ready to return to Macedon and prepare for the invasion of Asia. His route home took him through Pieria, where he lingered for nine days at Dium, celebrating the scenic festival in honour of the Muses and Olympian Zeus

---

[23] Arr. 1.8.5; Diod. XVII.12.3. Polyaenus IV.3.12 has the story of the side attack but makes the successful commander Antipater, not Perdiccas as in Diodorus.

which Archelaus had founded some seventy years before.[24] The sacrifices and entertainment were alike magnificent, dominated by banquets in the royal tent with its 100 couches, and the army as a whole rested, taking its ease after nearly seven months of continuous campaigning.

The following spring saw the opening of full-scale hostilities in Asia. It was none too soon. The Persian empire had achieved a degree of stability after two years of chaos. The grand vizier, the formidable eunuch Bagoas, had been the king-maker, first poisoning Artaxerxes III and elevating his youngest son Arses, and then eliminating the new king with his family after only two years on the throne. That disposed of almost the entire male line of Artaxerxes. The successor belonged to a collateral line of the royal house, a lineal descendant of Darius II.[25] This man, who is termed Artasata in the Babylonian documents,[26] assumed the regnal name of his great-grandfather and began his rule as Darius III in the summer of 336. He was impressive in appearance, tall and good-looking, and had distinguished himself in action against the Cadusii of the south Caspian coast. Before his accession he had probably collaborated with Bagoas, but once on the throne he immediately removed the vizier, who was assassinated on suspicion of conspiracy. Darius could now rule in his own right, and he first set himself to suppressing the various revolts that had broken out during the period of anarchy. Egypt had been estranged since the death of Artaxerxes III, ruled by a native dynast, Khababash, who claimed the monarchy of Upper and Lower Egypt.[27] There is also a strong probability that Babylonia was in ferment under a usurper whose name, Nidin-Bel, recalled the pretender who challenged Darius I in 522.[28] If there was a usurpation, it was soon over. The fragmentary king list from Uruk which mentions Nidin-Bel goes on to give Darius five years of rule, in which case he had re-established Persian control of Babylonia by 335. Egypt was reconquered with equal rapidity over the winter of 336/5. A Persian fleet penetrated the Delta, and the country was forced back to subjection under a satrap of the Great King. By the end of 335 the empire was quiet and Darius could turn his attention to the threat from the west. The fleet which had proved itself in Egypt was mobilised for war in the Aegean, and by the summer of 334 an armada of 400 warships, mostly Cypriot and Phoenician, was ready for action.

Meanwhile in Asia Minor the Macedonian offensive had faltered. The first season of campaigning, in the summer of 336, had been a success; the military operations had encouraged democratic revolutions as far south as Ephesus. In 335, however, the Persian defence became much more effective thanks to the activities of Memnon of Rhodes, a landholder in the Troad and an intimate and relative by marriage of the great Persian noble Artabazus. Memnon was

---

[24] Arr. 1.11.1–2; Diod. XVII.16.3–4; cf. Bosworth 1976b, 119–21; Hatzopoulos 1982a, 39–41.
[25] Diod. XVII.5.3–5; cf. Justin x.3.1–5; Strabo 736; Arr. II.14.5.
[26] Sachs 1977, 143. Justin x.3.3–4 gives Darius' pre-regnal name as Codomannus.
[27] Kienitz 1953, 110, 185ff.; Lane Fox 1973, 109–10.
[28] J. van Dijk, in *Vorläufiger Bericht über die ... Ausgrabungen in Uruk-Warka* 18 (Berlin, 1962), 53–60; J. B. Pritchard, *ANET*³ 566.

supplied with mercenaries by the Great King and began operations late in 336. Before the death of Attalus he had inflicted a defeat on a numerically superior Macedonian force outside Magnesia (by Sipylus?).[29] This did not apparently result in the capture of the city, but it was a shock to Macedonian morale, which was soon shaken further by the murder of Attalus. In the following season Memnon pressed his offensive northwards, crossing Mt Ida for a surprise attack on Cyzicus which was almost successful.[30] After ravaging Cyzicene territory he withdrew his forces to Parmenion's theatre of operations on the Elaitic Gulf. He was too late to prevent the capture and enslavement of Gryneium, but he forced the Macedonians to raise the siege of Pitane and threw them on the defensive. But Memnon was not the only Persian commander. There was a general mobilisation by the satraps of Asia Minor who pooled their military forces and concentrated them by the Propontis. This movement was not completed until the spring of 334, but one may assume that the Persian forces in the Aegean sector gradually increased throughout 335. Arsites and Spithridates, satraps of Hellespontine Phrygia and Lydia, must have been involved in the defence from the beginning. As a result of this activity Calas, Parmenion's colleague in command of the expeditionary force, found himself outnumbered even in the Troad and was forced back to the bridgehead at Rhoeteum (Diod. xvii.7.10). By the spring of 334 the Macedonian forces appear to have contracted to the Hellespont, where they kept the crossing points secure, but the rest of their territorial gains had evaporated. At Ephesus an oligarchic counter-revolution, supported by Memnon, had taken the city out of Macedonian control,[31] and there were presumably similar movements elsewhere. The Persians had now gained the initiative and their land forces were massing dangerously close to the Hellespont as their fleet gradually approached Aegean waters.

## III    **First victory**

The campaign began in the early spring of 334 B.C. Alexander had assembled his invasion army in Macedonia over the previous winter. It totalled 32,000 foot and approximately 5,000 cavalry; and, when it joined with the advance force operating in Asia, the entire complement was close to 50,000.[32] This was by far the largest and most formidable expedition that had ever left Greek shores, but as yet Macedonian numbers were far from exhausted. Alexander was able to leave a defence force in Europe that was nearly as powerful as his invasion army, with a nucleus of 12,000 phalanx infantry (Diod. xvii.17.5). For the moment Antipater, who was to act as Alexander's regent in Macedon and deputise as *hegemon* of the Corinthian League, had ample resources to

---

[29] Polyaenus v.44.4; cf. Badian 1966, 40–1, 63.
[30] Diod. xvii.7.3–8; Polyaenus v.44.5; cf. Goukowsky 1969.
[31] Arr. 1.17.11; cf. Badian 1966, 41–2; Heisserer 1980, 67–70.
[32] See below, p. 259.

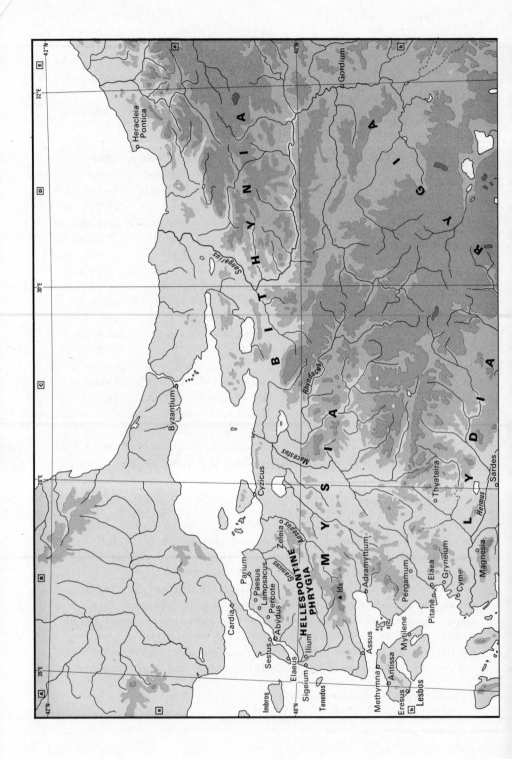

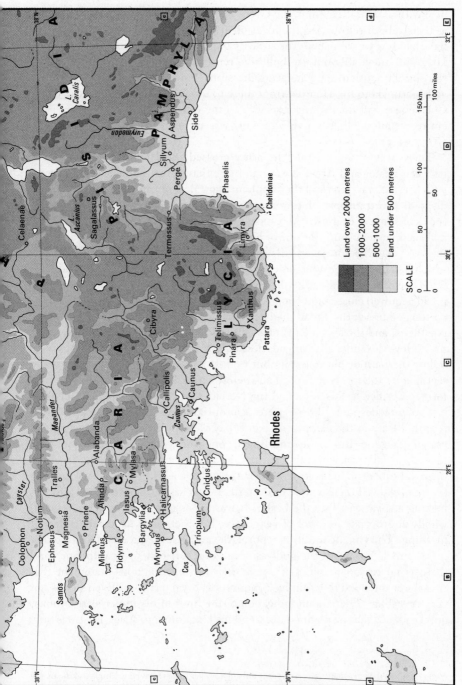

2. *Western Asia Minor.*

deal with any disaffection in the Greek world. That superiority was to be lost
as the strain of reinforcing the invasion army took its toll, but Alexander can
have had few worries about the security of his kingdom when he left it in 334.
His route, inevitably but symbolically, retraced the invasion route of Xerxes,
skirting the south of the Pangaeum massif to Philippi, proceeding via Abdera
and Maroneia to the Hebrus, from there to the river Melas at the head of the
Chersonese and finally turning south to the crossing-point at Sestos.[33] The
entire distance, slightly over 500 km, was covered in exactly twenty days
(Arr.1.11.5).

There was a pause while the army crossed the Hellespont. The straits
between Sestos and Abydus were no more than seven stades wide, but even
with the 160 warships and the supplementary fleet of cargo ships at the king's
disposal the transport of the army and baggage train would have been a
time-consuming exercise. Alexander was able to profit from the delay and
make a diversion south for one of his most impressive acts of propaganda. At
the tip of the Chersonese was Elaeus, the crossing-point for the Troad, an area
which had the strongest possible sentimental associations for him. It had been
the scene of the first great Panhellenic expedition into Asia and more recently
it had acquired close connections with the war of vengeance. Athene Ilias, the
patron goddess of the Troad, had been the principal victim of Persian sacrilege
at Athens, and the shrine of Protesilaus at Elaeus had also been plundered in
480. Now Alexander the Argead, descendant of Heracles and Achilles, was to
follow the path of his ancestors but against a greater foe. His first act was a
sacrifice by the tomb of Protesilaus before embarkation, to be followed by a
formal sacrifice to Poseidon and the Nereides in mid-crossing and a libation
into the Hellespont. These were appropriate acts of ritual propitiation,
repeated later in the campaign,[34] and they were probably traditional acts of
cult in Macedon. But at the same time no one who witnessed them would have
missed the contrast with the scourges and fetters of Xerxes. On the far shore
the royal squadron made its landfall at the Achaeans' Harbour, where the king
himself followed the example of Protesilaus and leaped ashore in full armour,
making a spear-cast into the beach. It was a classic statement of aggression,
wholly appropriate in a war of vengeance, but there may have been a deeper
meaning. The vulgate tradition reports Alexander subsequently declaring that
he accepted Asia from the gods as spear-won territory.[35] If authentic (and
there is no reason to reject it), it is the first unambiguous statement that
Alexander intended to retain his conquests as royal territory. Even so it is not
very revealing. There is no indication of the limit of his imperial ambitions,
only evidence that he planned to extend his kingdom into Asia. That was only

[33] Cf. Bosworth 1980a, 99–100; Engels 1978a, 26–9.
[34] Cf. Arr. VI.19.5; *Ind.* 20.10; VI.3.1; *Ind.* 18.11.
[35] So Diod. XVII.17.2. Justin XI.5.10 speaks only of a prayer to be received willingly as king by the
lands of Asia. It is fanciful to see any juridical significance in his actions: cf. Instinsky 1949,
29–40; Schmitthenner 1968; Mehl 1980–1.

to be expected. Philip had vastly expanded his dominions by conquests on the northern Aegean coast, and his son could hardly do less in Asia.

For Arrian (and possibly his sources) it was the invocation of the past that mattered most. The king made a formal visit to the sanctuary of Athene at Ilium and gained her blessing for the war, exchanging his own ceremonial armour for venerable relics in the shrine. In future the arms from the original Panhellenic war would be carried into battle before him. He also offered heroic honours to the great dead, notably his Aeacid ancestors, Achilles and Ajax.[36] But he did not follow the example of Herodotus and interpret the Trojan War as an early instance of the perpetual antagonism between Greek and Barbarian. He had Trojan blood in him through the Molossian royal line, which traced its origins to Achilles' son Neoptolemus and the captive Trojan princess Andromache; and he was eager to reconcile the two sides of his lineage. He showered benefactions upon the little community of Ilium in memory of Andromache (Strabo 594) and, more significantly, he made an apotropaic sacrifice to Priam on the supposed site of his murder, so expiating the guilt of Neoptolemus (Arr. 1.11.8). For Alexander the Trojans were not barbarians but Hellenes on Asian soil, and both in his person and in his propaganda he united the Greek communities on either side of the Aegean. The descendants of Achilles and Priam would now fight together against the common enemy. It was a most evocative variation on the theme of Panhellenism, and Alexander proceeded to battle with the ghosts of the past enlisted in his service.

He now rejoined his army, which was concentrated in the broad plain of Arisbe after its crossing, and began his march to meet the Persian army. The defending forces were assembled by the shore of the Propontis, in the vicinity of Zeleia, a small city 15 km inland from the mouth of the river Aesepus. There the Persian generals held a council of war to discuss their immediate strategy, an exercise complicated by the fact that there was a multitude of commanders and no clear hierarchy of command. Policy was apparently determined by majority decision.[37] The fundamental issue was whether to risk everything in a single pitched battle, and, given the relative strengths of the two armies, it was no easy decision. The Persians were far stronger in cavalry, with 20,000 horsemen levied from Asia Minor, but they were comparatively weak in infantry. Their forces of Greek mercenaries totalled less than 20,000 and their native troops, however numerous, were hopelessly inferior in calibre. Memnon of Rhodes argued against an immediate battle, pressing for the systematic destruction of all fodder in the path of the Macedonian army, a move which would have been particularly effective in the lean period before the harvest.[38] But there was strong opposition. Not surprisingly Arsites, satrap of Hellespontine Phrygia, was reluctant to see his territory devastated

---

[36] Arr. 1.12.1; Plut. *Al.* 15.7–8; Diod. XVII.17.3; Justin XI.5.12.
[37] Davis 1964; *contra* Badian 1977b, 283–4.
[38] Arr. 1.12.9; cf. Diod. XVII.18.2.

and spoke in favour of a full-scale engagement which would bring a quick end to the war. The limited Persian successes of 335 must have created expectations of victory over the young king, who was still an unknown quantity in Asia; and Arsites won over his fellow generals. As a Greek Memnon was distrusted and suspected (perhaps with some justice) of wishing to prolong the war for his own advantage. The decisions once taken, the Persians took up a defensive position on the main road west of Zeleia. They encamped above the plain of Adrasteia, an alluvial deposit intersected by the river Granicus, blocking any Macedonian movement east towards Zeleia and Cyzicus.[39] Alexander, they assumed, would not evade the challenge.

The Persians had begun their advance after the news of Alexander's crossing, and their choice of position must have been determined by their reconnaissance reports of the king's movements. Alexander himself was equally tentative, with no precise information about the Persian position. At first he led his forces to the head of the Hellespont, skirting Lampsacus and branching inland south of Parium, so as to avoid the rough passage of the coastline by Priapus.[40] During this latter part of the march he deployed an advance screen of scouts (Arr. 1.12.7, 13.1); and he was obviously expecting to make contact with the enemy. That contact came when he came within sight of the plain of Adrasteia, when his scouts reported the Persian army in position on the east bank of the Granicus, occupying the foothills around the modern town of Dimetoka. The strategic problem must have been immediately apparent. The river Granicus was sunk in a channel below steeply rising banks, which are now some three to four metres high. Its course, as the remains of a Roman bridge clearly show, has not changed significantly since antiquity, and its physical appearance will have been much the same then as now. In that case the depth of the river, scarcely more than a metre in early spring, would not have been a serious obstacle. The problem was the steepness of the banks, which precluded a frontal assault in extended line. Alexander's phalanx would inevitably have been dislocated and ran the risk of being slaughtered in the stream bed.

The Persian strategy was obviously designed to take maximum advantage of the river's disruptive effect, but how they actually deployed their forces is a deep mystery. Arrian (1.14.4–5) represents the entire Persian cavalry deployed along the edge of the river with the infantry stationed behind on high ground, which can only have been the range of foothills 1½ km east of the river.[41] That, as has often been observed, was a military absurdity, the cavalry separated from the infantry and placed in a position where their advantage was totally wasted. If they were to be an effective counter to the Macedonian forces, they should have been drawn up far enough away from the crossing-point to mount a full-blooded charge with the momentum to force the enemy back into the

[39] Janke 1904, 128–36; Foss 1977; Hammond 1980c, 76–80.
[40] Arr. 1.12.6–7. For the route see Bosworth 1980a, 107–9; Foss 1977, 496–8; Seibert 1985, 30–2.
[41] Janke, 1904, 129; Foss 1977, 501–2; Hammond 1980c, 80.

stream bed.[42] Stationary at the water's edge they were, themselves, vulnerable. But not all sources depict the Persian cavalry so close. In Diodorus' version of the battle they are deployed along the foothills so as to take advantage of the disruption of the Macedonian phalanx. The context is rhetorical and garbled by contraction, but the gist of it is found elsewhere[43] and the details of the battle reported by Arrian (1.15.7) suggest that part at least of the Persian line was capable of a charge at speed. There is certainly a good deal of colourful but uninformative writing in Arrian (and Plutarch), the fighting mysteriously transposing itself from the stream to the banks beyond (Arr. 1.15.2–4); and there is a chance that his narrative reflects an encomiastic court tradition designed to make the most of the difficulties of the crossing in defiance of the military possibilities. At all events the facts of the engagement are hopelessly obscured by the rhetorical predilections of the sources and the facts are probably lost for ever. One can only hazard the reconstruction that does least violence to the facts of topography.

A second problem is the time of the attack. Alexander approached the Granicus towards evening. Arrian (1.13.3–7) reports an exchange between the young king and Parmenion, in which the old general advised delay, pointing out the difficulties of the crossing and pressing for an assault at dawn. Alexander rejected his advice with the heroic (and fatuous) apophthegm that it would be shameful to baulk at the Granicus after crossing the Hellespont. The substance recurs in Plutarch (*Al.* 16.3), and the episode was clearly a favourite, part of a tradition of continuing disagreement between Alexander and his over-great subject.[44] On the other hand Diodorus speaks as though Parmenion's advice was acted upon and claims that Alexander crossed the river at daybreak, forestalling the Persian attack.[45] If he is correctly reproducing his source, we can only conclude that the most basic details of the engagement were contested in antiquity. The weight of evidence favours the tradition of Arrian and Plutarch, and it is quite possible that Diodorus' version comes from a confused abridgement of Parmenion's advice – what the old general suggested was misinterpreted as what happened. But it is also possible that the debate is fictional, designed to give Alexander's behaviour the strongest heroic colouring. Fortunately it makes little difference whether he attacked in the morning or the evening. What mattered was the strategic problem of the crossing. How could the king transport his battle line across the river without being thrown back by the massed Persian cavalry?

Alexander's forces were soon in battle array. His marching order already had the phalanx sandwiched between cavalry forces on either wing and he retained the same formation, the hypaspists and phalanx battalions in the centre, the Thessalian, Greek and Thracian cavalry on the left under

[42] So Judeich 1908, 389; Badian 1977b, 283–4.
[43] Diod. XVII.19.2; cf. Polyaenus IV.3.16.
[44] Cf. Arr. 1.18.6–9; II.25.2–3; III.10.1–2. The ultimate source may be Callisthenes.
[45] Diod. XVII.19.3; cf. *Itin. Alex.* 20 (*sub luce*).

Parmenion and on the right the Macedonian cavalry. In the right of the line there were two major groups. At the extreme right was Philotas with the bulk of the Companions and supporting light infantry, Agrianians and archers, and there was a composite force under Amyntas son of Arrhabaeus comprising the *prodromoi*, Paeonians and a single *ile* of Companions (Arr. 1.14.1). Amyntas' detachment came between the infantry and Companion cavalry, and the king himself took up position next to it. This was to be the fulcrum of his attack: Amyntas' men led the way across the river, followed by Alexander and the rest of the right wing. It looks as though they faced the easiest part of the river bank. The *prodromoi*, who on this occasion were armed with the long cavalry *sarisa*,[46] cannot have been expected to struggle up a sheer face. The most probable explanation is that, then as now, there were occasional stretches of the river where accumulations of gravel made the ascent and descent relatively simple.[47] These gravel slopes contrasted with stretches where the banks were steep and overgrown with vegetation. Access for an army was confined to a limited number of points, and we may assume that Amyntas' force took the easiest route, crossing the river without difficulty and continuing at speed up the opposite slope. Their mission was to get as far as possible from the bank and stem the initial charge of the Persian cavalry, so allowing the rest of the right wing to filter across the stream. As they crossed, Alexander brought the rest of the Companions into motion, following up the access slope. This movement naturally took him downstream to the left, and he kept his forces in a diagonal line,[48] so that they would be able to use the whole width of the gravel bed, sweeping up not in column but in successive waves, which would gradually assume the characteristic Macedonian wedge formation. If Diodorus (XVII.19.6) may be trusted, the same operation took place on the left of the line, where the Thessalian cavalry under Parmenion established the bridgehead.

At first the action favoured the Persians. The Macedonian vanguard was hopelessly outnumbered and faced the flower of the enemy cavalry, including Memnon and his sons. It was badly mauled and forced back towards the river. But it had achieved its main task. The momentum of the Persian charge was absorbed and there was free ground for Alexander to make a counter-charge. This he did in typically brilliant fashion, leading the assault himself and plunging into the most reckless hand-to-hand combat. It nearly ended the campaign. A secondary charge, led by a son-in-law of the Persian king, was directed at Alexander himself (the squadron may have been kept in reserve for that very purpose), and the young king was assailed from several quarters. The details are variously reported,[49] but it is clear that his main antagonists were the brothers Rhoesaces and Spithridates, that Alexander's helmet was

[46] Arr. 1.14.1; cf. 13.1.
[47] Cf. Janke 1904, 138; Foss 1977, 502; Badian 1977b, 281–2.
[48] Arr. 1.14.7, a *locus conclamatus*: for very different exegeses see Badian 1977b, 286–9; Hammond 1980c, 75–6.
[49] Arr. 1.15.7–8; Plut. *Al.* 16.8–11; Diod. XVII.20.5–7; Curt. VIII.1.20.

shattered and he would have received the *coup de grâce* but for the timely intervention of Cleitus the Black, commander of the Royal *ile*. It was a critical moment which underlined the fundamental weakness of the campaign. Alexander had embarked on the expedition childless and unmarried, apparently against the wishes of his senior advisers, Antipater and Parmenion. If he were suddenly killed, not only would the invasion be hamstrung but Macedon would inevitably face a destructive struggle for the succession. Few enterprises have ever been so dependent on the survival of a single man, yet Alexander's career was a continuing saga of heroic self-exposure. Each wound he incurred was fresh evidence of the fragility of the political structure which underpinned the campaign, renewed warning that every victory of his army could be nullified by a random missile or the assassin's knife. There must have been widespread expectation of his imminent death, and that expectation will have fuelled resistance to his regime.

At the Granicus the danger was averted. Alexander escaped without serious harm and the Macedonian cavalry rapidly proved its superiority. As at Plataea a century and a half ago, superior armament turned the scale. The Macedonian lances of cornel wood were more than a match for the light javelins of their opponents.[50] The bridgehead grew larger and, as more squadrons pressed over, the Persian cavalry was forced inexorably back. After the decimation of their commanders, eight of whom are specifically named among the fallen,[51] their line broke in the centre and the retreat became a rout. The Macedonians held their ground until all the army was across the river and then advanced against the mercenary infantry. These troops had taken no part in the battle, which to them must have seemed a confused and dust-veiled mêlée, until their own cavalry turned and left the field. Faced with this sudden reverse of fortune they held their position in the foothills, no doubt hoping for an armistice.[52] But in the heat of battle Alexander was in no mood for parley. The luckless mercenaries had to face the phalanx frontally while they were enveloped on the wings by the cavalry, and a massacre ensued. Forced to fight to the last, the mercenaries inflicted some of the heaviest casualties of the engagements; nine tenths of them were cut down where they stood, the remaining two thousand taken as prisoners-of-war. Alexander's first victory was complete and decisive, and it had been ominously rapid. Once his cavalry had cleared the crossing-point the battle was virtually over. The Persians had been demonstrably outmatched; they had lost a large proportion of their effective infantry and were in no position to contest the occupation of Asia Minor by land. That was acknowledged by the senior surviving Persian commander, Arsites, who retired from his satrapy to Greater Phrygia, where he committed suicide, conscious of his responsibility for the disaster.[53] The

---

[50] Arr. 1.16.1. See, however, Badian 1977b, 285–6.
[51] Arr. 1.16.3; cf. Diod. xvii.21.3.
[52] Plut. *Al.* 16.13; contrast Arr. 1.16.2.
[53] Arr. 1.16.3. Arsites' son was exiled to the Persian Gulf (Nearchus, *FGrH* 133 F 27–8).

other commanders who remained alive dispersed, Atizyes and Arsames to their satrapies of Phrygia and Cilicia and Memnon to the Aegean coast, where the next act in the drama would be played.

Master of the field, Alexander buried his dead, paying especial honours to the cavalry who had fallen at the opening of the battle and had been the real architects of his victory. A statue group in bronze was commissioned from the great Lysippus and graced Dium, the city of the Muses, until it was removed by Roman invaders in 146 B.C.[54] He also paid due honour to Athene, sending 300 Persian panoplies as a dedication for the Parthenon. They were the first fruits of the war of revenge, as Alexander stressed in the dedicatory superscription. He added that they came from all the Greeks except the Spartans.[55] It rankled that the expedition was not truly Panhellenic, and Sparta's abstention was duly noted. The captured mercenaries were guilty of a more heinous sin, Hellenes who had fought against Hellenes in violation of the decrees of the Corinthian League. They were accordingly transported to Macedonia, to redeem themselves by labour and possibly to augment the agricultural workforce, which Alexander had depleted for his invasion army. It was not an enviable fate, and the mercenaries remaining in Persian service were left no choice except to serve their paymasters to the bitter end.

IV     **The Aegean coast (summer 334 B.C.)**

The king did not pause long after his triumph. He briefly asserted his sovereignty over Hellespontine Phrygia, installing a satrap of his own in place of Arsites and demanding the tribute previously paid to Persia. The satrapal capital of Dascyleum, some 32 km south of Cyzicus, was occupied by Parmenion (Arr. 1.17.2), but otherwise the region was left untouched, its pacification reserved for the new satrap, Calas. Alexander had more pressing strategic concerns in the south, now that the Persian fleet was on the verge of entering the Aegean. His own fleet naturally followed the coast round towards Ephesus. The route of the army is not attested, except for Diodorus' vague statement that it marched through Lydia (XVII.21.7). Arrian (1.17.3) states baldly that he advanced to Sardes, and there is no tradition of any operations near the coast in the Troad or northern Aeolis. It is most probable that he followed the main inland route from the Propontis, driving south-east from Zeleia to the Macestus valley, then via the fertile plains of Balikesir and Kircağaç to Thyateira and finally to the Hermus valley.[56] That was a march of some 270 km, which brought him down quickly into the vicinity of Sardes, frustrating any attempt by the Persian garrison to remove its treasure. The garrison commander, Mithrenes, offered his surrender when Alexander's

[54] Arr. 1.16.4; Plut. *Al.* 16.16; Vell. Pat. 1.11.3–5; Pliny, *NH* xxxiv.64. Cf. Bosworth 1980a, 125–6, *contra* Hammond 1980b, 460–1.

[55] Arr. 1.16.7; Plut. *Al.* 16.18.

[56] For the route see Robert 1962, 50; Magie, *Roman Rule in Asia Minor* 797–9; Seibert 1985, 35–7; *contra* Engels 1978a, 30–3.

army was still 15 km away, and the city with its colossally strong citadel fell into Macedonian hands without a blow.

Alexander stayed at Sardes only long enough to install his own garrison and administrative officials (see below, p. 229) and to found a temple for the head of the Macedonian pantheon, Olympian Zeus, whose cult would coexist with that of the Persian Ahuramazda, also worshipped at Sardes in the guise of Zeus.[57] At the same time he granted the Lydians their ancestral laws and declared them free. That was mere propaganda. Alexander had indeed liberated them from Persian rule, but he substituted a regime that differed little, if at all, from the past. The visible attributes of subjection, satrapal government and the payment of tribute, remained. No doubt the great Persian landholders were dispossessed, but there is no evidence that the native Lydians were the beneficiaries. In any case there was no time for detailed organisation on the eve of the Aegean War; and the new satrap, Asander, can have made few concessions to Lydian autonomy during the stress of campaign. The Lydians had exchanged masters and probably had mixed feelings about the new despot who proclaimed that his service was perfect freedom.[58]

For the moment the king's concerns were military. An expeditionary force of allied troops was sent north to deal with Memnon's estates in the Troad, which had been left untouched before and after the Granicus. He himself took the main army south to the Cayster valley and westwards to the coast at Ephesus, which he reached on the fourth day out from Sardes, having covered about 100 km. The city lay open to him. His fleet was in the area, and its Persian garrison had abandoned it as indefensible. Ephesus itself was in the grip of a democratic counter-revolution. The previous oligarchic junta had been lynched as soon as their Persian protectors left the city; and Alexander prevented any further reprisals, forcing an amnesty on the Ephesians, an act of benevolent despotism but despotism none the less. He also restored the democratic leaders exiled in 335, who now became the backbone of the new government, and endowed the famous sanctuary of Artemis with the tribute formerly paid to the Great King.[59] His acts were clearly regarded as benefactions, designed to encourage submission elsewhere. In this they were immediately effective. Magnesia and Tralles, cities on the Carian border to the south, surrendered to him while he was still at Ephesus, and Alexander was inspired to a further gesture of magnanimity. Alcimachus, brother of the famous Lysimachus, was sent to the north to operate in the areas of Ionia and Aeolis where there were still Persian garrisons, and he was given specific instructions to establish democracies, restore autonomy and remit the tribute paid to the Persians.[60] This was no general manifesto. Alcimachus' commission was to win over occupied cities, and he was obviously given the utmost

[57] Arr. 1.17.5; cf. Robert 1975.
[58] Tibiletti 1954; Badian 1966, 44–5; Bosworth 1980a, 128–9.
[59] See below, pp. 251–2.
[60] Arr. 1.18.2. For fuller discussion see below, pp. 252–3.

latitude to make the conditions of surrender attractive. Other cities might receive their liberty, but the grant was not necessarily accompanied by remission of tribute, and Alexander reserved the right to intervene arbitrarily in the affairs of any city. Even in Alcimachus' case we have no indication that he was widely successful. There were bitter memories in Aeolis of Macedonian operations under Parmenion, and in the latter part of 334 the Persian fleet was able to operate almost unimpeded in the northern Aegean. The most generous offers may not have been sufficient to foment revolution in the occupied cities.

The interlude at Ephesus concluded with a sacrifice and solemn procession to Artemis, and Alexander moved south to Miletus while his fleet rounded the rocky peninsula of Mycale. Here the garrison commander decided on resistance.[61] The Persian fleet was now only a matter of days away, and Miletus, which was three parts surrounded by sea, would provide an ideal base for it. In the event, Alexander's fleet arrived first and occupied the offshore island of Lade, preventing access by the Persians. Their fleet was 400 strong, more than twice the number of Alexander's warships, but they were now helpless. Denied an anchorage close to Miletus, they had no alternative but to withdraw and establish a base under the foothills of Mycale, at least 15 km from the city. Meanwhile the action continued on land. There was no question of a sea battle against the seasoned crews from Cyprus and Phoenicia, and Alexander devoted his attention to the siege. A proposal by the Milesian oligarch, Glaucippus, offering Miletus as an open city for Persians and Macedonians alike, was rejected categorically (Arr. 1.19.1), and Alexander began operations. His first assaults were abortive, but once his siege engines were operative it was a different story. The rain of arrows and possibly stones from his siege towers stripped the walls of defenders, and his rams rapidly opened a breach over a narrow sector. Simultaneously his fleet formed a defensive barrier in front of the harbour entrances, so that the Persian warships were reduced to the role of observers, shadowing the action from a safe distance at sea (Arr. 1.19.2). In the city there was panic. The defence at the walls collapsed, and the Milesian civil population offered their surrender at the last moment.[62] That and their ancestors' resistance to Persia in the Ionian Revolt guaranteed the city's survival, although it must have been garrisoned and subjected to tribute. The defending forces were massacred, except for about 300 mercenaries who had taken refuge on one of the islets of Miletus. These Alexander took into his own service. It was his first act of conciliation with the Greeks on the Persian side, but it was too limited a gesture to outweigh the massacre at the Granicus.

The superior numbers of the Persian fleet had been totally frustrated. Even their base on Mycale was neutralised when Alexander sent his cavalry and three battalions of infantry to prevent their landing (Arr. 1.19.7–8). Shortage

---

[61] Arr. 1.18.4; cf. Diod. xvii.22.1.
[62] Diod. xvii.22.4–5; Arr. 1.19.6; cf. Bickermann 1934, 358; Bosworth 1980a, 140.

of water and provisions inevitably forced them to cross the straits to Samos, where the Athenian cleruchs allowed them to reprovision.[63] Even so, they had no secure base on land, and they could only patrol the coast in the hope that the Macedonian fleet would be rash enough to offer battle. Alexander's success had perhaps been too complete. He had given the classic demonstration that a fleet of warships, however large, could do nothing without a safe shore base. At the same time his own fleet had been at best accessory, unable to meet the Persians in the open sea and helpless without the army. Rather than build it up until it was a match for the enemy he took perhaps the most controversial strategic decision of his reign and demobilised altogether, except for a small squadron which he used for bulk transport.[64] In future his military actions would be confined to the land, and he would continue his tactics at Miletus, preventing the Persians landing and replenishing their provisions. That strategy worked admirably if the Persian fleet stayed close to him and contested his passage. If they took themselves elsewhere, the situation was very different. Alexander's satraps simply did not have the military resources to patrol the Aegean coast, and there was a real danger of a Persian reconquest of the north. That in fact nearly happened in the early months of 333, when Alexander had no choice but to commission a new fleet, tacitly admitting a military blunder.[65] The Persians could do incalculable damage along the winding coastline of Asia Minor, and Alexander had given them virtually *carte blanche*.

For the moment the king continued his march down the coast to the principal Persian arsenal at Halicarnassus. Set in a natural theatre, the city had been strongly fortified under Hecatomnid rule, its walls following the contour of the surrounding hills.[66] There were also powerful citadels within the wall circuit, Salmacis at the western extremity of the fortifications and the island fortress of Zephyrium, which contained the palace of Mausolus. Approach from the sea was easy, and, now that there was no challenge to the Persian fleet, it could be provisioned indefinitely. The defence was organised by Memnon of Rhodes, who had been promoted to the command of the war in the west. The report of the disaster at the Granicus had impelled Darius to commit responsibility to a single general, who was given power over the whole of the Aegean coast.[67] As a matter of courtesy he co-operated with the Carian satrap, Orontobates, but his authority was apparently overriding. News of the promotion will have reached Memnon on the eve of Alexander's arrival, and he took immediate action. He concentrated at Halicarnassus the mercenary forces which had been evacuated from the city garrisons in Alexander's path. He also ensured that the walls were in perfect shape and protected the

[63] Arr. 1.19.8; cf. Gell. *NA* xi.9.
[64] Arr. 1.20.1; Diod. xvii.22.5–23.3; cf. Bosworth 1980a, 141–3.
[65] Curt. iii.1.19–20; Arr. ii.2.3. See below, pp. 52–3.
[66] Cf. Bean and Cook 1955, 89–91; Hornblower 1982, 297–305.
[67] Arr. 1.20.3; ii.1.1; Diod. xvii.23.6, 29.1.

harbours with a screen of triremes. So defended, the city was the most formidable military challenge that the king had yet faced.

The Macedonian army approached by the coastal road, from Iasus and Bargylia, and the assault began at the Mylasa gate, towards the north-east salient of the walls. At first the operations were abortive, largely because Alexander had not assembled his full siege train. There was a short interlude while he made an unsuccessful attempt to capture Myndus, a dependent city on the western side of the Halicarnassus peninsula, and then the siege resumed, both sides using every refinement of military technique.[68] The Macedonians first filled the defensive moats in front of the city walls and then brought up siege towers to strip the battlements of defenders with a hail of arrows and stones from torsion catapults, while the walls were shaken at their foundations by rams and saps. The defenders retaliated by increasingly desperate sorties, attempting to set fire to the Macedonian siege engines. At the same time they strengthened their walls by a subsidiary lunette of brick. It is clear from Diodorus' narrative that they had considerable success. The most notable incident came when the walls were almost breached. Two towers and the intervening curtain wall had been demolished, and a night attack developed when two drunken members of Perdiccas' battalion tried to scale the defences in a fit of reckless bravado. More of the battalion followed their example, until there was a full-scale engagement. The Macedonians suffered heavy casualties, and the defenders were forced back into the walls only after intense fighting. The dead remained unrecoverable, thanks to the raking fire from Halicarnassus, and Alexander was compelled to parley for a truce, a humiliation unique in his reign.[69] Most of this is slurred over by Arrian, who focuses upon the Macedonian successes and represents the siege as a series of effortless victories.[70] The reality was very different. Even when the Macedonians penetrated the outer wall, they found themselves enclosed by the secondary crescent-shaped defence of brick, and they became vulnerable in the flank and rear. The defenders had even mounted a large wooden tower on the wall, which housed arrow-firing catapults.[71] Despite the losses the attack was pressed home and the situation of the defenders became critical. The hastily constructed lunette could not resist the massed attack of the Macedonian siege train indefinitely, and a last great sortie was launched. Led by Athenian mercenary commanders, Ephialtes and Thrasybulus, the Persian forces attacked the engines massed by the lunette. A smaller group simultaneously engaged other Macedonian units stationed by the triple gate on the west side of the city. Once more the attack was almost successful. Some of the siege towers were fired, and Ephialtes began to rout the Macedonian infantry under a covering barrage from the walls. At this crisis a group of veterans stiffened

[68] Diod. XVII.24.4–25.5; Arr. I.20.8–10. Cf. Marsden 1969, 100–2.
[69] Diod. XVII.25.5–6; Arr. I.21.1–4.
[70] Arr. I.20.8, 21.3, 21.6, 22.2–4; cf. Bosworth 1976a, 21–2.
[71] Arr. I.21.4, 23.2; cf. Diod. XVII.26.6.

the Macedonian resistance and turned the tide, repelling the sortie back into the city.[72] Ephialtes among others was killed.

At this point Memnon consulted with his senior commanders and decided to abandon the defence. While it was still night, he set fire to the arsenals of munitions and to the great tower on the walls and withdrew his men to the two inner citadels. The city was left to conflagration and to Alexander. When dawn broke, the king surveyed the ravaged city. It lay open to his army, but the enemy forces were still relatively intact occupying the citadels of Salmacis and Zephyrium, both easily supplied by sea. For all the labour and carnage of the siege he was hardly advanced in the main task. Halicarnassus was still occupied against him and the fleet, based on Cos, was fully operational, ready to take the offensive as soon as his back was turned. Alexander did not think of storming the citadels. Morale had flagged too much during the final sortie for him to risk a second protracted siege. Instead he razed the houses and walls of Halicarnassus, levelling at least the area around Salmacis (the Mausoleum remained intact to delight future ages). He also left a small garrison of 3,000 foot and 200 horse.[73] It proved insufficient to contain the Persian forces, and Halicarnassus remained a bastion of enemy strength until early 332. The siege had done Alexander more harm than it had the enemy. It had been costly in money and men and at the end of it all the strategic situation was unaltered. Memnon had a free hand to wreak havoc in the northern Aegean and that he proceeded to do, moving to Chios for the campaigning season of 333.

v    **From Halicarnassus to Cilicia (autumn 334 to summer 333 B.C.)**

Alexander left Memnon and the Persian fleet to their own devices and moved away from the Aegean coast, dividing his forces for the winter campaign. Caria was left in the hands of the Hecatomnid princess Ada, supported by the Macedonian general Ptolemy and his modest complement of troops at Halicarnassus (see below, p. 230). The king and his army went elsewhere. The men who had married immediately before the campaign began were sent back to Macedon for a winter with their wives. At the same time their officers were to levy troops to replace the losses of the summer.[74] The loss of these conscripts (3,000 infantry and 300 cavalry) would more than outweigh the contribution to the birth rate made by the newly married, and the human resources of the country began to be impoverished. In Asia Parmenion was sent with the allied troops to campaign on the Anatolian plateau, proceeding via Sardes and the Hermus valley into the interior of Phrygia, where the Persian satrap Atizyes still kept his forces under arms. Alexander himself pushed south into Lycia. Arrian (1.24.3) claims that his intention was to

---

[72] Diod. xvii.26.7–27.3; Curt. v.2.5; viii.1.36; contrast Arr. 1.22.1–3.
[73] Arr. 1.23.6; Diod. xvii.27.6.
[74] Arr. 1.24.1–2, 29.4.

command the coast and render the Persian fleet useless (German scholars have talked in terms of a 'Kontinentalsperre')[75], but the facts suggest otherwise. His route took him through Telmissus to the Xanthos valley, but then he diverged inland through Milyas, the mountainous corridor between northern Lycia and Pisidia, only reaching the coast at Phaselis.[76] He did send forces to occupy the cities of Lower Lycia, but the area was hardly blockaded against the Persian fleet. In the next summer Pharnabazus was able to operate in Lycia quite freely (Arr. II.2.1), where the rocky coastline provided any number of safe havens. It was for other reasons that the king turned his face away from the coast. In all probability he had already decided to follow in the footsteps of Cyrus and the Ten Thousand and to challenge the Great King for his empire. The following summer would see him push eastwards to the Cilician Gates. In the meantime his winter campaign annexed more territory from the Persian crown and freed the cities of the Aegean from the necessity of provisioning his army. He risked losing the gains of 334, but the lure of conquest in the east was irresistible.

Midwinter found Alexander at Phaselis, at the eastern extremity of the Lycian coast. There a curious correspondence took place with Parmenion over a Persian agent sent from Susa. This man, named Sisines, was captured in Phrygia and referred to the royal headquarters in the south. In Arrian (1.25.3–9) the story involves the Lyncestian prince, Alexander son of Aeropus, who commanded the Thessalian cavalry under Parmenion. Sisines is said to have implicated him in treasonable correspondence with the Persian court. Darius had offered the fantastic sum of 1,000 talents in gold for his namesake's assassination together with the throne of Macedon (which he was in no position to guarantee). After consultation with his council of Companions Alexander sent a secret despatch to Parmenion with instructions to arrest the Lyncestian. There the story ends, and Arrian says nothing of its sequel. In fact the Lyncestian was kept under close arrest until late in 330, when he was tried and executed in the aftermath of Philotas' alleged conspiracy.[77] It is hard to see why the legal proceedings were so long delayed if he had been as deeply incriminated as Arrian suggests. Indeed Diodorus (XVII.32.1) states that his arrest came nearly a year later, on the eve of Issus, and he mentions only vague suspicions evoked by a letter from Olympias. Given his past history of regicide there was ample reason for him to be placed in custody on suspicion alone. Concrete allegations of treason should have resulted in his immediate execution, son-in-law of Antipater or no. The story of the correspondence in winter 334/3 probably derives from allegations made at the trial in 330, when it was alleged that Sisines was an intermediary in a conspiracy against Alexander, and the allegations were retailed as fact by Arrian's source. The core of the story, the arrest of Sisines, is presumably

[75] Droysen 1952, 113; Schachermeyr 1973, 182.
[76] Arr. 1.24.4–6; cf. Bosworth 1980a, 156–8; Seibert 1985, 50–2.
[77] Diod. XVII.80.2; Curt. VII.1.5–9 (not reported by Arrian). See below, p. 103.

historical. Parmenion did capture an emissary from the Great King to his satrap in Phrygia, and he did send him to Lycia for questioning. What emerged from the interrogation we cannot know, but the incident supplies valuable evidence of communication between the two army groups. It may have been at this point that Gordium was fixed as the liaison point at the end of spring.

From Phaselis Alexander took his army into Pamphylia, sending the majority of his men across Mt Climax along a road specially constructed by Thracian pioneers. He himself travelled along the coast with his staff. Here the path was partially submerged. Southerly winds drove large waves against the narrow shoreline and made the going wet and uncomfortable (Strabo 667). At some point on the march the wind veered to the north, a flat calm ensued and the beach was left clear and dry for his passage. It was a not unusual quirk of the weather, but Alexander's entourage hailed it as a sign of divine favour.[78] Some time later the court historian, Callisthenes, elaborated on the appearance of the waves, which the wind had driven in arching rollers, producing an effect reminiscent of the oriental gesture of prostration (*FGrH* 124 F 31); even the sea recognised its change of masters and offered the appropriate act of obeisance to the conqueror. The fertile plain of Pamphylia now lay open to him, and he entered as the welcome guest of the Hellenised city of Perge, which served as his base for operations in the area. It was not a strikingly successful stay. The citizens of Aspendus were reluctant to comply with his exactions and had to be coerced into submission.[79] At Sillyum the garrison of mercenaries and Pamphylian natives was able to resist his initial assault (Arr. 1.26.5), and he left it untroubled while he dealt with the recalcitrant Aspendians, never apparently resuming the siege. Shortly afterwards Alexander moved north into Phrygia, leaving his boyhood friend, Nearchus of Crete, as satrap,[80] with a base at Perge, garrison points at Side and probably Aspendus, and the rest of the province to pacify and organise.

Alexander was now moving rapidly. Towards the beginning of spring 333 he took the road north from Perge to the mountain belt of Pisidia. His first objective was the stronghold at Termessus, which blocked the line of communication with the Maeander valley.[81] He was able to force the pass leading to the city proper (modern Gülük), but the citadel towered impregnable above the surrounding valley and defied his challenge. Without his siege train he was forced to retrace his steps, and with the help of the people of Selge (bitter enemies of their Pisidian neighbours) he made his way to a second stronghold at Sagalassus (modern Ağlasun). This was more accessible and less strongly defended. Alexander took his infantry frontally up the conical hill which led to the city and drove off the lightly armed defenders. The city then

---

[78] Arr. 1.26.1-2; cf. Plut. *Al.* 17.8; App. *BC* II.149.622; *FGrH* 151 F 1.2.
[79] See below, pp. 254–5.
[80] Arr. III.6.6; IV.7.2. Cf. Berve 1926, no. 544; Badian 1975, 149–50.
[81] Arr. 1.27.5–28.2; cf. Strabo 666; Bosworth 1980a, 170.

fell to him without a blow. He continued his march north, capturing the minor fortresses of Pisidia by storm or capitulation. The campaign was no conquest. Alexander apparently left no garrisons in Pisidia, and by the end of the reign the area was still stubbornly independent. The king's passage had a very limited deterrent effect. His march proceeded by the north-east corner of the inland salt expanse of Lake Ascanius (Burdur Gölü) and he soon reached the satrapal capital of Phrygia, Celaenae, where the springs of the river Marsyas welled out of the base of the citadel. Here Alexander encountered yet another garrison, a mixed force of Carian and Greek mercenaries. Once again they refused to surrender, and after a ten-day siege he agreed to a provisional capitulation: the acropolis would be surrendered if no relief force arrived within sixty days.[82] That he agreed to such a remarkable demand is strong evidence of his need for haste. He merely left Antigonus to police the agreement with a modest force of 1,500 mercenaries. At the same time Antigonus was appointed satrap of Greater Phrygia, a post which he held without interruption until the king's death. His task was evidently difficult from the start. The Macedonian army had passed through his satrapy at speed, engaging in only the most perfunctory military action, and Antigonus had to establish control with the bare minimum of forces – and a proportion even of this was later remitted to Alexander.

The next stage of the march, from Celaenae to Gordium, must have taken at least a month. No incidents are recorded, and the king may have been following the campaign route of Parmenion, reaping the benefits of his winter operations. The old general rejoined the main army at Gordium, as did the newly married men from Macedonia with their complement of reinforcements. Alexander also found an Athenian embassy awaiting him. It pressed unsuccessfully for the release of Athenian mercenaries captured at the Granicus. Alexander was reluctant to show any clemency before he met the Persian armies in the east.[83] But he could not devote his entire attention to the coming clash. Disturbing news was reported from the west. Memnon had begun operations in the northern Aegean with considerable success. The opening of the spring offensive saw Chios occupied without a blow, when the governing oligarchy opened its gates to the overwhelmingly strong Persian fleet. The same happened on Lesbos, where Antissa, Methymna and Eresus offered their surrender.[84] Only Mytilene held out, its resistance stiffened by a mercenary garrison sent by Alexander, and Memnon settled down to an intensive blockade by land and sea. There were rumours, if no more, that he was intending to cross to Euboea and threaten Macedon directly from the Greek mainland. Alexander did not for a moment contemplate retracing his steps, but he was sufficiently worried to reverse his strategic plans. He commissioned a new fleet in the west, sending Amphoterus to the Hellespont

---

[82] Arr. 1.29.1–2; Curt. III.1.6–8; cf. Briant 1973, 101–6.

[83] Arr. 1.29.5–6; Curt. III.1.9.

[84] Arr. II.1.1–2; Diod. XVII.29.2; see below, pp. 192–3.

and Hegelochus to liberate the islands. The expense was prodigious: 500 talents were sent with the admirals, a further 600 to Antipater, and in addition the cities of the Corinthian League were instructed to provide naval contingents (Curt. III.1.19–20). Even so, it was many months before this initiative bore fruit. Memnon died of an illness during the siege of Mytilene, in the summer of 333, but his nephew Pharnabazus pressed the city to capitulate. The Persian offensive then diverted towards the Hellespont, where the island of Tenedos surrendered, albeit with considerable reluctance. Hegelochus still had not amassed sufficient warships to give effective assistance, and the people of Tenedos yielded to *force majeure* (Arr. II.2.3). Their loyalty to the Macedonian cause is specifically noted, and it is only to be expected that cities less politically motivated welcomed the Persians with few reservations. Most of the details are lost, but it is certain that Miletus was back in Persian hands by late 333 (Curt. IV.1.37), and the fleet was able to sail almost unchallenged in the Cyclades. A small squadron under Datames was surprised by superior forces at Siphnos and lost eight triremes (Arr. II.2.4–5), but that was the only recorded setback. The bulk of the fleet made a demonstration in force in the western Cyclades and occupied Siphnos once again. This time there was no counter force from Euboea.

But the Persian supremacy at sea was already undermined. Even before Memnon's death, it seems,[85] Darius had decided to pool his military forces in the hope of crushing the Macedonian army in a single pitched battle, and from the spring of 333, if not earlier, he was building up a royal army at Babylon. The indispensable nucleus of his army was Greek mercenaries, and the Great King accumulated them from every quarter. The commanders in the west were duly ordered to transfer the bulk of their mercenary forces to Asia. This order arrived during the siege of Mytilene, and it was immediately obeyed. Pharnabazus took the forces requested south to Lycia, where he handed them over to Darius' emissary, another nephew of Memnon, Thymondas son of Mentor.[86] This contingent comprised a large proportion of the Persian fleet, perhaps as many as 200 ships (the 8,000 refugees from Issus were unable to use more than a fraction of them in their escape from Tripolis[87]). As a result the war in the Aegean flagged irretrievably, and the Macedonian admirals were able to reach parity with the enemy by the beginning of 332. But the transfer of mercenaries took place only in the late summer of 333. When Alexander was at Gordium, Memnon's offensive was at its height, his forces intact, and the king must have had very serious worries.

At this time of perplexity he visited the ancient palace of the Phrygian kings and inspected the legendary waggon of Gordius, the mythical founder of the Phrygian dynasty. The yoke of this vehicle was fastened to its pole by an elaborate fastening of cornel bark, the ends of which were invisible. According

---

[85] *Contra* Diod. XVII.30.1; Curt. III.2.1; Schachermeyr 1973, 194–6. Cf. Bosworth 1980a, 183.
[86] Arr. II.2.1; Curt. III.3.1, 8.1.
[87] Arr. II.13.3; Diod. XVII.48.2.

to a local legend, whether authentic or fabricated for the occasion, the person who released the fastening would be lord of Asia.[88] Alexander duly solved the problem, either cutting through the fastening to reveal the concealed ends or (as Aristobulus claimed[89]) removing the pin that secured the yoke and drawing it off, fastening and all. In both versions Alexander avoided the main task yet could be said to have fulfilled the prophecy. The divergence is admittedly puzzling. Perhaps what Alexander did with the yoke fastening was done in private and never officially explained. The mystery was then discussed in camp gossip, more or less informed. Callisthenes no doubt retailed the more dramatic story of the sword stroke, while Aristobulus remembered another, less drastic solution. Alexander put the unyoked waggon on display and sacrificed in acknowledgement to Zeus Basileus, who had conveniently greeted his achievement with thunder and lightning. How he interpreted the prophecy at the time we cannot say. He may merely have seen it as the legitimising of his sovereignty in Asia Minor, but on the eve of his march eastwards he probably gave it the widest possible significance. Both then and in the history of Callisthenes a little later his success at Gordium was hailed as divine endorsement for the entire campaign, which was not solely for vengeance but for permanent conquest.

It was now summer, perhaps the end of May. Alexander led his united army out of Gordium and drove quickly across Anatolia. He had every reason for haste. The fact that Darius was mobilising his full levy was an incentive, and (a more immediate consideration) he had begun his march before the harvest (nowadays wheat matures in August on the Anatolian plateau). The supply of foodstuffs was therefore at its lowest ebb.[90] He paused briefly at Ancyra to receive the submission of the Paphlagonian tribes of the Pontic shore. They were assigned to the satrapy of Hellespontine Phrygia and excused tribute, as they had been under Persian rule.[91] Apart from taking hostages he did not attempt to enforce his sovereignty, and the hard-pressed Calas was too involved with the Persians on the coast to trouble the Paphlagonians. He fought a brief campaign against them in 332 (Curt. IV.5.13), but it was apparently inconclusive. Paphlagonia was still unpacified territory at the end of the reign. It was a similar story in Cappadocia. Alexander probably took the most direct route via Lake Tatta to Tyana.[92] During the journey he appointed the native dynast Sabictas satrap of the southern satrapy (the north under Ariarathes he left entirely alone (see below, p. 231)). This was a token settlement. Alexander claimed sovereignty but left no forces and no admin-

---

[88] Arr. II.3.6–7; Curt. III.1.16; Justin XI.7.4; Plut. Al. 18.2; Marsyas, FGrH 135/6 F 4. Cf. Tarn 1948, 2.262–5; Fredricksmeyer 1961; Schmidt 1959; Kraft 1971, 84–92; Bosworth 1980a, 184–8.

[89] Arr. II.3.7; Plut. Al. 18.4 (= FGrH 139 F 7).

[90] Cf. Brunt 1976, 154; Atkinson 1980, 457–61; contra Engels 1978a, 37–42.

[91] Arr. II.4.1–2; Curt. III.1.22–4.

[92] Engels 1978a, 41–2; Bosworth 1980a, 188–9; Hornblower 1981, 240–3; contra Seibert 1985, 62–3.

istration. He was set on reaching the Mediterranean coast as quickly as possible. That he achieved by the end of summer. The Cilician Gates, the principal pass through the Taurus range (south of modern Pozanti)[93] was held by a skeleton force of Persian defenders, who were easily dislodged by his hypaspists and light infantry.[94] Meanwhile the satrap of Cilicia, Arsames, had decided to evacuate his capital and fell back to Syria to await the royal army. He had remembered Memnon's advice at the Granicus and began to devastate the Cilician countryside. As so often, Alexander arrived before he was expected. An advance column of cavalry and light infantry covered the 55 km from the Gates to Tarsus in a single day and prevented the firing of the capital.

VI     The campaign of Issus

Cilicia was to be Alexander's base for the next months. Proverbially fertile, its plain had been a major contributor to the Achaemenid treasury, and it was encircled by the Taurus and Amanus ranges, which provided strictly limited access. Alexander set out to make it a fortress, sending Parmenion ahead to occupy the passes along the Royal Road to Syria.[95] These were the defiles extending from the Pillar of Jonah, where the foothills of the Amanus come down in a spur to overlook the sea, to the Belen Pass which controls access over the Amanus to the inland Amik plain.[96] These southern defiles were soon cleared of Persian outposts, and the Macedonians effectively occupied Cilicia as far as the Syrian border.

For the moment the position remained static. Alexander had fallen ill, the result of an imprudent swim at Tarsus.[97] Hot from his ride through the stifling and malarial plain, he had been tempted by the clear waters of the Cydnus, which then flowed through the city, and plunged in directly. Unfortunately it was fed by the snows of the Taurus and was intensely cold, even in summer. Alexander was soon in difficulties, suffering cramps and severe chill. A tropical fever developed, accompanied by persistent insomnia, and his life was in question for a time.[98] Finally his senior court physician, Philip the Acarnanian, administered a drastic purge. The medication may have been effectual or merely fortunate in the time of its application. At all events the fever subsided, and Alexander slowly recovered. The illness had incapacitated him for several weeks, and it created an atmosphere of intense insecurity at precisely the time that the Persian army was approaching Cilicia. Intrigue must have been rife among the high command, as the possibility of the king's

[93] Janke 1904, 98–111; Schachermeyr 1973, 663–6.
[94] Arr. II.4.3–4; Curt. III.4.3–5.
[95] Arr. II.5.1. For the chronology see Schachermeyr 1973, 203; Bosworth 1980a, 192–3.
[96] Cf. Janke 1904, 21–31; 1910, 139–42; Engels 1978a, 44.
[97] Arr. II.4.7–11; Plut. *Al.* 19.2–9; Diod. XVII.31.4–6; Curt. III.5.1–6.20; Justin XI.8.3–9; *FGrH* 151 F 1.6.
[98] Engels 1978b suggests that the disease was pernicious *falciparum* malaria. Green 1974, 220, opts for bronchial pneumonia.

3. Cilicia and Northern Syria

death became more concrete. It was probably at this point that Alexander's treasurer, Harpalus son of Machatas, fled to Europe. His motives are not recorded, except that he was persuaded to do so by an adventurer named Tauriscus,[99] but it it likely enough that he had decided that Cilicia was a most undesirable place to be if his king died. If there was to be a succession crisis he would be much better placed in the vicinity of Macedon. But whatever plans he had were frustrated by the king's recovery and the victory at Issus. Harpalus vegetated in the Megarid for nearly a year until he was recalled to court and resumed his duties as treasurer in the spring of 331. His offence was not treason or embezzlement: otherwise his reinstatement is inexplicable. The political speculation, whatever its nature, was not serious enough to compromise his value as a financial manager. But his desertion is symptomatic of unrest at Macedonian headquarters during the king's illness, and it will not have been unique.

Meanwhile the Persian army was approaching. Darius had mustered his levies at Babylon in the spring and early summer of 333, summoning forces from the central satrapies of the empire. The formidable cavalry of the north-east frontier did not appear because of pressure of time, but the entire levy of Persis and Media was mobilised. Darius also contracted what was probably the greatest number of Greek mercenaries ever to serve in a Persian army. The sources give a figure of 30,000[100] and it may not be too great an exaggeration. On the other hand the total figures for his army are shamelessly magnified for the greater glory of Alexander, and it is impossible to give even an educated guess at the reality. There is relative unanimity, however, that Alexander's forces were greatly outnumbered; and contemporaries expected to see him trampled into the Cilician plain by the hordes of enemy cavalry (Aesch. 3.164). Darius had decided to risk his fortunes on a single battle. It was a controversial decision and there are traces of the debate in our sources. The Athenian Charidemus argued for a division of forces, the king remaining at Babylon while a smaller army (led by himself!) would tackle the Macedonians. His ambitions were undermined by the jealousy of the Persian nobles, which had earlier hampered Memnon, and he himself was apparently executed for his untimely frankness in debate. This disagreement over strategy was to persist (another tradition records the Macedonian deserter, Amyntas, opposing the decision to move from the base at Sochi later in the campaign), and the lack of unanimity, together with the mutual suspicions of Greek and Persian commanders, was a major weakness in the Persian high command.[101] But the vital decision was made by the early summer, and the grand army began its slow march north from Babylon, its progress slowed by the vast baggage train which conveyed the royal treasure and, most impor-

[99] Arr. III.6.7; cf. Badian 1960b; Heckel 1977b; Jaschinski 1981, 10–18; Worthington 1984; Kingsley 1986.
[100] Callisthenes ap. Polyb. XII.18.2; Arr. II.8.6; Curt. III.9.2.
[101] Curt. III.2.10–19; Diod. XVII.30 (Charidemus); Arr. II.6.3–6; Plut. Al. 20.1–4 (Amyntas). Cf. Berve 1926, 2 nos. 58, 823.

tantly, the princesses and concubines of the court. Shortly before Darius reached the Euphrates crossing at Thapsacus, news arrived of Alexander's illness, and he pressed on hurriedly, crossing the river in five days and advancing towards the Amik plain. The bulk of his baggage train was sent to Damascus, some 300 km to the south, and the combatant forces encamped at Sochi, a site in the Amik plain on the fringes of the Amanus range. His journey from Babylon had taken at least three months and he took up position at Sochi some time in September.[102]

Meanwhile Alexander had recovered and was active in Cilicia. From Tarsus he moved to the coast and went west to the city of Soli, at the extremity of the plain. Here Alexander's settlement was draconian. He introduced a garrison and exacted a vast fine of 200 talents for alleged pro-Persian sympathies. Hostages were taken to ensure payment. This ferocious treatment contrasts with the remission of tribute conceded to the city of Mallus at the opposite side of the plain. Soli, like Mallus, attributed its origins to the Argive hero Amphilochus, but Alexander only recognised the claims of one community. Curtius may be right that the fine on Soli was a disguised impost;[103] the city was isolated, far to his rear, and it could not give any significant assistance to the Persian cause, whereas Mallus was far more strategically sited, its goodwill far more important. From Soli Alexander plunged into the coastal foothills of the Taurus, the area later known as 'Rough Cilicia', and conducted a seven-day campaign with a select force of infantry. The episode was too brief for it to be seen as a major strategic exercise. It was probably a show of force, designed to impress the hillmen with the military efficiency of the conquerors and to deter raids on the plain. Certainly Alexander had no worries about the immediate proximity of the Persian army, or he would not have diverged so far in a direction diametrically opposite that of the anticipated offensive. After this diversion he returned to Soli for a sacrifice and festival, as a thank-offering to Asclepius for his recovery. While he was there news arrived of a victory over the Persian commander, Orontobates, achieved by his satraps in the west. It was not final or even decisive, for Halicarnassus remained in Persian hands and the enemy fleet was still unchallenged in the Aegean.[104] But, following soon after the news of Memnon's death, it was a welcome boost to Macedonian morale and for the Persians an ominous indication that the withdrawal of mercenaries had destroyed the offensive in the west.

Alexander now began his march eastwards, moving along the coast to Mallus, where he received reports that the Persian army had encamped at Sochi. At the news he accelerated his pace, first to Castabulum at the head of

---

[102] Engels 1978a, 42–3, argues for 48 days to cover the 577 miles from Babylon (cf. also Marsden 1964). Probably an underestimate. Compare the rate of progress of Cyrus' army (Diod. XIV.21.5; cf. Atkinson 1980, 460–1).

[103] Curt. III.7.2; Arr. II.5.5. Cf. Welles 1930, 136–40 (no. 30) with Bosworth 1980a, 195. For the Argive origins of the Cilician cities see below, p. 254.

[104] Arr. II.5.7; Curt. III.7.4 (cf. Arr. II.13.4, 6).

the gulf of Issus,[105] where he met Parmenion, and then to Issus. Leaving his sick and wounded there, he advanced into the coastal defiles, crossing the spur of the Pillar of Jonah. At this point the sources diverge fundamentally. Arrian represents the king as eager to come to grips with the Persians but delayed in his camp by an autumn thunderstorm, whereas Curtius claims that his strategy was defensive, to give battle in the coastal defiles.[106] What seems certain is that there was a delay before the battle. Darius' baggage train was able to cover the 300 km from the vicinity of the Amik plain to Damascus by the time the battle was fought, a journey which would have taken it at least three weeks. The Persian army was accordingly based at Sochi for perhaps a fortnight before the battle took place. It was most likely that there was an element of defensive strategy on both sides. Darius chose the plainland most suitable for deploying his superior numbers, whereas Alexander opted to meet the Persians in the coastal narrows. His march from Mallus brought him to a position where he had the Pillar of Jonah in the rear with the sea and Amanus range protecting his flanks.[107] If the Persians followed the royal road through the Belen Pass, they would meet him in the narrows, their numbers neutralised. It was now a question of waiting. Which army would risk fighting on the other's chosen ground?

In the end it was Darius who moved. Ancient writers with the advantage of hindsight suggest that he was deluded by overwhelming arrogance, and there may be some basis to the claim. The Great King, a military hero in his own right, would not be inclined to wait indefinitely for a numerically inferior adversary. There was also the question of supply. In the Amik plain Darius was dependent on land transport for his provisions and, the harvest long over, supplies would soon dwindle. Alexander on the other hand was easily supplied by sea from Cilicia. Logistical factors would inevitably force the Persians to take the initiative, and move they did. But it was in an unexpected direction. Darius led his army on a flanking move to the north, a circuitous march of at least 150 km through the Bahçe Pass and the narrows of Toprakkale.[108] His forces were unopposed and swarmed down into the plainland north of Issus, severing communications between Alexander's army and his bases in Cilicia. This northern march came as a complete surprise, and Alexander did not believe the news until he had sent some of his staff by sea to verify it (Arr. II.7.2; Curt. III.8.17). He was either ignorant of the northern passes, which

---

[105] Curt. III.7.5–6. On the possible site of Castabulum see Ruge, *RE* x.2336; Atkinson 1980, 470–1. It is not to be identified with Hieropolis some 42 km north-east (*contra* Engels 1978a, 48ff.; Devine 1984). For the site of Issus see Seton-Williams 1954, 159–61; Hellenkemper 1984.

[106] Arr. II.6.1–2; Curt. III.7.8–10. For various interpretations of strategy see Seibert 1972a, 99ff.; Bosworth 1980a, 199–201 (most recently Murison 1972; Wirth 1977; Engels 1978a, 42–53, 131–4; Hammond 1980a, 94–110). Most scholars start from the assumption, based on Arr. II.6.2, that Alexander made a forced march from Mallus to Myriandrus in two days. See, however, Brunt 1976–83, 1. 458–9; Atkinson 1980, 177; Bosworth 1980a, 220.

[107] On the topography see Janke 1904, 12–31; 1910, 137ff.

[108] Callisthenes *ap.* Polyb. XII.17.2; Arr. II.7.1; Curt. III.8.13; cf. Janke 1904, 37–44.

would be extraordinary after two months or more in Cilicia or had discounted them as a serious route for the Persian army. For once he had been taken off his guard, but there was the consolation that the enemy had been tempted into his ground, even if the direction of approach was unexpected. He could not assume that the entire Persian force was to the north. For all he knew a second contingent might be poised to force the Belen Pass and catch his army in the rear. He probably left the allied infantry (who are not attested in the battle) with supporting units to monitor the southern passes. The bulk of his army retraced its steps north, spending the night before the battle at the summit of the Pillar of Jonah, the narrowest point of the coastal defiles (Arr. ii.8.1–2; Curt. iii.8.22–4).

The Persians had established a defensive position south of the Pinarus, one of the many streams discharging into the sea from the Amanus. Its exact location is a mystery which, given the changed hydrography of the area, may never be resolved.[109] It may be that the battle was fought in the vicinity of the Kuru Çay, some 15 km north of the Pillar of Jonah, where the plain is relatively narrow, about 4 km wide (the contemporary Callisthenes (Polyb. xii.17.4) claimed that the battlefield was 14 stades from sea to foothills). This terrain suited the Macedonians, but the Persian forces were uncomfortably compressed. Cavalry were massed by the sea to the right; mercenary infantry occupied the centre, while the Persian national infantry continued the line into the foothills of the Amanus, extending forward almost at right angles to envelop the Macedonian flank. The rest of the army was massed in depth to the rear of the line. To meet this solid wall of defenders Alexander prepared his battle line well in advance. At dawn the Macedonian army moved down to the plain, first infantry and then cavalry. The process of filtering through the narrows was of necessity slow and took up most of the morning. As the plain widened the infantry was able to deploy itself into battle formation, at first 32 ranks deep, then 16, finally 8.[110] It was a gradual process. Files would move up to the front as spaces opened up for them and the phalanx would gradually expand in length and contract in depth. Consequently Alexander had a battle line capable of facing and repelling any cavalry sortie during his advance to battle. There were inevitable delays, as the army crossed the ravines and streams that intersected the plain, but as the afternoon began the Macedonian line closed on the Persians. Cavalry were interposed to right and left of the phalanx, the Thessalians and allies on the sea side, Macedonians to the mountains. Thrown back at an oblique angle were archers and light infantry, positioned to counter the Persians on the mountainside. Alexander himself was at the head of the Macedonian cavalry immediately to the right of his infantry phalanx. There was a last-minute adjustment, as he transferred two

---

109 Endlessly discussed. For summaries of the controversy (stimulated by Janke's work) see Schier 1909; Seibert 1972a, 99–100; Atkinson 1980, 471–6. Engels' calculations (1978a, 131–4) of the time required to funnel the army through the narrows preclude any battle site far to the north of the Pillar of Jonah. See also Hammond 1980a, 97–100.

110 Callisthenes *ap.* Polyb. xii.19.5–6; cf. Arr. ii.8.2; Curt. iii.9.12.

*ilai* of Companions to deepen the cavalry forces at his right and extended his line, which had hitherto been kept clear of the foothills, so as to counter the Persian infantry on the upper reaches of the Pinarus. That entailed a transfer of Agrianians, archers and mercenaries from the flank and rear.[111] They were intended merely to hold their ground and prevent an outflanking push by the Persian infantry. The main attack, as always, was launched by Alexander and the Companion cavalry.

Darius stood firm behind the Pinarus, leaving the offensive to the Macedonians. It was carefully launched, a measured advance in slow time to preserve the alignment of the phalanx and then, at missile range, the charge led by Alexander himself. His cavalry was attacking across a stream and its momentum cannot have been enormous, but, even so, the lightly armed Persian infantry could not cope with the shock. Alexander's cavalry drove forward, pushing left towards Darius, who was in the centre of the Persian levy, surrounded by his personal guard. Elsewhere things went less well. The phalanx could not keep pace with Alexander's charge, and a gap opened between infantry and cavalry. What was worse, the cohesion of the infantry line broke down while they were forcing the river and further gaps developed.[112] The mercenary hoplites in Darius' service could then insinuate themselves between the lethal *sarisae* and attack the Macedonians from the side, where they were most vulnerable. It was the tactic used by the Romans to destroy the Macedonian armies of the second century B.C., and at Issus the phalanx was more closely challenged than at any other time in the reign. There was a real danger of its being dislocated and routed. On the extreme left towards the sea the Persian cavalry with its massed weight of numbers was almost irresistible, forcing the Thessalians back across the river.[113] Now the Macedonian line was aslant and disrupted, the king on the far side of the Pinarus, his left thrust back to its own bank, and the phalanx stationary in the stream bed.

Fortunately the Persian line was weakest at the apex of Alexander's attack. The Persian infantry gave way before the lances of the Macedonians, and the king forged gradually closer to Darius. Alexander's court historians, eager to denigrate his rival, suggested that Darius fled at the very start of the engagement.[114] That is most improbable, given his earlier record of personal bravery. The vulgate tradition on the contrary gives a vivid account of Darius fighting from his high war chariot until his guard was annihilated before him and he himself was on the verge of capture. That is the scene depicted on the celebrated mosaic from the House of the Faun at Pompeii, which was certainly inspired by a contemporary painting (the work perhaps of Philoxenus of

---

[111]  Arr. II.9.1–2; cf. Callisthenes *ap*. Polyb. XII.21.5–6; Curt. III.11.2; Bosworth 1980a, 209–12.
[112]  Arr. II.10.4–7; cf. Curt. III.11.4–6.
[113]  Callisthenes *ap*. Polyb. XII.18.11–12; Arr. II.11.2; Curt. III.11.1.
[114]  Arr. II.11.4 (cf. 10.1); Callisthenes *ap*. Polyb. XII.22.2. Cf. Berve 1926, 2 no. 124; Schachermeyr 1973, 209–10; Bosworth 1980a, 215–16.

Eretria) based on eyewitness reports.[115] Darius did resist more stubbornly than Arrian suggests, but, even so, the engagement did not last long. The Persians with their missile javelins could not cope with the stabbing lances of the Macedonians. Eventually Darius took flight to avoid capture, first in his war chariot and then, for greater speed and anonymity, on a newly foaled mare. His retreat infected the morale of the troops around him and, as the panic deepened, the whole of Darius' left between the king and the hills started to withdraw, while Alexander moved consistently seawards to relieve his hard-pressed phalanx. Darius' mercenaries now had to face a cavalry push at their flank at the same time that the Persian contingents to their left took flight (Arr. II.II.I). As they wavered, the Macedonian phalanx recovered its alignment and the hedge of *sarisae*, now intact, drove the mercenaries from the stream. Under this double offensive they broke and the retreat became general. By the sea the Thessalians under Parmenion observed the movement and counter-attacked at the moment that their enemies' morale sagged at the rumour of the flight of their king. The last portion of the Persian line now turned and the rout began.

During the battle the Persian numbers had given them no advantage. In retreat they were a lethal liability. Each unit added to the chaos. By a cruel stroke of fate the cavalry, the fastest and heaviest part of the army, was the last to flee, and to make their escape the horses had to plunge through the whole mass of infantry. The process was irreversible, and the victorious Macedonians pressed forward the pursuit until nightfall, keeping the rear of the retreat under constant harassment. The carnage was worst at the stream crossings, where the natural obstacle provided even more resistance for the masses in flight. Ptolemy claimed, perhaps with little exaggeration, that his cavalry were able to cross one ravine upon a bridge of corpses.[116] The retreat, far more than the battle, had destroyed the Persian army. According to the sources Alexander had lost some 500 men, the Persians 100,000. These are propaganda figures, designed to underscore and extol the Macedonian victory, but even so the Persian losses were disproportionately high. The grand army was effectively destroyed and the Syrian coast lay open to the young conqueror.

That ended the campaign in Cilicia. The Persian king withdrew to Thapsacus with a portion of the stragglers from the battle, including 4,000 mercenaries. Another body of survivors branched northwards through the Cilician Gates, where they joined with insurgents in Cappadocia and Paphlagonia. This was a serious offensive. Curtius (IV.1.34) speaks of their intention to recapture the Anatolian plateau, and Antigonus, the satrap of Phrygia, was fully extended, his scanty forces depleted by Alexander's demands before Issus. Eventually he won three victories over the Persian forces and continued

---

[115] Diod. XVII.34.2–7; Curt. III.11.7–12; Justin XII.9.9. On the Alexander-Mosaic see Seibert 1972a, 55–8; Rumpf 1962.
[116] Arr. II.11.8 = *FGrH* 138 F 6; cf. Callisthenes *ap*. Polyb. XII.11.3.

his campaigns into the remote mountain country of Lycaonia,[117] but it took a solid year of fighting. Even so, the interior of Cappadocia remained troubled and its conquest required the presence of Perdiccas and the grand army in 322.[118] The defeat had destabilising effects elsewhere. A large group of mercenaries, 8,000 strong, made their way south to Tripolis and took ship to Cyprus.[119] One body, led by the fugitive Macedonian Amyntas, sailed south to Egypt, where they attempted to annex the country. Amyntas occupied Pelusium and moved on Memphis, claiming to be the proper successor of the satrap Sauaces, who was killed at Issus. His forces were too undisciplined and were cut to pieces by a sortie from the city. Egypt for the moment remained in Persian hands. The remainder of the mercenaries appear to have sailed west to Crete, where they assisted the Spartans with their campaign in the island (see below, p. 199). It was a confused situation, but the balance had definitely tipped towards the Macedonian forces in the west. The news of Issus broke when the Persian fleet was at anchor in Siphnos, and it sent the commanders post haste to the coast of Asia Minor to suppress rebellion there.[120] They were too late. At the advent of spring 332 the fleet disintegrated. The city contingents from Phoenicia and Cyprus returned home to make their peace with the conqueror, and Pharnabazus and Autophradates were left with a mere fraction of their original forces. They could no longer mount an effective challenge to the newly constituted Macedonian fleet, and their strongholds fell one by one in the course of the campaigns of 332. Tenedos, Chios, Lesbos and Cos were occupied without resistance and Pharnabazus himself was taken by surprise, later to escape at Cos.[121] The entire Aegean coast was liberated from Persian occupation and was settled by Alexander's *fiat*. As before, democracies were imposed, even when oligarchies had been sanctioned by the Corinthian League, and partisans of the king enjoyed power. The remains of the Persian fleet found refuge in Crete, where the last act of the Aegean War was played (see below, pp. 199–200).

Alexander meanwhile was enjoying the fruits of victory. Immediately after the battle he had annexed the Great King's baggage train, both at Issus and at Damascus. The treasure comprised more than 3,000 talents, and there was a far more valuable acquisition than money. The princesses of the royal house, including Darius' wife Stateira and the queen mother Sisygambis, were captured in the camp to the rear of the Pinarus, and a distinguished group of noble ladies fell into Parmenion's hands at Damascus.[122] All were treated with extreme deference and the princesses retained their royal entourage and titulature. Alexander refused to ransom them, but kept them with him,

---

[117] Curt. IV.1.34–5, 5.13. Cf. Burn 1952, 82–4; Briant 1973, 53–80.
[118] Cf. Errington 1970, 60–1; Bosworth 1978, 233–4.
[119] Diod. XVII.48.2–6; Curt. IV.1.27–33; Arr. II.13.2–3; Anaximenes, *FGrH* 72 F 17.
[120] Arr. II.13.4–6; Curt. IV.1.37; cf. Badian 1967, 175–7.
[121] Arr. III.2.3–7; Curt. IV.5.14–22. For events on Lesbos and Chios there is considerable epigraphic evidence (Tod, *GHI* nos. 191–2; see, more fully, Heisserer 1980, 27–110).
[122] Cf. Arr. II.12.3–8 with Bosworth 1980a, 220ff.; Curt. III.13.12–14 (Damascus).

terming Sisygambis his 'mother' (as he had Ada in Caria) and promising dowries for Darius' daughters. In effect he took over Darius' role, and these royal ladies were an important factor in his claim to be the proper King of Asia. When Stateira died in 331, she was duly given a royal burial, and, more significantly, when Alexander left the royal ladies in Susa, he gave instructions that they should be given an education in Greek (Diod. xvii.67.1; Curt. v.2.17). The transfer of royal power to the Macedonians could not be made clearer. The princesses were to learn the customs of their conquerors, and Alexander completed the process in 324 when he and his staff contracted formal marriages with them (see below, p. 156). But in 333 the war of revenge was still in process and marriage with a Persian princess was unthinkable. Instead Alexander took a mistress, Barsine.[123] This lady had been the wife in turn of Mentor and Memnon of Rhodes and was the daughter of Artabazus and a descendant of Artaxerxes II. She had also had a Greek education and was one of the beauties of the age. From the liaison came a son, Heracles, who was for two brief moments a pawn in the game of empire but never considered in any sense his father's heir.

## VII    The conquest of the Syrian coast (322 B.C.)

Alexander left Cilicia and northern Syria in the hands of two of his Companions, Balacrus and Menon (see below p. 232). He entered Phoenicia and received the surrender of Straton, crown prince of Aradus, principal city of the north. Aradus itself was built on an island and so was spared the presence of the Macedonian army. Alexander paused on the coast to the south, at Marathus (modern 'Amrīt), where he received the first diplomatic overtures from Darius. If we can believe the reports of Arrian and Curtius, which have a large measure of agreement,[124] there was little that was conciliatory. The king offered to ransom his family but made no territorial concessions. He was however prepared to treat Alexander as friend and ally. That in itself was a significant psychological step for the Great King, who in theory had no rival and dictated terms to his inferiors. But for Alexander in the flush of victory it was wholly unacceptable. His answer was uncompromising. He was not the aggressor in the war but avenging Persian wrongs: the invasion of 480, the assistance to Perinthus in 340 – and the instigation of Philip's murder. That was not all. Darius was a usurper on the Persian throne, the creature of Bagoas, and now Alexander had established his right to the kingship of Asia, acknowledged by the Persian nobles in his service. Accordingly he was only prepared to parley if Darius approached him as subject to king. Otherwise the issue would be settled by battle. That closed negotiations,

[123] Plut. Al. 21.7–9; Justin xi.10.2–3; xii.15.9; cf. Errington 1970, 74; Brunt 1975; contra Tarn 1948, 2.330–7.
[124] Arr. ii.14; Curt. iv.1.7–14; Diod. xvii.39.1–2. On the sources see Bosworth 1980a, 227–30; Atkinson 1980, 271–7 and, for discussion of detail, Griffith 1968; Mikrogiannakis 1969; Schachermeyr 1973, 222–7.

and Darius began assembling a second army to defend Mesopotamia against the invader. Against all expectations he had nearly two years to wait.

Alexander continued his progress through Phoenicia. Byblos and Sidon came over to him enthusiastically; and the Sidonian king Straton II, a friend of Darius, was rejected by his people and deposed. The pattern seemed about to continue at Tyre, which followed the example of Aradus and offered submission through a delegation led by the crown prince (the reigning king, Azemilk, like Gerostratus of Aradus, was still with the Tyrian contingent to the Persian fleet in the Aegean). All went well until the king expressed his desire to sacrifice at the state temple of the city god Melqart, whom he regarded as a manifestation of his ancestor Heracles.[125] It so happened that his presence coincided with the main festival of Melqart, in February 332,[126] and a sacrifice at that time would have been a striking display of his sovereignty. So the Tyrians seem to have interpreted his request. They were willing to allow him to sacrifice on the mainland, at Old Tyre, but the island sanctuary was to remain (as Aradus had been) closed to Macedonians and Persians alike. This was in effect a declaration of neutrality, which Alexander was as little disposed to allow Tyre as he had been Miletus. He dismissed the ambassadors in anger and prepared to lay siege to the island city. Strategically this was unnecessary. Tyre, like Celaenae, could have been left supervised by a garrison on the mainland and held in check by her neighbours' enmity. Eventually she would have to make her peace with the invader. But Alexander's sovereignty had been frontally challenged and he was not prepared to leave the contumacy unpunished. He would sacrifice to Melqart whatever the cost.

It was prodigious. The island of Tyre was separated from the mainland by a strait four stades wide, and Alexander began the construction of a vast siege mole, demolishing Old Tyre for the fill. When it reached the deeper water close to the city walls, the work lagged as the Tyrians harried the labourers from the sea.[127] The construction work needed the protection of two vast siege towers which cleared the city battlements of skirmishers. Even so the towers themselves were vulnerable. The Tyrians took advantage of a strong sea breeze and drove a fire ship onto the end of the mole, totally destroying both the towers. Further damage was done by an equinoctial gale which disrupted the stone infrastructure (Curt. iv.3.6–7; Diod. xvii.42.5). Meanwhile Macedonian forces had been active elsewhere. Parmenion was driving through the interior of Syria, and Alexander himself led a punitive raid into the Antilibanus to take reprisals for an attack on his men, who had presumably been felling timber for the siege work.[128] The siege itself had become bogged down, thanks to the Tyrian naval superiority. A change came in early

125 Arr. II.15.7; Curt. IV.2.2–3; Diod. XVII.40.2. Cf. Brundage 1958; Picard 1964.
126 Curt. IV.2.10; cf. Menander of Ephesus, *FGrH* 783 F 1.
127 For details of the siege see Arr. II.18.3–24.6; Curt. IV.2.8–4.18; Diod. XVII. 40.4–46.6, and, on the characteristics of the sources, Rutz 1965; Bosworth 1976a, 16–25; Atkinson 1980, 315–19.
128 Arr. II.20.4; Curt. IV.2.24–3.1; Plut. *Al.* 24.10–12; Polyaenus IV.3.4.

summer, when the defectors from the Aegean fleet returned home. Eighty ships from Phoenician cities other than Tyre put into the port of Sidon, where they were joined a little later by 120 warships from Cyprus, whose kings now offered formal submission. Three of them, the kings of Salamis, Curium and Amathus, participated in the campaign with their contingents. That put the siege on a different footing. Alexander had the advantage in ship numbers and was able to pen the Tyrians inside their island. Now preparations for storming the city could be pressed ahead. The siege mound was gradually extended towards the walls and Alexander's military engineers, notably the brilliant Thessalian Diades, constructed the most formidable offensive arsenal yet seen in Hellenic siege warfare.[129] The most famous were the shipborne siege towers equipped with scaling bridges, but there were also powerful torsion catapults capable of firing stones of considerable dimensions. On the other hand the Tyrians had built up a defensive armament which was almost as effective, strengthening their walls at the most vulnerable points and adding fire bases lavishly equipped with incendiaries and anti-personnel equipment. There were also defensive screens of padded leather to cushion the impact of the catapult stones, and revolving wheels to block and break the arrows.[130] For a time there was little military action. What there was concentrated on clearing the defensive breakwater in front of the walls (Arr. II.21.4–7). There was a lull before the final assaults. A last-minute naval sortie from Tyre caused panic but little harm.

Finally, at some time in July 332, the attack began. The siege mole was now proved ineffective. With so much time to prepare, the Tyrians had built an inner wall and filled the gap with earth and stones. In that quarter the defence was impregnable. Elsewhere the attack was launched with shipborne rams, and it was at the south part of the circuit that the fortifications were breached. The cost was heavy as the Tyrians retaliated with their entire defensive arsenal, and the first attempt to use the scaling bridges was unsuccessful. At nightfall the operations ceased, and the king allegedly contemplated breaking off the siege.[131] He stood firm, but contrary winds prevented the resumption of the attack for the next two days. In the final attack Alexander extended the breach in the fortifications and stripped the wall of defenders. Then the scaling bridges were brought to bear and the hypaspists stormed onto the walls together with men from Coenus' phalanx battalion. The battlements were first secured, then the Macedonian troops stormed down through the palace complex into the city proper. As the defender. withdrew from the walls, the Phoenician and Cypriot fleets forced through the harbour barricades. The city had fallen, and a gruesome massacre followed, as the Tyrian military population was systematically slaughtered. The Macedonians thoroughly

---

[129] Berve 1926, 2 no. 267 (cf. nos. 656, 789, 821). For the siege engineering see Marsden 1969–71, 1.62–3, 102–3; 1977.

[130] Diod. XVII.43.1–2 (cf. Goukowsky 1976, 197–8), 43.9–44.5: Curt. IV.3.24–6.

[131] Diod. XVII.45.7; Curt. IV.4.1 (glossed over by Arr. II.22.6–7); cf. Bosworth 1976a, 16–20.

vented the frustrations of the long siege, and 8,000 of the defenders perished. Some 2,000 of them were crucified along the coast, a grim warning of the futility of resisting the conqueror. The rest were enslaved, except for a group of dignitaries who had taken refuge in the temple of Melqart. These included the king and a small group of Tyrian nobles and more interestingly, a delegation from Carthage, Tyre's famous colony. Originally the Carthaginians had come in their traditional role as observers at the festival of Melqart and so witnessed the opening of the siege. Later a delegation of 30 had returned to the city, regretfully refusing military assistance, and had been trapped by the opening of the naval blockade. Alexander respected their persons but considered the actions of Carthage those of an unfriendly power, and he sent them away with threats of future reprisal.[132]

The new victory demanded celebration. In the debris of the ravaged city the king fulfilled his intention of sacrificing to Heracles/Melqart and held a great procession, his army and fleet parading in full regalia, then competing in an athletic festival (Antigonus, son of Callas, won a double victory in the stadion and the race in armour), finally staging a torchlight review.[133] It was a copy of his thank-offering at Soli for recovery from his illness, but this time the ceremony commemorated mass slaughter and enslavement, and Melqart received a savagely ironical dedication from his self-proclaimed descendant, the siege engine which had done most to destroy his city. Tyre itself was cleared of its former population, which was either sold into slavery or spirited away by the good offices of the Sidonians. New settlers were recruited from the hinterland and there was a resident garrison with a Macedonian commander. It was not a very impressive result from seven months of siege. A single city had been destroyed at vast expense, material and human (Arrian's figure (II.24.4) of 400 casualties for the entire siege is the merest propaganda), and the main value of the exercise was its deterrent effect on resistance elsewhere.

Alexander was now ready to move on Egypt. Its satrap, Mazaces, was already in communication with him and had probably given guarantees that he would admit the Macedonian forces. Such resistance as was left on the Levantine coast was concentrated at Gaza, where Batis,[134] the city commander, had hired mercenaries and stockpiled provisions to sustain a protracted siege. As usual, the challenge was met frontally. Alexander took his army south from Tyre and marched directly down the coast to Gaza. A second siege ensued and was to last two months (Diod. XVII.48.7; Jos. AJ XI.325). The delays were caused by the sandy soil around the city walls, which prevented the effective use of the few siege towers which his engineers were able to construct from the scanty local resources.[135] The defence was also unexpec-

---

132 Curt. IV.4.18 (cf. 2.10), 3.19); Arr. II.24.5. For subsequent relations with Carthage see Justin XXI.6.1–7 (with Berve 1926, 2 no. 52); Arr. III.24.5 (with Bosworth 1980a, 354).
133 Arr. II.24.6; Diod. XVII.46.6; Moretti, ISE no. 113.
134 So Arr. II.25.4. The name is usually said to be Iranian, but Hegesias (FGrH 142 F 5) implies that he was Babylonian.
135 Curt. IV.6.8ff., more credible than Arr. II.25.2ff.

tedly spirited. A sally from the city caused serious difficulties for the besiegers and Alexander himself was wounded through the shoulder by a catapult bolt. As a result direct assaults were postponed until the walls of Gaza were subverted by mines, easy enough to construct in the soft sand. Finally the siege armament from Tyre was transported south by sea and mounted on a large siege mound, and presently the city walls were shaken by bombardment as well as undermined by subterranean excavation. Three assaults on the ramparts were repelled, but they were gradually stripped of defenders by the artillery barrage and the walls were finally occupied, the hypaspists as usual heading the attack. Alexander was in the forefront and received a second, minor, wound in the leg (Curt. IV.6.23). His blood was up and his troops were ready for the slaughter, their temper soured by the weeks of hardship preparing for the assault (water in particular would have been in very short supply over the months of September and October).[136] The predictable massacre followed, as the fighting men of Gaza were exterminated, resisting until the end. The women and children became the prizes of war. Arrian's account ends here, but there is an episode even more sombre related by Curtius (IV.6.25–9). It was probably retailed by Cleitarchus and was certainly written up (in flat and tasteless prose) by Hegesias of Magnesia (*FGrH* 142 F 5). According to this tradition, the commandant of Gaza was captured alive and executed in gruesome style by having his heels pierced and being dragged to his death at the tail of a chariot. The story cannot be proved false, certainly not on the basis of its omission in Arrian,[137] and there was every reason why Alexander, irked by the long delays at Tyre and Gaza, should have wished to give a terrible object lesson to any community or commander who might have the temerity to resist his progress. The fact that the episode is singularly revolting is no argument against its historicity.

VIII    **The occupation of Egypt (winter 332/1 B.C.)**

Gaza was reconstituted with a native population recruited from its hinterland and established as a military fortress to guard the access to Egypt. Alexander was at last ready to move west to take control of the satrapy. First he sent a recruiting expedition to Macedon, led by the phalanx commander Amyntas son of Andromenes, who was given a squadron of ten triremes and sent across the winter seas to Macedon.[138] The king's business could not wait until the spring and his need for fresh manpower was urgent after a year of almost unremitting siege warfare. Even so the mission was long and painstaking. It was to be more than a year before Amyntas returned with his reinforcements (see below, p. 87). For the moment there was no military problem. Egypt lay

---

[136] Cf. Engels 1978a, 57–8.
[137] Cf. Tarn 1948, 2.268; Pearson 1960, 248; Hammond 1983a, 126; see, however, Radet 1931, 104–5; Schachermeyr 1973, 220 n.242; Lane Fox 1973, 193; Green 1974, 267.
[138] Diod. XVII.49.1; Curt. IV.6.30–1; VII.1.37–40.

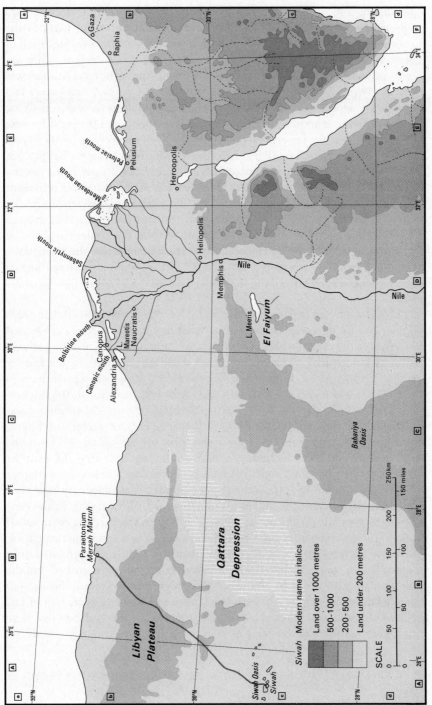

4. *Northern Egypt and Siwah.*

open to him, and Alexander had employed the two months of the siege of Gaza to prepare a triumphal and bloodless entry. The march from Gaza to the Egyptian border was uneventful. It took seven days to come within reach of Pelusium (Curt. IV.7.2; Arr. III.1.1), a distance of about 200 km. This was rapid travelling, but hardly a forced march, through terrain that was notoriously inhospitable. The fleet probably carried water,[139] and there had been ample opportunity to prepare supply dumps during the delay at Gaza. Accordingly the army reached Egypt without incident, and the great fortress of Pelusium, at the eastern extremity of the Delta, received his fleet into harbour. The Pelusiac mouth had been the first line of defence for Egypt since Pharaonic times and had frustrated successive Persian invasions during the fourth century. It was here that the Macedonians would encounter resistance if Egypt was to be held against them. Instead they were welcomed and the native Egyptians flocked in their thousands to Pelusium where they greeted Alexander as a liberator. As his fleet sailed up the Nile Alexander took his land forces through the desert to Heliopolis and from there across the river to the capital at Memphis, where the last Persian satrap, Mazaces, offered formal submission and surrendered the city with its treasury and royal appurtenances intact.

The welcome had been impressive and it left Alexander in no doubt of his popularity with the indigenous inhabitants of Egypt. He therefore celebrated his arrival in the capital with a general sacrifice, including the Apis bull among the deities honoured. This was a totally Hellenic celebration, marked by gymnastic and musical contests in which the most distinguished performers in the Greek world competed (Arr. III.1.4). Apis was included in the celebrations as an act of deference to the native Egyptian religion.[140] Alexander was well aware of the traditions that both Achaemenid conquerors of Egypt, Cambyses and Artaxerxes III, were responsible for the killing of Apis bulls, and no act could have had more potent symbolism, pointing the contrast between the new monarch and his Persian predecessors. There was no attempt or intention to adopt Egyptian religious ceremonial. Alexander may have been curious enough to visit the bull in his sanctuary (cf. Hdt. II.153; Strabo 807) or even to view the great funerary temple at Saqqara, where the mummified bulls were preserved after decease and worshipped as a conglomerate entity, Osiris–Apis (Wsr–Hp), lord of the underworld;[141] but the Egyptian deities remained alien, to be honoured and respected but in no way absorbed into the Macedonian pantheon. In the same way Alexander received the age-old nomenclature of the Pharaohs: king of Upper and Lower Egypt, Son of Ra, beloved of Amun and selected of Ra, and as Horus, he was god manifest. The titles were naturally given him, as they were the Persian kings, in official

[139] Engels 1978a, 60; Bosworth 1980a, 216.
[140] Cf. Diod. 1.84.8 (= Hecataeus, *FGrH* 264 F 25). On the supposed Persian sacrilege see Kienitz 1953, 57–9; Schwartz 1948.
[141] Cf. Wilcken 1922–37, 1.7ff., esp. 25–9.

inscriptions, but there is no reliable evidence that he received the kingship at a formal investiture in Egyptian style. Although the Alexander-Romance (Ps.-Call. 1.34.2) records a ceremony of enthronement at Memphis, the immediate context is so larded with fantasy that no individual detail can be isolated as factual.[142] It is most likely that Alexander assumed the kingship as his right and dispensed with native ceremonial. His stay in the capital was brief and he had no time for more than a cursory acquaintance with the native institutions.

Far more important was the sanctuary of Ammon in the oasis at Siwah. In Alexander's eyes the Libyan Ammon was a local manifestation of Zeus. That is clear from the remains of his first historian, Callisthenes, who referred to the god simply as Zeus, and, writing at court, he surely echoes Alexander's own thinking.[143] The god and his cult were, however, familiar in the Greek world, and the central sanctuary at Siwah had been the focus of pilgrimage since the fifth century B.C., its oracles celebrated and respected. There were also offshoots in mainland Greece, the most famous at Aphytis in Chalcidice, where there was a temple of Zeus Ammon, built in the second half of the fourth century, and whose coinage long before Philip's reign depicted the Libyan god complete with ram's horns.[144] Alexander must have known of the cult since his infancy and he was already disposed to see himself as the son of Zeus (see below, p. 282). He was attracted by the reputation of the oracle, with which he was so closely associated by birth, and further stimulated by a tradition that his Argead ancestors, Heracles and Perseus, had visited the sanctuary.[145] The story that Cambyses had lost an army en route to Siwah[146] may also have inspired emulation, just as similar stories about Cyrus and Semiramis were later to attract him to the Gedrosian desert. The motivation to visit Siwah was complex but it was indubitably strong and far more than a casual impulse. In all probability his wishes were known before he entered Egypt and inspired a number of rival oracles from Asia Minor, confirming his divine sonship. After a brief stay at Memphis and perhaps an excursion south to the Thebaid[147] he addressed himself to the serious business of the visit.

---

[142] See, however, Koenen 1977, 30–1.

[143] *FGrH* 124 F 14a. Cf. Bosworth 1977a. For the early history of Ammon in Greece see Classen 1959; Woodward 1962.

[144] Cf. E. Leventopoulos-Youri, *AAA* 3 (1971) 356–7; *Arch. Delt.* 25, Chron. 2, 354–61; *Arch. Delt.* 29, Chron. 677. For the coinage see *BMC Macedonia* 61; Head, *HN*² 210; R. Plant, *Greek Coin Types* (Seaby, 1969), nos. 1488, 1544, 2105.

[145] Callisthenes, *FGrH* 124 F 14a; Arr. III.3.1–2; Curt. IV.7.8. For literature see Seibert 1972a, 116–25. Note particularly Wilcken 1970, 1.26off.; Tarn 1949, 2.353ff.; Kraft 1971, 53–60; Bosworth 1977a, 69ff.

[146] Hdt. III.25.3–26.3; cf. Curt. IV.7.6–7; Plut. *Al.* 26.11–12.

[147] Curtius IV.7.5 implies that he went upstream to Upper Egypt and settled affairs there. That could be correct. Arrian is very sketchy at this point and could easily have omitted an excursion which he saw as unimportant. A river journey even as far as the Thebaid would not have taken an undue time. In 654 the princess Nitocris took seventeen days in all to make a state voyage from Sais to Thebes (Breasted, *Anc. Records* 4. 677ff., nos. 944–5). Memphis was closer, and Alexander will have needed no more than fourteen days upstream and even

With a small force of light infantry and the royal *ile* he sailed down the Nile, following the western arm of the Delta towards the Canopic mouth. He paused to investigate the shores of Lake Mareotis and was impressed by the potentialities of the narrow isthmus between lake and sea which accommodated the harbour station of Rhacotis. That was to be the site of his first great foundation, Alexandria in Egypt (see below, p. 246). For the moment he did no more than decide upon a new city. The formal inauguration of the site and the marking of its boundaries was reserved for his return from Siwah.

Alexander now moved westwards to the city of Paraetonium (Mersah Matrūh), about 290 km from the future foundation. There the road went westwards again to the village of Apis before plunging south into the desert for another 260 km to the oasis of Siwah, which Strabo (799) claims could be reached in five days. Alexander paused briefly to receive an embassy from Cyrene, which offered rich presents including war-horses and chariots and invited him to visit their territory (Diod. XVII.49.3; Curt. IV.7.9). Presumably the civil conflict which was to attract Thibron to Cyrenaica in 324/3 (see below p. 291) was already brewing and the established city governments hoped to use Alexander's forces to entrench their dominance. Alexander, however, was set on visiting Ammon and contented himself with a treaty of peace and alliance. For the moment Cyrenaica was to remain outside the empire, but his attention had again been attracted to the western Mediterranean and embryonic ideas of intervention and conquest may already have formed in his mind. But in 331 it was the desert that called him, and Alexander's party followed the road south. Their journey was vividly written up by Callisthenes, whose account was later excoriated as a piece of blatant flattery (*FGrH* 124 F 14; cf. Timaeus, *ap*. Polyb. XII.12b.2). Romantic it certainly was; a deluge of rain providentially averting the threat of thirst, a violent southerly obliterating the desert landmarks, and a pair of crows appearing to guide the party to Siwah. But it seems an elaboration upon actual known features of the Libyan desert – the discomfort of the southern sirocco, the variable winter rainfall, the presence of crows near oases in the Sahara, all of which the travellers may well have encountered. Callisthenes emphasised aspects of the journey which suggested divine intervention in Alexander's interest and prepared the ground for his reception at Siwah. His account, though exaggerated, provided the basis for later writers, even eyewitnesses like Ptolemy and Aristobulus (Ptolemy went so far as to make the guides to Siwah not crows but a pair of snakes), and all sources, including the vulgate tradition, speak of difficulties in the desert. Difficulties there may have been (Alexander's journey time of eight days (Diod. XVII.49.3–4; cf. Curt. IV.7.10, 15) is longer than the normal time for a small caravan) but there is unlikely to have been serious danger on a track so well-beaten.

Once at Siwah, Alexander duly consulted the oracle in the central sanctuary

less down (cf. Hdt. II.175.2). If he did visit the Thebaid, the entire journey need not have taken more than a month.

The occupation of Egypt 73

at Aghurmi.[148] As successor of the Pharaohs he was admitted directly to the inner sanctum, where he consulted the god in private. The mode of questioning was curious, corresponding to oracular procedure in Egypt attested from the second millennium B.C. and fully documented in a papyrus of the reign of Psammetichus I (651 B.C.).[149] The cult image, not the familiar Ammon with his characteristic ram's horns but an archaic omphalos-shaped stone studded with emeralds, was carried on a gilded litter in the form of a boat. Eighty priests bore the load[150] and their movements and the swaying of the litter were interpreted as the response of the god. In Saitan Egypt the symbolism was relatively simple: if the litter advanced it denoted approval, if it backed, the reverse. At Siwah, however, there was apparently a whole repertory of movements to be interpreted, and Alexander himself was physically separated from the cult image in the inner chamber of the temple, which measured only ten feet by eighteen. His questions were probably given in private to the officiating priest, who observed the movements of the cult image and returned to the inner sanctum to deliver his interpretation. The details must remain obscure.[151] All that is certain is that Alexander consulted the oracle in the temple apart from his staff, who posed their own questions outside the sacred area. What he asked therefore remained private.[152] Later tradition, perhaps beginning with Cleitarchus, evolved a series of questions concerning world empire and the punishment of Philip's murderers, but none can be traced to any source close to Alexander. Ptolemy and Aristobulus merely claimed that he was satisfied with the responses he received (Arr. III.4.5), and the flattery of Callisthenes did not apparently include precise oracular questions and answers. All we hear of any reliability is that Alexander later claimed that Ammon had authorised him to sacrifice to certain gods (Arr. VI.19.4), but it is uncertain whether that authorisation was given at Siwah or at some later consultation – or even in a recent dream.[153] One thing can be stated with confidence. Alexander was openly addressed by the priest as son of the god (see below, pp. 282–3). This may have been Greek interpretation of the Pharaonic titulature (as king of Egypt Alexander was by definition son of Amun, the Egyptian manifestation of the god of Siwah), but it is more

[148] Steindorff 1904; Fakhry 1944; Parke 1967.
[149] Parker and Černy 1962.
[150] So Diod. XVII.50.6: the number may be exaggerated. Parker and Černy 1962, 47 n. 5 (cf. Goukowsky 1976, 205), suggest that there were only eight priests.
[151] The issue is complicated by Strabo 814, who reports Callisthenes as follows: 'the god's responses are not given in words, as at Delphi and Branchidae, but by nods and symbols for the most part, just as Homer's Zeus "spoke and nodded assent with his dark eyebrows", the prophet interpreting Zeus'. These last words (τοῦ προφήτου τὸν Δία ὑποκριναμένου) are usually construed to mean that the priest acted the part of the Homeric Zeus and gave the signs and nods through his facial expressions (cf. Pearson 1960, 34). That is inconsistent with the rest of the tradition and implies that there were two wholly different modes of oracular response at Siwah. I assume either that there was some misunderstanding by Strabo or that ὑποκρίνεσθαι should be understood as *interpreting*, not acting the part of the god.
[152] Callisthenes, *FGrH* 124 F 14a; cf. Wilcken 1970, 1.267–71, 321–6.
[153] So Ehrenberg 1965, 455, citing an earlier note of Wilcken.

probable that he was acknowledged the actual son of Ammon, and of the Greek Zeus. That at all events is how he represented himself officially. Callisthenes portrayed him as son of Zeus (not Ammon) and to the end of his reign, in word and action, Alexander commemorated his divine paternity. He had visited Siwah to consult the deity which, in some form, he considered his father and he was emphatically confirmed in his belief.

After a short stay in the oasis, including a viewing of the celebrated 'spring of the sun' ('Ain el Hamman), Alexander made his way back to Egypt. Aristobulus claimed that he retraced his path, while Ptolemy apparently talked of a direct march back to Memphis.[154] The conflict of authority may be only apparent. If Ptolemy referred simply to a return to Memphis, mentioning none of the intermediate stages, Arrian may well have inferred that he meant a different route, directly east through the desert. In any case the weight of evidence supports Aristobulus. The ceremonial foundation of Alexandria is generally placed after the visit to Siwah, during the return journey to Memphis, and the date of the city's inauguration, as celebrated in the Roman period, was 25 Tybi, which (in 331 B.C.)[155] fell on 7 April. If the date is based on sound tradition (and is not a later approximation to supply an Egyptian equivalent for an original foundation date by the Macedonian calendar), it would follow that the new Alexandria came into being in the spring, shortly before the king left Egypt finally. Alexander returned from Siwah to the coast, retraced his route to the Canopic mouth of the Nile and personally supervised the demarcation of the central civic area of the future city (see below, p. 246). He reached Memphis soon afterwards and celebrated his arrival with a major sacrifice to Zeus the King, the deity whose Libyan manifestation he had consulted at Siwah and whose son he now claimed to be (Arr. III.5.1). His army was waiting for him, refreshed by the winter in the Nile valley, and he could take up the threads of his campaign.

IX     **The campaign of Gaugamela**

Some time in April the army left Memphis, marching rapidly along a prepared path, pontoon bridges having been constructed in advance across the Nile and its principal canals (Arr. III.6.1). Alexander crossed the Sinai and moved north towards Phoenicia. Nothing is recorded of his progress except that he carried out a brief punitive campaign in Samaria, where his governor, Andromachus, had been captured and executed (see below, p. 233). By the summer he had temporarily installed himself at Tyre, and he honoured Melqart with yet another grandiose celebration. The Cypriot kings of Salamis and Soli were especially prominent and had taken pains to hire the most celebrated actors of the day, Athenodorus and Alexander's personal friend

---

154 Arr. III.4.5; cf. Borza 1967; Bosworth 1976b, 136–8.
155 Ps.-Call. 1.32.10; cf. Jouguet 1940; Welles 1962, 284; Bagnall 1979; *contra* Wilcken 1970, 1.263; Fraser 1972, 2.2–3, n. 6.

Thessalus. The lure of the royal court was already irresistible, and Athenodorus violated a contract to appear at the Athenian Dionysia, choosing instead
the dramatic competitions in Egypt and Syria (Plut. *Al.* 29.5). The Athenians
imposed a fine but were powerless to prevent the efflux of professional actors
and athletes. They themselves sent an official embassy led by Achilles and
Diophantus.[156] In part this was congratulatory. The delegates of the Corinthian league had met at the Isthmian games of 332 and voted to send a
golden crown in commemoration of his achievements 'for the salvation and
freedom of Greece' (Curt. IV.5.11; Diod. XVII.48.6). At Athens it was felt
prudent to do the same (*IG* II².1496, lines 52ff.), and the official embassy duly
appeared in Tyre in the summer of 331. In addition to offering congratula-
tions it also sued for the release of the prisoners-of-war captured at the
Granicus, and Alexander complied with the request, granting what he had
categorically refused early in 333 (Arr. 1.29.6). The change of attitude is
certainly connected with the situation in Greece proper. Since 332 there had
been war in Crete between Macedonian forces and the mercenary army of the
Spartan king Agis and there was an acute danger of hostilities spreading to the
mainland. Alexander had responded by sending his admiral Amphoterus with
a substantial fleet to intervene in Crete and bolster Macedonian allies in the
Peloponnese (see below pp. 199ff.), but he did not intend to deal with the
troubles in person. His aims were exclusively focused on the next campaign
against Darius, and the only resources he would divert to the west were ships
and money. Antipater and his allies would have to cope without the assistance
of his army, and their own reserves were depleted. There was no suggestion of
cancelling or delaying Amyntas' recruiting mission in Macedon, and by the
spring of 331 an army corps 15,000 strong was on its way to Mesopotamia (see
below, p. 87). Under those circumstances it was vital to ensure the neutrality
or friendship of Athens, and the promise to release the prisoners of the
Granicus was a cheap and effective way of securing good will. In the turbulent
summer of 331 Athens did keep aloof from the Spartan alliance and one of the
factors must have been the expectation of the imminent release of the
prisoners (we do not know how soon they were repatriated by Antipater).

There had also been some diplomatic exchange with Darius, but here
Alexander was much less conciliatory. The Persian king had come to terms
with some of the bitter realities of defeat, and he was increasingly prepared to
make territorial concessions in the hope of averting military catastrophe.
During the siege of Tyre he apparently renewed his offer to ransom his family
and ceded to Alexander the old Lydian empire, Asia Minor between the
Hellespont and the Halys.[157] That was an unparalleled concession for the
Persian king, but hardly an attraction for the Macedonians, who had left the
Halys far behind in their triumphal progress. The last and most serious
overture came in the summer of 331. It is placed at different points of time by

156 Arr. III.6.2; Curt. IV.8.12. Cf. Will 1983, 71–7.
157 Curt. IV.5.1–8; Diod. XVII.39.1–2; Justin XI.12.3; cf. Val. Max. VI.4 *ext.* 3.

the various sources, but apart from Arrian (II.25), who dates it (erroneously)
to the siege of Tyre in 332, there is agreement that it took place in the period
immediately before Gaugamela.[158] This time the offer was impressive indeed.
Darius offered all territory as far as the Euphrates together with a treaty of
friendship and alliance and a colossal ransom of 30,000 talents for his captive
family. Alexander was also invited to marry his eldest daughter, Stateira.
There was clearly strong inducement to accept and enjoy the fruits of
conquest, reserving the future action against Persia until such time as the
territory already acquired was pacified and organised. Philip might well have
paused at that juncture, and there was probably strong pressure from the older
members of staff to do so. It is universally recorded that Parmenion urged
acceptance of the terms, to be crushingly answered by his king, that he would
do so, were he Parmenion. Whether or not the altercation took place in exactly
those terms is perhaps debatable, but there can be little doubt that there was
disagreement over policy, Parmenion objecting to the risks of further campaigning while the west was still unsettled and Alexander pressing for total
conquest. Ultimately (after the death of Parmenion) the episode was given its
definitive presentation by the court historian, Callisthenes, who represented
Parmenion as prosaic and unimaginative, an obstruction to the heroic
aspirations of the young king, and a series of similar dramatic exchanges
evolved, showing Parmenion as consistently over-cautious, his caution proved
unjustified by the event.[159] His inclination to accept the Persian overtures
was, however, shared by many of the staff (Diod. XVII.54.3–4), and Alexander
must have been aware of the opposition. Nevertheless he had no hesitation in
rejecting Darius' proposals categorically, in an impressive display of autocracy. He once again made open claim to the Persian kingdom and declared
that he would only make terms if his opponent submitted unconditionally to
his jurisdiction. That ruled out any further compromise or negotiation.
Alexander prepared for the new campaign with his usual panache, but his staff
and army was probably less united behind him than they had ever been in the
past.

The army that faced him was perhaps more formidable than the army
defeated at Issus. Darius no longer had the resources of the west, except for
detachments from Syria, Cappadocia and Armenia which had not fallen under
Alexander's sway or had retreated in the face of the conquest. Instead he was
able to exploit the manpower of the east and north-east of the Empire. The
most effective were the cavalry from Bactria and Sogdiana, their numbers
augmented by auxiliaries from western India and the Saca peoples of the
steppes to the north and west of the Sogdian frontier. Led by their satrap
Bessus, who was related by blood to the Great King (Arr. III.21.5, 30.4), they

---

[158] Plut. *Al.* 29.7–8 (Tyre 331); Diod. XVII.54.1–5 (before the battle); Curt. IV.11.1–22; Justin
XI.12.9–15. Cf. Mikrogiannakis 1969, 87ff.; Bosworth 1980a, 228–9, 256; Atkinson 1980,
320ff., 395–6.

[159] Plut. *Al.* 33.9–10 = *FGrH* 124 F 37. For other elements of the hostile tradition against
Parmenion see Cauer 1894, 33–4; Bosworth 1980a, 29–32.

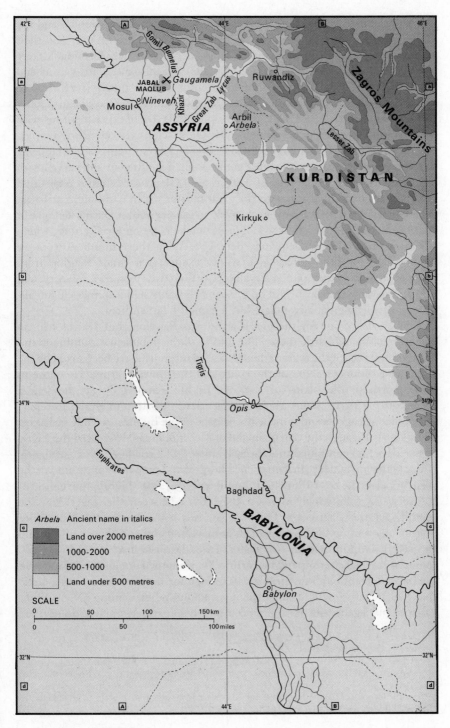

5. *Assyria and Babylonia.*

formed a unified corps of a calibre comparable to the Companions, and the Saca horsemen at least were heavily armed cataphracts, both they and their mounts encased in flexible laminated armour.[160] Hardly less formidable were the cavalry of the central satrapies, Areians, Arachosians, Parthyaeans and their allies. As usual the foot soldiers were of inferior quality with little to recommend them but their numbers. Their weaponry may have been slightly better than before, since Darius had apparently been experimenting with swords and lances of longer dimensions (Diod. XVII.53.1; cf. Curt. IV.9.3), but they remained no match for the Macedonian heavy infantry. The Hellenic mercenary forces were now almost gone. A small contingent still served with Darius under the leadership of Patron and Glaucus,[161] but it was quite insignificant in comparison with the great muster which had fought at Issus. The Persian strength was now exclusively in cavalry and, if Darius' defence of his empire was to succeed, it would need to take place on level terrain, where his numbers could be adequately deployed. What those numbers were we cannot say, for the sources give wildly exaggerated totals ranging from 200,000 infantry and 45,000 cavalry (Curtius) to 1,000,000 infantry and 400,000 cavalry (Arrian).[162] The Persians certainly had a numerical advantage, probably a great advantage, but it cannot be quantified.

The muster point for the grand army was Babylon, but Darius had no intention of giving battle there. The loyalty of the populace was dubious and the food reserves of the region, though abundant, must have been taxed by the prolonged residence there of the court and the growing army. He chose to move north to the plains of Assyria. In the summer of 331 he sent a reconnoitring party under Mazaeus, his erstwhile satrap of Syria, to report Alexander's progress and impede his passage of the Euphrates while he led his army slowly through the rich plainland of Mesopotamia. He crossed the Tigris in five days and continued to Arbela. Eventually he reached his chosen battle site at Gaugamela. Here he entrenched himself and prepared his ground in the plain between the river Bumelus (Gomil) and the Jabal Maqlub, the highest of the series of hills which intersect the terrain between the Tigris and the foothills of the Zagros.[163] This was an unashamedly defensive position. Darius was waiting for his antagonist to meet him and had chosen his ground to make maximum use of his cavalry. In addition he had in readiness two hundred scythed chariots and had artificially smoothed out any undulations in the battle terrain to allow them greater scope for manoeuvre. It was a tactic that had failed signally against the Ten Thousand at Cunaxa (Xen. Anab. 1.8.20), but against an inexperienced and disorganised opposition scythed

---

[160] Curt. IV.9.3; Arr. III.13.4. Cf. Rubin 1955; Eadie 1967, 161–3; Bernard 1980a, 452–7.

[161] Arr. III.11.7, 16.2; cf. Curt. V.8.3, 12.4.

[162] Arr. III.8.6; Curt. IV.12.13; cf. Diod. XVII.53.3; Plut. Al. 31.1. For an attempt at a precise estimate of numbers see Marsden 1964, 32–7, contra Brunt 1976–83, 1. 511; Bosworth 1980a, 293.

[163] For the location of the battlefield see Schachermeyr 1973, 270, contra Stein 1942. On Darius' line of march see Marsden 1964, 11ff.

chariots could be singularly effective.[164] Xenophon made them a decisive factor in his fictitious battle of Thymbrara (*Cyrop.* VII.1.30–2) and noted that they were an important weapon in the arsenal of every Persian king (VII.1.47). No doubt they had enjoyed some success in pitched battles in the Near East, and Darius hoped that their impetus would dislocate Alexander's line of battle and create gaps for his heavy cavalry to exploit. Victory would come through weight of numbers and Darius did all he could to make them effective.

By midsummer 331 Alexander was ready to move from Tyre, and as far as the Euphrates his route had been well prepared. At Thapsacus two bridges spanned the Euphrates. The presence of Mazaeus with a substantial cavalry force had prevented their completion until the eve of the king's arrival (Arr. III.7.1–2), but as his army approached the Persian defenders melted away and his crossing was unopposed. Unlike Cyrus and the Ten Thousand the Macedonian army did not follow the course of the Euphrates south into Babylonia but struck eastwards to the Tigris. The reason given by Arrian (III.7.3) is that fodder and provisions were more plentiful and the heat less intense. The latter is perhaps dubious, but there is little doubt that northern Mesopotamia was more fertile and productive than the south: the forests around Nisibis were famous even in Trajan's time (Dio LXVIII.26.1). What is more, Darius' army had certainly begun its march north from Babylon and there was no secret about its direction. Alexander had every reason to move directly towards the plainland of Assyria. His route from Thapsacus to the Tigris was estimated in antiquity at 2,400 stades (Strabo 90), around 440 km, and it probably took him from Thapsacus to Harran and then eastward via Rhesaena and perhaps Nisibis to the Tigris, which he was to cross slightly north of the modern city of Mosul.[165] His movements had been observed by scouting parties, and some of them were captured and indicated, probably with intent to deceive, that Darius intended to contest the passage of the Tigris. The news had accelerated Alexander's march through Mesopotamia, but when he reached the river there was no opposition in sight. Darius was clearly content to wait on his prepared ground. He had sent out ravaging parties to collect the harvest and burn the stubble in the face of Alexander's advance, but even this action was not achieved widely enough to cause him serious hardship (Curt. IV.10.11–15). In any case he had approached the Tigris in September, when it was at low water, and it was passable on foot without any artificial means of flotation. The current was still strong and made the crossing an exhausting business. Alexander rested his troops for two days and on the eve of his departure, at 9 p.m. on September 20, there was an eclipse of the moon, a portent of disaster for the Persian army and the one secure dating criterion for the Alexander period.[166]

[164] Xen. *Hell.* IV.1.17–19; cf. Anderson 1970, 184–8.
[165] Marsden 1964, 18–21; Engels 1978a, 68–70. We cannot assume that the crossing-points in antiquity were the same as those of today.
[166] Arr. III.7.6; Curt. IV.10.1–7; Plut. *Al.* 31.8; Pliny, *NH* II.180.

From the crossing-point the Macedonians continued in a vaguely eastward direction, with the Kurdish mountains on their left. On the fourth day his scouts sighted an advance guard of Persian cavalry. Alexander himself led a sortie and managed to capture a few of the stragglers, who supplied him with information about the precise position of the Persian army, 150 stades away, concealed by the massif of the Jabal Maqlub. Alexander responded by pitching camp and resting his troops for four days.[167] During that time he will have sent out detachments to reconnoitre the approach to the battlefield and by the end of the stay in the rest camp he must have been fully informed about the size and location of the opposing forces. Accordingly he moved up his army to a base camp below the northern outliers of the Jabal Maqlub,[168] where he deposited his baggage and non-combatants, and in the course of the following night he took his fighting force across the intervening hills. His approach had been shadowed by enemy cavalry under Mazaeus, but, as was usual with Persian armies, they were reluctant to spend the night in close proximity to the enemy and the Macedonians were able to occupy the slopes overlooking the plain of Gaugamela. Now Alexander could rest his men again and carry out a detailed survey of the battlefield, as Parmenion doubtless advised him (Arr. III.9.3–4). The Persians were 30 stades away, in full view, already drawn up in their defensive position, and Alexander could examine them at his leisure while keeping his own forces in semi-readiness in case of attack.

According to Aristobulus (*FGrH* 139 F 17) the Persian *ordre de bataille* fell into Alexander's hands after the engagement, and it gave a detailed analysis of the line, listing the national contingents in order. In the centre, as usual, was the Great King with his élite squadron of Kinsmen and his royal guard of *melophoroi*, buttressed by the remnants of his Greek mercenary army. Immediately to his front were 50 scythed chariots and his small contingent of elephants and to the rear, packed in depth, was the bulk of the infantry, drafted mainly from Mesopotamia. To the right were the troops from Syria and Mesopotamia together with the Median levy and peoples from the Caspian shore as far east as Parthyaea. The strongest part of the line was the left wing which was intended to face Alexander and the Companion cavalry. Here were placed the horsemen of the north-east, the Bactrians with their Saca auxiliaries, Dahae and Massagetae, followed by the levies of Arachosia and Persis proper. The wing was strengthened by an advance guard of heavy

---

167 Arr. III.9.1; Curt. IV.10.15.
168 This reconstruction is based on Arrian III.9.1–2, supplemented by Curtius' fuller but confused account. As it stands, however, Arrian's narrative is defective. There is a day missing. Plutarch (*Al.* 31.8) states that the night before the battle was the eleventh after the eclipse, but Arrian's narrative allows only ten days (Atkinson 1980, 486–7). There is also some confusion between two rest camps. Curtius makes a clear distinction between the encampment 150 stades from the battle site and another fortified camp below the foothills (IV.12.17). The discrepancy is best explained if we assume that Arrian's text conflates the rest camp with the advance camp. Cf. Bosworth 1980a, 294; Wirth 1980–1, 23–31. For bibliography on the battle in general see Seibert 1972a, 127–30.

cavalry with no less than 100 scythed chariots (there was a balancing formation on the right – Armenian and Cappadocian cavalry together with 50 chariots). Persian strategy was necessarily simple, to create gaps in the enemy line which could be exploited by the cavalry and at the same time to maintain the integrity of their own formation. So long as the line was intact there was no scope for a direct attack by Alexander's own cavalry, and, if the scythed chariots did their work, there would be wide openings carved in the Macedonian front.

By the evening the situation was clear; Alexander summoned and briefed his senior officers. He sacrificed in front of his tent to *Phobos* and conducted secret rites under the supervision of Aristander of Telmissus (Plut. *Al.* 31.9). The army took what rest they could. It was probably little enough, but more than the Persians could hope for, kept as they were in their battle positions overnight, because of their generals' traditional and paranoid fear of surprise attack (Arr. iii.11.1; Curt. iv.13.11; cf. Xen. *Anab.* iii.4.34–5). At dawn Alexander appeared, resplendent in ceremonial armour, addressed his Greek allies and, according to Callisthenes (*FGrH* 124 F 36) he prayed for succour to his purported father Zeus (the prayer was immediately answered by the appearance of an eagle flying directly at the Persian line). Alexander now marshalled his army, creating a compact and relatively narrow formation. The front followed its traditional pattern, the Macedonian infantry phalanx at the centre, the hypaspists to the right and blending into the Companion cavalry, brigaded in its eight squadrons, the Royal squadron with Alexander again on the right. On the left the Greek allied cavalry and Thessalians performed the same function as the Companions on the right, the squadron from Pharsalus forming a *corps d'élite* around the person of Parmenion. Parallel to the front was a second line of infantry, the Hellenic troops of the Corinthian League and any mercenaries and troops from the Balkans not deployed elsewhere. On each flank there was a formation thrown back *en échelon*. On the right were light troops, Agrianians and archers, and the 'old mercenaries' led by Cleander. These closed the gap between the two parallel fronts, and in advance of them was a cavalry screen, first the Scouts and Paeonians and then, at the apex of the line, a contingent of mercenary cavalry led by Menidas. On the left flank there was a comparable formation, first Thracian infantry closing the gap between the two lines and then squadrons of allied mercenary cavalry. The entire formation was roughly rectangular in shape.[169] Alexander had realised the inevitability that he would be outflanked and was ready to meet an attack from any direction, while the cream of his army at the front would be ready to exploit any gap in the enemy line.

The preliminary formation is relatively clear, but the details of the battle are variously transmitted by the sources and are impossible to reconcile *in toto*. Even at the time it must have been a virtually hopeless task to reconstruct the course of the engagement, for all participants necessarily had a very partial

[169] Arr. iii.12.1–5; Curt. iv.13.31–2. On this formation see Griffith 1947, 77–9; Devine 1975, 374–8.

experience limited to their own sector. Nobody, certainly not Alexander, had a synoptic view, even if such a view had been possible. As it was, the battle took place at the end of summer, and the dust created by this predominantly cavalry encounter was prodigious and enveloped the action in an opaque, choking pall (cf. Diod. XVII.61.1; 60.4; Curt. IV.15.32). Only a few pivotal events are recorded and it is difficult to put them in a sensible context. At first it seems that Alexander was massively outflanked to his right. He personally faced Darius at the centre of the Persian line with the entire Persian left overlapping his flank guard. Accordingly he moved to the right, keeping the Royal squadron at the apex of the line, which inevitably became oblique.[170] The Persians attempted to counter the movement, but their forces were too deeply massed to be quickly deployed as a whole, and the scythed chariots necessarily remained on their prepared ground. The Macedonian line forged inexorably rightwards and equally inexorably the overlap on the Persian side transferred from the left to the right. Parmenion and his troops on the left had an increasingly greater mass of Persians to counter, and their function was obviously to stand firm and take the brunt of the attack while Alexander found the crucial gap on the right. As he reached the extremity of the Persian line, the Bactrian and Saca cavalry which acted as flank guard (Arr. III.11.6) wheeled forward to block any further advance. The first part of the battle proper now began as Menidas' mercenary cavalry on the extreme right met the Persian flanking force. Shortly afterwards Darius launched his scythed chariots, while Alexander was still within the levelled ground prepared for them. The tactic failed totally. A screen of light infantry, Agrianians and javelin-men, showed terrifying skill and agility in shooting down the horses and diverting the chariots. The few that penetrated their defence passed harmlessly through the Macedonian lines, as gaps were made to let them through, and they were neutralised by the grooms of the Companions and men from the rear ranks of the hypaspists, who were also affected by the charge.[171] Arrian only describes the situation on the right wing. It is clear that the left was under severe pressure from the beginning. Mazaeus, the commander of the Persian right, had fewer chariots but he used them in conjunction with cavalry, and was able to exploit the few gaps made in the Macedonian line. At the same time he sent a detachment of cavalry to attack and pillage the Macedonian base camp, a movement which was rapidly successful but which had no effect upon the progress of the battle. Later it generated myth. It was claimed that the Queen Mother Sisygambis was in camp and proudly declined to be liberated.[172] There was also a story that Parmenion sent messages urging Alexander to save his camp, only to be heroically repulsed,[173] but it is hard to see how such a message could have reached the king at his exposed position on

[170] Arr. III.13.1; Curt. IV.15.1; Diod. XVII.57.6.
[171] Arr. III.13.5; Curt. IV.15.4. Cf. Bosworth 1980a, 306–7.
[172] Curt. IV.15.9–11; Diod. XVII.59.6–7. Cf. Burn 1952, 89–90; Wirth 1980–1, 30–8.
[173] Plut. Al. 32.5–7; Curt. IV.15.6–8.

the apex of the right, harder to see how he could have taken cognisance of it. The message and its repulse is part of the picture of the fearful and sluggish Parmenion which Callisthenes originated for propagandist reasons, but its core, the Persian attack on the camp, is surely historical.

The left held its ground, increasingly beleaguered, while the decisive events of the battle took place on the right. A large-scale cavalry battle developed as Menidas' mercenary cavalry were progressively reinforced by the rest of Alexander's cavalry flank guard. On the Persian side there was an increasing movement left by the Bactrian units under Bessus, until finally a gap developed between the Persian left and rest of the line. This was a climactic moment. Alexander was now at the head of a wedge, the Companions thrown forward obliquely with the phalanx continuing the line on one side, the Agrianians and the infantry flank guard receding on the other. The formation appeared like a flattened lambda, with the Royal squadron at its point.[174] This apex now drove into the gap in the line, and progressively widened it. The Companions then pressed inwards, driving at the exposed flanks of the Persian troops while the phalanx in close formation rolled back the front with its hedge of *sarisae*. As at Issus, Darius at the centre was placed under increasing pressure as the Macedonian assault came gradually closer and the press of fugitives confused his own ranks. At some stage he took flight. He was hardly the first to take to his heels, as Arrian claims (III.14.3), but equally he cannot have waited until Alexander came within spear range, as is stated in the vulgate tradition – otherwise escape (in his ceremonial chariot) would have been impossible. The details of the rout are impossible to reconstruct, but it is clear that it was inevitable once the Persian line had been breached. Nothing on the Persian side could resist the impetus of phalanx and cavalry combined.

Alexander's main intention appears to have been the capture of his rival, dead or alive, and he pressed the pursuit onwards as the centre of the enemy line disintegrated. But that was hardly the end of the story. It was impossible for the Macedonian army to maintain the pursuit as a single entity. The left wing was still hopelessly outflanked and could not press forward with Alexander. Inevitably a gap developed towards the left of the phalanx. The two leftmost battalions stood their ground to preserve continuity with the rest of the Macedonian front while the rest pressed onwards diagonally through the centre. The gap was penetrated by a few units of Persian and Indian cavalry who were stationed in the vicinity of Darius, but it was a limited irruption, soon neutralised by the reserve phalanx in the rear.[175] Menidas and the cavalry of the flank guard were also left isolated against the Bactrians when Alexander launched his assault, but Bessus was in a position to observe the destruction of the centre and drew his forces off to retire in good order,

---

[174] Arr. III.14.1–2; Curt. IV.15.20–1. Cf. Schachermeyr 1973, 237; Bosworth 1980a, 307; Devine 1983, 214–16.

[175] Arr. III.14.4–6. The passage is problematic; cf. Griffith 1947, 84–5; Burn 1952, 88–90; Marsden 1964, 59–60; Wirth 1980–1, 41–8; Welwei 1979, 225–8; Bosworth 1980a, 308–9.

virtually unharmed (Arr. III.16.1). More important by far was the left wing, which was still vastly outnumbered and sustaining attack on the flank. All sources agree that Parmenion sent a message to the king reporting the seriousness of the situation, but the fate of that message is variously reported. According to Plutarch (who may have followed Callisthenes) the appeal reached Alexander and prevented his overhauling Darius, and Arrian similarly maintains that the king retraced his steps and resumed the pursuit only when he was assured of the safety of his army. On the other hand Diodorus (partly supported by Curtius) states that Parmenion's despatch riders found Alexander separated from the rest of the battle line and gave up hope of overhauling him.[176] That is surely true. The dust that shrouded the engagement would have effectively prevented the king's whereabouts being known and no messengers could hope to catch up with him once he was launched in the pursuit. The other versions of the episode are overlaid with propaganda, with the intention either of inculpating Parmenion for premature panic or exculpating Alexander from allegations of recklessness. All that seems certain is that Alexander pressed the pursuit until the approach of evening, following the fugitives in the direction of the river Lycus (Great Zab), some 30 km from the battlefield. He was as usual at the head of the Companions, far in advance of the rest of his line, which was separated into two parts: the majority of the phalanx continued to sweep the remains of the Persian centre in front of their advance, while the left of the line was stationary, still under attack. Gradually the news of the rout of the centre and the flight of the Great King penetrated to the Persian right, and the assault flagged. The Thessalian cavalry, which had fought superbly, rallied and threw the enemy into retreat there also. One last, unplanned, engagement remained. As the Companions returned from the pursuit they crossed the path of a large body of stragglers from the left of the Persian line, Persians, Parthyaeans and Indians, who had probably retreated in the face of the Macedonian phalanx.[177] They were riding in deep formation and clashed frontally with the returning Companions, who barred their line of retreat. The result was one of the most savage mêlées of the day, in which some sixty Companions fell, but it was a mere tailpiece to the battle. The Persian survivors dispersed and the Companions were reunited with the rest of the victorious army.

It is impossible to estimate the losses on either side, for the figures given by the ancient sources shamelessly exaggerate the Persian casualties and equally shamelessly minimise those on the Macedonian side. The pivotal event of the engagement, Alexander's destruction of the Persian centre, was over relatively quickly and the carnage was probably limited. There was

[176] Plut. *Al.* 33.9–10; Arr. III.15.1–2; Curt. IV.16.1–7; cf. Diod. XVII.60.7. For various interpretations see Griffith 1947, 87–8; Marsden 1964, 61–2; Devine 1975, 382; Bosworth 1980a, 309–11.

[177] Arr. III.15.1–2 (not, as usually assumed, the cavalry, which broke the Macedonian line earlier in the engagement (III.14.4)).

nothing like the defiles at Issus to slow down the retreat, and most of the Persian cavalry at least will have made their escape relatively easily. On the other hand there was fierce prolonged fighting on the left which must have mauled both sides badly, and we are explicitly told that the cavalry flank guard suffered more losses than their heavily mailed Bactrian and Saca opponents (Arr. III.13.4). The relative casualties may not have been so disproportionate as they were at Issus, but even so the victory was decisive. Alexander had deployed his smaller forces with consummate skill. His march to the right and the cavalry engagement on the flank had drawn away Persian cavalry and created a gap at just the point where his most effective units were concentrated. But his strategy entailed sacrifices. The mercenary cavalry, scouts and Paeonians had to sustain the attack of superior, more heavily armed opponents and the left was exposed to outflanking by enemy forces that were vastly more numerous. It was vital that the left held firm and Parmenion's achievement in keeping it so was considerable. He deserved better than the shabby insinuations of Alexander's propagandists, who represented him as slack and incompetent, a brake upon his king's heroic progress.

Darius did not regroup his shattered forces. He fled back to Arbela and without pausing diverted eastward into Media, crossing the Zagros by way of the Spilik pass and the modern town of Ruwandiz. With him was a nucleus of his royal guard and the remains of his mercenary army. He was also joined by Bessus and his cavalry, who had survived the battle more or less intact. The rest of the Persian survivors dispersed, the biggest group adhering to Mazaeus, who made a wide detour behind the Macedonian army, crossed the Tigris and took refuge in Babylon. Alexander himself resumed the pursuit the night after the battle. He stormed to Arbela but found Darius already gone. Abandoning any designs of further pursuit, he prepared for the invasion of Babylon which lay open to his army. It was now early in October. Alexander had taken a giant step towards destroying Darius and ending the war of revenge. Both themes were reflected in his public actions. On the one hand he was proclaimed king of Asia, the true Great King, the acclamation reflecting the reality that he had taken the place of Darius in all lands west of the Zagros. At the same time he evoked the memory of the Persian War, promising the restoration of Plataea and remitting a portion of the spoils to distant Croton in honour of the services of Phayllus in 480 B.C.[178] The successor of Xerxes was still the avenger of Xerxes' sacrilege, and the despot of Asia claimed to be the champion of the liberty and autonomy of the Hellenes.

x      **Babylonia and Persis (winter 331/0 B.C.)**

Alexander stayed on the battlefield only long enough to bury his dead and moved south through Babylonia, intent on securing the lowland capitals of the

---

[178] Plut. *Al.* 34.1–4. Cf. Hamilton 1969, 90–2; Schachermeyr 1973, 276ff.; *contra* Altheim and Stiehl 1970, 195ff.

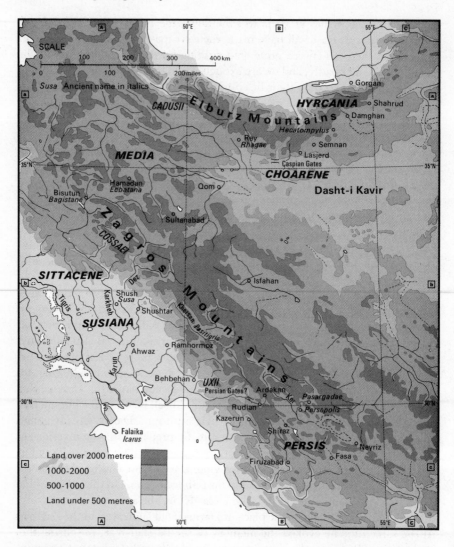

*6. The Iranian heartlands.*

Persian Empire. As in Egypt he was welcomed as a liberator. When he reached Babylon there was no attempt to hold the city against him. After its history of revolt the Persians had taken care to render it indefensible;[179] and its garrison, virtually imprisoned in the old palace of Nebuchadnezzar, could not withstand an attack from outside if it were abetted by a hostile populace within the city walls. Negotiations for its surrender must have taken place during the three weeks or more that Alexander required to cover the 460 km from Arbela

[179] Cf. Schachermeyr 1970, 56–7 (interpreting Hdt. 1.180.1, 181.2).

to Babylon. A magnificent spectacle ensued as the Macedonian army advanced in full battle array, to be met by the Persian general Mazaeus with his grown-up sons, the offspring of a marriage with a Babylonian lady.[180] In Mazaeus the two cultures met, and there could be no better person to surrender the capital to its conqueror. There followed Bagophanes, the Persian citadel commander, and representatives of the Babylonia priesthood, all with an exotic selection of gifts. The king entered his new capital in triumph along streets strewn with flowers, breathing the heady odour of incense from altars on either side of his progress. He immediately took possession of the palace and treasury and made a formal sacrifice to the city god, Bel-Marduk, following the protocol prescribed by the local priesthood. Like his Achaemenid predecessors Alexander accepted the formal titulature of the old Babylonian kingship and he may even have undergone the traditional rite of investiture, grasping the hands of Marduk.[181] As king of Babylon he was caretaker of the great temple complex of Esagila, which had suffered considerable dilapidation under Persian rule. The damage was attributed to Xerxes, and the priesthood had high expectations that their new ruler would restore Esagila to its traditional splendour. They were soon disabused. Alexander was willing enough to concede the rebuilding of the sanctuary but he did not personally address himself to the task. The Babylonians themselves were to have the labour (and expense) of the reconstruction,[182] and he himself showed no interest in the project until his return from India (see below, p. 168). He might in his public pronouncements flatter Babylonian national sentiment but he had no serious intention of acting as a Babylonian monarch. The bullion from the treasury went to a more immediate and practical purpose, the payment of gratuities to his troops (Diod. xvii.64.6; Curt. v.1.45). There was also a need for rest and recreation, and for more than a month the army enjoyed the fleshpots of the capital. It was towards the end of November 331 that Alexander began his march to Susa, leaving Babylonia in the hands of his first Persian satrap Mazaeus, supported and supervised by Macedonian military commanders (see below, p. 235).

There was no military problem to be faced. Immediately after Gaugamela Alexander had sent one of his officers, Philoxenus, to ensure the surrender of Susa and its legendary treasures (Arr. iii.16.6). There was no resistance. The satrap Abulites readily opened his capital to the king's emissary and allowed the bullion to be impounded. Alexander had only to take occupancy. His army was now at full strength, the losses of Gaugamela more than balanced by the arrival of a huge convoy of reinforcements from Macedonia. Amyntas had finally returned with more than 15,000 troops, recruited from Macedonia, Thrace and the Peloponnese, and this fresh manpower brought the army back

---

[180] Curt. v.1.17–23; cf. Badian 1965b, 175; Bosworth 1980a, 341.
[181] Arr. iii.16.5; cf. Schachermeyr 1973, 282; Lane Fox 1973, 248.
[182] Arr. iii.16.4; vii.17.3; Strabo 738; cf. Bosworth 1980a, 314.

at least to its strength before Issus.[183] The new arrivals were as usual apportioned to their appropriate ethnic units, and a modest reorganisation of the command structure took place; sub-commanders were appointed both to the Companion cavalry and to the hypaspists, selected wholly by merit irrespective of their local affiliations (see below, p. 268). It was a change on a small scale but important none the less. It foreshadowed the major regrouping of the Companion cavalry after the death of Philotas and is an indication that the king was less than satisfied with the traditional command structure which perpetuated regional divisions and ensured a natural bond between commander and subordinate. The new appointments were made during a rest period in the rich province of Sittacene, east of the Tigris, and Alexander marched on to Susa at his leisure, covering the 365 km from Babylon in twenty days (Arr. III.16.7). There the events at Babylon were repeated. Alexander was received at the river Choaspes (Karkheh), some three kilometres west of Susa. The satrap brought gifts of regal splendour, including racing camels and Indian elephants, and ceremonially escorted him to the city, the principal capital of the Achaemenid empire. There he took possession of the treasury, which contained accumulated reserves of 40,000 talents of gold and silver bullion and 9,000 talents in gold darics.[184] This was the greatest single sum that had ever fallen to any European dynast, yet it was a fraction of the total Persian reserves which he was to acquire within the month. Unlike his Achaemenid predecessors Alexander had no intention of husbanding his new resources, and the rest of his reign witnessed an outpouring of wealth on a scale that is probably unique in history. Immediately after he secured the treasure Alexander sent Menes to the Levantine coast with a massive reserve of 3,000 talents of silver, which he was to disburse (in part) as a subsidy to Antipater.[185] The war against Agis was at its height (see below, p. 201) and the regent had difficulties mustering an adequate army. There was no question of remitting troops to help him in the crisis, but there was a superabundance of money which would attract mercenaries and sustain political intrigue. Persian darics could prove as fatal to Agis as they had to Agesilaus in 394. The war was over before they could come into play, but the message was painfully clear: Macedonian supremacy was underwritten by Persian gold and could not be seriously challenged.

The next target was Persis proper, the heartland of the empire. The winter was well advanced (late December 331) but Alexander was prepared to take the risk of snow blocking the Zagros passages. The longer he delayed in the plainland of Khuzestan, the greater the resistance he could expect to meet when he forced his way through the mountains the following spring. The army set out from Susa, crossing pontoon bridges over the Dez and Pasiti-

[183] Diod. XVII.65.1; Curt. v.1.39–42; Arr. III.16.10.
[184] Diod. XVII.66.2; cf. Strabo 731; Plut. *Al.* 36.1; Justin XI.14.9; Curt. v.2.11; Arr. III.16.7; Bellinger 1963, 68 with n. 148.
[185] Arr. III.16.9; cf. Diod. XVII.64.5; Curt. v.1.43. See Bosworth 1974, 53–64; *contra* Goukowsky 1978–81, 1.179.

gris,[186] and entered the territory of the Uxii, which formed a corridor between Susa and Persis proper. It comprised two distinct sectors, the lower terrain on the foothills of the Zagros between the modern centres of Ramhormoz and Behbehan and the mountains proper. The inhabitants of the lower terrain were agriculturalists, their land proverbially fertile (Diod. xvii.67.3), and they were governed by a satrap, a relative of Darius. The mountaineers, who were pastoralists, were more intractable, independent of the Achaemenid satrapal organisation and regular recipients of gifts when the Great King traversed their land (Arr. iii.17.1; Strabo 728). Alexander had troubles, it seems, with both groups. As usual the sources are vague and imprecise, but two separate actions seem to be recounted.[187] On the one hand Medates, governor of the lowland Uxii, allegedly planned to block the highway into Persis, but he was rapidly outmanoeuvred by Alexander. The king attacked frontally at dawn while a light column of Agrianians and mercenaries circumvented the enemy position by a side path which brought them out above the defenders.[188] Medates and his men retreated to a fortress where he briefly negotiated a capitulation on very generous terms (the Queen Mother Sisygambis sent a message from Susa, pleading for her kinsmen by marriage).[189] There was also a campaign against the mountain Uxii, who requested their traditional passage money. Alexander invited them to meet him at the narrows which they controlled and then staged one of his most impressive displays of rapid mobility. The nearest Uxian villages were sacked and looted and Alexander then made a forced march to occupy the narrows before the Uxian warriors could muster there. Craterus was sent ahead to occupy the heights overlooking the pass. As a result the Uxians were caught between hammer and anvil, decimated by the superior Macedonian troops, and the survivors were subjected to a heavy annual tribute of livestock (Arr. iii.17.2–6). The two episodes are superficially similar, in that both involved turning movements, but they are completely distinct actions – the crushing of resistance in the Uxian lowlands and a punitive campaign against the mountaineers. Given the vagueness of the topographical data, there is no likelihood of a secure identification of either theatre of operations. Medates' abortive holding position seems to have been relatively close to the northern border with Susiana, the campaign against the mountain Uxii further on in the march, but there is no single detail explicit enough to pinpoint a location. What is certain is that the resistance in Uxiana was not determined enough to slow Alexander's progress or inflict losses. Medates may have delayed him for a few days but the mountaineers, if anything, accelerated his progress. Neither inflicted any casualties.

---

[186] Strabo 729; cf. Diod. xvii.67.1; Curt. v.3.1; iii.17.1.

[187] So Briant 1982b, 161–73; Hammond 1983a, 130. But cf. Badian 1985, 441 with n. 2.

[188] Diod. xvii.67.4–5; Curt. v.3.4–10.

[189] Curt. v.3.12–15. Ptolemy also referred to the Queen Mother's intervention, but Arrian (iii.17.6) couples it with the action against the mountaineers. That seems impossible (Bosworth 1980a, 323–4).

Shortly before he reached the borders of Persis Alexander divided his forces. The allied and mercenary forces together with the baggage train were left under Parmenion's command to take what Arrian describes as the carriage road to Persepolis (Arr. III.18.1; cf. Curt. v.3.16). The king himself took his Macedonian troops, cavalry included, along with the indispensable Agrianians and archers, and struck directly through the mountains at the Persian capital. Once more the exact route is difficult to identify. There are several paths across the Zagros which would have been accessible to a force as expert in mountain conditions as was Alexander's. At present the most acceptable is the route proposed by Sir Aurel Stein, which has its difficulties in relating to the ancient sources but as yet is the only one to have supplied evidence of use in the Achaemenid period.[190] On this hypothesis the united army went as far as the modern town of Fahlian. There Parmenion diverged south, following the modern highway to Kazerun. He may have made a long loop south via Firuzabad, taking the most gradual ascent to Shiraz and the plain of Persepolis. It was the easiest route and he could afford to take his time. Once Alexander had penetrated the defences of Persis he could bring up the baggage at leisure and without opposition. The king now took the direct route, along the Fahlian river and its eastern extension, the Tang-i Layleh. Towards the head of the valley, in an open space known as Mullah Susan, the route bifurcates; one path continues east over the Bolsoru pass and onwards to Ardakan, another branches up a narrow gorge until recently known as the Tang-i Mohammad Reza,[191] rising to a watershed at 2167 metres and giving access to the plain of 'Aliabad. This gorge is probably what the Greek historians termed the Persian (or Susian) Gates, and Alexander found it occupied by a Persian army under the satrap Ariobarzanes. It was a well-prepared position. Ariobarzanes had blocked the gorge with a wall (Arr. III.18.2–3), probably across the narrows underneath the watershed, and his men commanded the heights on either side. The encampment will have extended back to the watershed and it was equipped with a series of outer fortifications. On the heights of the Kuh-i Rudian overlooking the gorge there were probably scouts deputed to watch for any turning movement. It was an almost ideal defensive position, and it was hardly the only defence established. The Persians could not calculate Alexander's route with mathematical precision, nor could they predict that he would choose to force their position at the gates.

Alexander as usual took up the challenge. He first attacked frontally but was unable to penetrate the defences. A rain of missiles from the heights above the Tang-i Mohammad Reza took a heavy toll on his infantry and he was forced to retreat, leaving his dead in the defiles.[192] A second assault was impracticable;

190 Stein 1940, 18ff.; Hansman 1972. A critique of Stein's arguments by Henry Speck is to be published shortly in the *American Journal of Ancient History*.
191 Stein had erroneously named it the Tang-i Khas, which in fact runs parallel but some 10 km further west.
192 Diod. XVII.68.2–3; Curt. v.3.17–23; cf. Arr. III.18.3.

to abandon his dead (or sue for their return) was unthinkable. Interrogation of the prisoners-of-war revealed a turning path, and Alexander set off by night with the majority of his forces, leaving Craterus in camp with two phalanx battalions and a nucleus of archers and cavalry. Alexander crossed the Bolsoru pass under cover of darkness and instead of continuing to Ardakan he veered south-east along the base of the Kuh-i Rudian. There was a second division of forces at this point. Alexander led an advance party, comprising roughly half of the infantry and cavalry, while the rest under Philotas and three of the phalanx commanders followed by a slightly different route. There is some divergence in the sources about the function of this second group, but Curtius is reasonably convincing when he suggests that it acted as a second assault group, exploiting the confusion caused by Alexander's initial attack.[193] Arrian's account is distorted, probably thanks to Ptolemy, who annexed for himself the credit of the second assault and suggested that Philotas and his party were despatched to bridge the river Araxes, more than 100 kilometres from the Persian encampment. At all events there is no doubt that the king led the turning movement, probably over two nights (Curt. v.4.17, 22–3), and using the forest vegetation as a cover against Persian reconnaissance groups on the Kuh-i Rudian. He came down on the Persian defences from the north-east, destroying two advance fortifications and driving the occupants of a third into the mountains. Now he attacked the Persian camp proper, sited around the watershed, and Craterus was immediately alerted by a prearranged trumpet signal. The Persians were caught by surprise and thrown into confusion by the double attack. Those who could make their retreat withdrew to the defences on the southern side of the camp complex, but they were vulnerable to the second assault led by Philotas, which compounded the chaos. To the north of the gorge Ptolemy had been left to deal with any stragglers who were able to circumvent Alexander's attack. The Persians were unable to meet any of the three prongs of attack and were cut down *en masse*. Ariobarzanes made his escape with a small body of cavalry and a somewhat larger infantry guard. He attempted to enter Persepolis but was excluded by its garrison and fell in battle against the advancing Macedonian army (Curt. v.4.33). The rest of the Persian defenders died in battle or capitulated. It was a complete and decisive victory for Alexander, who had once more displayed a genius for rapid and inconspicuous movement and had attacked at the time that the enemy was most vulnerable both physically and psychologically. The initial abortive attack, however, had been a rash blunder and the losses would have been resented, however quickly Alexander managed to retrieve the situation.

Persepolis lay open to the invading army. Its citadel commander, Tiridates, was ready to make his peace with the victors, first excluding Ariobarzanes from the capital and then writing to Alexander to take possession of the

---

[193] Curt. v.4.20, 30; *contra* Arr. III.18.6–9. Cf. Bosworth 1980a, 327–9, and (for another approach) Heckel 1980.

treasury before it was looted. The king accepted the invitation, riding at speed to the Pulvar, which he crossed on an improvised bridge. The capital was defenceless before him, but it was treated very differently from Babylon and Susa. Alexander invoked the official propaganda of the war and turned over the city to his troops in retaliation for Xerxes' wrongs to Greece.[194] Only the palace complex was exempted – for the moment. The private homes of the Persian nobility were sacked without mercy, the men cut down and the women enslaved. It was an act of outrage on a helpless populace and was coldly calculated. Alexander's men had seen the Persian treasures at Arbela, Babylon and Susa pass into their king's hands and apart from the gratuity paid at Babylon their material rewards of victory had been meagre. Now they had the wealth of the Persian nobility to satisfy them (the promise of plunder had probably been a potent stimulus over the past months) and the looting had the pious justification of revenge. The capital itself was to be downgraded, its resources transferred elsewhere, and Persis was to be a satrapy like any other, a subordinate part of the empire of the new king whose principal centre of government would be Babylon (Strabo 731). Its titular governor might be Persian, but there was a permanent garrison of Hellenic troops (Curt. v.6.11; Plut. Al.69.3) to enforce the will of the victor. Persepolis bore the brunt of the invasion, intimately associated as it was with Darius I and Xerxes. The older capital of Pasargadae was treated with more respect. Its modest treasury of 6,000 talents was impounded, but the monuments were left intact, in particular the tomb of Cyrus the Great for which Alexander was to show an especial veneration (see below, p. 154).

The Macedonians were to stay four months in Persis (Plut. Al. 37.6) while they waited for the winter snows to disperse. During that time the Treasury of Persepolis was stripped of its accumulated reserves of gold and silver bullion, which the vulgate sources estimate at the colossal figure of 120,000 talents (Diod. xvii.71.1; Curt. v.6.11). At the very minimum the haul was at least as great as that from Susa. Alexander had no intention of leaving any of it in its traditional repository, and he requisitioned a vast convoy of camels and pack animals from the Mesopotamian lowlands (the main carriage road at least was kept clear of snow). Some of the bullion was redirected to Susa and some reserved to travel with the army to Media but none was to remain at Persepolis. No single gold or silver object of any size was to be found in the Treasury by its twentieth-century excavators.[195] While the convoy was being formed, Alexander and his men rested at Persepolis and were reunited with the rest of the army under Parmenion. There was a short diversion towards the end of March,[196] when Alexander took a small force of infantry and cavalry for a 30-day campaign in the Zagros. This brought him into contact with the

---

[194] Diod. xvii.70.1–6; Curt. v.6.1–8; Plut. Al. 37.3–5. The details are pathetically exaggerated, but there is no reason to doubt the historicity of the sack.
[195] Cf. Schmidt 1953–70, 1.179; Bosworth 1980a, 332.
[196] Curt. v.6.12 – sub ipsum Vergiliarum sidus; cf. Borza 1972, 237 with n.29; Engels 1978a, 73–7.

Mardi, another mountain people on the southern border of Persis, and involved the devastation of some Persian territory (Curt. v.6.17), but its scale was too small to have lasting effects.

At the capital his army received him in the palace of Xerxes, which was now stripped of bullion. Diodorus (XVII.71.3) interpreted that as a sign that he intended to destroy Persepolis completely, and he may not be altogether wrong. The fate of the palace must have been discussed during the months of occupation. Was it to be destroyed to repay the burning of the Acropolis or was it to remain as the satrap's residence, a garrison centre which would be a perpetual symbol of the change of dynasty? Arrian (III.18.11–12) reports an exchange between Parmenion and Alexander which is probably apocryphal as it stands but which may reflect a genuine debate over the palace and its future use. The question was resolved dramatically after Alexander had offered ceremonial sacrifices in honour of his recent successes. A feast followed with a prolonged drinking session at which several courtesans were present, including the Athenian Thais, future mistress of Ptolemy. According to Cleitarchus (whose account is at the basis of the tradition in Diodorus, Curtius and Plutarch) she precipitated the crisis, suggesting that the palace be burned then and there as a reprisal for Xerxes' sacrilege at Athens.[197] The banqueters, Alexander included, sprang into action, seized torches and set fire to the palace, whose ceiling of cedar wood was soon burning uncontrollably (there are traces of the conflagration in the Hall of 100 Columns and the Treasury). The army, which had been attracted by the blaze, joined the revel and went wild in an orgy of destruction in which the remaining contents of the Treasury, notably the royal tableware, were smashed and vandalised.[198] The palace was gutted, and in the sober light of day there was some doubt whether the destruction was justified. There is a measure of agreement that Alexander regretted the action at the time,[199] and when he returned to Persepolis nearly six years later he was apparently ready to admit error (Arr. VI.30.1). But the propaganda was ready to hand. The town of Persepolis had already been sacked as an act of revenge and the burning of the palace was its culmination, commemorated as such in the thank-offering to Zeus which was later made by the cavalry contingent from Thespiae.[200] In the spring of 330 there was still some point in stressing the official pretext of the war.[201] Antipater was embroiled with Agis, and it would have some sentimental value, if nothing else, to emphasise that his king's victories had been won in the cause of the Greeks. Unlike the Spartans, who had sold themselves to the Great King,

[197] Cleitarchus, *FGrH* 137 F 11; Diod. XVII.72.1–5; Curt. v.7.2–7; Plut. *Al.* 38.1–8; cf. Strabo 730. For the various interpretations of the episode see Seibert 1972a, 132–4; Bosworth 1980a, 331–2. Note particularly Badian 1967, 189–90; 1985, 443–6; Wirth 1971, 149–52; Borza 1972.

[198] Cf. Schmidt 1953–70, 1.178–9; Olmstead 1948, 521–3.

[199] Plut. *Al.* 38.8 (ὁμολογεῖται); Curt. v.8.11 (*paenituisse constat*).

[200] *Anth. Pal.* VI.344; cf. Bellen 1974, 60–4.

[201] Cf. Badian 1967, 188–90.

Alexander had destroyed the centre of his power. But the reality fell short of the propaganda. The palace was indeed uninhabitable but the city around it remained to serve as the satrapal capital (Diod. XIX.21.2, 46.6). Nor was the populace totally alienated. Most Persians had not been affected by the rape of their capital and they were prepared to accept the invader long after the shock of defeat and conquest had passed. There was no unrest in Persis even at the height of Bessus' counter-offensive (see below, p. 105) and from 324 the regime of the Macedonian Peucestas was positively welcomed by the native population.

XI     **The occupation of Eastern Iran**

For Darius the end of the campaign and his life were imminent. He had established himself in the Median capital of Ecbatana and awaited events there. A few counsellors of distinction remained, the chiliarch Nabarzanes, the veteran Artabazus and the satraps of the eastern empire, dominated by Bessus, kinsman of Darius and master of the northern marches of Bactria and Sogdiana. As yet there were forces still untapped, and Darius had called upon new levies from Bactria and the tribes of the Caspian shore, notably the Cadusii who had distinguished themselves at Gaugamela (Arr. III.19.4; Diod. XVII.73.2). The intention was to stage one last desperate defence of the imperial heartland, always assuming that Alexander moved north to Media and was not distracted by rebellion in Persis or even in Greece (Arr. III.19.1). All optimism, however, proved ungrounded. Alexander left Persepolis in May, undeterred by the situation in the west, and the reinforcements had not arrived. The eastern satraps no doubt had too candid an appraisal of the prospect of holding Media to commit more of their domestic levy. Darius had too few forces to risk battle – 3,300 cavalry, mostly Bactrians under Bessus' command, and a larger force of infantry, still including a nucleus of Greek mercenaries. There was no choice but withdrawal. The eastern satrapies were to be the next battleground and Media was of necessity abandoned to the invader. Darius vacated the capital and moved north-east to the Caspian Gates, the complex of defiles which separated Media from Parthyene and the eastern satrapies.[202] There he joined the convoy of waggons which he had sent ahead with the royal household and began the long trek east.

It was already too late. At the news of Darius' planned resistance Alexander left the vast bullion train with the treasure from Persepolis and took his army at speed through the border satrapy of Paraetacene. After eleven days' march he was met by a Persian noble, Bisthanes (allegedly a son of Artaxerxes III), who brought the news that Darius had left Ecbatana at least five days previously, taking with him the contents of the Median treasury. Alexander reacted instantly. The march on the Median capital was now supererogatory.

---

[202] Curt. v.8.1ff. (rhetorically embellished); Arr. III.19.1–2. On the strategic importance of the Gates see Standish 1970.

What mattered to him was to overhaul Darius and to do that he needed speed. Accordingly he reduced his forces to a minimum – the cavalry (Companions, *prodromoi* and mercenaries), the bulk of the Macedonian phalanx and the indispensable light infantry, Agrianians and archers, in all less than 20,000 men. With this *corps d'élite* he diverged from the main road to Ecbatana,[203] probably in the vicinity of the modern Sultanabad, and struck north-eastwards to Rhagae (now Rey, 12 km to the south of Tehran). The rest of the army was left to take possession of Media under the direction of Parmenion. He was to ensure that the convoy of bullion, now far to the south under the formidable protection of 6,000 Macedonian phalanx troops, reached its destination in Ecbatana. Then he was to carry out a pincer movement along the Caspian coast, crushing Darius' Cadusian allies and blocking any Persian retreat north of the Elburz mountains.[204] Those instructions were soon countermanded, and the old general remained at Ecbatana with the garrison forces, finally detached from Alexander's person and gradually to be isolated from the troops he had known.

Alexander reached Rhagae after ten days of forced marching, but he failed to intercept Darius, who, travelling light, had already reached the Caspian Gates. At this point he paused, to refresh and consolidate his army (he could not tell whether the Gates would be held against him). After a five-day rest period the pursuit resumed (Arr. III.20.2–4). Two days' rapid march took him some 90 km east of Rhagae, through the Gates which were in fact undefended and into the fertile district of Choarene (Khar). While he was amassing provisions to sustain the anticipated journey through desert country he received yet more news of affairs in the enemy camp. There the Persian high command was on the verge of disintegration, thanks to an internal power struggle. Darius was retreating to the eastern marches of his Empire, lands that he had not apparently visited in person (nor had any of the late Achaemenid kings), and his satraps there were unwilling to accept his leadership, marred as it was by a series of catastrophes. Shortly after the evacuation of Ecbatana there were suggestions[205] that the supreme command should be transferred, temporarily at least, to Bessus, the most powerful and distinguished of the eastern satraps (cf. Curt. v.9.8). The chiliarch Nabarzanes supported the intrigue and Darius was left with only the support of the westernised Artabazus (whose family had for generations been associated with Hellespontine Phrygia) and the Greek mercenaries who continued to support the king they knew. The internal dissensions necessarily slowed the progress of the Persian column and in their wake came increasing demoralisation, as a

---

[203] Curt. v.13.1. Arrian (III.19.5) states that Alexander actually entered Ecbatana, but that must stem from a misunderstanding of his source. Cf. Bosworth 1976b, 132–6; 1980a, 335–6; *contra* Badian 1985, 447.

[204] Arr. III.19.7. Cf. Goukowsky 1978–81, 1.35–7; Bosworth 1980a, 336–8.

[205] Repeated in a series of speeches in Curtius (v.8.6ff.; cf. 9.3–8); cf. Berve 1926, 2 nos. 244, 543.

stream of deserters abandoned Darius' cause in despair and fell back to make their peace with the victor.

The first news of the crisis was brought by the Babylonian noble Bagistanes, and Alexander immediately resumed the pursuit with his cavalry and the fittest of his infantry. It was to be the most celebrated forced march of the reign, covering nearly 200 km. in three stages.[206] From the plain of Choarene he struck into the desert, along the northern rim of the Dasht-i Kavir. At the oasis of Thara (Lasjerd?) he received further news of the troubles in the Persian camp. Darius had finally been arrested by Bessus and his accomplices and was transported in a waggon, a prisoner in golden chains. This had precipitated the final split. Artabazus and his sons, the few remaining loyalists, took the Greek mercenaries and withdrew north into the Elburz mountains.[207] All that remained of the royal army were the forces of the eastern satraps, no longer a military problem for Alexander. The final stage of the pursuit was conducted by horse alone, the pick of the infantry mounted for the last push. Aided by local guides, this force of 6,000 cavalry swept across the desert by a direct, waterless route and overhauled the Persian stragglers shortly after dawn. Now the end came quickly. At the first indication of the Macedonian advance Darius was stabbed by his captors. According to Arrian (III.21.10) the assassins were Satibarzanes, satrap of Areia, and Barsaentes, satrap of Drangiana and Arachosia, but the murder was primarily instigated by Bessus and Nabarzanes. They now went their separate ways to their satrapies, Nabarzanes to hiding in Hyrcania, leaving their mortally wounded king to die, minutes before his conqueror reached his side.[208] Their motives are variously stated in the sources, but it is clear that they had no intention of allowing the Great King to fall into Alexander's hands and be seen as his vassal. If he could have been saved from the pursuit, he could serve as a figurehead for resistance in the far east under Bessus' de facto leadership. As it was he was better dead.

The chase had ended a little short of the city of Hecatompylus, recently located at Shahr-i Qumis.[209] Alexander used the capital as a temporary base while the infantry which he had left in the desert caught up with his pursuit party. Meanwhile he treated the body of his rival with every courtesy, remitting it to Persepolis for royal burial (though not in the tomb Darius had intended for himself, which remained unfinished).[210] This marked the end of an epoch. The last Achaemenid was dead, and there was as yet no rival to Alexander, the self-proclaimed King of Asia. In every sense the war of

206 Cf. Arr. III.21.3–10; Curt. V.13.3–13. For the variants and details of topography see Bosworth 1980a, 340–5; contra Radet 1932.
207 Arr. III.21.3–5; Curt. V.12.14–18.
208 Arr. III.21.10; Diod. XVII.73.3. For more romantic stories see Plut. Al. 43.3–4; Curt. V.13.23–5; Justin XI.15.5; and for the tradition of a meeting between the two kings see Diod. XVII.73.4; Ps.-Call. II.20.5ff. with Merkelbach 1977, 28ff.
209 Hansman 1968; Hansman and Stronach 1970.
210 Arr. III.22.1. Cf. Schmidt 1953–70, 3.80ff., esp. 107.

vengeance could be said to be complete, now that every capital of the Persian Empire was in his hands and the palace of Xerxes reduced to smoking rubble. For his Greek allies the war was indeed over. As soon as the pursuit of Darius ended, the king sent word to Ecbatana,[211] authorising the demobilisation of the troops of the Corinthian League and diverting no less than 2,000 talents from the treasure of Persepolis for a discharge bonus. Any who wished to continue in service were enrolled as mercenaries. The rest were conveyed to the Syrian coast, to be shipped to Euboea and released. This was a largely symbolic decision. The Hellenic infantry had never been used in the front line (see below, p. 264) and its departure did not significantly impair the effectiveness of Alexander's army. For secondary functions, particularly the supply of garrisons, there was an increasing pool of mercenaries, and the Hellenic forces were becoming an encumbrance, more and more annexed to the command of Parmenion. But the demobilisation was a dangerous precedent. It evoked a strong reaction among Alexander's troops, who agitated for return and may have come close to mutiny.[212] The tensions implied by Parmenion's recommendation to accept a frontier at the Euphrates had now become apparent and the army was unequivocally expressing its reluctance to press indefinitely into Asia. There was now no Parmenion to champion the cause, and Alexander was able to assert his will over his men. In an assembly he harangued his Macedonians in a powerful speech, stressing the dangers of rebellion if they vacated Asia, dangers that would come in the first instance from Bessus, unconquered in Bactria.[213] That was the crux. Alexander was talking not of revenge but of an empire. He was Darius' successor, with claims to his entire realm, and he would not tolerate any part of it remaining independent. He would impose his royal authority whatever the cost and, though in theory his men were the beneficiaries of empire (Plut. *Al.* 47.3), in practice the issue was his categorical insistence on total unchallenged autocratic power. His men were prevailed upon to advance that ambition, fired by the king's rhetoric and perhaps more by the hope of donatives present and future (Diod. XVII.74.4), but the opposition had been serious and it was to gather momentum over the next years.

Alexander's first concern was to deal with the remnants of Darius' army which had taken refuge in the Elburz. He left Hecatompylus and after three days' march, near the modern city of Damghan, he divided his forces, intending to drive through the mountains by three different routes. His own column, comprising hypaspists, select phalanx men and light infantry, took the most direct route, pressing towards the Caspian via the Shamshirbun Pass and the upper reaches of the Dorudbar, while Craterus and Erigyius used other passes, the latter taking the cavalry and baggage train by the main

---

211  Justin XII.1.1–3; Curt. VI.2.17; cf. Diod. XVII.74.3 (garbled); Arr. III.19.5–6; Plut. *Al.* 42.5. see Bosworth 1976b, 133ff.
212  Curt. VI.2.15–16; cf. Diod. XVII.74.3; Justin XII.3.2–3; Plut. *Al.* 47.1–3.
213  Curt. VI.3.1–4; Justin XII.3.3; similar material in Plut. *Al.* 47.1–2 (cf. Diod. XVII.74.3).

carriage road (via Shahrud and the Chalchanlyan Pass).[214] There was no
attempt to defend the passes. Alexander's rearguard of Agrianians easily beat
off a desultory attack by some native tribes (Arr. III.23.6); otherwise his
progress was unchallenged. But it was not unobserved. At his first halting-
place on the banks of the river Rhidagnus (Neka) he received overtures from
Nabarzanes, the fugitive chiliarch and regicide,[215] which he answered cour-
teously, offering pledges of safe conduct. A little later Phrataphernes, satrap
of Parthyaea and Hyrcania, surrendered in person. By this time Alexander
had reached the Hyrcanian capital of Zadracarta, and he had joined forces
with Craterus and Erigyius. The peoples of the eastern Elburz had capitulated
without resistance and Autophradates, the satrap of the mountain district of
Tapuria, also submitted in person, to be confirmed in his office (unlike
Phrataphernes, who was replaced by Amminapes, a Persian noble who had
helped surrender Egypt two years before). Capitulation now became general.
The most impressive act of surrender took place near the western border of
Hyrcania. Artabazus came to the Macedonian headquarters with his sons and
representatives of the Greek mercenaries who had deserted the Persian camp
with him. He was treated with warm respect. The mercenaries, justifiably
wary after the fate of their colleagues at the Granicus, asked for a guarantee of
good faith. Unlike Nabarzanes, they were categorically denied it. The king
invoked the prohibitions of the Corinthian League and insisted on unconditional surrender. They had no choice but to comply.

There was a brief interlude, a five-day campaign against the independent
Mardi, who inhabited the territory on the south-west border of Hyrcania.
Their independence was their only provocation and they were taken completely by surprise. Many fled into the densely wooded mountains, where they
were systematically hunted down until they offered submission and hostages.
They were now absorbed into the empire as an annexe of Tapuria.[216]
Alexander returned to find the mercenaries at his base camp, awaiting his
judgement. Despite his threats it was mild, simply enlistment into his service;
veterans who had joined Darius before the declaration of war in 337 were
given the option of demobilisation. Once submission was made the king was
clement and conciliatory. It was only a party of Spartan ambassadors,
representatives of a state still (he believed) openly at war, that he treated at all
harshly, placing them under close arrest. The remainder of the refugees were
taken into the court or the army, even Nabarzanes, who surrendered himself
when Alexander returned to the Hyrcanian capital.[217] The fact that he had
instigated the arrest and murder of his king did not stand in the way of his
friendly reception, which he owed in part to the charms of the royal eunuch,

[214] Arr. III.23.2; Curt. VI.4.2–3; cf. von Stahl 1924, 324; Pédech 1958, 75–7.
[215] Curt. VI.4.8–14; cf. Arr. III.23.4 (compressed).
[216] Arr. III.24.1–2; Curt. VI.5.11–21; Diod. XVII.76.3–8; Plut. *Al.* 44.3–5. On the Mardi see
Marquart 1907, 57–8; von Stahl 1924, 328.
[217] Curt. VI.5.22–3. His chronology is generally preferable to that of Arrian (cf. Badian 1958a,
144–7; Bosworth 1980a, 350).

Bagoas, one of his many presents to the victor.[218] The crucial factor was his acceptance of the new regime, and for the moment it looked as though Alexander was accepted by all factions of the old Persian court, by Darius' murderers and by his defenders. He had good reason for the sacrifices and games which he held during his fifteen-day stay in Zadracarta.[219]

The union of hearts was temporary. A challenge came almost immediately. Alexander moved back across the Elburz into Parthyaea and advanced eastwards to the borders of the satrapy of Areia. At Susia (probably to be identified with the town of Tus, north-west of Meshed) he met the satrap, Satibarzanes, who made formal submission, and was confirmed in office.[220] He was to co-operate with a Macedonian officer, Anaxippus, who commanded a surprisingly small unit of forty mounted javelin men (see below, p. 271). Alexander clearly did not anticipate serious trouble. He was immediately disabused. The news broke that Bessus had laid claim to the Achaemenid throne. During the interlude in Hyrcania the regicide had made his way to his home satrapy and once there had assumed the insignia of kingship, the flared upright tiara, and adopted regal nomenclature, terming himself Artaxerxes, the fifth of that name.[221] Not only was he determined to resist Alexander, he was arrogating the kingship itself in the anticipation that the satrapies of the far east would stand united behind him. Alexander's reaction was predictable, to come to grips with the usurper immediately. From Susia he planned to drive east, along the foothills of the Kopet Dag massif, to invade Bactria from the west. He was travelling light and, according to Curtius,[222] he burned his transport waggons before beginning the march. The aim was clearly to crush Bessus immediately, before he could concentrate his forces. That was the military reaction. There was also a political one. Alexander adopted some items of Persian court dress: the diadem, the white-striped tunic and the girdle, which he combined with the distinctively Macedonian *kausia* and cloak. At the same time he issued senior Companions with the scarlet robes of Persian courtiers, introduced court chamberlains of Asiatic stock and added a group of Persian nobles to his entourage, most prominently Darius' brother Oxyathres.[223] It was an effective demonstration that Alexander took his claims of kingship seriously. He was no transient conqueror but the genuine successor of the Persian monarchs, supported and served by the brother of his predecessor. Such a move might be hoped to cut some of the ground away from Bessus. It also had its dangers. The Macedonians, already reluctant to continue eastwards, now saw their king assimilate himself, in part at least, to

218 Gunderson 1982, 184ff., revives Tarn's view that Bagoas is a fiction. So also Hammond 1980a, 322 n. 114.

219 Arr. III.25.1; cf. Curt. VI.5.32; Diod. XVII.77.3.

220 Arr. III.25.1–2; Curt. VI.6.13; cf. Heckel 1981, 69.

221 Arr. III.25.3; Curt. VI.6.12–13; *Metz Epit.* 3. Cf. Ritter 1965, 6ff.

222 Curt. VI.6.15–17; cf. Plut. *Al.* 57.1; Polyaenus IV.3.10 (dated before the invasion of India). See Engels 1978a, 86; *contra* Hamilton 1969, 157.

223 Diod. XVII.77.4–7; Curt. VI.6.1–10; Justin XII.3.8–12; *Metz Epit.* 1–2; cf. Plut. *Al.* 45.1–2; Arr. IV.7.4–5. See Ritter 1965, 31–55; Bosworth 1980b, 4–8.

Persian court protocol. It was a blatant breach with tradition and necessarily angered the more conservative of the nobility. But there was apparently no focus for the opposition. Parmenion was isolated in Media, soon to be deprived of his phalanx infantry (his mercenary cavalry and Thessalian volunteers had gone ahead to join Alexander in Areia), and the troops under his command at Ecbatana were largely Thracian. His influence suffered a further blow when his son Nicanor, the hypaspist commander, died of illness at the time that Alexander began his march against Bessus. The king declined to stay for the obsequies but detached Philotas with a substantial body of troops to give his brother fitting burial.[224] For the first time none of Parmenion's family was close to Alexander, and it probably facilitated his experiment with court ceremonial.

Now came the crisis. Once Alexander was launched on his invasion of Bactria, revolt erupted behind him. Satibarzanes declared himself for Bessus, massacred the minuscule force of Anaxippus and began mobilising his subjects against the Macedonian king. Alexander broke off his march east. Leaving Craterus to bring up the bulk of the army, he took the Companions, light infantry and two phalanx battalions and allegedly covered 600 stades in two days and nights of forced marching, to reach the Areian capital (near modern Herat). Satibarzanes took flight to the east with 2,000 cavalry, leaving his people to defend a heavily wooded hill citadel near the capital.[225] The resistance was determined, but the defenders were overcome by a forest fire, deliberately started and fanned uncontrollably by the fierce late summer north-westerly gale. A brief punitive campaign put the satrapy back in his hands, and he conferred it upon another Persian noble, Arsaces. But he was not disposed to move directly against Bessus. Immediately south of Areia lay the satrapies of Drangiana and Arachosia, the realm of the other regicide, Barsaentes. After his experiences with Satibarzanes Alexander did not intend him to remain undisturbed, a potential threat inside his empire. What was more, there was regicide to avenge. Immediately after Darius' death Alexander could make peace with the murderers, but Bessus' declaration and Satibarzanes' rebellion had transformed the situation. Now Alexander himself was challenged and it made excellent propaganda to assume the role of avenger. Bessus was a traitor and usurper, and Alexander played on the issue to buttress his own legitimacy in the eyes of the Iranian populace. In the face of the invasion Barsaentes took flight into India, beyond the borders of the empire,[226] and the Macedonian army moved south to the Drangian capital of Phrada (Farah).

[224] Curt. VI.6.18–19 (cf. Arr. III.25.4). The 2,600 troops included Nicanor's men, the hypaspists, who (uniquely) were not under Alexander's command during the Areian campaign (Arr. III.25.6).

[225] Diod. XVII.78.2; Curt. VI.6.22–3; cf. Arr. III.25.7. Engels' identification of the fortress with Qalat-i Nadiri (1978a, 87–91) cannot be sustained. For another view see Goukowsky 1976, 231; Seibert 1985, 120.

[226] Arr. III.25.8; Curt. VIII.13.3–4.

XII     **Conspiracy and intrigue: the downfall of Philotas**

At Phrada occurred one of the great scandals of the reign, which involved the execution of Philotas and the assassination of his father Parmenion. The story is sensational and variously reported in the sources, which cover a whole spectrum from Arrian's misleadingly brief and apologetic account (explicitly based on Ptolemy and Aristobulus) to the detailed and lurid narrative of Curtius Rufus with its battery of forensic speeches.[227] What seems agreed is that a plot was initiated against Alexander's life. Its central figure was Demetrius the bodyguard, and there were a number of minor conspirators (Curt. VI.7.15), none of whom appears to have had any particular importance. The conspiracy was revealed fortuitously, when Dimnus, a minor associate of the king, attempted to recruit his young favourite to the cause. The young man panicked and used the offices of his brother, Cebalinus, to reveal the details of the movement. At this point Philotas became involved. Cebalinus approached him outside the royal apartments, informed him of the plot and asked him to act as intermediary with the king. Nothing happened, and Cebalinus repeated his request the following day. Finally he despaired of Philotas and approached the king directly. The sequel was the arrest of Dimnus, who killed himself (or was killed) when the guards came for him,[228] and the rest of the alleged conspirators were also secured. After consultation with his friends, in particular Craterus, Hephaestion and Coenus, Alexander ordered the arrest of Philotas, and arranged for him to stand trial before the army on the following day.

There are many points of obscurity in the story, and the degree to which Philotas was involved is a hotly contested question.[229] It can be admitted that the conspiracy was a serious attempt on Alexander's life. Demetrius and Dimnus may have had purely personal motives, but it is equally possible that they were antipathetic to Alexander's claim to the Achaemenid succession and wished for some limitation of empire. Philotas may have sympathised with their aims, but he was not a principal in the conspiracy. He was not explicitly named and Cebalinus would never have approached him if he had known him to be privy to the movement. But he did not divulge what he had heard. That is admitted by all sources and for Arrian it is prima-facie proof of his complicity (III.26.2). Philotas claimed that he considered the details of the plot to be fictitious, the product of Cebalinus' over-heated imagination, but, if so, it is incomprehensible that he compromised himself by not reporting it or investigating the charges further. It is perhaps best to concede that he had some sympathy with the conspirators without being actively involved in the

---

[227] Arr. III.26–7; Curt. VI.7.1–VII.2.38; Diod. XVII.79–80; Plut. Al. 48–9; Justin XII.5.1–8; Strabo 724. For analysis of the sources see Cauer 1894; Goukowsky 1978–81, 2.118–34; contra Egge 1978, 41ff.

[228] Curt VI.7.28–30; Diod. XVII.79–2; cf. Plut. Al. 49.7.

[229] The seminal work is Badian 1960a. See also Hamilton 1969, 132–8; Schachermeyr 1973, 326–36; Heckel 1977a; Bosworth 1980a, 359–63.

plot. That is implied by an obscure episode reported by Curtius, in which Philotas, on the point of execution, was able to inculpate a certain Calis as an accomplice of Demetrius, even though he had not been named by Cebalinus.[230] Possibly he had caught wind of seditious meetings but held his own counsel, preparing for action if the conspiracy should succeed. If so, it was passive disloyalty, and his enemies made the most of the situation. Craterus had already suborned Philotas' mistress and through her channelled reports of his increasing disaffection from Alexander (Plut. *Al.* 48.4–49.2). Now he pressed for his elimination and organised the arrest with Alexander's full concurrence.[231] Philotas had exposed himself fatally and too many of the court had an interest in his removal for the opportunity to be ignored.

The trial was carefully stage-managed before an army assembly, which Curtius (VI.8.23) claims numbered no more than 6,000 (it was obviously not a plenary gathering).[232] Alexander produced the corpse of Dimnus and on general grounds of probability accused Philotas of organising the conspiracy. He was supported by passionate speeches from the phalanx commanders, Amyntas son of Andromenes and Coenus (Philotas' brother-in-law); and Philotas' oration in his own defence was undermined by a minor officer, Bolon, who was popular with the troops and made a personal attack on the accused, harping on his notorious arrogance. As a result the assembly, in which his own troops (the cavalry) were necessarily a minority, was easily induced to clamour for the death penalty. Subsequently Philotas was put to the question, and under extreme duress he made various admissions of disloyalty, some of them perhaps involving his father. But Parmenion could not be associated with the conspiracy of Dimnus; the most that could be extorted from Philotas was a story involving seditious conversations with Hegelochus, who was conveniently deceased by 330.[233] That was insufficient to secure a condemnation, even from the Macedonian army, and Alexander was reduced to political assassination. He had determined on the eradication of the family and had no intention of letting the father survive the son. Parmenion was still at Ecbatana but without the support of any Macedonian troops – the phalanx infantry which had escorted the bullion train was well embarked on its long march east to rejoin Alexander.[234] Accordingly the king intrigued directly with Cleander, the mercenary commander at Ecbatana and brother of Coenus, one of the principals in the arrest of Philotas. Instructions for the assassination were conveyed by racing camel across the desolation of the Dasht-i Lut, their bearer a friend and adjutant of Parmenion. Eleven days' hard travel brought the despatch to the Median capital, and Cleander and his fellow commanders acted immediately, striking down the old general while he

---

[230] Curt. VI.11.36–7; cf. Goukowsky 1978–81, 2.130.
[231] Curt. VI.8.2–10, 17–18; cf. Berve 1926, 2 no. 446 (p. 222); Badian 1960a, 337–8.
[232] Lock 1977a; Errington 1978, esp. 86–91; *contra* Aymard 1967, 156–7; Briant 1973, 287ff.
[233] Curt. VI.11.22–30; cf. Berve 1926, 2 no. 341.
[234] Curt. VII.3.4; cf. Bosworth 1980a, 338, 356; *contra* Goukowsky 1978–81, 1.38–9.

was reading a letter from his king.[235] Brilliant and totally ruthless, the coup was wholly effective and Parmenion had his reward for a lifetime of service to the Macedonian throne. His disagreements over policy had become too strong to be tolerated by the increasingly autocratic Alexander, who seized upon the first opportunity to eliminate him.

Meanwhile in Drangiana Philotas had met his end, broken by torture and stoned to death along with the conspirators named by Cebalinus. That was not the end of the affair. There were other prosecutions, motivated in part by private spite. The most important were the sons of Andromenes (Amyntas, Simmias and Attalus) who had been intimates of Philotas and were dangerously compromised when their younger brother Polemon panicked at the report of his interrogation by torture and took flight from the camp.[236] No doubt Amyntas' enemies suggested guilt by association, and the phalanx commander was forced to defend himself. This he did effectively and secured his exoneration, while his brother returned of his own accord. Clearly Alexander had no personal reason to wish the downfall of the sons of Andromenes (Amyntas had participated in the indictment of Philotas), and the younger brothers survived the reign with prestige apparently undiminished. Amyntas, however, died in battle shortly after his acquittal (Arr. III.27.3). Another casualty was Alexander the Lyncestian (see above, p. 50), who was brought out of close arrest and put on trial for treason. Three years of confinement had their inevitable effect. Wandering in speech and mind, he could not make any defence against the charges levelled at him and was summarily executed.[237] This had nothing to do with the conspiracy. Alexander exploited the hysterical mood of the army, which he had created, to remove a man who was an embarrassment and potential threat to him, a possible figurehead for future conspiracies. Son-in-law of Antipater he might be, but he was better removed and the charges of treason, however flimsy, could carry conviction after the execution of Philotas, when any person at court, no matter how exalted, might have been thought capable of seditious intrigue.

The king had served notice in the starkest fashion that opposition would not be tolerated and disloyalty in any form would receive the most condign punishment. Rank was no protection. On the other hand there were commands to be filled. Alexander had no intention of replacing Parmenion in the command structure. Instead there was a process of fragmentation. Large permanent commands tended to disappear, and a policy evolved of separating commanders from their units and cutting across the regional ties that had previously existed between officers and men (see below, pp. 268ff.). The first step came when the cavalry command was divided. Philotas was replaced by two hipparchs, Cleitus the Black and Hephaestion. This was a combination of

[235] Curt. VII.2.11–32; Diod. XVII.80.3; Arr. III.27.3–4; Plut. *Al.* 49.13; Strabo 724.
[236] Curt. VII.1.10ff.; Arr. III.27.1–3. Cf. Bosworth 1976a, 12–14; Heckel 1975.
[237] Curt. VII.1.5–9; Diod. XVII.80.2; cf. Berve 1926, 2 no. 37; Badian 1960a, 335–6.

the old and the new, an officer of the previous generation associated with one of the rising stars of the court, and its purpose, we are told (Arr. III.27.4), was to prevent the cavalry developing allegiance to any single figure. Any odium accruing from the execution of Parmenion would be mitigated by the promotion of Cleitus, already commander of the royal *ile*, but his influence was countered by the parallel appointment of Hephaestion. By contrast the hypaspists remained under a single commander, Neoptolemus, who was a relative of Alexander himself, associated by birth with the royal house of Epirus.[238] More significantly, the senior positions, the commands of army divisions operating separately from Alexander, became monopolised by a small pool of marshals, dominated by the men who had engineered Philotas' downfall: Craterus, Hephaestion, Perdiccas and Coenus. These were the intimates of the king, his counsellors and marshals. Collectively they occupied the position Parmenion had enjoyed at the beginning of the reign, but no single person was dominant and there were antipathies between them, notably that between Hephaestion and Craterus. At the same time Alexander's coevals acquired court positions, displacing the older generation of Philip. Demetrius' replacement as bodyguard was Ptolemy, son of Lagus, who had been exiled in 337/6 in the aftermath of the Pixodarus scandal (Arr. III.27.5). The promotions were balanced by demotions, most of which we cannot trace. There was, however, a special disciplinary company, known as 'the unit of insubordinates', into which Alexander drafted any Macedonian troops who were known to have expressed criticism of the removal of Parmenion.[239] The number of disaffected was obviously considerable, but Alexander was in no mood for conciliation. The criticisms of his policies were to be stifled at all levels and no critic, however great or humble, was safe from reprisals. The punishment of the conspiracy had been adeptly transformed into a political purge, and its effect was to deter opposition, for the next two years at least.

XIII    **The conquest of the North-east Frontier**

From Phrada, which Alexander renamed Prophthasia ('Anticipation')[240] to commemorate the detection of the conspiracy, the army moved south to the complex of freshwater lakes which receive the effluent of the river Helmand. This was one of the granaries of ancient Iran, with ample reserves to tide the Macedonians over winter. Alexander remained in the area for some sixty days (Curt. VII.3.3), enjoying the hospitality of the Ariaspians, whom the Achaemenids had honoured as benefactors after they had given succour to the starving army of Cyrus the Great. Impressed by their civic institutions (and the traditional sanctity of the district), he extended their boundaries and

---

[238] Plut. *Eum.* 1; cf. Arr. II.27.6; Berve 1926, 2 no. 548.
[239] Diod. XVII.80.4; Curt. VII.2.35–8; Justin XII.5.5–8.
[240] Steph. Byz. s.v. Φράδα; Plut. *Mor.* 328F. Cf. Diod. XV.18.4 (festival of Prophthasia at Clazomenae).

conferred nominal freedom – under the supervision of a satrap responsible for both them and the Gedrosian tribes to the south.[241] During his stay disquieting news arrived of a second revolt in Areia. Satibarzanes had returned with cavalry supplied by Bessus and was reasserting his control over the satrapy. This invasion was linked with wider agitation. Bessus had nominated a certain Brazanes satrap of Parthyaea[242] and sent troops along the northern corridor from Bactria to fuel revolt as far as Media. It took some time for the extent of the rising to be revealed and Alexander did not return in person to cope with the situation in Areia. In any case the army from Media, comprising 6,000 phalanx infantry, was on its way to join him (it had probably gone as far as Drangiana) and could be relied upon to prevent the insurrection spreading south. The containment of the unrest was placed in the hands of Erigyius and two other commanders, who operated in conjunction with the veteran Persian noble, Artabazus.[243] Phrataphernes, recently reinstated in Parthyaea (see below, p. 236), was ordered to join the operations from the north but was too preoccupied by the threat to his own position to co-operate. The expeditionary force entered Areia in the spring of 329 and rapidly came to grips with Satibarzanes. The insurgent leader was killed by Erigyius in hand-to-hand combat and Alexander received his head at Bactra by midsummer (Curt. VII.4.32). That was far from the end of the affair. The native satrap of Areia had shown little sympathy with the Macedonians, and Alexander ordered his replacement by Stasanor, a Companion of Cypriot origin (Arr. III.29.5). Stasanor had to struggle to establish himself, and it was not until the winter of 328/7 that he was able to report success, along with Phrataphernes, who had captured the usurper Brazanes. The troubles had lasted for almost two years and Alexander's control of the satrapies of the north was severely challenged.

The king himself was eager to settle accounts with Bessus. He entered Arachosia without opposition and finally joined forces with the convoy from Media (Curt. VII.3.4). That enabled him to leave a substantial garrison army with his new satrap, Menon, sufficient to stifle revolt in the months ahead. He led the rest of his troops along the Helmand valley, driving into the Hindu Kush and the passes which gave access to Bactria. Late in March 329 he began to cross the region of Parapamisadae, centred on the Kabul valley, which formed the crossroads between Bactria, India and Arachosia. The journey had been plagued by snowfalls and shortage of supplies, and the passes were still snowbound. Alexander had no alternative but to wait, provisioning his army from the well-stocked villages of Parapamisadae[244] and founding a new

---

[241] Arr. III.27.4–5; Diod. XVII.81.1–2; Curt. VII.3.1–3; Strabo 724; *Metz Epit.* 4. On the location see Fischer 1967, 195–9; Bosworth 1980a, 365–6; *contra* Brunt 1976–83, 1.498–9.
[242] Arr. IV.7.1 (identified as the ex-chiliarch Nabarzanes by Heckel 1981, 66, and Gunderson 1982, 187–8.
[243] Curt. VII.3.2–3; Diod. XVII.81.3; Arr. III.28.2. On this campaign see Bosworth 1981, 20–4.
[244] Strabo 725; Curt. VII.3.18. For the chronology see Jones 1935; Hamilton 1969, 98–9, and for the route Fischer 1967, 129–232; Engels 1978a, 93–5.

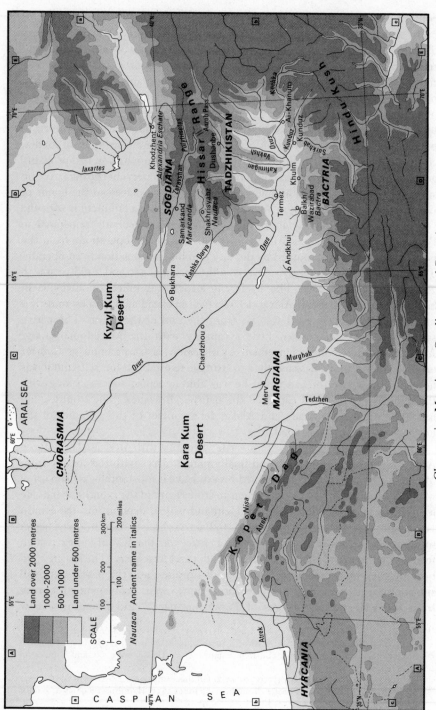

7. *Chorasmia, Margiana, Sogdiana and Bactria.*

Alexandria near Begram (see below, p. 247) to command the Shibar and Khawak passes and prevent any incursion from Bactria later in the season.

Meanwhile Bessus had been preparing to defend Bactria. He laid waste much of the arable land on the northern slopes of the Hindu Kush, probably concentrating on the approaches to the main route through the Bamian and Gorband valleys. But he could do no more than impede Alexander's passage. Despite his regal pretensions he was unable to unite the Bactrian nobility in a concerted defence of their territory. The Bactrian cavalry he mobilised numbered no more than 7,000,[245] a mere fraction of the invading army. Accordingly he withdrew north of the river Oxus (Amu Darya), accompanied by a few nobles from Sogdiana, and planned guerrilla warfare in the northern provinces, with the help of the nomad Saca peoples of the surrounding steppes. Alexander had left his new foundation as soon as the passes were clear enough of snow to allow his army's transit. If, as is probable, he had heard of Bessus' ravaging operations, he took one of the less frequented routes (the Khawak pass is the most popular choice) and after fourteen days of uncomfortable travel he reached Drapsaca (Kunduz?), one of the chief centres of Bactria.[246] There had been no resistance and few problems apart from a shortage of food and firewood in the high country, which for a time reduced the rank and file to feeding on the flesh of their pack animals, marinated in the juice of the native asafoetida plants. But Bactria lay open to him and he occupied the capital without striking a blow. It had been deceptively easy. Alexander paused briefly to appoint garrison commanders to the Bactrian citadels and nominated Artabazus over the satrapy (see below, p. 237). He then continued the hunt for Bessus, driving northwards to the Oxus across the desert.

It was a 75-km journey across waterless terrain under the unrelenting midsummer heat. The Macedonian army was unprepared for the conditions and suffered badly from thirst and exposure, straggling across the desert in a long column.[247] When the river was finally reached, there were a large number of deaths from uncontrolled drinking. The crossing itself was more arduous than anticipated. Bessus had commandeered and burned all available boats (Arr. III.28.9), and the Oxus, wide and fast-flowing, could not be forded. Accordingly the army, as it had done at the Danube in 335, made the crossing on improvised rafts of skins stuffed with dried grasses. Even so it was five days before all the contingents were across. The pursuit, however, was nearly over. Bessus was victim of the increasing lack of morale among his followers. It was patent that Alexander's first priority was to seize him, the self-proclaimed Artaxerxes V, and equally patent that his forces were inadequate for anything other than flight. Alexander had skilfully announced that his quarrel was with

---

[245] Arr. III.28.8; 8,000 according to Curt. VII.4.20.

[246] Arr. III.28.4–29.1; Strabo 725; Curt. VII.4.22–4. On the passes across the Hindu Kush see Foucher 1942, 1.20ff.; Schachermeyr 1973, 336–7, 676–81.

[247] Curt. VII.5.1–16; Diod. XVII arg. ιθ (not mentioned in Arrian). Cf. Strasburger 1982, 1.464–5; Engels 1978a, 100–2.

Bessus alone and had welcomed and rewarded a deserter from his camp.[248] The Sogdian nobles, Spitamenes and Dataphernes, decided to make their peace with the greater monarch by surrendering the lesser. Then, like his Achaemenid master, Bessus was overpowered and thrown in chains. Alexander received word of his arrest shortly after he crossed the Oxus and sent Ptolemy ahead to supervise the surrender. In his memoirs Ptolemy was later to describe a breakneck chase through Sogdiana to snatch Bessus from his captors, who were wavering in their resolve to surrender him. Other sources, notably Aristobulus, recorded an uneventful transaction: Ptolemy accompanied the Persians, captive and captors alike, to the presence of Alexander, and the Sogdian nobles themselves formally surrendered Bessus.[249] The second version is probably correct, contrasting soberly with the romanticism and self-glorification of Ptolemy's account. But there is a relative agreement about Bessus' fate. He was surrendered naked and fettered, to be first scourged, then remitted to Bactra where he suffered mutilation of his nose and ears, and was finally despatched to Ecbatana for execution. In his public declarations Alexander claimed to be avenging the betrayal and murder of Darius.[250] That was of course true, but not the whole truth. Alexander had been prepared to coexist with the regicides in the immediate aftermath of Darius' death. The change of attitude came when Bessus assumed the upright tiara, and the punishment eventually meted out to him was the punishment suffered by usurpers in the Achaemenid period. Like Bessus, Fravartish, who was proclaimed king of Media at the accession of Darius I, suffered mutilation, public exposure and death by impalement at Ecbatana. Alexander followed Achaemenid precedent and he had the pretext of pious vengeance.

The spirit of vengeance had already shown its ugly face that summer. While Ptolemy was occupied with the surrender of Bessus, the main army had reached a small town, inhabited by a community of Greek origin, allegedly the descendants of the Branchidae who had surrendered the temple at Didyma to Xerxes in 479 B.C. Alexander received the surrender but on the following day he allowed the town to be looted, its population massacred in final expiation of the ancient sacrilege. It is a strange story and it has been repeatedly discounted as romantic fiction.[251] But it is hard to dismiss the tradition of the massacre. It was recorded by Curtius and Diodorus, who presumably derived their accounts from Cleitarchus, and it also appears in Strabo in a context which is apparently based on other sources.[252] Whether or not the victims actually were the descendants of the Branchidae is immaterial. The allegation may have

---

[248] Diod. xvii.83.7–8; Curt. vii.4.18–19; cf. Berve 1926, 2 no. 196.

[249] Arr. iii.29–30.5 (Ptolemy, *FGrH* 138 F 14; Aristobulus, *FGrH* 139 F 24); cf. Curt. vii.5.36–42; Diod. xvii.5.36–42; Diod. xvii.83.8; *Metz Epit.* 5–6. On the peculiarities of Ptolemy's version see Welles 1963, 109–10; Seibert 1969, 14–16; Bosworth 1980a, 376–7.

[250] Arr. iii.30.4–5; Curt. vii.5.38–9.

[251] See most recently Bigwood 1978, 36–9, essentially following Tarn 1948, 2.272–5, and Pearson 1960, 240. There is no apparent reason for invention, which certainly cannot be laid at the door of Callisthenes. The story is accepted by Bellen 1974, 63–5 and by Parke 1985, 62ff.

[252] Curt. vii.5.28–35; Diod. xvii *arg.* x̃; Strabo 517–18 (cf. 634).

been made by Alexander's own staff and used to justify an act of savagery
which his troops clearly relished, exacerbated as they were by the desert march
and the painful crossing of the Oxus. Looting and murder were a cathartic
release which Alexander could justify retrospectively by involving the theme
of revenge. The wrongs of a Greek sanctuary were redressed – one moreover
that had had the prudence and diplomacy to recognise his divine sonship (see
below, p. 282). On every level the episode was repellent – and the behaviour of
the army was not a theme which would have endeared itself to Aristobulus or
to Ptolemy, who was probably elsewhere at the time. Its omission in Arrian is
certainly no argument against its historicity. A massacre probably did take
place, an appalling act of violence against a defenceless population, and it was
a sinister augury for the summer's campaign.

Alexander now continued to the satrapal palace at Maracanda (Samarkand),
suffering a leg wound (minor fracture of the fibula) in an engagement against
local tribesmen who had attacked his forage parties.[253] From there he
proceeded north to the banks of the modern Syr-Darya, the effective northern
limit of the Persian Empire. The river was known locally as the Jaxartes, but
Alexander and his staff considered it the same river as the European Tanais
(Don). They may have been primarily influenced by the current Greek
geographical framework of eastern Asia. Aristotle (*Met.* 1.13, 350a24–5) held
that the Syr-Darya, which he termed the Araxes, rose in the Hindu Kush but
sent off a branch stream which became the European Tanais and discharged
into the Sea of Azov. Alexander was clearly disposed to make the equation,
and the abundant stands of silver fir in the vicinity of the Syr-Darya were
reminiscent of the European firs, which, it was erroneously believed, did not
grow in Asia. One arm of the river, it was conceded, discharged into the
Caspian (there is no evidence to suggest that the Macedonians knew of the Sea
of Aral), and Polycleitus of Larisa went so far as to claim that the Caspian and
the Sea of Azov were interconnected lakes.[254] That was speculation, but
Alexander took it seriously enough in 323 to commission an expedition to
establish whether there was any linkage between the two seas (see below,
p. 169). In 329 he assumed without question that he had come to an eastern
affluent of the European Tanais. There were important corollaries. For
centuries it had been assumed that the Tanais formed the boundary between
Europe and Asia, and the sources are unanimous in describing the peoples to
the north of the river as European Scyths. In his view Alexander had come to
the extremity of Asia and the peoples he encountered were not remote from
the familiar Scyths of the Black Sea. There are several indications that he
considered the Black Sea easily accessible from the Tanais/Syr-Darya and
made some attempts at reconnaissance in that direction.[255] In that case return

253 Curt. vii.6.1–9; Arr. iii.30.10–11; cf. Bosworth 1980a, 379. For an attempt at location see
   von Schwarz 1906, 40.
254 *FGrH* 128 F 7 = Strabo 509–10. Cf. Hamilton 1971, 108–10; Schachermeyr 1973, 398–401.
255 Arr. iv.1.1–2, 15.1; Curt. vii.6.12; viii.1.7; cf. Berve 1926, 2 no. 250.

to Europe was a definite option, but it was not an option that he entertained while there were areas of Asia outside his empire. Significantly he was prepared to enter into treaty relations with the Sacae to the north of the river: they were to be his friends and allies, not subjects.[256] In a real sense the Syr-Darya was to be a boundary of empire, for the moment at least.

The king established a new city, Alexandria Eschate, on the south bank of the river, in the vicinity of the modern city of Khodzhent/Leninabad (see below, p. 248). While he was in the first stages of planning, he received word of general insurrection throughout the great Bactrian satrapy. Alexander's garrison forces were massacred in the north and the magnates of Bactria and Sogdiana unleashed a common front of rebellion. Behind the movement were Spitamenes and Dataphernes who demonstrated that their surrender was a mere expedient, to be revoked when the time was ripe. The local nobility with justifiable suspicions of a general assembly which Alexander had announced at Bactra were more than willing to revoke their allegiance.[257] Alexander was taken by surprise and set to the task of reconquest with understandable ferocity. His first objective was seven major fortresses in the immediate vicinity of the Syr-Darya. With their outer walls of mud brick they were ill equipped to resist the sophisticated siege tactics of the Macedonians and the majority fell at the first assault. As a matter of policy the conventions were strictly enforced, the males massacred and women and children enslaved (Arr. IV.2.4). There was some determined resistance, notably at Cyropolis, the largest fortress, allegedly founded by Cyrus the Great (modern Kurkath)[258] and, if we accept Curtius' account, at a mysterious city of the Memaceni.[259] The population suffered the usual fate but the Macedonians were mauled to some degree. Craterus and other senior officers were wounded, and the king himself incurred a debilitating head and throat wound which concussed him and rendered him almost inaudible.

The first sector of the rebellion was contained, but there were other threats. The news of the uprising had penetrated to the Sacae north of the river, and hordes of cavalry were massing opposite Alexandria Eschate (Arr. IV.3.6). Equally serious was an attack on Maracanda by Spitamenes, who had besieged the Macedonian garrison in the citadel. Alexander returned to the frontier, where with feverish haste he completed the fortifications of his new foundation in twenty days.[260] With his population of Graeco-Macedonian settlers and a semi-servile rural work-force of native Sogdians, it was to serve as the primary fortress of the northern frontier, capable of withstanding an attack from the nomads of the north. Alexander reinforced the lesson in person. He had been building wooden vessels and skin rafts for the crossing and, once his preparations were complete, he made a direct attack on the Saca cavalry on the

[256] Arr. IV.1.2, 15.5; see below, p. 251.
[257] Arr. IV.1.5; Curt. VII.6.13–15.
[258] Benveniste 1943–5.
[259] Curt. VII.6.17–23; cf. Arr. IV.2.5.
[260] Arr. IV.4.1; cf. Curt. VII.6.25–6; Justin XII.5.12.

far bank. The leading vessels had missile-firing catapults mounted at their prows and their preliminary barrage created panic in the enemy and cleared a space on the bank, which was then occupied by an advance screen of light infantry.[261] The phalanx infantry then landed and extended the bridgehead while the cavalry filtered across the river. Now the army was safely on the far bank, Alexander attacked with his own cavalry. There was a minor setback as the advance squadrons of mercenaries and *sarisa*-equipped Macedonians were baffled and out-manoeuvred by the classic circling tactics of the nomads. Alexander adapted quickly to the challenge. He combined his cavalry and light infantry forces, using the archers and javelin men to frustrate any ouflanking movements. The hit-and-run tactics were neutralised, and Alexander launched his own attack, an advance on a broad front by three hipparchies of Companions and the mounted javelin men and a massed charge by the rest of his cavalry, drawn up in a deep column.[262] The details are obscure, but the result of the manoeuvre was dramatic. The Saca cavalry gave way in the face of the frontal assault and, unable to wheel and attack the Macedonian flanks, they took to flight. Alexander pressed the pursuit for some 15 km until he was forced to halt, incapacitated by his recent wound and a violent attack of diarrhoea caused by drinking contaminated local water. Even so, it was a brilliant victory, and the losses suffered by the Sacae were disproportionately large. As a result Alexander received an embassy from the Sacan King and possibly neighbouring tribes as well, apologising for the provocation and offering submission (Arr. IV.5.1). There was little danger of more hostile action in the immediate future.

Now that the north of Sogdiana was pacified, he could turn his attention to the south, where he had suffered a serious reverse. He had sent a small expeditionary force to relieve the defenders of Maracanda, a force of mercenary cavalry and infantry led by their commanders, Caranus, Andronicus and Menedemus, and supported by a nucleus of sixty Companion cavalry. At the news of their approach Spitamenes raised the siege of the citadel and withdrew westwards along the Zeravshan valley. In the course of his retreat he was reinforced by horsemen from the Dahae, the westernmost of the Saca nomads, and he was encouraged to lay an ambush for the Macedonian expeditionary force, which had pressed in pursuit despite the poor quality of their mounts, which were debilitated by fatigue and lack of fodder. The engagement that followed was variously reported by Ptolemy and Aristobulus,[263] both alleging deficiencies in the Macedonian command, either lack of co-ordination or sheer reluctance to assume responsibility, and it is clear that the defeat was subsequently laid at the door of the commanding officers, possibly in order to exculpate Alexander from any allegation that he had sent inadequate forces.[264]

---

261  Curt. VII.9.2–9; *Metz Epit.* 11–12. Arr. IV.4.4 apparently places the artillery on the south bank. *Pace* Marsden 1969–71, 1.165–6, Curtius is more circumstantial and should be accepted.
262  Arr. IV.5.4–7; cf. Curt. VII.9.10–13.
263  Arr. IV.5.2–9 (Ptolemy); 6.1–2 (Aristobulus); cf. Curt. VII.7.31–9.
264  Plut. *Al.* 50.8; cf. Schachermeyr 1973, 366.

Certainly there was ample scope for speculation. The one thing that is agreed is that Alexander's men were harassed by the more mobile enemy, driven to panic and eventually succumbed under the relentless archery of their enemy. The majority of the Macedonians were killed, and Arrian (IV.6.2) alleges that no more than 300 foot and 40 horse escaped. Those few survivors, none of them commanders, would have had confused and conflicting recollections of the action and it is hardly surprising that the source tradition is divergent. What was undeniable was that the king had suffered a major reverse and the morale of the rebels had been stiffened. The news reached Alexander on the banks of the Syr-Darya, and he rapidly concluded negotiations with the Sacae before marching south with half the Companions, the hypaspists and the pick of the phalanx infantry. He covered the 290 km to Maracanda at maximum speed (Arrian claims exaggeratedly that it took three full days and nights)[265] and forced Spitamenes to break off the siege once again. Once more he withdrew to the western desert and Alexander reluctantly gave up hope of overhauling him, delayed as he was by the necessity to visit the battle site and give his men decent burial. Then he turned to reprisals. Rightly or wrongly, he considered that the native populace had collaborated with Spitamenes, and he systematically devastated the valley of the Zeravshan, possibly the richest and most populous sector of Sogdiana. Its fortresses were stormed, the defenders massacred in a calculated campaign of terror comparable to that against the rebels in the north (Arr. IV.6.5). The end of the season saw the west of the satrapy a wasteland and Alexander withdrew his forces to the relatively secure haven of Bactra, where he established his court for the winter.

It was still a delicate situation with pockets of unrepressed rebellion not only in the Bactrian satrapies but all over the north-east. Alexander accordingly paused only for the minimum period, until the worst of the winter was over and a number of large convoys of mercenaries had reinforced his army.[266] As soon as the season permitted military activity, he drove eastwards, following the fringes of cultivation along the Oxus valley and clearing any insurgent strongholds that remained in the foothills.[267] In due course he reached the valley of the Kokcha and crossed the Oxus in the vicinity of the site of Ai-Khanum, which he probably designated for future settlement (see below, p. 248). Here he divided his forces, leaving four phalanx commanders to garrison Bactria proper, under the general supervision of Craterus. The campaign now continued into Sogdiana. Immediately to the north of the Oxus Alexander established a network of six city foundations, each on an elevated site, which would serve as a nucleus for his occupying forces (see below, p. 248). Next he made a further division of his army, sending off senior

---

[265] Arr. IV.6.4; cf. Curt. VII.9.21; Brunt 1976–83, 1.505–6.
[266] Arr. IV.7.1–2; Curt. VII.10.10–12.
[267] Curt. VII.10.13–15; *Metz Epit.* 14; cf. Arr. IV.15.7–8. On the problems of the sources and the conjectural route of Alexander see Bosworth 1981, 23–9.

commanders with small compact forces to overrun and control separate sectors of insurgent territory. The general thrust of the advance was towards the Hissar Range, the great natural barrier that separated east and west Sogdiana, and the east of the satrapy was systematically reduced, stronghold after stronghold falling to the Macedonian forces.[268] The most spectacular engagement was an attack on a rock fortress commanded by a certain Ariamazes. There is a disagreement between Arrian and the vulgate tradition over the precise date of the engagement, but the weight of evidence inclines towards the summer of 328. On that occasion Alexander sent an élite group of mountaineers to scale the cliff face out of sight of the defenders, attracting them by the promise of a huge cash reward, 12 talents for the first to reach the summit. After an arduous climb and some fatalities the scaling party reached the highest point of the cliff, overlooking the natural amphitheatre in which Ariamazes had organised his defence. Once they saw the Macedonian 'winged men' above their stronghold, the morale of the defenders collapsed and they surrendered to Alexander, to be resettled as the agrarian work-force of the new foundations.[269]

As the summer ended, the various expeditionary forces converged on Maracanda, the base of operations for the end of the campaigning year. Here the king received a number of embassies from Saca tribes to the north and west of the Syr-Darya. They had approached him the previous summer and subsequently entertained Macedonian emissaries sent to inspect their lands. Impressed by the campaign across the Syr-Darya and the punitive operations in Sogdiana, they considered it prudent to confirm their allegiance.[270] They were accompanied by the Chorasmian king, Pharasmanes, whose realm (in the lower reaches of the Syr-Darya) was the most centralised and powerful of the lands north of the frontier.[271] With an escort of 1,500 horsemen, heavily mailed cataphracts, he visited the new monarch of the south and concluded a treaty of peace and alliance. He was aware of Alexander's geographical investigations and his belief that the Black Sea was relatively close, and he attempted to use the Macedonian army to expand his domains, insinuating that there were Amazons on his borders. The king tactfully declined Pharasmanes' invitation, declaring that India was his first objective but foreshadowing a later project of conquest in the Black Sea, when he would call upon Chorasmian help. For the moment his ambition was the subjugation of Asia. When that was achieved he would resume operations in the west, settling the many troubled areas of Asia Minor and connecting his European and Asian

[268] The most coherent narrative is that of Curtius VII.11.1ff. (cf. *Metz Epit.* 15ff.; Diod. *arg. λε*). Arrian's account is difficult and fragmented (IV.16.1ff.) and contains a number of doublets. The principal aberration from the vulgate account is the dating of the capture of Ariamazes' stronghold to the spring of 327 (Arr. IV.18.4ff.). The chronology adapted in the text is advocated by Bosworth 1981, 29–39. For a narrative based on Arrian (but dating the siege to midwinter) see Tarn 1948, 1.72–6.

[269] Curt. VII.11.28; *Metz Epit.* 18; Arr. IV.19.4–5 (cf. IV.16.3).

[270] Curt. VIII.1.7–9. Arr. IV.15.1–6 places these embassies at Bactra, some months earlier.

[271] Tolstov 1953, 112–13; Herzfeld 1968, 325–6; Altheim and Stiehl 1970, 188ff.

domains.[272] This initial project, ambitious though it was, was to be totally eclipsed by the wider plans of Mediterranean conquest which Alexander evolved during his return from India (see below, p. 152), but we have no reason to believe that it was not seriously mooted in 328. Another invitation which had a more immediate effect came from a Sacan ruler who offered his own daughter as a bride for Alexander and the offspring of his most prominent subjects as marriage partners of the Companions.[273] Alexander refused diplomatically, but the idea of taking a Persian noblewoman as consort took root in his mind and bore fruit a few months later.

The stay at Maracanda was relatively protracted, and included an excursion to a reserve at Basista, where a huge hunt took place and wild game left undisturbed for generations was slaughtered *en masse* (Curt. VIII.1.11–19). After the return to the capital there was a festival and a ceremonial sacrifice to the Dioscuri. The feasting continued into a symposium and under the influence of the local wine, court flatterers excelled themselves in praise of Alexander and denigration of his father. Our three principal sources for the affair give different accounts of the conversation,[274] which in the very nature of things must have been imperfectly recollected by participants after they regained sobriety. There is some agreement, however, that there were two strands of flattery, one comparing Alexander's birth with that of the Dioscuri and implicitly disowning Philip (see below, p. 283), the other mocking the generals who perished at Spitamenes' hands at the Zeravshan and implying that the Macedonian successes rested solely on Alexander's generalship.[275] This provoked resentment among the older generation of Macedonians who rejected the king's monopoly of military glory. Cleitus, son of Dropides, the cavalry commander, acted as spokesman. Whether there were motives at work deeper than inebriation and exasperation we cannot say. Cleitus had recently been nominated Artabazus' successor as satrap of Bactria/Sogdiana and it is possible that he saw the appointment as a demotion,[276] a prelude to destruction like Parmenion's command in Media, but there is no evidence that he was out of favour or a personage important enough in his own right to be undermined and eliminated. We cannot penetrate beneath the evidence of the sources, that Cleitus had been alienated by the increasing trend to oriental despotism at court and that on this occasion, his combativeness fortified by alcohol, he gave expression to the general disquiet. With the help of an apposite quotation from Euripides' *Andromache* (693ff.) he suggested that the king's glory was parasitic upon the lives of his men.[277] That was offensive enough, but Cleitus went on to eulogise Philip's actions at the expense of

[272] Arr. IV.15.4–6; cf. Robinson 1957, 336; Kraft 1971, 127–8.
[273] Arr. IV.15.2, 5; Curt. VIII.1.9; Plut. *Al.* 46.3.
[274] Arr. IV.8.1–9; Curt. VIII.19–51 (cf. Justin XII.6.1ff.); Plut. *Al.* 50–2; cf. Brown 1949b, 236–8; Hamilton 1969, 139ff.; Bosworth 1977a, 62–4.
[275] Plut. *Al.* 50.8–10; Curt. VIII.1.20ff.; Arr. IV.8.5.
[276] Curt. VIII.1.19, 35; cf. Lane Fox 1973, 311–12, and, for further speculation, Carney 1981.
[277] Plut. *Al.* 51.8; Curt. VIII.1.29; Julian, *Conv.* 331B.C. Cf. Aymard 1967, 51–7; Instinsky 1961.

Alexander's and harped on his own merits in saving Alexander's life at the
Granicus. On both sides tempers became uncontrollable. Alexander called on
his hypaspists, breaking into Macedonian,[278] but they were commendably
slow to react to their native tongue, and the king was physically restrained by
his bodyguards, complaining that he was another Darius, betrayed by his
court. Meanwhile Cleitus' friends attempted to hustle him out of the hall.
Aristobulus claimed that Ptolemy got him outside, past the castle moat, and
that Cleitus turned back out of sheer perverseness (Arr. iv.8.9 = FGrH 139 F
29), but his account is slanted to exculpate the king as far as it could be done.
Other sources claim that Cleitus could not be controlled and returned at the
height of his drunken rage.[279] In the confusion as the company left the hall,
Alexander seized a weapon from one of the guards and struck down Cleitus.
The circumstances of the act are as blurred as the prelude. We are not told why
the king's friends ceased their restraining role (cf. Arr. iv.8.8). Possibly the
king's fury was such that they feared for their own lives if they crossed him
further or their concern for Cleitus may have been a front. All that is clear is
that the king was free to act when his temper was most uncontrollable, and
Cleitus died almost instantaneously.

Drunken remorse followed the drunken rage. One tradition portrayed the
king attempting to kill himself with the fatal weapon[280] but restrained by his
bodyguards, who were now attentive. All sources agree that he spent three
days in seclusion without food or water, prostrated by paroxysms of self-
reproach. He was finally consoled. Callisthenes played some role but he may
have been eclipsed by Anaxarchus, the sceptic philosopher from Abdera, who
is accredited with a nihilistic speech drawing the analogy between Alexander
and Zeus and alleging that all the actions of a king must be considered just
since he is the embodiment of justice.[281] The sentiment can readily be
paralleled, in Xenophon's Cyrus (Cyrop. viii.1.22) or Aristotle's ideal
monarch (Pol. iii.1284b 25–34),[282] but in the highly charged atmosphere of
flattery that pervaded Alexander's court it was dangerous doctrine, a justification of every and any act of despotism. The episode may not be historical
but it is consistent with the attested themes of court flattery and cannot be
summarily rejected. At all events Alexander left his tent, to general relief.
There was no lasting resentment for the death of Cleitus as there had been for
Parmenion. Indeed the army condemned his contumacy and was apparently
prepared to deny him burial (Curt. viii.2.12). Cleitus may have had his
followers and sympathisers, but they were a small minority and unable or
unwilling to make capital out of his death. Significantly his nephew Proteas
remained in high favour at court, a famous drinker who by a curious twist of

---

[278] Plut. Al. 51.6; cf. Arr. iv.8.8; Badian 1982, 41.
[279] Plut. Al. 51.8; cf. Curt. viii.1.48–51.
[280] Arr. iv.9.2; Plut. Al. 51.11; Curt. viii.2.4.
[281] Arr. iv.9.7–8; Plut. Al. 52.3–7; Mor. 781A. Cf. Brown 1949b, 239–40.
[282] Cf. Volkmann 1975, 65–73; Braunert 1968; Farber 1979.

fate inspired Alexander to perform his last and fatal feat of drunkenness (Ephippus, *FGrH* 126 F 3).

The serious business of campaigning remained. There were still pockets of resistance in Sogdiana, and Spitamenes was particularly effective in a series of surprise attacks on Macedonian garrisons aided by Massagetic cavalry from the steppes. An attack on Bactra itself failed narrowly and a heroic sortie by its small garrison of mercenary cavalry ended in disaster. It took the intervention of Craterus to drive the raiders out towards the desert. He inflicted a defeat on the Massagetae but could not prevent their finding sanctuary in the desolation of the Kyzyl Kum (Arr. IV.16.4–17.2). Earlier in the season Alexander had sent out Coenus to make a direct attack on Spitamenes' nomad allies. Now he was given two phalanx battalions and a large mixed force of cavalry and deputed to continue operations from Maracanda. Alexander himself moved south to Nautaca, where Hephaestion had established winter quarters for the army.[283] This was one of the last areas of rebellion, which Alexander had visited briefly in his pursuit of Bessus but had since left undisturbed. The local ruler, Sisimithres, had withdrawn to a supposedly impregnable citadel, which was well watered and wooded, its access blocked by a deep ravine.[284] As usual Alexander accepted the challenge and began siege operations, painfully bridging the chasm with a causeway of earth which his army piled up on a bed of stakes skilfully cantilevered over the narrowest part of the gap.[285] This display of siege engineering overawed the defenders, who surrendered before their inner defences were stormed. Sisimithres was reinstated in his dominions and the rock with its vast store of provisions fell into Macedonian hands to tide the army over the winter.

Meanwhile events had gone well to the north. Coenus had faced an invasion by Spitamenes and his Massagetic allies and inflicted a heavy defeat on them. As a result the Sogdian insurgents deserted Spitamenes and made their peace with the Macedonians. Spitamenes himself fled for the last time into the desert. He had failed once too often and his nomad allies killed him at the news that Alexander himself was taking the field against them. His head was sent to Alexander, and the other rebel leader, Dataphernes, was surrendered in chains.[286] By the time the winter set in, the revolt could be said to have ended. The vast majority of the Bactrian and Sogdian magnates had surrendered, the native populace had been terrorised and decimated and the nomadic tribes beyond the frontier were either allied or intimidated. On a wider front the troubles had abated. During the winter Stasanor and Phrataphernes announced the successful completion of operations in Parthyaea and Areia/ Drangiana (Arr. IV.18.1–3; Curt. VIII.3.17). Alexander's writ now ran

[283] Arr. IV.18.1; Curt. VIII.2.19; *Metz Epit.* 19.
[284] Curt. VIII.2.19–33 (*Metz Epit.* 19); cf. Strabo 517. Arr. IV.21.1–9 sets the siege slightly later and names the ruler Chorienes (who appears in a different context in the vulgate tradition: *Metz Epit.* 29; Curt. VIII.4.21). See further Bosworth 1981, 30–2.
[285] Arr. IV.21.4–5; Curt. VIII.2.23–4.
[286] Arr. IV.17.4–7; cf. Curt. VIII.3.1–16 (*Metz Epit.* 20–3). Cf. Berve 1926, 2 no. 718.

unchallenged throughout the eastern satrapies and the general insurrection which Bessus had inspired was at last over.

It was time for reconstruction. The revolts in Bactria and Sogdiana had taken nearly two years of active campaigning to suppress, and it was apparent that the satrapy needed an exceptionally large garrison force. Accordingly its satrap Amyntas had a considerable army, comprising 10,000 infantry and 3,500 cavalry, and he had the backing of the many thousand European colonists who, whatever their feelings about their domicile, had a vested interest in eradicating rebellion. At the same time Alexander enlisted large numbers of the native cavalry in his own army and instituted a training programme for 30,000 youths to be formed into a native phalanx, armed and disciplined in Macedonian style (see below, p. 272). Eventually the satrapy was to lose a considerable fraction of its military manpower, and the remainder of the populace would be more tractable for the new hellenic ruling class. Finally he took a wife from the Bactrian nobility. His choice was Rhoxane, daughter of the Bactrian magnate Oxyartes, who had fallen into his hands during the campaign of 328. Her favourable treatment won over the father to collaborate with the conqueror, and in the early spring of 327[287] Alexander formally celebrated the marriage in Macedonian style,[288] encouraging some of his court (probably the commanders of the occupation force) to do the same. This was practically the final act in the process of conquest. Alexander underscored his claims to lordship by taking a wife from the conquered territories, following in part the example of his father. But this was his first marriage and it was not to a Macedonian but to a Bactrian princess. However politic it may have been, it aroused resentment among the circle antipathetic to the increasing trend of orientalism at court, resentment which was to surface explicitly in the disturbances at Babylon after the king's death (cf. Curt. x.6.13–16).

The spring witnessed the end of the Sogdian war. Alexander first began to move after two months in winter quarters (Curt. viii.4.1), but his army suffered badly in a lightning storm accompanied by a sharp drop in temperature and was barely resuscitated by a caravan of provisions sent by Sisimithres.[289] After some minor operations north of the Oxus he took his main force south to Bactra, the assembly point for the forthcoming invasion of India. Craterus and three phalanx commanders were left to deal with the two remaining insurgent leaders, a task soon expedited with little loss and total success (Arr. iv.22.1–2; Curt. viii.5.2; cf. Metz Epit. 23). Even so, it was some time before the army was reunited at Bactra. In the mean time there occurred the famous and abortive experiment with proskynesis (see below, p. 284), which was followed by the sensational episode of the Pages' Conspi-

---

[287] Arr. iv.19.5ff.; Curt. viii.4.21–30; Metz Epit. 28–31; Plut. Al. 47.7–8; Strabo 517.
[288] Curt. viii.4.27; cf. Renard and Servais 1955; Bosworth 1980b, 10–11.
[289] Curt. viii.4.1–19; Metz Epit. 24–7; Diod. xvii arg. אθ; cf. Strasburger 1982, 1.465; Bosworth 1981, 35–6.

racy. That was a serious attempt upon the king's life, initiated by his closest attendants. The story is retailed with an unusual degree of unanimity in the sources. It is agreed that the ringleader was Hermolaus, son of Sopolis, who had forestalled the king at the kill during a hunt and had been rewarded by a public flogging. He then recruited a small group of intimates who plotted to assassinate Alexander one night that they shared the guard of the bedchamber.[290] As it happened, the plot was frustrated. The king drank until dawn and did not need his watch. Then it was too late. One of the conspirators confided too far and the news was taken to the king by Charicles, brother of the imprudent Page. All the plotters were immediately arrested and under rigorous torture admitted their guilt. Execution by stoning then followed.

The affair remains a mystery. There is nothing known to have united the attested conspirators in a political nexus. Apart from Sopolis (father of Hermolaus) and Asclepiodorus (the father of Antipater) their parents are unknown and they themselves only figure in this single episode. It is unlikely that the affront to Hermolaus' *amour propre* was sufficient to motivate all the conspirators,[291] and the wider grounds of discontent adumbrated in the vulgate tradition have something in their favour.[292] The growing despotism of the court may have alienated the younger members of the nobility as much as it did their seniors, and the recent attempt to introduce *proskynesis* could have served as a catalyst to their disaffection. At all events it is agreed that the group was influenced by Callisthenes: Hermolaus is said to have been an intimate, and the historian may have had conversation with the Pages in general (Curt. VIII.6.24). Callisthenes' opposition may then have inspired the conspirators to assassinate their king. If so, he was not privy to the plot, as Ptolemy and Aristobulus alleged (Arr. IV.14.1). The consensus of ancient authority was that the Pages, who incriminated themselves and others under torture, could not be induced to give evidence against Callisthenes.[293] None the less, he was thought to have encouraged their treason and was placed under arrest. If we may believe Ptolemy (who had no obvious axe to grind), he too was tortured and executed. The other tradition, that he was kept in close arrest and died of illness is probably apologetic,[294] a reaction against the outrage which his death provoked in the Greek world.[295] His sin had been opposition to the prevailing political current at court and his enemies took advantage of the treason of his intimates to suggest guilt by association. It was much the same technique as had been used against Philotas, and it was equally successful. The king had

[290] Curtius (VIII.6.11) claims that it took a month for the opportunity to arise (cf. Arr. IV.13.4).
[291] Hamilton 1969, 154–5; Schachermeyr 1973, 388.
[292] Arr. IV.14.2, expanded in the rhetorical speeches of Curtius (VIII.7.1–8.23).
[293] Arr. IV.14.1; Plut. *Al.* 55.6; Curt. VIII.6.24, 8.21.
[294] Arr. IV.14.3 (Aristobulus, *FGrH* 139 F 33); Plut. *Al.* 55.9 (Chares, *FGrH* 125 F 15). Cf. Hamilton 1969, 156; Badian 1981, 50–1; *contra* Hammond 1980a, 198.
[295] Testimonia in Jacoby, *FGrH* 124 T 19 (cf. *RE* x.1683–4). The fact that Theophrastus wrote a monograph in his honour ('Callisthenes or On Grief': Diog. Laert. v.44) should not be taken as evidence for a Peripatetic vendetta against Alexander; cf. Badian 1958a, 153ff.; Mensching 1963; Bosworth 1970.

been genuinely threatened, his life placed in jeopardy, and he reacted savagely. Despite their tender age the Pages were treated to every rigour of Macedonian criminal procedure, and Callisthenes, who had been the chief proponent of opposition was eliminated ruthlessly and without trial.

## XIV    The advance to India

By the end of spring 327 the army was ready to begin the invasion of India. It was a project that had been maturing in Alexander's mind for some time, since at least the summer of 328 (Arr. IV.15.6). There had already been representations from Indian rulers who hoped to use the invader's army to expand their own domains.[296] The most important was the ruler of Taxila, who had approached him in Sogdiana to offer his services in the conquest of his country (Diod. XVII.86.4; Curt. VIII.12.5). There were also refugees like Sisicottus, who had first served with Bessus and then co-operated with Alexander throughout the Sogdian campaigns (Arr. IV.30.4). Such men had every reason to encourage the king to invade, and he himself needed little encouragement. It is a matter of controversy how far Persian control of India extended. According to Herodotus (Hdt. IV.44) Darius I had taken his empire as far as the Indus and the southern Ocean, but it is doubtful whether the Persian presence was obtrusive or lasting. By Alexander's time Persian suzerainty, even nominally, extended no further than the Kabul valley, the inhabitants of which had sent cavalry and elephants to Darius' army at Gaugamela.[297] But that, if anything, was an inducement to re-establish and expand the empire he had conquered, and he may already have entertained the idea of pressing his conquests to the Ocean, which he and his entourage clearly envisaged as relatively close to the Punjab. There was also the factor of heroic emulation. Ctesias had already retailed the legend of Semiramis' conquests in India, and there was probably a tradition that Dionysus had begun his triumphal progress west from the Indian lands.[298] The impulse to follow and surpass was clearly strong, and Alexander's staff was ready to point out evidence of the mythical passage both of Heracles and Dionysus. The son of Zeus would retrace the path of his forebears (cf. Curt. VIII.10.1) and establish a lasting empire. Ten days' marching from Bactra took him across the passes of the Hindu Kush and into Parapamisadae, where he reinforced his newly founded Alexandria (see below, p. 247) with extra settlers. Then he began the invasion proper, driving down the valley of the Cophen (Kabul River) towards the plain of the Indus.

The invasion force was divided into two columns. Approximately half the Macedonian troops and all the mercenaries were assigned to Hephaestion and

---

[296] For (over-rational) analysis of the motives for invasion see Andreotti 1957, 140ff.

[297] Arr. III.8.3, 16. The mountain Indians of III.8.4 were probably part of the Arachosian satrapy, occupying the hills east of the main road into Parapamisadae (Arr. III.28.1). See now Badian 1985, 461–2, arguing for 'some remnant of Achaemenian control' in Gandhara.

[298] Diod. III.65.7 (Antimachus of Colophon); cf. Goukowsky 1978–81, 2.11–14.

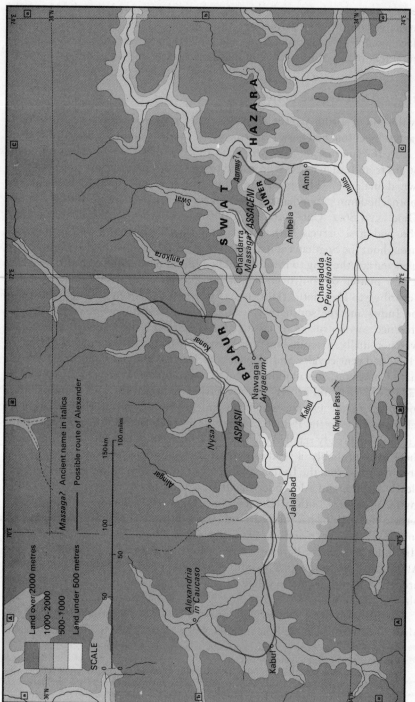

8. *The Kabul valley.*

Perdiccas and commissioned to secure the main road into India, destroying
any centres of resistance. Alexander himself took the élite troops, notably the
hypaspists, Agrianians and the *asthetairoi* of Upper Macedonia (see below,
p. 259), and concentrated on the peoples north of the river in the mountain
country of Bajaur and Swat. From the beginning he considered the inhabitants as his subjects, expecting immediate submission and punishing resistance
with massacre and enslavement. At the outset of the campaign he made a grim
example. Crossing the river Choes (Alingar?)[299] he found that the inhabitants
had retired to fortresses against the hills, and the first stronghold he attacked
offered resistance, a chance arrow wounding him lightly in the shoulder. The
following day it was stormed. All defenders who failed to make their escape
were systematically massacred and the settlement was destroyed (Arr.
IV.23.4–5; Curt. VIII.10.6). Under the impact of this act of terror the
neighbouring city of Andaca capitulated, and Craterus was left with an
infantry force to organise the territory and destroy any remaining centres of
resistance. Alexander then crossed into the Kunar valley, where the inhabitants simply fled to the mountains after burning their homes. He attacked the
fugitives but did not bring them to capitulation. The same happened when he
crossed the mountains into the region of Bajaur. Here, according to Ptolemy
(*FGrH* 138 F 18), he was able to bring the refugees to bay in their retreat, and
he took numerous prisoners and a huge number of prize cattle, the pick of
which he intended to transfer to Macedon. There was also a new foundation in
the most strategic location of the territory (Arr. IV.24.7). The procedure,
military intimidation and settlement of a garrison population, was exactly that
used so effectively in Sogdiana.

Not all communities required intimidation. Between the Choes and the
Kunar valley Alexander was approached by an embassy which surrendered to
him, asking for special consideration because of the sanctity of their city.[300]
The local god (whether Indra or Çiva) was identified by Alexander's staff as
the Greek Dionysus, and he was willing to believe that the populace was
descended from the god's entourage. This impression was strengthened when
he found ivy and bay trees growing on the neighbouring mountainside.
Accordingly the city was named Nysa after the mythical nurse of Dionysus,
and the mountain's local name was represented as Meros and considered the

[299] The topography of the campaign is highly controversial. The fixed point is the river Guraeus
(Arr. IV.25.7), which is usually identified with the modern Panjkora (Gauri in Sanskrit).
Before reaching the Guraeus the Macedonians had crossed a mountain pass (Arr. IV.24.6;
Curt. VIII.10.10) from another river valley (Arr. IV.24.1), which can only be that of the
Kunar. The area of operations there was at least two days' rapid march from the Choes valley,
which I assume was distinct from the Kunar. The lower reaches of the Alingar seems the
obvious choice. Alexander then crossed to the Kunar by way of the Dunda pass. Cf.
Eggermont 1970, 108; Goukowsky 1978–81, 2.23–4; *contra* Stein 1929, 41; Brunt 1976–83,
1.508; Seibert 1985, 150–1.
[300] On this episode see Goukowsky 1978–81, 2.21–33; Brunt 1976–83, 2.437–42. There is no
warrant for dismissing the story as late fiction. It was known in some form to Theophrastus
(*HP* IV.4.1) and was retailed by at least one of Arrian's major sources (the Nysaean cavalry
mentioned at IV.2.3 recur at VI.2.3 in the course of the main narrative).

inspiration of the Greek legend that the god was nurtured in the thigh (*meros*) of Zeus. Alexander celebrated the discovery with a formal sacrifice and there is a tradition (reported first in Theophrastus) that he held a Bacchic revel there, crowning himself and his army with ivy.[301] The city benefited materially. Alexander approved of its aristocratic government in the hands of 300 notables and he conceded its freedom. It was a freedom like that of the Euergetae of the Helmand, to continue with the local laws and customs under the existing ruler, who nevertheless came under the supervision of Alexander's satrap. At the same time he insisted that the community supply a contingent of cavalry and took the ruler's son and grandson as hostages. Alexander's behaviour was not essentially different from (say) his behaviour at Mallus, where he had acknowledged the Argive origins of the city and rewarded it accordingly. He took the claims of the locals at face value when it suited him and enthusiastically commemorated the traces he found of his mythical forebears. But his enthusiasm was conditional upon surrender. Had the people of Nysa resisted him he would have been deaf to their protestations. No appeal to Dionysus could have saved them.

Alexander faced more severe fighting when he planned an invasion of the kingdom of the Assaceni in the valley of the Lower Swat. Its eponymous ruler had a sizeable army, estimated by Arrian (IV.25.5) at 30,000 foot and 2,000 horse, which was strengthened by mercenaries recruited from the plains. This was not strong enough to meet Alexander in the field, and the defenders dispersed themselves into local strongholds, the most important of which was Massaga, a fortress with walls of mud brick and stone situated somewhere to the north of the Swat in the vicinity of the Katgala pass.[302] There Alexander concentrated his main assault and prepared an impressive battery of siege towers. The only hope for the Assaceni was to keep their walls manned, but during four days of artillery fire from the Macedonian engines the battlements were damaged and their defenders decimated. After the commandant of Massaga had been killed by a stray catapult bolt[303] and capture was imminent, overtures were made to Alexander, who agreed to the surrender of the fortress on condition that the imported mercenaries should join his own army. The mercenaries accordingly left the city with their arms and baggage and encamped on a hill some distance from the Macedonian forces. According to Arrian, Alexander had word that they intended to decamp, surrounded the hill and exterminated the entire contingent. The episode is variously narrated in the sources, with some criticism of Alexander's good faith. Possibly there was some misunderstanding, the Indians not realising that they should enlist

[301] Theophr. *HP* IV.4.1; Arr. V.2.5–7; Curt. VIII. 10.15–17; Justin XII.7.6–8; *Metz Epit.* 36–8.
[302] Caroe 1962, 51–3; Eggermont 1970, 66.
[303] Arr. IV.27.2. He is presumably not to be identified with King Assacenus, who died before the siege began (Curt. VIII.10.22; *Metz Epit.* 39). He may be the king's brother, 'Amminais', who brought the mercenaries into Massaga (*Metz Epit.* 39). The other brother, who led resistance in the eastern mountains (Arr. IV.30.5), is a different individual again.

with the Macedonian king, but the fact remains that they were massacred on a flimsy pretext after they had placed themselves at the conqueror's mercy.

The lesson was well taken, and the defences were stiffened elsewhere. The city of Bazira, which had been attacked by Coenus, probably at the same time as the siege of Massaga, held out stubbornly. Another Macedonian force laid siege to Ora with equal lack of success, until Alexander transferred his main army group there and took the city at the first assault (Arr. IV.27.9: cf. Curt. VIII.11.1). Elsewhere the Assaceni followed the example of the people of the Kunar, evacuated their settlements and took refuge in the mountain fortress of Aornus. The rock was associated in local legend with the Indian deity Krishna, and Alexander's staff evolved the story that Heracles (Krishna's counterpart in Greek mythology) had once made an unsuccessful attempt to storm it. The challenge to emulate and surpass was irresistible. Despite the formidable dimensions of the fortress and the fact that it was abundantly provided with spring water and arable land (Arr. IV.28.3),[304] he made preparations for the siege, leaving garrisons at Massaga, Ora and Bazira and securing the lowlands near the Indus in the vicinity of Aornus (Arr. IV.28.7). The invaluable Craterus was based at Ecbolima, the nearest town to the fortress, and deputed to stockpile enough grain to sustain a lengthy siege. That precaution proved unnecessary. Alexander used local guides and took a position high up on a saddle leading directly to the citadel (if Stein was correct in his identification, this was on the slope of the Little Una, nearly 8,000 feet above sea level and 5,000 above the river Indus). If we may believe Arrian's account,[305] the saddle was first occupied by a small column of Agranians and light infantry led by Ptolemy, and Alexander led the rest of his assault force under enemy attack to establish himself directly under the main fortress. The rest of the story was another triumph of Macedonian siege engineering. Alexander constructed a siege mound along the saddle so that his anti-personnel catapults could gradually be brought to bear on the defenders of the topmost plateau. After four days of construction work the mound was immediately below the main defences and, faced with the overwhelming Macedonian firepower, the Indians began negotiations, intending to evacuate the fortress under cover of night. Alexander's reconnaissance parties alerted him to the withdrawal, and he was able to climb unopposed onto the plateau and attack the enemy in retreat. The slaughter was considerable. Despite its awe-inspiring inaccessibility Aornus was captured with a small force (light infantry and selected phalanx troops) with relatively little loss, and an object lesson had been given of the Macedonians' total pre-eminence in military technology.

The resistance of the Assaceni now collapsed. Alexander's marshals had

---

304 This was one of Stein's main reasons (1929, 131–2) for identifying Aornus with the ridge of Pir Sar, a level plateau with wheat fields along practically its whole length, some 2½ km.

305 Arr. IV.29.1–30.4. The other accounts (Curt. VIII.11.3–25; Diod. XVII.85.3–86.1; *Metz Epit.* 46–7) differ from Arrian and are mutually inconsistent.

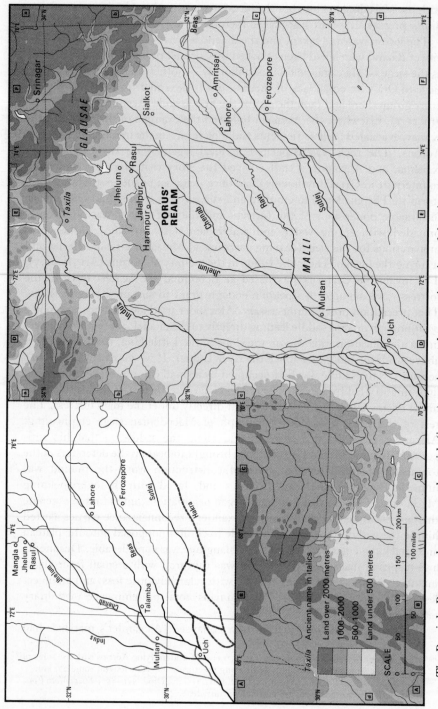

9. *The Punjab. Present-day topography with (inset) conjectural approximation of the river system in the 8th century* A.D.

been continuing operations in the lowlands while he attacked Aornus, and the last enemy forces were holding out under a native prince in the mountains of Buner.[306] At Alexander's advance the population left the cities and, as he moved towards the Indus, along a road specially built by his pioneers, the enemy killed their leader and sent his head to the conqueror. Most of the men under arms crossed the river to find refuge with Abisares, prince of what is now Hazara, and left their elephants roaming wild, to be hunted down by Alexander and attached to his army. Behind him, to the borders of Parapamisadae the land was secure – for the moment. Hephaestion and Perdiccas had pushed quickly along the Cophen valley. The prince of Peucelaotis attempted resistance and defended his capital (Charsadda)[307] for thirty days, until it was stormed and he lost his life. There was no further serious fighting in the lowlands. Hephaestion and his expeditionary force were soon at the Indus and had built a bridge well before Alexander began the siege of Aornus. All was ready for the crossing. Alexander could appoint a Macedonian satrap over the conquered territory, to supervise a number of native rulers (hyparchs), many of whom had records of disaffection from the previous regime (see below, p. 238). This new order was barely tolerated. Within the year there was a revolt by the Assaceni which resulted in the death of the satrap Nicanor[308] and served notice that there was considerable depth of feeling against the invaders. But in the spring of 326 Alexander could press forward to the Indus, confident that an autumn and winter of terror and repression had secured the Cophen valley, the vital link that connected his existing empire with the new world of India.

xv  **The campaign of the Hydaspes**

The army crossed the Indus, probably in the vicinity of Ohind (Udabhandapura) using the bridge constructed by Hephaestion and a number of vessels built on the spot for the crossing. It was a significant moment, which Alexander commemorated by lavish sacrifices and athletic games (Arr. v.3.5; Diod. xvii.86.3). He was now in friendly country. The native prince Omphis (Ambhi), who had visited Alexander in Sogdiana (see above, p. 120), now came to meet his new master in person with an impressive entourage which included thirty elephants. He had provisioned Hephaestion during the bridge-building (Curt. viii.12.6), and now he brought lavish presents to Alexander. His reward was confirmation in his father's princedom (under a Macedonian satrap) and largesse which more than outweighed his own gifts. Together the great king and his vassal entered the capital of Taxila (Takshi-

[306] Arr. iv.30.5–9; Curt. viii.12.1–4; Diod. xvii.86.2–3; cf. Eggermont 1970, 93–102.
[307] Arr. iv.22.8. For the location see Wheeler 1962; 1968, 95–8. This city must be distinct from Peucelaotis by the Indus, which first surrendered to Alexander on the eve of the siege of Aornus (Arr. iv.28.6; Strabo 698; see, however, Eggermont 1970, 68ff.; Seibert 1985, 148–9).
[308] Arr. v.20.7; cf. Berve 1926, 2 no. 556; Bosworth 1983, 37–8.

çila), some 30 km north-west of modern Islamabad,[309] which Arrian claims
was the largest city between the Indus and the Hydaspes, and a new round of
games and sacrifices ensued. In the mean time there were diplomatic contacts
with the two most important neighbouring princes, both enemies of the ruler
of Taxila (Curt. VIII.12.12, cf. Arr. V.18.6) against whom he hoped to enlist
the Macedonian army. One of these dynasts, Abisares, was prudent enough to
offer token submission, but the other, Porus, was adamant in his refusal.[310]
He ruled the rich and populous country between the rivers Hydaspes
(Jhelum) and Acesines (Chenab), which, Strabo (698) alleges, contained
almost 300 cities. The size of the army he could muster is variously
reported,[311] but in terms of infantry and cavalry it was certainly smaller than
Alexander's. Its main strength was its elephant division, which was greater in
numbers and quality than anything Alexander had yet encountered. There
was to be no question of a pitched battle on equal terms. Porus intended to use
the Hydaspes as his main line of defence, hoping to beat back all attempts to
cross it and ultimately to deflect the Macedonians to easier targets.

When news came of Porus' recalcitrance, Alexander left Taxila immediately, despite the exotic attractions of the new civilisation. He and his staff had
been deeply impressed by the local customs, not least by the ascetic practices
of the Brahman sages, and he was able to recruit one to his entourage, the
famous Calanus, whose death in Persis was one of the great spectacles of the
expedition (see below, p. 155) and whose advice must have been of material
assistance in dealings with the native Indians.[312] But for the moment scientific
curiosity took second place to military demands. It was essential to reach the
Hydaspes before the river reached high water, swelled by the melting of the
Himalayan snows and still more by the advent of the monsoon rains, which
usually begin late in June. Accordingly he took his army across the Great Salt
Range and established his base camp on the banks of the Hydaspes. The exact
location is unknown,[313] and, given the radical changes in the course of the
rivers of the Punjab over the centuries,[314] it is most unlikely that the battle site

[309] Marshall 1951, 1.1ff.; Wheeler 1968, 102ff.
[310] Berve 1926, 2 no. 683. The name is a Greek approximation to the Indian Paurava. Like the
other royal names, it is also the name of the people he ruled: Porus was monarch of the
Paurava, just as Assacanus was monarch of the Açvaka.
[311] Maximum 4,000 cavalry, 300 chariots, 200 elephants, 30,000 infantry (Arr. V.15.4);
minimum 85 elephants, 300 chariots, 30,000 infantry (Curt. VIII.13.6; Metz Epit. 54). Cf.
Diod. XVII.87.2 (total resources of Porus); Plut. Al. 62.1.
[312] Cf. Nearchus, FGrH 133 F 23 (Strabo 716), commenting on the widespread use of Brahman
advisers by Indian princes. See also Megasthenes, FGrH 715 F 19b (Strabo 703) for their
public duties in the time of Chandragupta.
[313] For the various locations see Seibert 1972a, 158–60; 1985, 156–7. The most popular has been
that of Stein 1932; 1937, 1–36, which places the base camp at Haranpur, 176 km from Taxila
(cf. Pliny, NH VI.62), and the crossing-point at Jalalpur, 28 km upstream. A rival location
north of Jhelum was proposed by Breloer 1933 and has had limited acceptance (Radet 1935:
see, however, 1938).
[314] The phenomenon was noted already by Aristobulus (FGrH 139 F 35 = Strabo 693). Stein's
claim (1932, 62) that the course of the river has not changed markedly is unfounded and
improbable. See particularly Wilhelmy 1966.

will ever be fixed, unless Alexander's commemorative foundations of Nicaea and Bucephala (see below, p. 248) are unearthed and identified. It was certainly backed by the Great Salt Range which formed a headland some 30 km upstream (Arr. v.11.1) and there were a number of islands in the river which facilitated a crossing. On the other side of the stream was the Indian army, its elephants placed in full view to deter any venture across.

Alexander prepared meticulously for the campaign. The vessels which he had used for the crossing of the Indus were dismantled and transported laboriously some 300 km to the Hydaspes, and he amassed grain from all quarters of the realm of Taxiles, giving the impression that he was prepared to wait until low water in September (Arr. v.9.3–4). At the same time he organised regular diversions by land and water, by day and night. Porus' forces were continually marching and counter-marching to frustrate any attempt at crossing, and there were skirmishes on the islands in midstream (Curt. VIII.13.12ff.; Arr. v.9.3). Meanwhile he had determined on his crossing-point at the headland, where there were dense woods and an island conveniently placed to cover his fleet in transit. Here he hid the majority of his ships, taking every precaution to conceal his actual crossing-place. The base camp was left under the command of Craterus with a substantial body of cavalry and infantry, equipped and ready to cross the river, while the mercenary forces, infantry and cavalry, were dispersed along the riverside under the command of three phalanx officers, Meleager, Attalus and Gorgias.[315] These units acted as distractions, diverting the Indians' attention from the main crossing-point, where Alexander was concentrating his striking force. According to Arrian's enumeration (v.12.2) it was fairly small, approximately half the Macedonian hipparchies alongside Bactrian and Saca cavalry from the north-east frontier, the hypaspists *in toto* together with two phalanx battalions and the light infantry. If he is correct in his account of the dispositions there are a considerable number of units omitted, at least three phalanx battalions and three cavalry hipparchies. Our accounts of the battle are admittedly defective and may have simply glossed over an important detail of the fighting, but Arrian is relatively consistent in his total for Alexander's force, claiming that it numbered 6,000 foot and 5,000 horse immediately after the crossing (Arr. v.14.1). No source suggests that there was any increment before the battle proper,[316] and there is surely a possibility that the army was not at full strength at the Hydaspes – a second column, otherwise unattested, may have been attempting a passage elsewhere. Alexander was not facing the levy of the Persian empire but that of a single Indian prince, with a restricted territory

---

[315] Arr. v.11.3–12.1; cf. Curt. VIII.18.22 (same strategy but different names).

[316] Arrian v.18.3 calculates infantry losses at the Hydaspes and repeats that the total was 6,000 at the first onset. He gives no indication of any other infantry forces present at the battle, and *a fortiori* there were none. Interpretations which presuppose that extra troops filtered across the river after the first crossing (notably Tarn 1948, 2.190–1; Hammond 1980a, 270) must be discarded. The figures for Alexander's forces may well be minimised, but there is no reason to question Arrian's list of units present at the crossing.

and beleaguered by his enemies to the east and west. Alexander could afford to divide his army and divert precious forces from Porus' defence. The main problem was the crossing. When that was effected, he did not need vast numbers for victory.

The crossing took place safely under cover of a spring thunderstorm. Alexander's forces, transported on boats and skin rafts stuffed with chaff, crossed just before dawn as the rains eased[317] and were not seen by Porus' scouts until they had skirted the side of the midstream island and were almost on the shore. The landing was uncontested, but there was an unforeseen difficulty when a secondary stream of the Hydaspes intersected their path and could only be forded after considerable time and trouble. Once fully across the river, Alexander deployed his cavalry in a defensive screen, the Sacan horse archers in the van, and moved ahead to counter an advance force of Indian cavalry led by one of Porus' sons. This was routed by Alexander's totally superior cavalry, which attacked in column, repulsed the horsemen and captured the cumbersome six-man chariots which were immobilised by the rain-soaked mud.[318] The fugitives returned to Porus and reported that Alexander was present in person and that the main Macedonian army had crossed. Porus now concentrated his army on Alexander, leaving only a small detachment of elephants and troops so as to deny passage to Craterus, and chose a clear sandy plain to mount his defence. His main hope was in his elephants. These he stationed at intervals along his line,[319] filling the gaps with infantry and placing cavalry and war chariots on the wings. The elephants, he assumed, would be invulnerable to cavalry (the horses would not attack them frontally) and would cause havoc in the infantry phalanx.

It was a logical strategy, but the Macedonians had acquired experience of elephants over the previous months and could cope with them. Alexander realised that his infantry would take the brunt of the fighting, and under the screen of the cavalry he deployed his phalanx in extended line, allowing it time for rest before the battle proper. The preliminaries were in the hands of the cavalry, far superior to their counterparts in Porus' army, which had already suffered one defeat. Alexander removed his cavalry screen. The bulk of the horse he led in person, taking it across the front of the phalanx to threaten the cavalry on Porus' left wing. A smaller force of two hipparchies under Coenus' command attacked the Indian right.[320] The manœuvre was strikingly success-

[317] Arr. v.12.3–4. Cf. Curt. VIII.14.23–4; Plut. Al. 60.3–4 (exaggerated).
[318] Variant accounts from Aristobulus and Ptolemy are reported by Arrian (v.14.3–15.2), differing on the size of the Indian force and the time that the encounter took place. Curtius VIII.14.2–8 gives details which are different again but agree with Ptolemy in placing the skirmish relatively close to the site of the main battle.
[319] Arr. v.15.5 (200 elephants, each a plethron (30 m) apart from the next – the number is clearly exaggerated); cf. Curt. VIII.14.13; Diod. XVII.89.4–5.
[320] Arr. v.16.3 (cf. Curt. VIII.14.15; Plut. Al. 60.10). Arrian's language is compressed and obscure and has led to much debate (see particularly Hamilton 1956). The difficulties ease when it is accepted that the Indian cavalry was outnumbered on the left by Alexander's forces

ful. Alexander began his attack with a foray by his horse archers and exploited the confusion they caused, wheeling to the right at the head of the Companions and driving into the exposed left flank of the enemy line. Outnumbered and wavering, the Indian cavalry needed reinforcement from the right of their line, and units began to be filtered across the rear of Porus' elephant phalanx. While they were in transit, Coenus charged from the right, and the luckless Indian horse found itself under attack on both fronts. Under the impetus of the Macedonian onset they gave way and took refuge in the infantry column, where they inevitably generated confusion and ran the risk of causing the elephants to panic. At this point the infantry action began. The Indian infantry, whose archers were impeded by the wet conditions (Curt. VIII.14.19), had no answer for the Macedonian *sarisae*. It was the elephant attack that was serious, but the Macedonians were able to open their ranks as they had for the scythed chariots at Gaugamela and with their long *sarisae* they were able to dislodge the mahouts and strike upwards at the elephants, driving them back into their own line.[321] This was the time of greatest confusion, but the Macedonians showed the greater discipline. An Indian cavalry sortie was repelled, and Alexander's own cavalry forces, united in a single body, exploited any gaps in the Indian flank and rear and spread the chaos (Arr. v.17.3–4). At the front of the line the elephants, mostly without their drivers, were uncontrollable and trampled down their own troops indiscriminately. The Macedonian phalanx regained its integrity and pressed forward its hedge of *sarisae* while the cavalry virtually enveloped the rear (Arr. v.17.7). Attacked from all sides and crowded under the feet of their elephants, the Indians were slaughtered ruthlessly until pressure of numbers opened a gap in the Macedonian cavalry cordon and allowed some of the infantry to escape. The cavalry was largely exterminated and the surviving elephants captured. Porus himself held out until the very end, a gigantic figure more than two metres tall, visible to all on the back of the largest elephant.[322] He refused to parley until he was wounded and his army routed. Left almost isolated on the field he surrendered to his conqueror's mercy. Meanwhile Craterus had crossed the Hydaspes (the defence of the passage probably dissolved at the news of Alexander's victory) and his troops, supplemented by the mercenary forces stationed along the bank upstream, took on the pursuit of the Indian foot, which was hounded to annihilation (Arr. v.18.1).

It was a shattering victory and Alexander commemorated it as such. He held athletic and gymnastic games at the site of his crossing and planned two new foundations, one at the site of the victory, duly named Nicaea, and the other at the base camp, named Bucephala in honour of his great horse, who

and needed to transfer horse from the right to have any chance of holding the wing. Whether or not Coenus' forces were visible, the transfer was a necessity.

[321] Arr. v.17.3; cf. Curt. VIII.14.16; Diod. XVII.88.2–3. The Agrianian light infantry was also active (Curt. VIII.14.24).

[322] Arr. v.18.4–19.1; Curt. VIII.14.31–6; Diod. XVII.89.2–3; Plut. *Al.* 60.12–13. Cf. Goukowsky 1972.

had died during the battle.[323] Later the Babylon mint was to issue a series of tetradrachms depicting the two foes he had overcome – an elephant on the reverse and an Indian bowman on the obverse. Still more spectacular were the great decadrachms which portrayed Alexander on horseback, armed with a *sarisa* and attacking a pair of Indians mounted on an elephant.[324] At one level the celebration was justified. The fighting was exotic and spectacular, and victory was complete. On the other hand the dimensions of the battle were not large. As always, the true figures are obscured by propaganda, which minimised the Macedonian losses and exaggerated the number of Indians in the field, but it can hardly be denied that Alexander fought with a fraction of his army and even so outnumbered the enemy in cavalry and maybe in infantry also. As a commander he showed considerable brilliance in crossing the Hydaspes and deploying his forces to neutralise the threat of the elephants, but Porus' resistance was doomed from the moment the Macedonian forces secured their landing.

## xvi     From the Hydaspes to the Southern Ocean

Alexander was more than content with his victory. Porus, who had impressed him deeply by his heroism, he did not depose but confirmed as ruler of the lands beyond the Hydaspes, still a king to his own subjects but a vassal of the Great King. He was further rewarded by the enlargement of his territories. While his new foundations were taking shape under the expert supervision of Craterus, Alexander campaigned against the Glausae, who occupied the mountainous timber-rich country to the north-east.[325] This terrain was to provide him with the material for the fleet which took him to the Southern Ocean later in the year. If we may believe Nearchus (*FGrH* 133 F 20), he was impressed by the discovery of crocodiles in the Indus and, somewhat later, of Egyptian beans at the Acesines and drew the conclusion that the rivers of the Punjab were in fact the source of the Nile; one branch of the Indus at least swung through desert country south of the Persian gulf (which he envisaged as an inland sea), and ultimately reached Egypt as the Nile. His geographical speculation was promptly disabused by the native Indians, who confirmed that there was only a single channel in the lower reaches of the Indus and that it discharged into the Southern Ocean,[326] but his curiosity remained fired and he intended to inspect the phenomenon for himself and take his conquests south to their natural terminus. There is li*t*¹. doubt that the plan was in his mind at the time of the battle and he took steps to secure the timber for a fleet

[323] Arr. v.19.4 (precise location); cf. Strabo 698–9; Curt. ix.1.6; Diod. xvii.89.6. Cf. Radet 1941, *contra* Tarn 1948, 2.236–7.

[324] For these coins see Dürr 1974.

[325] Arr. v.20.2–4; cf. Strabo 698–9 (mentioning Taxiles' presence: he left for home immediately after the campaign against the Glausae); Diod. xvii.89.4–5; Curt. ix.1.4–5.

[326] *FGrH* 133 F 20 = Strabo 699; cf. Arr. vi.1.2–6. For Alexander's geographical concepts see Schachermeyr 1973, 443–51.

large enough to transport the bulk of his army. The campaign against the Glausae, which Alexander conducted with select infantry and cavalry, was uneventful. The inhabitants surrendered without resistance and their land was added to Porus' domains. Taxiles, who had accompanied Alexander up to that point, was 'reconciled' with his former enemy and sent home to his capital (Arr. v.20.4). He cannot have been particularly satisfied. The man he had tried to destroy had displaced him in Alexander's favour and looked like becoming the main beneficiary of the invasion.

Porus' enemies were now Alexander's. The peoples east of the Acesines had previously been at loggerheads with him and suffered an abortive invasion at his and Abisares' hands (Arr. v.22.2), and Porus' immediate neighbour, a homonymous cousin, had offered submission to Alexander before the battle of the Hydaspes (Arr. v.21.3). Now he took fright at the unexpected promotion of Porus and fled across the Hydraotes (Ravi) with the bulk of his army. That was enough to provoke Alexander's intervention. Abisares, who had apparently revoked his new allegiance and promised aid to Porus,[327] was merely threatened with invasion and ordered immediately to Alexander's presence. The thrust of the march was to the east. Alexander sent Porus to levy an army from the military reserves that remained after his defeat (see above, p. 126) and left Coenus at the Acesines to direct his foraging parties after the main army (Arr. v.21.1). The military task was not formidable, but the weather was deteriorating and creating problems of logistics and morale. The battle at the Hydaspes had been fought around May and the dispositions and minor campaigning afterwards had taken nearly a month.[328] By the time Alexander encamped by the Acesines the spring thunderstorms were replaced by continuous drenching monsoon rain, and the river was flooding adjacent plainland. That was uncomfortable and the river crossing was positively dangerous, with the stream at its fullest and fastest (see Ptolemy's description, cited by Arrian v.20.8–10). It was the time of the summer solstice and the deluge was not to subside until the rising of Arcturus, late in September.[329] From the Acesines onwards the campaign was to be fought in appalling conditions. They were totally ignored in Ptolemy's history, if we can trust Arrian's version of it, which never even mentions rain during this period.[330]

At first there was little or no resistance. The Macedonians overran the lands of Porus' cousin, leaving garrisons in salient positions to help the foragers strip

---

[327] Arr. v.19.5; Curt. VIII.14.1, IX.1.7; Diod. XVII.90.4.
[328] Diod. XVII.89.6. This statement has been disputed (cf. Brunt 1976–83, 2.456–7) on the grounds that Arrian (v.9.4: but cf. v.19.3) seems to place the battle about the time of the summer solstice. But Arrian in turn is inconsistent with Nearchus' date for the encampment by the Acesines (Strabo 692; Arr. *Ind.* 6.5), and his language is imprecise. It may be that his source claimed that the Indian rivers were at full spate around the solstice (so Nearchus), and Arrian wrongly inferred that the battle was fought around that time. Cf. Anspach 1903, 40–1; Schachermeyr 1973, 423.
[329] So both Aristobulus (F 35) and Nearchus (F 18) in Strabo 691–2.
[330] There is one retrospective reference to storm damage at Nicaea and Bucephala (Arr. v.29.6; cf. Strasburger 1982, 1.465–6).

bare the countryside under the command of Coenus and Craterus. Hephaestion was left to consolidate the conquest while his king crossed the Hydraotes
and attacked the so-called autonomous Indians, who organised the first
resistance at their principal stronghold, the city of Sangala (its site, in the
vicinity of Lahore and Amritsar, has yet to be identified). Yet again the
Macedonian expertise in siege warfare was demonstrated to appalling effect
and Ptolemy, who distinguished himself in action, chose to give a full
description. The Indians used a triple defence of waggons to protect the city
defences, but they could not withstand the pressure of Alexander's phalanx,
reinforced by the infantry of the rearguard. After the first day they were
imprisoned within their walls, hemmed in by a double palisade, awaiting the
completion of the Macedonian siege towers. A sortie was attempted but
repelled by Ptolemy. Finally, when Porus had joined the siege with a freshly
levied army and more elephants, the attack proper began. The brick walls of
Sangala were undermined even before the towers came into operation and the
city was taken by storm – with the usual consequences.[331] Perhaps the rains
had been a greater problem than the defenders. Visibility must have been
impaired, mistakes easy to make, and the wounded were noticeably numerous
(Arr. v.24.5). Even so, the siege was decisive. The inhabitants of the
neighbouring cities abandoned their homes rather than submit to the vicissitudes of conquest and they were ruthlessly pursued; the sick and fatigued
who were overhauled were chivalrously slaughtered by the army. Sangala
itself was razed and its territory annexed to the peoples in the vicinity who had
accepted the Macedonians. Porus was once again the ultimate beneficiary,
allowed to install his own garrisons even in the cities which had surrendered
(Arr. v.24.8).

Alexander now proceeded unopposed to the Hyphasis (Beas), receiving the
surrender of the local rulers as he went. It is a matter for conjecture how far he
intended to go. All sources agree that he intended to cross the Beas and attack
the peoples beyond. Arrian (v.25.1) speaks of a populous, aristocratically
governed people rich in elephants.[332] But he does not give its name or
location. The vulgate tradition, based ultimately on Cleitarchus, mentions the
monarchy of the Prasii and Gangaridae, centred on the great river Ganges,[333]
and there seems little doubt that it referred to the Nanda dynasty, whose
capital Pataliputra (the Greek Palimbothra) was sited at the confluence of the
Son and the Ganges, by the modern city of Patna.[334] This first came into
prominence after the visits of Megasthenes to the court of Chandragupta
shortly before 300 B.C., but it seems perverse to deny that Alexander heard
reports of it and was inspired to conquest. Hieronymus at least seems to have

[331] Arr. v.22.5–24.5 (*FGrH* 138 F 35); Curt. IX.1.15–18.
[332] See also Strabo 702 *fin.* for the same tradition. If Arrian's source was referring to the kingdom
of the Prasii, we must conclude that the aristocratic rulers were the host of royal officials
whose number impressed Megasthenes (Strabo 707ff.; Arr. *Ind.* 12.6–7).
[333] Diod. XVII.93.2–4; Curt. IX.2.2–7; *Metz Epit.* 68; Plut. *Al.* 62.2–3.
[334] Wheeler 1968, 130ff.

believed the story.[335] But what cannot be determined is the accuracy of Alexander's information. (The vulgate tradition speaks of a twelve-day desert journey to the borders of the kingdom, which hardly corresponds with the actual 330 km of populated country between the Beas and the upper Ganges.) He presumably had reports of the great river Ganges and the kingdom which dominated its upper plain, but detailed measurements of distance would only have come after the conquest.[336]

That was not to be. The frustration that had been building up in the Macedonian army since the eve of Gaugamela finally vented itself. By this time the monsoon deluge had lasted seventy days (Diod. xvii.94.3), damaging clothing, arms and morale, and the prospect of another hazardous river-crossing and indefinite campaigning against armies equipped with elephant squadrons of legendary strength was too much. The demand to stop, return and enjoy the fruits of conquest now became irresistible. Meetings were held in camp and complaints were voiced, too strong and numerous to be ignored. Alexander attempted to placate his men and summoned a council of senior officers to test the level of feeling.[337] His appeal to cross the Hyphasis and continue the conquests was met with silence, and finally Coenus, son of Polemocrates, a phalanx commander of unchallenged seniority, expounded the cause of his men, insisting that a further advance to the east was unacceptable.[338] This intervention clearly represented the spirit of the meeting, which Alexander angrily dismissed. A second meeting the following day was no more successful. Alexander retired like Achilles to his tent and nursed his wrath for three days, waiting for signs of a change in heart. It did not come. Finally, as Ptolemy reported (Arr. v.28.4), he made the regular sacrifice for the crossing (cf. Arr. v.3.6), and the omens proved appropriately unfavourable. Alexander could now accept the verdict of the gods and renounce the passage of the Hyphasis. To commemorate the renunciation he erected twelve massive altars of dressed stone as a thank-offering to the deities who had blessed his success. The king's ambitions were frustrated but it was the gods to whom he deferred, not his men. The rank and file reacted with hysterical acclamation, confirming their deep opposition to any further advance. Alexander had bowed to their pressure and he never forgot it. From this point he was prepared to demobilise and dispense with his veterans and those who had represented their views. Coenus himself was dead, the victim of an unspecified disease, a matter of days after his actions at the Hyphasis. He received a magnificent funeral, but the circumstances of his

---

[335] Diod. xviii.6.1–2; ii.37.1–3; cf. Meyer 1927; Hornblower 1981, 84–6.
[336] Cf. Schachermeyr 1955; Brunt 1976–83, 2.463–5; contra Kienast 1965.
[337] Arr. v. 25.2 (probably based on Ptolemy). Other sources (Curt. ix.2.13ff.; Diod. xvii.94.5; Justin xii.8.10–16) less plausibly speak of a plenary assembly of the army.
[338] Arr. v.27.1ff.; Curt. ix.3.3–5. Coenus had been left in the rear to co-ordinate foraging parties (Arr. v.21.1, 21.4), but like Hephaestion (Arr. v.21.5; cf. Curt. ix.1.35) he had clearly rejoined the army at the Hyphasis (Brunt 1976–83, 2.88–9; contra Tarn 1948, 2.287ff.).

death were suspicious and worthy of comment.[339] Similarly Craterus, last-ingly popular with the Macedonians for his defence of national tradition, was treated with ostensible honour but kept on missions away from court.[340] Alexander's entourage was to comprise men who would approve his ambitions.

Those ambitions were now firmly fixed on the Southern Ocean. Alexander ratified Porus' *de facto* control of the territories eastwards to the Hyphasis. Unlike Taxiles he had no European satrap to coexist with, and the only constraints upon him were the city foundations on the Hydaspes and the Acesines (see below, pp. 239–40). Alexander had practically lost interest in the area. As he returned to the Hydaspes, he confirmed Abisares in his realm, expanding it at the expense of his neighbour, Arsaces (Berve 1926, 2 no. 147), but imposing tribute. That was the end of his annexations in northern India. Alexander reached the Hydaspes shortly before the rising of Arcturus in late September[341] and devoted himself to the construction of his river fleet. His base was the new foundations of Bucephala and Nicaea, where an artificial harbour had been built, and the timber floated down from the mountain forests was gradually transformed into navigable craft. Alexander's courtiers acted as trierarchs, presumably helping the construction with their own resources and holding honorary rank during the journey downstream.[342] The actual command of the fleet was placed in the hands of Nearchus of Crete, Alexander's boyhood friend and ex-satrap of Lycia and Pamphylia, seconded by the helmsman of the royal flagship, Onesicritus of Cos. It was a miscell-aneous collection of vessels, including commandeered local river boats. All were light; the nucleus of two-banked triaconters which had been originally built for the Hydaspes crossing was supplemented by further light galleys and transport vessels.[343] This was no war fleet designed for battle but solely to provide transport for horses, men and provisions. According to Nearchus the total number of ships was 800, and Ptolemy put the figure as high as 2,000.[344] It was certainly a formidable armament, and Alexander's departure cere-monies were solemn and impressive. There was a round of musical and athletic games, sacrifices to the ancestral gods of Macedon and the deities of ocean and river, and finally Alexander poured libations from his flagship, first

[339] Arr. VI.2.1; Curt. IX.3.20. Cf. Badian 1961, 20.
[340] Plut. *Eum.* 6.3; cf. Bosworth 1980, 7.
[341] For the chronology see Aristobulus, *FGrH* 139 F 35 = Strabo 691. The rains ceased just before the rising of Arcturus, when Alexander was back at the Hydaspes; the voyage began a few days before the rising of the Pleiades (early November, 326) and ended at Patalene around the rising of the Dog Star (mid-July, 325). The Macedonians were concerned with the fleet all autumn, winter, spring and summer, a total of ten months (corresponding to the time from the rising of Arcturus to the rising of the Dog Star, from the return to the Hydaspes to the arrival at Patala).
[342] Arr. *Ind.* 18.3–9; cf. 20.9.
[343] See particularly Arr. VI.3.2, 5.2, 18.3 with Berve 1926, 1.163–6; Casson 1971, 123ff.
[344] Arr. *Ind.* 19.7 (Nearchus); VI.2.4 (Ptolemy); cf. Diod. XVII.95.5; Curt. IX.3.22; *Metz Epit.* 70.

to the Hydaspes and then to the other deities in turn.[345] At a trumpet signal the fleet cast off and began the voyage downstream. To the right and to the left army columns under Hephaestion and Craterus marched along the banks. It was an exotic and festive scene, as the beat of thousands of oars, echoing in the confined space between the river banks, attracted spectators from far and wide, who stayed to accompany the fleet with song and dance.

The rivers had passed their peak after the monsoon period, but there were still hazards, notably at the confluence of the Hydaspes and Acesines, where the combined channel was particularly narrow and the current fast enough to throw Alexander's galleys out of control.[346] The loss of vessels and lives was high and required a period of reconstruction, during which there were minor campaigns against neighbouring tribes. But the main thrust of Alexander's advance was directed against the Oxydracae and Malli (Ksudrakas and Malavas), who were reputed to be the most warlike people of the lower Punjab and were at the moment preparing to resist his invasion (Arr. vi.4.3). Their territories are hard to locate, given the fact that the courses of the main rivers were very different in antiquity (the Hyphasis, for instance, apparently flowed into the Hydraotes and did not, as today, join the Sutlej and make an independent confluence with the Indus),[347] but it seems agreed that the Malli, the chief object of Alexander's attack, occupied the land on either side of the Hydraotes, some distance from its junction with the Acesines.[348] The king accordingly divided his forces. Nearchus took the fleet southwards from the Acesines to the borderlands of the Malli, while Craterus and Philip son of Machatas (the satrap of northern India) led a large column down the west bank. Hephaestion and Ptolemy were to take two other army groups down the east bank, their march timed to be eight days apart so as to intercept stragglers and refugees from Alexander's invasion. It was he of course who led the main column, a lightly equipped force comprising hypaspists, a single phalanx battalion, light infantry, half the Companion cavalry and the now indispensable Dahan mounted archers. Driving rapidly towards the Hydraotes across desert terrain he attacked the Malli from the north, taking them entirely by surprise. What followed is depressingly familiar.[349] The settlements in his path west of the Hydraotes were taken by storm, the inhabitants who attempted flight ridden down by the cavalry. The slaughter continued at the river, as Alexander's men fell on the civilians who were evacuating the west bank, and the attack was transferred to the east of the Hydraotes, where recalcitrant cities were stormed and the bulk of the populace forced to seek

[345] Arr. vi.3.1–2; Ind. 18.11–12.
[346] Arr. vi.4.5–5.4, romantically embroidered in Diod. xvii.97.1–3; Curt. ix.4.9–14.
[347] Megasthenes ap. Ind. 4.8 (cf. Arr. vi.14.5, where the southern confluence is said to be that of the combined Acesines and Hydraotes). Cf. Lambrick 1964, 105–7; Wilhelmy 1966, 271ff.; 1969.
[348] Probably in the general area north-east of modern Multan; cf. Mughal 1967, esp. 16–23.
[349] The campaign on the Hydraotes is known only from Arrian (vi.6–10), whose account is unitary and apparently based on Ptolemy (vi.10.1 = FGrH 138 F 25). It is not, however, based on autopsy, since Ptolemy was far away with the rearguard on the Acesines (vi.5.6–7).

refuge in the desert. The Malli even evacuated their capital and transported the refugees there back across the Hydraotes, intending to hold its steep banks against the Macedonian army. In the event they did not even contest the passage, withdrew from the river and occupied the strongest city of the region.

Alexander began the siege as normal, investing the town with a ring of cavalry until his infantry was in place and then storming the walls with almost effortless ease. As usual, the citadel was the last to fall. Here the assault flagged, for reasons that are not clear. If we may believe Arrian (vi.9.2) there was a shortage of scaling ladders and some reluctance among the hypaspists to mount the assault (Arr. vi.9.3; cf. Curt. ix.4.30). Alexander had detected (or thought he had detected) similar battle-weariness some days before and had set a personal example, leading the attack on the battlements in person (Arr. vi.7.5). The Macedonians may indeed have lost some of their alacrity in the seemingly endless sequence of skirmishes and sieges that had marked their campaign in India, and their perceptible loss of morale, compounding the effect of their refusal at the Hyphasis, galvanised the king into one of his most heroic feats of arms. Once more he led the assault, but once he was on the battlements his hypaspists broke the ladders behind him by sheer weight of numbers, leaving him temporarily isolated with a handful of companions, notably Peucestas, the bearer of the sacred shield from Ilium. Precariously teetering on the battlements and transported by battle fury he leaped down into the citadel, to become the single target of the defenders. Finally an arrow pierced his corselet and penetrated his right chest, perhaps even damaging a lung.[350] As he collapsed, Peucestas and (perhaps) Leonnatus took the brunt of the attack and prevented further injury until the hypaspists stormed the mud brick walls, opened the citadel gate and killed every living person in the citadel in a savage act of reprisal (Arr. vi.11.1; Curt. ix.5.20; Diod. xvii.99.4).

The episode rapidly became the stuff of legend. The identity of the heroes who protected the king was hotly disputed. Peucestas was agreed to have played the principal role but the presence of Leonnatus was contested. Ptolemy later was silent about the achievements of his enemy Aristonous,[351] and his own historians, notably Cleitarchus, falsely alleged that he was present in person.[352] Given the sensational nature of the episode and the propaganda value later of a claim to have preserved Alexander's life, it is hardly surprising that the tradition was contaminated from the outset. At the time the prevailing emotion was anxiety, if not panic. The king was dangerously wounded and might shortly die, precipitating a crisis of command. The news of the wound penetrated quickly to the base camp at the confluence of the Acesines and Hydraotes and was received with deep consternation – the rank and file had no illusions about their prospects, in hostile territory under the command of

[350] Ptolemy *ap.* Arr. vi.10.1; Diod. xvii.99.3; Curt. ix.5.9–10; Plut. *Al.* 63.6. See, however, Lammert 1953.
[351] Curt. ix.5.15 (contrast Arr. vi.11.7; Plut. *Al.* 63.8); cf. Errington 1969, 235–6; *contra* Roisman 1984, 382.
[352] Curt. ix.5.21 (= *FGrH* 137 F 24); Arr. vi.11.8; Paus. 1.6.2.

quarrelling marshals, if their one unchallenged leader died (Arr. vi.12.2–3). Back outside the Malli town Alexander underwent emergency surgery at the hands of Critobulus of Cos, lost great quantities of blood and came close to death. It was some time before he could be moved, and a small flotilla was dispatched from the confluence to transport him to his base. He took pains to parade himself before the army at his arrival and, in a scene of high collective emotions, he was able to mount his horse and demonstrate that the reports of his death had been greatly exaggerated (Arr. vi.13.2–3). Even so, a lengthy period of convalescence was necessary, during which the fleet was repaired and augmented and an embassy of submission was received from the Malli and Oxydracae, who had been demoralised by the slaughter in their territories and preferred submission to extermination. Accordingly they were annexed to the satrapy of Philip, whose authority was now to run as far south as the final confluence of the Acesines and Indus. That was where the fleet now proceeded. As before, the peoples close to the river were forced to submission. Perdiccas led a column through the territory of the Abistani while Alexander received the surrender of the tribe on the riverside.[353] Similarly the people at the confluence welcomed him into their lands and he established an Alexandria at what was previously their capital, a future garrison and naval base on the frontier between northern and southern India.[354]

Alexander already had designs on the southern Indus valley. At the confluence of the Indus and the Punjab rivers he declared Peithon, son of Agenor, satrap of all the lands south to the ocean (Arr. vi.15.4). The neighbouring Indian prince, Musicanus, had omitted to pay homage, which was seized upon as a *casus belli*. Alexander unceremoniously invaded his territory, and the news of his approach was sufficient for Musicanus to offer gifts and surrender his lands, begging forgiveness for his error. Alexander magnanimously confirmed him in his princedom, visited his capital, probably at the ancient site of Alor (the medieval capital of Sind)[355] and allegedly admired the country and its institutions. His helmsman, Onesicritus, was even more impressed and later devoted an excursus of his work on Alexander to an encomium of the land of Musicanus, which he saw as a paradigm of social moderation, reminiscent of Dorian Crete and Sparta.[356] But, as always, Alexander's first thoughts were military. The city was fortified and garrisoned to provide a control centre for the region (Arr. vi.15.7), and, assured of Musicanus' loyalty, he turned against his neighbours. The riverain territory south of Sukkur, ruled by a dynast variously named Oxycanus or Porticanus, was rapidly subdued after the capture by storm of two major cities. More serious was a revolt by Sambus, ruler of certain mountain tribes to the west of the Indus. He had apparently surrendered to Alexander before the invasion

353  Arr. vi.15.1; cf. Diod. xvii.102.1–4; Curt. ix.8.4–7.
354  Diod. xvii.102.4; Curt. ix.8.8. There are two reports in Arrian (vi.15.2, 4), which may be variant accounts of the same foundations (Bosworth 1976b, 130–2).
355  Lambrick 1964, 108; Wilhelmy 1966, 272–3; Eggermont 1975, 7–9.
356  Strabo 701–2 = *FGrH* 134 F 24. Cf. Brown 1949b, 56–61; Pearson 1960, 100–6.

(Arr. VI.16.3) but, like Porus' cousin the previous year, he renounced his allegiance after his enemy, Musicanus, had entrenched himself in the conqueror's favour. A show of force was sufficient to scare the capital, Sindimana, into submission. Other towns were stiffened in their revolt by the influential Brahman ascetics[357] and were captured and sacked with the usual frightful toll of lives (Cleitarchus claimed that there were 80,000 casualties).[358]

During the campaign against Sambus there was a second revolt, this time by Musicanus, whose surrender had been strictly a temporising measure. It was enough to send the satrap Peithon against him, while Alexander systematically captured, razed and garrisoned the cities to the south of his country. The insurgent prince was captured by Peithon and crucified in his capital along with his Brahman advisers (Arr. VI.17.1–2; Curt. IX.8.16). That was the end of resistance for the time being. Appalled at the atrocities committed on his borders the ruler of Patalene, the land of the Indus delta, approached Alexander well in advance and surrendered himself and his realms unconditionally. There was no opposition now to his advance to the southern ocean, and it was at this point, if not earlier,[359] that he detached a large column of veterans under Craterus' command. Three phalanx battalions, the whole elephant corps, and all Macedonian troops, infantry and cavalry, whom he considered unfit for active service were sent directly west over the Bolan or the Mulla Pass to the Helmand valley, where they were to make their way via Sistan to Carmania. Alexander himself decided to take the more arduous coastal route (see below, pp. 144–6) and felt that he could dispense with many of the men who had voiced their disinclination to further hardship. The main army could now move south, Alexander sailing with the fleet and Peithon and Hephaestion leading expeditionary forces on either side of the Indus. They came without incident to the capital of Patala, which is generally identified with the ruins of Bahmanabad, some 75 km north-east of Hyderabad.[360] The country he entered was deserted, abandoned by the inhabitants in sheer terror at his approach. To obtain provisions for his stay and a labour force for his military projects he was forced to give guarantees of safety and immunity under Macedonian occupation, and in due course many of the Indians did grudgingly return (Arr. VI.17.5; Curt. IX.8.28). The events of the last months had proved the futility of military resistance, but they had made him an object of terror. The Indians would leave their possessions and make token submission, but they would always see him as an

---

[357] Arr. VI.16.5. The Brahman resistance became a popular literary topic in Hellenistic times: cf. Plut. *Al.* 64; *FGrH* 153 F 9; *Metz Epit.* 78–84; with Hamilton 1969, 178–9; Wilcken 1970, 1.174–207; Martin 1959.

[358] Curt. IX.8.15 (= *FGrH* 137 F 25); Diod. XVII.102.6.

[359] Arr. VI.17.3–4. For the earlier date see VI.15.5 (perhaps a doublet: Bosworth 1976b, 127–9; *contra* Brunt 1976–83, 2.146–7); Strabo 721; Justin XII.10.1–2. For details of the route via Chaarene (Strabo 725) see Goukowsky 1978–81, 2.105–7.

[360] Cf. Wilhelmy 1968b, 258ff.; Eggermont 1975, 27 (see, however, 189–90 – unconvincing).

invader and destroyer and hate him for it. It was a bad augury for lasting conquest.

## XVII    The march through Gedrosia

The Macedonian forces arrived at Patala at the time of the rising of the Dog Star, in the middle of July 325 (Aristobulus, *FGrH* 139 F 35). Once there Alexander began preparations for the next part of the campaign, the passage of the Makran coast. It was to be a double journey, by land and sea, and it is clear that the king's concerns and anxieties were primarily for his fleet. Nearchus (Arr. *Ind.* 20.1–6) gives a vivid description of his agonising over committing the fleet to the Ocean, a description which is no doubt biased in his own favour to exaggerate the confidence the king reposed in him[361] but which none the less reflects a genuine worry. The fleet was committed to a voyage of detailed reconnaissance (*Ind.* 32.11) along an unknown coast, and the risks were literally incalculable. Accordingly the preparations he made were as painstaking and meticulous as any recorded in the course of the expedition. In the first place he turned Patala into a military base with a ship-station and dockyards to accommodate the existing fleet and left Hephaestion in command of the citadel while he explored the principal arms of the Indus delta. His first venture, down the western arm, was abortive. His light ships foundered in a sudden gale and needed to be replaced. He also needed local knowledge, and his light infantry was dispatched to capture some of the elusive native population to act as guides. Finally, despite the intermittent southerly gales and the extreme tidal variations, which occasionally grounded the ships,[362] he reached the island of Cilluta towards the mouth of the river. Beyond Cilluta was another island in the Ocean proper which Alexander visited and sailed out further south to offer sacrifice to Poseidon and the gods of the sea.[363] The ceremonial echoed that at the outset of the expedition, when he had sacrificed to Poseidon and the Nereids in the Hellespont. Now there was a greater hazard than the mere crossing of the army, and Alexander did his utmost to propitiate the deities who would preserve his fleet. At the same time he achieved his ambition to sail the circumambient Ocean which he had reached by conquest – some small consolation for the frustration at the Hyphasis.

The preliminary exploration was not yet finished. Alexander returned to Patala and made a second voyage down the eastern arm of the river (Arr. VI.20.2). Here he had less difficulty, apparently untroubled by winds or tide. A large saline lake provided a base for his land forces while he took his lightest vessels out into the Ocean again, and he came to the conclusion that the Ocean

---

[361] Cf. Badian 1975, 153–6; *contra* Brunt 1976–83, 2.365.
[362] Arr. VI.18.5–19.2; Curt. IX.9.1–26 (rhetorically embellished).
[363] Arr. VI.19.5; *Ind.* 20.10; Plut. *Al.* 66.1–2; Diod. XVII.104.1; Curt. IX.9.27. For a conjectural reconstruction of the coastline in 325 and an identification of the island (Aban Shah) see Lambrick 1964, 113; Wilhelmy 1968a.

fleet should use this eastern route,[364] even though it prolonged the total journey. The lake was intended as a secondary harbour. It was equipped with a naval station and docks, while his land forces were busy sinking wells on the coastline to the west of the river mouth. Now the fleet had a base at Patala, turned into a fortress by Hephaestion, an intermediate station at the Indus lake, and water supplies for the beginning of the voyage. There was also a four-month supply of grain stockpiled to meet the demands of provisioning before Nearchus was ready to start the voyage.

There could be no immediate departure. The onset of the south-west monsoon was imminent. Its effects were beginning to be felt when Alexander sailed down the western arm of the Indus but it was not strong enough to prevent his venturing into the Ocean. In modern times the monsoon begins in South Pakistan around mid-July, but it can be delayed for three weeks and more, and in 325 it clearly had not begun until August at least. But by the time Alexander was ready to leave Patala, the southerly winds had set in consistently, and he was informed by the natives that sailing would be impossible throughout the monsoon period. Navigation would only be possible from the time of the setting of the Pleiades (c. 5 November), when the monsoon winds had retreated (Arr. VI.21.2).[365] He knew that it would be nearly three months before the fleet could safely move, but he was leaving it in a heavily fortified base, well supplied with provisions and with secondary harbour facilities near the Indus mouth. As it transpired, the elaborate arrangements went for nothing. The harbour facilities in the great lake were never used, and Nearchus sailed down the western arm of the Indus, not the eastern, as Alexander had intended. He also sailed prematurely, around the evening rising of the Pleiades, early in October (Strabo 721; Arr. Ind.21.1 (= FGrH 133 F 11a)), while the winds were still adverse. He was obliged to make a cut through the coastal sand bar to gain access to the Ocean and then was marooned on an offshore island for 24 days, until the monsoon southerlies subsided (Ind. 21.5–6, 12–13). The reason Nearchus gives is pressure from the hostile natives, and that is easy to believe. The inhabitants of Patala had disappeared in the face of Alexander's invasion army and had to be hunted out (Arr. VI.17.5–6, 18.5). Even when the Macedonian forces were present in full strength they had attacked working parties in the desert (VI.18.1), and it is not surprising that, when Alexander left the area, they turned on the fleet. Presumably the installations in the great lake were overrun and destroyed, and the fleet, besieged at Patala, was forced to withdraw in the direction that was militarily safest, even if it was not the most advantageous for the voyage.

---

[364] Arr. VI.20.4 is difficult and perhaps corrupt (for translation see Hammond 1980b, 467–8). It does not entail that Alexander intended to use the western arm: the naval installations on the lake (Arr. VI.20.5) clearly imply that his preparations were centred on the eastern stream. Cf. Lambrick 1964, 114–15.

[365] Nowadays the monsoon winds cease by early October. In the Roman period the earliest date for the return voyage from South India was 28 December (Pliny, NH VI.102; cf. Böker, RE Suppl. IX.403–12).

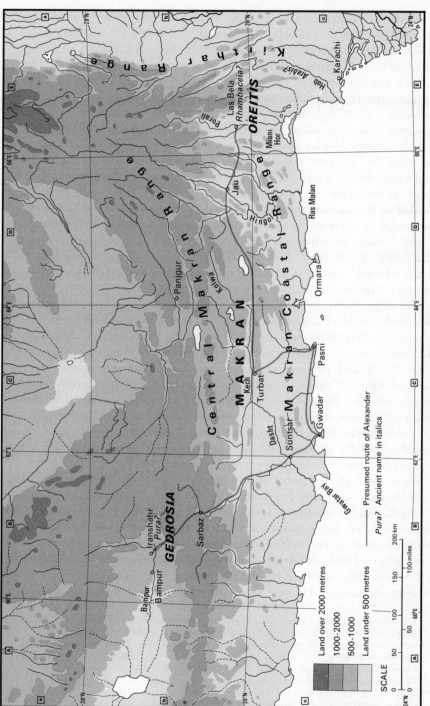

10. *Las Bela and the Makran.*

Alexander himself struck out from Patala with the majority of his land forces. Their number can only be guessed at. The vast forces of Indian troops which had swelled his army during the Indus voyage (Arr. *Ind*.19.5, cf. Plut. *Al*. 66.5) were dispersed, and the nucleus of permanent troops remained. That in itself was large enough, the Macedonian troops not included in Craterus' column, the Hellenic mercenaries, the auxiliary cavalry from the eastern satrapies. There was also a considerable baggage train with a host of non-combatants, including the concubines and children of the army. The total is a matter of pure guesswork, but the absolute minimum cannot have been less than 30,000[366] and even that was a dangerously large number for the arid wastes that lay ahead. At first the army was able to use the wells dug in the desert in the vicinity of Patala (Arr. VI.18.1), and his army marched by the foothills of the Kirthar range to the mouth of the river Arabis (Hab?).[367] From the Arabis he followed the coastline to make a surprise attack on the Oreitae, an independent Indian people domiciled in the plain area around what is now Las Bela in Baluchistan. A party was there deputed to dig wells along the coast, while Alexander went ahead with a striking force to invade Oreitan territory. Hephaestion followed with the baggage train.

Alexander crossed the coastal desert north of the Arabis in a single night and launched an attack on the unsuspecting Oreitae. Three columns ravaged the plain of Las Bela (which was considerably narrower then than now, given that the shoreline has advanced by as much as 35 kilometres, thanks to silt from the river Purali and deposits of sands from the south-west monsoon),[368] Alexander himself attending to the fertile tract of Welpat in the north, which has always been the most densely populated area of Bela state. The chief village of the area, Rhambaceia, was destined for a new city,[369] and Hephaestion, newly arrived with the baggage, was deputed to deal with the synoecism. But this time the Oreitan resistance was confined to the west of the plain, concentrated around the passes leading into the Makran, almost certainly blocking the route between Las Bela and the head of the Kolwa valley (the Kumbh pass across the Jau Lak). The Oreitae had been joined by their Gedrosian neighbours from the Makran who had a common interest in barring the passage, but they prudently shied away from a direct encounter with the Macedonian army and made formal surrender (Arr. VI.22.2). The Oreitae were subjected to direct satrapal rule under Apollophanes, and Leonnatus was left behind with a mobile force of Agrianians, archers and mercenaries, both infantry and cavalry. His task was to organise the territory, to populate the

---

[366] For estimates see Strasburger 1982, 1.479–80 (too dependent on Plut. *Al*. 66.5); Engels 1978a, 111–12 (*contra* Brunt 1976–83, 2.482); Kraft 1971, 109–18 (impossibly low).

[367] So Stein 1943, 213–14; Eggermont 1975, 89–93; Engels 1978a, 138; Brunt 1976–83, 2.478. For the alternative, less convincing, identification of the Arabis with the Purali see Goukowsky 1978–81, 2.92–100; Seibert 1985, 173–4.

[368] Cf. Snead 1966, 37–8; Engels 1978a, 139–40.

[369] Arr. VI.21.4; Curt. IX.10.7. On the location see Stein 1943, 213–16; Engels 1978a, 138–9; *contra* Hamilton 1972, Goukowsky 1978–81, 2.96–100; Seibert 1985, 175.

new city and to arrange matters for the passage of the fleet. According to Diodorus (xvII.104.8) Alexander had ambitions to establish a city by the coast, and finding a sheltered harbour he planned an Alexandria nearby. That seems to be a conflation: Alexandria is clearly the synoecism on the site of Rhambaceia, which Arrian describes, but the coast foundation, if it existed, can hardly be anything other than the depot on the coast where Leonnatus stockpiled grain for the fleet (Arr. *Ind.*23.6). There were obviously two areas of concentration: the coast, where the fleet would need to be provisioned, and the hinterland which was secured by a new foundation, populated by settlers from Arachosia to the north (Curt. IX.10.7). Leonnatus was the vital link in Alexander's overall strategy, such as it was. He was to keep the Oreitans submissive, to arrange for a permanent citadel to maintain the alien domination and to ensure that the coast was friendly for Nearchus' fleet. Not surprisingly the natives refused to acquiesce. Leonnatus' forces were attacked and apparently defeated soon after Alexander left the territory (Diod. xvII.105.8), and shortly before Nearchus arrived on the coast there was a full-scale battle in which Leonnatus confronted an army of Oreitae and allied peoples and cut down 6,000 of them at minimal loss to his own forces (Arr. vII.5.5; *Ind.* 23.5). The victory cleared the coast, and Nearchus was able to provision his fleet with ten days' supply of grain, the only supplies he encountered in his entire coastal voyage. That was in November. Leonnatus had been in Oreitan territory throughout the monsoon season and was able to requisition the harvest as it matured.[370] The natives were naturally provoked to desperation after the depredations of Alexander's initial invasion, and the two blows of famine and defeat will have threatened them with depopulation. Leonnatus had amply earned the crown he received at Susa.

Alexander left Oreitan territory perhaps in early October. The monsoon season had certainly set in, and the scanty autumn crops of the Makran would have been well into their growing cycle. The Macedonian army now moved west to begin the long journey to Carmania and the Persian Gulf. The territory it traversed was notoriously desert. According to Nearchus, Alexander was well aware of the fact, having heard stories that the legendary Semiramis and Cyrus the conqueror had both lost armies there (Arr. vI.24.2–3; Strabo 686, 722), but instead of being deterred he was inspired to succeed where they had failed.[371] At the same time there was his intention to provision the fleet along the coast (Arr. vI.23.1, 4–6, 24.2). Given the proverbial desolation of the Makran, that might seem a preposterous ambition, but Alexander was marching at the best season of the year, in the eastern areas at least, taking advantage of the growth from the monsoon run-off. In later years the Makran, though formidable, was no impassable

---

[370] For the growth cycle in Baluchistan and its dependence on the summer rainfall see the *Baluchistan District Gazetteer* Series vII (1906), 31ff., 147ff.

[371] Cf. Strasburger 1982, 1.458–9. Nearchus' evidence, embarrassing to some, has been variously discounted (Kraft 1971, 106ff.; Engels 1978a, 111ff.; Hammond 1980a, 234). See now Badian 1985, 471–3.

barrier. In A.D. 711 the seventeen-year-old conqueror of Sind, Muhammed ibn Qasim, traversed the terrain at roughly the same season as Alexander, with a land and sea force. His army was much smaller and more mobile, comprising cavalry and camels, and his expedition took place when the Makran was firmly in Arab hands, his passage evidently well prepared for. Nevertheless he crossed the territory without serious losses and embarked immediately on a major campaign in Sind. Alexander's forces could expect to encounter provisions of a kind, and there might be sufficient surplus to supply the coast. His line of march inevitably took him inland, through the more populous centres of Gedrosia. Had he marched along the coast, he would inevitably have stripped the area bare, ruining it for the fleet. Indeed Nearchus gives no indication that there were any traces of the army's passage. He suggests that Alexander went through the interior (Arr. *Ind*. 26.1, 32.1) and the communities he exploited for provisions obviously had not had the pleasure of entertaining Alexander previously. Arrian (VI.23.1) emphasises that Alexander was anxious to sink wells and provide depots, but his reconnaissance of the coast proved disappointingly negative. His route took him mainly inland. Strabo (721) claims that Alexander kept no more than 500 stades from the coast, to make it accessible for the fleet, but it is hard to see how the distances could be accurately measured. The king would be at the mercy of haphazard reports from reconnaissance parties and would rarely have a reliable estimate how far distant he was from the sea.

Most probably he took the main road west across the Jau Lak pass, narrow and steep but apparently accessible for laden animals in dry weather, and from there in a westerly direction along the line of the Kolwa and Kech valleys.[372] This took him through some of the most fertile and accessible parts of Gedrosia. Foraging parties were sent far afield to acquire provisions and the northern sector of Gedrosia (the area of modern Panjgur) was directed to send supplies south to the fleet – a directive which was promptly ignored when Alexander was out of range. In this first part of the journey he actually managed to amass a surplus of provisions and turned south to convey them to the fleet. That was probably at the oasis of Turbat, some 400 kilometres (238 miles) from Las Bela, where there is a fairly clear track south to the Ocean at Pasni, a distance of 120 kilometres.[373] The exercise proved futile. The troops allotted to the baggage convoy, themselves driven frantic by hunger, broke the royal seals on the consignment and consumed most of the provisions. Alexander discovered this only when close to the sea (Arr. VI.23.4) and abandoned any idea of provisioning the fleet. The demands of his army were insistent and became ever more so as he moved eastwards, into territory that was not affected by the monsoon stream. In autumn the Persian Makran is almost entirely arid, the winter rains beginning only in November after five

---

[372] So Stein 1943, 216ff.; Engels 1978a, 137–43; Brunt 1976–83, 2.478–9. For the coastal route see Strasburger 1982, 1.459–62, 487–90; Hamilton 1972, 607–8; Seibert 1985, 171–6.

[373] Stein 1943, 220–1; 1931. For the distances see the *Baluchistan District Gazetteer* 348–9.

months of near-total drought.[374] The difficulties would necessarily have increased as the army struggled west, along the coast for seven days from Pasni before veering north again to rejoin the inland road. The route took them through the Dashtiari plain and north to the Bampur river, the centre of civilisation in eastern Gedrosia. There at the palace of Pura (modern Iranshahr?)[375] the army rested, after a desert march which all sources agree took sixty days (Arr. VI.24.1; Strabo 723; Plut. *Al.* 66.7). The Bampur basin was on the direct line of communication with Sistan (Drangiana), one of the major granaries of Iran, and it had been associated with Drangiana as early as 329, when its inhabitants had surrendered to Alexander (Arr. III.28.1; Diod. XVII.81.2). In response to messages sent during the desert crossing Stasanor, satrap of Drangiana, had sent a contingent of foodstuffs on racing camels (Diod. XVII.105.6–7; Curt. IX.10.17: Plut. *Al.* 66.7). That supplemented the scanty resources of the Gedrosian capital, but even so Alexander allowed his famished army no more than a few days' rest before pushing west through the Jaz Murian depression to the borders of Carmania. There he encountered further supplies from Drangiana and as far afield as Parthyaea (Arr. VI.27.6; Curt. IX.10.22). The rigours of the desert march had now definitely ended.

It is hard to assess the effect of the passage of Gedrosia. Plutarch (*Al.* 66.4–5) speaks of massive losses, which reduced the army to a quarter of its former size, but he is operating from an exaggerated basic figure, the total of forces present at the start of the Hydaspes voyage, and what he says is suspect. Certainly the Macedonians were not decimated. At least 18,000 infantry made their way to Opis.[376] Approximately half had come with Craterus through Arachosia and Drangiana and had a relatively comfortable journey, but it is evident that Alexander's party did not sustain calamitous losses. Admittedly the fighting troops may have suffered less and received better supplies than the rest of the convoy, but there was no unqualified military disaster. There is no doubt that the march inflicted unparalleled discomfort, and the hardships were reported luridly by survivors. Diodorus and Curtius stress the absence of victuals and the ensuing spectre of starvation, while Arrian and Strabo have a vivid tale of misery, extracted from a common source, almost certainly Nearchus.[377] This stressed the heat and length of the marches, the difficulties of finding water, the perils of flash flooding, and the effects of progressive exhaustion. Now Nearchus was not personally on the march and he may have given an excessively one-sided picture to underscore the relative absence of casualties in his own passage of the coast. Certainly all sources stressed the hardships of the march, even the narrative source used by Arrian to describe the attempt to provision the fleet

---

[374] Statistics in the *Cambridge History of Iran* 1.246.
[375] Stein 1937, 104ff.; see, however, Cook 1983, 190.
[376] For details see Bosworth 1986 and the discussion below, p. 267.
[377] See particularly Strasburger 1982, 1.449–70; Brunt 1976–83, 2.475–6. The older attribution to Aristobulus still has adherents: e.g. Pearson 1960, 178; Schachermeyr 1973, 464; Hammond 1980a, 320 n. 105.

(Arr.vi.23.4), but the hardships were probably not uniform. The baggage animals were slaughtered for food as famine set in (Arr. vi.25.2), but that took time. In the first stages of the march, as far as Turbat, the animals were in service, suffering from the terrain and climate, but patently surviving. There was fodder for the beasts of burden and surplus victuals for the men. The stresses became progressively worse as the army left the terrain affected by the monsoon. Hunger and thirst took their toll and the baggage train dwindled to nothing. At the same time the weaker non-combatants, the wives and children of the soldiery, fell victim more readily to hunger, deprivation and accident (Arr. vi.25.5). The losses were no doubt great, but they were not suffered in equal measure throughout the army. The fighting men will have suffered least, while we can well believe that the livestock was virtually exterminated. In retrospect, however, the episode would have appeared a nightmare of forced marches, thirst and starvation, and the king will have gained little popularity from it. His motives may have been laudable in part, to supply the coast for the fleet, but his prior knowledge of the coast was inadequate and the egotism of his ambition reprehensible. Nothing justified his taking the straggle of non-combatants with him, and the size of the army was out of all proportion to the military objectives at issue. He had eclipsed Semiramis and Cyrus and taken an army through, but the suffering was appalling. And Alexander's army was not the worst affected. One should spare a thought for the wretched inhabitants of the Makran, whose harvest was stripped bare by Alexander's passage inland and Nearchus' along the coast (cf. Arr. *Ind.* 28.1,7–9). Their prospect of starvation was more certain and the ordeal would be longer than sixty days.

XVIII    **From Carmania to Susa**

At the Gedrosian capital Alexander resumed contact with the outer world, and the news was not good. Even on the march he had probably heard of a reverse suffered by his troops in Oreitis (Diod. xvii.105.8). He responded by deposing the satrap, Apollophanes (Arr. vi.27.1),[378] but almost at once he received news of Leonnatus' victory and Apollophanes' death in battle (Curt. ix.10.19, cf. Arr. *Ind.* 23.5). From the north came a report from Craterus, now only a matter of days away from the king, announcing a native rebellion which he had successfully crushed. At the same time there were disturbing reports of insurrection in the Iranian provinces and authoritarian behaviour on the part of his satraps (see below pp. 240–1). At first he was in no position to respond violently, with his army divided and weakened by the Gedrosian desert, but he assumed a façade of amiability, welcoming Astaspes, the native satrap of neighbouring Carmania, despite the allegations that he had plotted revolution during the Indian campaign (Curt. ix.10.21).

The army meanwhile began its march into Carmania, across the Jaz Murian

378 Cf. Badian 1958, 148; 1961, 21; Bosworth 1971b, 124.

depression into the valley of the Halil Rud. At some point after he crossed the
Carmanian border he was joined by Craterus' army column together with
massive convoys of food and livestock from the central satrapies. At the same
time the natives of Carmania made available their own produce, above all the
wine for which the region was famed (Curt. ix.10.25; Arr. vi.28.1; cf. Strabo
726–7). The relative abundance naturally led to excess, as the troops
compensated for their starvation diet in the desert. The vulgate tradition
records a thoroughgoing revel, in which Alexander masqueraded as Dionysus,
carousing on a raised platform drawn by eight horses and followed by the rest
of his staff, also riding on carriages; the whole army marched for seven days in
a state of drunken exaltation. Arrian dismissed the story, which he alleges was
not mentioned by Ptolemy or Aristobulus or, for that matter, by any reliable
authority (this must include Nearchus).[379] Some of the story, the imitation of
Dionysus, may be a late accretion, but the majority of the details, independently described by Plutarch and Curtius, look authentic. If the carousing was
not described by Aristobulus, it was because he had a general aversion to
recording the details of Alexander's insobriety, and Ptolemy need not have
thought the episode worth describing. It was fundamentally a matter of
therapy. The hardships of the Gedrosian march needed to be ameliorated, if
they could not be forgotten, and a general debauch served the purpose well.

The excess lasted for seven days and Alexander then turned to serious
business. Astaspes was the first victim, summarily executed during the actual
revel (Curt. ix.10.29). The Macedonian generals in Media followed him.
Cleander, Agathon, Sitalces and Heracon had brought the bulk of their forces
down to Carmania. They had come at least 1,700 km from the Median capital
of Ecbatana with a marching column of 6,000 men and had clearly been
summoned before the king left India. His displeasure was already known or
guessed, for a number of aggrieved notables had travelled down from Media
with them and brought accusations of gross misconduct, including sacrilege
and rape. The complaints of the subjects were corroborated by their own
troops (Arr. vi.27.4), and the culprits (Cleander and Sitalces at least) were
imprisoned and executed, no less than 600 of their men sharing their fate. It is
a deeply mysterious episode (see below, p. 241), but it seems reasonably clear
that the culprits had no intimation of their fate; they expected to override the
complaints which were made against them. Instead Alexander proved inex-
orable. He had been deeply shocked by the evidence of insubordination and
decided to give the terrible warning which would impress all governors of
whatever rank. There was another consideration. The delinquents had
engineered the assassination of Parmenion and their execution was probably
received with some satisfaction by the army at large. Like the Carmanian revel
it could be set on the credit side of the ledger, to help counterbalance the

---

[379] Plut. *Al.* 67 (cf. Hamilton 1969, 185–7); Diod. xvii.106.1; Curt. ix.10.24–9; cf. Arr.
vi.28.1–3. Arrian's scepticism is usually followed in modern discussions, but see Goukowsky
1978–81, 2.47–64.

sufferings in the desert. This was the first of a series of purges of satraps, predominantly Iranian (see below, p. 240), and the shock waves percolated throughout the empire.

At this stage came one of Alexander's most controversial actions.[380] While in Carmania he issued letters to all satraps and generals in Asia, instructing them to dismiss their mercenary armies forthwith. The episode is reported only by Diodorus (XVII.106.3, 111.1), who connects it with the repression of satrapal insubordination. Mercenaries serving in the provincial forces had been used as instruments of personal despotism (the decimation of the Median garrison shows how seriously Alexander regarded the phenomenon), and Alexander was determined to stop the process. There had been a precedent in the recent past. In 359/8 Artaxerxes III had instructed the satraps of the west to disband their mercenary armies – and thereby caused the revolt of Artabazus (see above, p. 14). That was a security measure pure and simple, and Diodorus suggests that Alexander was operating on similar principles. But other factors were probably at work. The mercenaries discharged from satrapal armies were not merely demobilised; they were intended for Alexander's own service. In the eighteen months after the initial order there were a number of convoys of mercenaries to the heart of the empire culminating in the joint arrival of contingents from Caria and Lydia, led by their respective satraps.[381] Pausanias (1.25.5; cf. VIII.52.5) even talks of a general intention to transfer to Persia all the Greeks who had served under Darius and the satraps. That is an exaggeration, but it contains a nucleus of truth. Alexander's reserves of mercenaries must have been low after the numerous settlements in the north-east and India and the constant demands for garrison forces in the satrapies (see below, pp. 247ff). The problem could be ameliorated by dismissing satrapal forces in the west and ordering the incumbent governors to bring up their men to court. The policy probably originated in the instructions issued long before in India, commissioning the Median and Babylonian (?) commanders to bring their forces to join the royal army.[382] When they arrived in Carmania, Alexander was sufficiently moved by the evidence he found to make the action more general. There was no intention to strip the satrapies of their armies. He cannot have left them defenceless against internal rebellion, and satraps must have been allowed to replenish their armies. Peucestas, appointed to Persis early in 324, was able to raise an army of more than 20,000 native troops within a year.[383] All satraps and generals in Asia apparently had the same instructions, and in due course even Antipater was ordered to bring out the home army from Macedonia to replace Alexander's own veterans. The result was chaos and dislocation. Mercenaries, it seems, were demobilised, but not all were willing to join the

[380] Cf. Badian 1961, 26–8; Jaschinski 1981, 45–61.
[381] Arr. VI.23.1, 24.1; cf. Berve 1926, 1.183–5.
[382] Arr. VI.28.3; VII.18.1.
[383] Arr. VII.23.1, 24.3–4; cf. Jaschinski 1981, 56–60.

convoys to Asia. Many became renegades, forming themselves into bands to live off the countryside by force and intimidation. A considerable number of them followed the leadership of the Athenian Leosthenes, who transported them out of Asia and settled them at Taenarum in Laconia, a great mercenary depot even after the failure of Agis' war (see above, p. 216). The satraps' capacity to make mischief was reduced, but the resulting price in instability was high. There were also lasting tensions among all officials. A summons to court was a matter for deep anxiety (Arr. VII.18.1), and the atmosphere of fear and suspicion is neatly caught by Hypereides (*Dem.* col. 19; cf. Diod. XVII.106.2). His allegation that many satraps and generals were on the point of revolt in the summer of 324 may be an exercise in retrospective wishful thinking, but it does reflect a general atmosphere of fear and suspicion throughout the empire.

The first and most important effect was the flight of Harpalus from Babylon.[384] He may have been summoned by Alexander along with the satrapal forces under the command of Apollodorus. Harpalus stayed firm at his headquarters. He may have had some inkling of what was to come, and he certainly had grounds to be apprehensive of his reception at court. Whatever the quality of his financial administration, his pretensions to regal status had been blatant – his enemy Theopompus accused him of establishing his Athenian mistress Glycera as a queen in her own right in Cilicia (Ath. 586c, 595D–E = *FGrH* 115 F 254). Accordingly, when news arrived of the executions in Carmania, he felt directly threatened. Like Cleander he originated from the old kingdom of Elimiotis, and Ecbatana had been one of the financial centres under his direction (see below, pp. 242–3). Whether or not he had collaborated with him, it was likely that he would be inculpated in Cleander's alleged misdemeanours, and he promptly took flight to the west with 5,000 talents and a small army of mercenaries (Diod. XVII.108.6), impinging on the Greek world in the spring of 324, a potent and dangerous political factor (see below, pp. 215ff.). The news of his departure came as a shock to Alexander, who arrested the first informants as malicious liars (Plut. *Al.* 41.8). As he became convinced of the defection of his old friend, shock turned to hostility. At court sometime before the summer of 324[385] a topical satyr play, the *Agen*, was staged. It was understandably eulogistic of Alexander (the 'Agen' of the title) and Harpalus appeared to be pilloried, for his relations with his Athenian mistress (the temple to Pythionice is explicitly mentioned) and his generous dealings with Athens. At the time of performance Harpalus was still on the Levantine coast, his flight to Athens still in the future, but both he and the city are threatened with retribution (Ath. 586D, 596B). The diplomatic situation worsened further after the Athenians

384 For bibliography see Seibert 1972a, 167–9. The fundamental article is still Badian 1961. On Harpalus' flight and arrival in Athens see now Jaschinski 1981, 23–44; Goukowsky 1978–81, 2.72ff.; Ashton 1983.

385 The exact date is hotly disputed. Cf. Sutton 1980, 75ff.; Goukowsky 1978–81, 2.65–77; Jaschinski 1981, 35–7.

admitted Harpalus into Piraeus, and for a short tense time war with Alexander hung in the balance (see below, p. 225). For the moment, in the winter of 325/4, Harpalus' movements were still nebulous and reprisals were necessarily deferred, but Alexander's suspicions of his subordinates were compounded. As his journey continued the native satraps were subjected to a rigorous and intimidating audit and the new appointees, all European, were not in general men of great distinction. Insubordination would in the future be less likely and less threatening.

As the winter deepened, Alexander approached the Carmanian capital, which Diodorus (XVII.106.4) names Salmus. It was, according to Nearchus (Arr. Ind. 33.7), five days' journey from the coast. The site remains a mystery,[386] but it was probably at the western side of the valley of the Halil Rud, in the general vicinity of the modern town of Khanu. The army was in an area of relative plenty but close enough to the coast to receive news of the progress of Nearchus' fleet. There Alexander sacrificed to commemorate his Indian victory and the emergence from the Gedrosian desert, and he held a musical and athletic festival, a drunken and festive affair, notable for the general acclaim achieved by Alexander's favourite Bagoas when he entered the winning chorus.[387] During the celebrations, if not before, news came of Nearchus' safe arrival at Harmozeia, the principal seaport of Carmania. The details are supplied for us by Nearchus, and they are open to justifiable suspicion. Nearchus has a rich story, full of dramatic *peripeteia*, in which he unexpectedly learns of the king's presence in the near vicinity, marches up country with a small escort, strangely missing the search parties sent out by his anxious king, and is finally retrieved, unrecognisable from brine and fatigue, to give the glad news of the fleet's survival to Alexander in person. The details of this Odyssey are beyond verification and there is very probably a good deal of imaginative embellishment.[388] What is certain is that the fleet arrived at Harmozeia without serious loss and that its arrival was announced to Alexander by Nearchus in person. It was a moment of general exaltation, and, if we may believe Nearchus (Arr. Ind. 36.3), Alexander renewed the sacrifices and prolonged the games. The celebrations which had begun commemorating the delivery of the army from Gedrosia ended with thank-offerings for the safe arrival of the fleet.

Nearchus now gave a formal report of his experiences, a report which later became the core of his literary memoirs, summarised by Strabo and Arrian.[389] It was a detailed log of times, distances and places, with picturesque details of the principal adventures on the voyage. After the monsoon winds sank, at the

---

[386] Stein 1943, 223; Goukowsky 1978–81, 2.54–8; Cook 1983, 187.

[387] Plut. Al. 67.8; Athen. 603A–B. Cf. Badian 1958a, 150ff.; *contra* Tarn 1948, 2.322.

[388] Pearson 1960, 134–5; Badian 1975, 160–2. For the traditional assessment of Nearchus' narrative see particularly Lehmann-Haupt in Papavastru 1936, 117–37.

[389] For the older bibliography see Seibert 1972a, 163–5. The most influential work has been Tomaschek 1890. See also Schiwek 1962; Eggermont 1975, 33–55; Brunt 1976–83, 2.518–25.

end of October, Nearchus sailed along the coast. He went westward from the mouth of the Indus, pausing at the mouth of the Arabis, where there was no trace of the wells dug by Alexander earlier in the season (Arr. VI.21.3; cf. *Ind.* 22.8). The natives had presumably filled them in, so forcing Nearchus' men to go 40 stades inland to find fresh water. It was only in Oreitis that they found provisions, which Leonnatus had stockpiled at the port of Cocala (see above, p. 143). From Oreitis they were in *terra incognita*, the land of the Ichthyophagi. The miserably poor inhabitants with their fire-hardened wooden spears could not deny the fleet a landing and were unceremoniously routed, but their resources were minimal. During the passage of the coast the explorers were confined to a sparse diet of fish supplemented occasionally by mutton and green dates. (cf. *Ind.* 26.7). The problems of the voyage become the problem of provisioning, and Nearchus' men descended like locusts on each settled community, stripping bare what scanty stores existed. A small walled town, not even named by Nearchus but probably sited near the mouth of the Dasht river, suffered particularly badly. Its inhabitants approached the strangers with meagre presents of food and allowed Nearchus to enter the walls. They were rewarded by a general attack and the promise that the town would be destroyed unless the harvest was surrendered (Arr. *Ind.* 27.7–28.9). Despite this successful extortion the fleet was reduced in a matter of days to the hearts of wild date palms and the lucky find of a herd of domestic camels (*Ind.* 29.5). Once they entered Carmania conditions became easier, with greater accessibility of cereals, fruits and vines. They finally beached at Harmozeia at the mouth of the Minab river, near the modern Bandar Abbas, where there was at last an abundance of provisions. From the mouth of the Indus they had travelled some 1,300 km and the voyage had taken around sixty days (Nearchus' record as preserved by Arrian is defective and allows no precise summation). It had been relatively free of disaster. Nearchus admitted that one vessel disappeared during the voyage with its entire Egyptian crew (Arr. *Ind.* 31.3) and occasional heavy winds caused damage, especially on the earlier part of the voyage (*Ind.* 23.3, 25.1). But the fleet had completed its passage relatively unscathed, despite the strange conditions and the inhospitality of the coast. Even an encounter with a school of whales passed without incident, as the creatures dived beneath the fleet and came up well astern (Arr. *Ind.* 30.2–7; Strabo 725). The prevailing south-easterlies, as predicted (cf. Arr. VI.21.2), had brought the expedition safely to Carmania.

Nearchus was duly commended for his report and had his commission extended to explore the coast between Carmania and Susa (Arr. VI.28.6, *Ind.* 36.4–5; cf. Curt. X.1.16; Diod. XVII.107.1). But he had set more in motion than schemes of coastal exploration. He had proved that it was possible for a fleet to traverse an unfamiliar desert coast without support from the land. That was the underpinning for plans of further conquest and exploration on such a gigantic scale as to be incredible to many modern scholars.[390] Alexander intended to conquer the western Mediterranean from Egypt to the Atlantic and apparently envisaged a circumnavigation of Africa by his fleet. The project is variously attested by sources of dubious authenticity, but there is no cogent reason to dismiss it as apocryphal. It would be naive to suppose that Alexander had no further ambitions of conquest, when even the contemporary Aristobulus noted that his appetite for empire was insatiable.[391] In fact he had a long-standing grievance against Carthage, having threatened war for her moral encouragement of Tyrian resistance in 332, and early in 328 he had evolved plans of expansion from the Black Sea (see above, p. 151). These embryonic projects had developed into a general ambition for conquest in the Mediterranean, and his last months of life were dominated by preparation for it. At his death papers were published revealing plans for the construction of 1,000 warships on the Levantine coast and a military road across North Africa as far as the Pillars of Heracles, together with naval installations in strategic locations. The number of ships involved is vast and the dimensions are equally impressive: all were to be larger than triremes (Diod. xviii.4.4). The supply of sailors alone must have exhausted the manpower, trained and untrained, of the Phoenician coast (Alexander recruited free men and slaves alike (Arr. vii.19.5)). But the ports of Cilicia and Phoenicia did produce a large number of vessels which turned the balance of the Lamian War in 322 (see below, p. 209), and Alexander had every reason to build up a fleet of unparalleled magnitude, intending as he was to attack both Carthage and Sicily. He knew his Philistus well[392] and will have been familiar with that historian's famous description of Dionysius the Elder's great arsenal amassed for the siege of Motye (*FGrH* 556 F 28). Dionysius was alleged to have built up a fleet of 400 warships, including quadriremes and quinqueremes, and the Carthaginian counterforce was even larger (cf. Diod. xiv.54.5).[393] The numbers have been criticised as suspiciously inflated, but there was no reason for Alexander to discount them or underestimate the military challenge he faced. If he was to conquer the Western Mediterranean he needed a naval force of unparalleled size.

The first steps to implement the new programme of conquest were taken in Carmania. It was to begin with a push south from Babylonia, down the west coast of the Persian Gulf. For that Alexander needed ships, ships that could not be supplied from the treeless plainland of Mesopotamia. Both Plutarch (*Al.* 68.2) and Curtius (x.1.19) mention instructions that warships be constructed in Phoenicia and Cilicia and then be transported in sections to the Euphrates. This scheme has nothing implausible in it. Warships had been

[390] See particularly Wilcken 1970, 2.369–84; Schachermeyr 1954; Badian 1968. The main sceptical discussions are Tarn 1948, 2.378–98; Hampl 1953; Andreotti 1957, 133–40; Kraft 1971, 119–27.
[391] Arr. vii.20.6; Strabo 741 (*FGrH* 139 F 55–6); cf. Arr. v.24.8.
[392] Plut. *Al.* 8.3. See, however, Brown 1967.
[393] Cf. Berve 1967, 1.241–4.

dismantled for easier transport in Pharaonic Egypt[394] and Alexander himself had used the technique in India on a small scale (Arr. v.8.5: Curt. VIII.10.3). Now the timbers of the Amanus and Lebanon were to be exploited massively for fleets which would operate in the Mediterranean and the Persian Gulf. When Alexander reached Babylon in the spring of 323 he found a vast new harbour under construction, capable of accommodating 1,000 warships, and the first of the warships from the Levant, 47 in all, had arrived.[395] At the time of his death an expeditionary force was poised for departure, ready to begin the work of colonisation and conquest in the Persian Gulf and Arabia which was the first stage of the western plans (see below, p. 169). Further fleets manned from Phoenicia and Syria would follow in due course, and ultimately the forces would divide, a fleet dispatched around the coast of Africa while Alexander took the main army to the Mediterranean coast to open the war of conquest.[396] That was the nucleus which had taken shape in Carmania. The details would have been modified over the following months and years as the results of the coastal voyages of reconnaissance which Alexander commissioned in 324 became available. The somewhat daunting reports of Archias, Androsthenes and Hieron of Soli must have had some negative effect (cf. Arr. VII.20.7–9). Whatever Alexander may ultimately have decided, there is no reason to doubt that in the early months of 324 he was fired by Nearchus' success to plan a much more ambitious naval project, a total circumnavigation of Africa which would take up the challenge of the Achaemenid voyages of discovery and solve the mysteries they had failed to unravel (cf. Hdt. IV.42–4).

In the depths of winter Alexander left the Carmanian palace and with a small detachment of cavalry and light infantry he went direct to Pasargadae, the ancient capital of Persis (Arr. VI.29.1). His exact route cannot be traced, but in all probability he pushed north towards the head of the Halil Rud and diverged eastwards through Sirjan and Sahr-i Bahbek, passing to the north of Lake Neyriz into the plain of Pasargadae.[397] Meanwhile Hephaestion took the bulk of the army, including the elephants, by a milder route closer to the coast (perhaps *via* Lar, Fasa and Shiraz). For the moment Alexander was isolated, with comparatively few men, and he had a delicate situation to face. The satrap of Persis, Orxines, had not been appointed by Alexander, but had usurped the position after the death of Phrasaortes, relying on his descent from Cyrus and his command of the Persian levy at Gaugamela (see below, p. 240). Alexander had no intention of ratifying the situation and had already determined Orxines' successor (cf. Arr. VI.28.3), but he had no way of

---

[394] Casson 1971, 136. For the transport of timber from the Lebanon in Babylonian times see Herzfeld 1968, 67–71.

[395] Arr. VII.20.3; Strabo 741.

[396] Plut. *Al.* 68.2; Arr. VII.1.1–3 (cf. IV.7.5; V.26.2). This tradition is usually discounted (see, however, Schachermeyr 1973, 539), but it is circumstantial and may derive from one of Arrian's major sources.

[397] Cf. Herzfeld 1908; Goukowsky 1978–81, 2.60–2.

gauging his popularity and was forced to move with extreme care, as he had done in Carmania.

Orxines was well aware of his peril and met his sovereign with an impressive entourage and even more impressive gifts (Curt. x.1.24). He was received politely, but scandal soon struck. Alexander had decided to pay his respects at the tomb of Cyrus, the small gabled chamber on its stepped stone base which today dominates the ruins of Pasargadae.[398] Once the tomb was unsealed, its contents proved sadly inferior to expectations. A couch and a battered coffin were all the funerary equipment and the corpse of the conqueror lay in pieces on the floor. The tomb, it was alleged, had been violated and an investigation was immediately launched. It was inconclusive. The group of Magi who had the hereditary task of guarding the monument were put to the torture but proved totally ignorant of the violation and were released. Orxines himself was under suspicion but was vindicated by circumstantial evidence (Strabo 730), and the identity of the culprits was (it seems) never known. The tomb itself was repaired and sealed under the supervision of Aristobulus, who left his personal account of the mysterious affair,[399] and Cyrus received decorations worthy of his greatness in life. But the episode had ugly repercussions. The tomb robbery was taken as evidence of lawlessness during Alexander's absence, and further allegations were soon to come. Alexander moved south to Persepolis, where the sinister Bagoas, his favourite eunuch, orchestrated an attack upon the satrap.[400] He was variously accused of despoiling royal tombs and arbitrary executions of his subjects, and he was summarily crucified (Arr. vi.30.2). Some of the allegations may have had substance – at all events a senior Macedonian official (the garrison commander?) was also executed (Plut. Al. 69.3); but Orxines' cardinal sin was surely his usurpation. Alexander had recently tried and punished a usurper in Media who had assumed the upright tiara of royalty (Arr. vi.29.3), and Orxines with his royal lineage had come dangerously close to doing the same in the heart of Persis. It was desirable that a future satrap should be non-Iranian but at the same time acceptable to the native populace. The chosen incumbent was Peucestas, Alexander's saviour at the Malli town, and he set himself to absorbing Persian *mores*. With his king's full approval he adopted Persian dress and learned the Persian language, and he was totally successful in wooing the Persians. By 317 he was wholly accepted by his subjects, who protested bitterly when Antigonus removed him (Diod. xix.14.5, 48.5). His orientalism evoked the resentment of the Macedonian rank and file as much as it pleased Alexander and it certainly was not widely copied by the other Macedonian satraps. Indeed Diodorus suggests, rightly or wrongly, that Peucestas was the sole

---

[398] Stronach 1978, 24–43.

[399] *FGrH* 139 F 51. Of the two versions Arrian's (vi.28.4–8) is the fuller and apparently the more reliable. He says nothing of an earlier visit to the tomb, which is unique to Strabo (730) and is suspect.

[400] Curt. x.1.30–7. Cf. Badian 1958a, 147–50, *contra* Tarn 1948, 2.321; Gunderson 1982, 190–5; Hammond 1983a, 157.

satrap whom Alexander allowed to assume native dress,[401] and that his position was unique. In Persis, the old imperial heartland, an alien ruler was more resented than elsewhere and conformity to local *mores* more essential. Peucestas was encouraged to assimilate himself to the local culture and win acceptance. He could then rule Persis without internal revolution, but he could never unite the populace to rebel against the royal authority. Elsewhere European satraps did not and were not encouraged to adopt the customs of their subjects. They remained obvious symbols of alien despotism, with more problems of internal security but with very little potential for insurrection in their own interests.

Hephaestion had now brought the bulk of the army safely to Persepolis, where under the gutted shell of the Achaemenid palace a second, smaller conflagration took place. The Indian sage, Calanus, was overcome by illness[402] and insisted on suicide by fire. He was drawn to the pyre on a royal Nesaean horse and was given a solemn farewell by the entire army, even the elephants joining in the valedictory war-cry (Nearchus ap. Arr. VII.3.6). Calanus died, silent and immobile, a paradigm of endurance commemorated in all Alexander histories,[403] and his death was celebrated by gymnastic and musical competitions. Less dignified was a competition in drinking unmixed wine which resulted in forty-one fatalities.[404] The intemperance of the court was now assuming legendary proportions, and the excesses of the transit of Carmania were to recur periodically throughout Alexander's last months of life. Alexander now took his united army along the royal road to the winter capital of Susa, which he reached in March 324,[405] spending around twenty-four days on the road (Diod. XIX.21.2). Just before he entered Susa he crossed a pontoon bridge, where he found Nearchus waiting with the fleet (Arr. *Ind.* 42.7–8). The voyage from Harmozeia had been relatively uneventful. Despite the desert shoreline they were amply supplied with food from the offshore islands, and Alexander had managed to do what he so signally failed to achieve in Gedrosia – he had sufficient grain stockpiled at the mouth of the Sitacus to provision the fleet during an overhaul which lasted for three weeks.[406] But, viewed in terms of exploration, the voyage was not a success. The coast was plagued by shallows and offered few anchorages. Even where the shore was approachable, strong tides made landing hazardous. As a result Nearchus kept mostly to the open sea, and explained later that he was unable to give accurate details on anything other than mooring places and sailing times.[407] The

---

[401] Diod. XIX.14.5; cf. Bosworth 1980b, 12.
[402] He fell ill at Pasargadae (Strabo 717) and died shortly afterwards in Persis (Arr. VII.3.1). Diodorus' localisation (XVII.107.1) is extremely vague.
[403] Strabo 717–18; Arr. VII.3.1–6; Plut. *Al.* 69.6–7; Diod. XVII.107.2–5. Cf. Berve 1926, 2 no. 396.
[404] Chares, *FGrH* 125 F 19 (Athen. 437A–B; Plut. *Al.* 70.1).
[405] Onesicritus *ap.* Pliny, *NH* VI.100 (in the seventh month after his departure from Patala); cf. Brunt 1978–81, 2.500.
[406] Arr. *Ind.* 38.9. See, however, Engels 1978a, 118.
[407] *Ind.* 40.9; cf. Strabo 732. For the itinerary see Schiwek 1962, 69–86.

voyage ended at the mouth of the Euphrates, where news came that Alexander had begun his journey to Susa. The fleet then went east to the mouth of the Pasitigris to meet the main army at the bridge, 60 stades from the capital (Strabo 729).[408] Alexander's forces were again united, in the third month after the separation in Carmania, and it was a merry meeting. As before there were sacrifices and games, and the senior officers were crowned for their achievements: Peucestas for his heroic behaviour at the Malli town (he had temporarily left his satrapy), Leonnatus for his victory in Oreitis, and Nearchus and Onesicritus for their successful voyage in the Indian Ocean. Hephaestion and the other bodyguards also received crowns (Arr. VII.5.4–6; Ind. 42.9–10). The celebrations marked the end of an epoch. The king had returned triumphant and honoured the humbler architects of his success.

A far more brilliant pageant was to follow. When he had left Susa late in 331, Alexander had installed there the royal princesses with instructions to learn Greek. They were waiting for him on his return, and Alexander honoured his earlier promise to establish them with husbands (Diod. XVII.38.1). That posed a problem. If they were married to their peers in the Persian aristocracy there was the danger that they would become instruments of revolution. Orxines and the Iranian pretenders recently executed were a warning that the conquest of Persia was not yet an accomplished fact, and it was dangerous to give Persian nobles the prestige of a royal marriage. On the other hand a precedent for mixed marriage had been established in Bactria/ Sogdiana, where Alexander had married the daughter of Oxyartes and apparently persuaded some of his nobles to do likewise. Now Alexander staged an elaborate, colossally expensive, marriage ceremony.[409] He and ninety-one other members of his court took wives from the Persian nobility in a five-day celebration, accompanied by musicians, dancers and actors recruited from all over the Greek world. The marriages took place in a special enclosure with a bridal chamber for each couple, and the ritual, unlike that of Alexander's first marriage, followed the Persian mode. Alexander himself took two princesses, the eldest daughter of Darius and the youngest daughter of Artaxerxes III. Hephaestion married Drypetis, another daughter of Darius, while Craterus had her cousin Amastris, a niece of the Great King. Perdiccas took the daughter of Atropates of Media, and Nearchus, Ptolemy and Eumenes married into the family of Artabazus, himself an agnate of the royal line. Finally Seleucus married Apame, a daughter of the Bactrian insurgent Spitamenes. Over eighty other marriages were celebrated, each pair receiving a dowry from the king, and all Macedonians who had taken Asian concubines were paid a gratuity.

The ceremony was clearly important and symbolic, but its nuances are lost to us. It has often been seen as the foreshadowing of a general fusion of the

---

[408] For the location and its problems see Bosworth 1987.

[409] Arr. VII.4.1–8; Plut. Al. 70.3; Diod. XVII.107.6; Justin XII.10.9–10. Note the vivid eyewitness description of Chares (FGrH 125 F 4 = Athen. 538B).

Greek and Persian aristocracies into a single ruling class.[410] That was certainly
not the case. There is no parallel process of promoting the Persian aristocracy,
none of whom was prominent at court. The only known Iranian Companions
are Oxyathres, Darius' brother (who was with Alexander hardly more than a
year), and Bagoas, son of Pharnuches. Apart from the quite extraordinary
response to the mutiny at Opis there was no attempt to use Persians in
positions of military command or political power. A select group of young
nobles was drafted into the *agema* of the Companion cavalry and equipped
with Macedonian weapons (Arr. VII.6.4–5), which may suggest some degree
of integration, but it was on a small scale: members of carefully selected
families were placed in the élite Macedonian cavalry squadron, but they were
not in positions of command and they were vastly outnumbered by Macedonians. The chiliarchy (or grand viziership) had fallen to Hephaestion,[411]
while his Companions assumed the purple robes of Achaemenid courtiers.
Indeed the predominance of Europeans in positions of power increased in the
latter years of the reign as Iranian satraps were removed from their posts in the
purges of 325/4 (see below, p. 240). The Susa marriages continued the trend.
Now the princesses of the Achaemenid house and the senior ladies of the
previous court were given husbands of Macedonian stock. Power had passed
to the European conquerors and the marriages symbolised the fact. Alexander
himself, the self-proclaimed successor to Darius and Artaxerxes, had married
a daughter of each of his immediate predecessors, and, as in the past, the
women of the royal house gave continuity to the regime. He was not only the
son of Philip but the proper King of Asia. The claims he had made at
Marathus (see above p. 64) were completely realised.

The bridegrooms were less happy with the new arrangement. (Arr.
VII.6.2). The king had used his powers of persuasion – or coercion – and his
senior staff accepted the marriages, even Craterus, who was otherwise notable
for his devotion to Macedonian tradition. But the unions did not last. Less
than a year after Alexander's death Craterus had divorced his bride and
betrothed her to Dionysius, the petty tyrant of Heracleia Pontica (Memnon,
*FGrH* 434 F 1 (4.4)), and apart from Seleucus' wife, Apame, none of the
Persian ladies is recorded playing any role in the age of the Successors. Taking
wives from the vanquished, even the nobility of the vanquished, was a
degradation, and there was hostility to Alexander's Asian consorts, culminating in the resistance at Babylon to the nomination of Rhoxane's child as the
future king (Curt. X.6.13, Justin XIII.2.9–10). The uneasiness of the senior
staff was echoed and amplified by the rank and file, who were increasingly
alienated by Alexander's assimilation to the role of King of Kings. His

---

[410] See particularly Droysen 1877, 1.2.241–2; Berve 1938; Schachermeyr 1973, 479–87; *contra*
Hampl 1954. For a full review of the problems see Bosworth 1980b.

[411] Schachermeyr 1970, 31–7. Compare Ptolemy's position as ἐδέατρος (Chares, *FGrH* 125 F 1),
which Berve 1926, 1.39–40, denied was a Persian court position. That runs contrary to the
explicit evidence of the lexicographers (Ael. Dion. *ap*. Eustath. *Od*. 1403.40; *Etym. Magn.*
315.37–40; 'Suda' s.v. ἐδέατρος).

adoption of Median dress had been a long-standing grievance (see above, p. 99), and now it was a consistent feature of court life; Alexander's regular costume was the white-striped purple tunic of the Persian king (worn with a Macedonian cloak) and the Persian diadem.[412] The court at Susa was now resplendent with the accoutrements of Achaemenid ceremonial. The old royal bodyguard of *melophoroi* was revived and attended the king, not replacing the Macedonian hypaspists but serving as a separate and complementary corps. Resentment gradually increased and as the fantastic extravagance at Susa continued day by day it must have been generally felt that Alexander had lost contact with his Macedonian origins. He was an absolute monarch, ruling in a markedly oriental style, and there was little, if anything, to distinguish the victorious army from the Persians they had conquered. Their mood was further exasperated by the arrival of the 30,000 Iranian youths from the north-east satrapies, specially trained in Macedonian arms and tactics (see below, p. 272). Their drill was impressive, their numbers more so, and their name, *Epigoni*, was ominous. They could replace the Macedonian phalanx as the striking arm of the royal army and in an emergency might even be used against the native Macedonians.[413] The disenchantment of the soldiery, exacerbated by the hardships of the desert march, was profound. Accordingly, when Alexander offered to discharge the debts of his troops, an act of largesse to commemorate the Susa marriages, his motives were queried. The registration of debtors which he required was interpreted as a means to compile a dossier of the improvident, and the men held aloof until Alexander promised automatic payment on the production of a loan contract. It is an instructive episode, revealing a disturbing lack of faith in the king's altruism and a surprising level of indigence in the army (the lowest figure for the debts discharged is 9,870 talents).[414] The conquests, despite the vast hoards they realised, had not enriched the bulk of the army, and the incubus of debt had obviously been oppressive.

XIX     **The final year**

In the spring of 324 the army left Susa, most of the land force marching with Hephaestion directly to the Persian Gulf. Alexander himself placed his infantry guard and some of the Companions on shipboard and sailed to the mouth of the Eulaeus (Karun), retracing the last stage of Nearchus' voyage.[415] As he had done in India, he went out into the open sea and sailed with a small fast squadron to the mouth of the Tigris. The majority of the fleet followed a

[412] Ephippus, *FGrH* 126 F 5; cf. Ritter 1965, 31ff.; Bosworth 1980b, 5–8.
[413] Diod. XVII.108.3; cf. Briant 1982b, 30–9; Bosworth 1980b, 17.
[414] Arr. VII.5.1–3 gives the full story with a total of 20,000 talents (so, more briefly, Justin XII.11.1–3). Plutarch has essentially the same story at the same time (*Al.* 70.3–6; cf. *Mor.* 339B–C) but gives the figure as 10,000 less 130, exactly the same as in Curtius' version, presented as a flash-back from the Opis mutiny (X.2.9; so Diod. XVII.109.2).
[415] Arr. VII.7.1–2.

cross canal which connected the Eulaeus with the lower Tigris, and the army was reunited close to the great estuary into which the Tigris then discharged. That was the site for yet another Alexandria, the later Spasinou Charax.[416] A native city, Durine, was transplanted to provide the agrarian populace and an élite of superannuated Macedonian veterans settled in a special quarter named Pellaeum after the Macedonian capital (see below, p. 249). Few of the settlers will have been happy with their new lot, and the ill feeling among the troops can only have increased.

From the meeting-point Alexander followed the Tigris northwards into Mesopotamia. As he went he demolished the series of artificial cataracts which made the river impassable to navigation. It was the late spring, the river at high water, and water was flowing in torrents over the holding dams which in quieter seasons diverted some of the flow to irrigation channels. The system was explained to Alexander as a defence against a naval attack and he contemptuously set the native labour force to work, removing the dams and making the Tigris accessible for his fleets.[417] Part of the motivation was certainly to prepare for the next year's offensive against Arabia, which would require an armada from Mesopotamia, and Alexander was making the Tigris amenable to his purposes; the river would receive naval traffic in either direction, and the new settlement at the mouth would serve as an arsenal. Alexander had no hesitation in destroying vital works of irrigation in the interests of improved navigability. On the Euphrates, on the other hand, there were no artificial barriers to naval transport and his preparations were wholly beneficial, improving the existing canal system, so that there was always an adequate flow of water (see below, p. 170). Nothing was to impede the passage of his fleets once the new campaign began. Reconnaissance expeditions were also commissioned, and the Arabian coast was surveyed as far as the straits of Hormuz. The intensity and scale of the preparations (see above, p. 152) are eloquent testimony of the importance in Alexander's eyes of his new projects of conquest. They were as yet scheduled for the indefinite future but they dominated his present actions.

By midsummer the army had reached Opis, a city on the Tigris slightly above the level of Babylon. There Alexander made a declaration that he would discharge all Macedonians who were unfit for service because of age or injury.[418] It was a logical enough move. The veterans would be replaced by fresh blood from Macedonia in ample time for the campaigns in the west, and after their return they would serve as a reserve for the home army. But the announcement brought to a head all the pent-up frustration of the past months and there was a wave of protest which was understandable if illogical. To return home might be intrinsically desirable but it was seen as a rejection. The

[416] Pliny, NH vi.138; cf. Nodelman 1960; Hansman 1967.
[417] Arr. vii.7.6–7; Strabo 740; cf. Schachermeyr 1973, 539.
[418] Arr. vii.8.1 (cf. Hammond 1980b, 469–71); Plut. Al. 71.2–9; Diod. xvii.109.2–3; Curt. x.2.13ff.; Justin xii.11. See Wüst 1953–4b; Badian 1965a.

king was discarding his old guard on the eve of new and profitable conquests.
At the same time the immediate prospect of staying on in an army now
dominated by oriental troops was by no means attractive, and both parties,
those retained and those discharged, shared a common discontent. That was
expressed in abuse and demands that the discharge should be general –
Alexander could continue the campaign with his father Ammon.[419] This
protest can hardly be dignified with the term mutiny that is universally applied
to it. The troops confined themselves to verbal complaints, but they were
contumacious and wounding. Alexander was no longer accustomed to traditional Macedonian frankness. Abuse, particularly from the men who had
refused his leadership at the Hyphasis, was intolerable and the implied
disobedience a challenge to his regal authority. He responded violently,
arresting thirteen of the most obvious demonstrators and having them
summarily executed. The rest he upbraided in a memorable harangue,
accusing them of rank ingratitude and rejecting the protests totally. They
could go home and leave him if they liked; he would turn to the conquered
peoples for support.[420] The final threat was rapidly put into effect. Alexander
stormed into the palace and secluded himself. Superficially his behaviour
recalls the Hyphasis mutiny, but this time there was to be no relenting. After
two days of seclusion he summoned selected Persians and offered them
commands. The Macedonian military titles were to be transferred to Persian
units.[421] Now, it seemed, the Macedonian veterans had no function in the
scheme of things, and the Persian units might not merely replace them but be
deployed against them. How far Alexander might have gone we cannot say, for
the Macedonians capitulated totally, throwing their arms before the palace
door and asking for forgiveness in the most abject terms. After a few days
Alexander received them and accepted their homage. He exchanged kisses
with their spokesman Callines and in a grandiloquent gesture embraced them
all as his kinsmen. The tension was broken, the hysterical lamentation
replaced by equally hysterical rejoicing.

Alexander had acts of his own to expiate. He had deliberately played on the
deep hostility between Macedonian and Persian and the deliberate promotion
of Persians had inflicted a profound shock on his rank and file. To salve the
wounds he held an enormous banquet of reconciliation, allegedly attended by
more than nine thousand guests. Appropriately he was surrounded by
Macedonians with Persians in the next circle and picked representatives from
other nations on the periphery. It was the same general arrangement as he had
observed in his receptions at Susa,[422] but on this occasion the preference
shown to the Macedonians was emphatic and significant. He and his entourage

[419] Arr. VII.8.3; Justin XII.11.6; Diod. XVII.109.2. Cf. Bosworth 1977a, 64ff.; contra Kraft 1971,
    64–5.
[420] Speeches are given by Arrian (VII.9–10) and Curtius (X.2.15ff.). On the question of
    authenticity see Tarn 1948, 2.290–6; Wüst 1953–4a; Brunt 1976–83, 2.532–3.
[421] Arr. VII.11.1–4; Plut. Al. 71.4–6; Curt. X.3.5ff.; Diod. XVII.108.3.
[422] Phylarchus, FGrH 81 F 41; cf. Bosworth 1980b, 8.

drew wine from the same crater and poured a solemn libation in which all guests joined. Alexander himself offered a prayer which among other things sought 'concord and community in empire for Macedonians and Persians' (Arr. VII.11.9). Concord was a natural concept to invoke after a period of conflict (cf. Diod. XVI.20.6), and community in empire was equally natural for a ruler whose imperial army comprised Iranian and Macedonian troops. The prayer indicated that both peoples figured in Alexander's imperial projects and that they should coexist peacefully. There was no deeper hint that he envisaged a hybrid master race fused from both nationalities or that he saw humanity as a brotherhood under his universal rule.[423] The prayer rather took its proper place in the ceremony of reconciliation, a pragmatic (almost cynical) device to relax the tensions he had played upon for his own ends. There was no alteration in policy. The Iranians continued to dominate within the army, in terms of numbers at least, and positions of power at court and in the satrapies continued to be monopolised by Europeans. Community in empire remained a pious prayer – nothing more.

The discharge was now put into effect. Ten thousand Macedonian veterans (and 1,500 cavalry) were selected for repatriation, over half the native component of his army (see below, p. 267). They were munificently paid, each man receiving a talent in addition to his full pay, and the column was placed under the leadership of Craterus and a number of senior officers, including Polyperchon and Cleitus the White. Craterus' health was not perfect (Arr. VII.12.4) and he was the natural choice for the command of the formidable army of veterans. It was probably a relief to have him away from court. He had been most outspoken in his defence of Macedonian tradition (Plut. Eum. 6.3; Al. 47.9), and, like Parmenion, had been regularly kept away from court on important but isolated military tasks. Alexander gave him a moving farewell, stressing his deep affection (Arr. VII.12.3), but no doubt breathed more easily after his departure. His assignment was complex. First he was deputed to Cilicia, to supervise the build-up of armaments for the forthcoming campaign in the Mediterranean,[424] and in due course he would bring his troops back to Macedonia and replace Antipater as regent in Europe, with overall responsibility for Macedon, Thrace and the Corinthian League. Antipater himself was to join his king in Asia with a fresh army of prime recruits. Superficially this was yet another preparatory move for the forthcoming war: Antipater, like the other officials in the western empire, was to bring his surplus forces to swell the royal armies (see above, p. 148). But in this case there were additional factors at play. Relations between the king and his regent had deteriorated over the years, and they had not been helped by a series of virulent letters from Olympias. The Queen Mother had retired to

---

[423] On these fantasies, whose most eloquent representatives are Berve 1938 and Tarn 1948, 2.399–440, see Andreotti 1956, Badian 1958b with Merlan 1950, and Bosworth 1980b, 2–4.
[424] Diod. XVIII.4.1, 12.1. Craterus was still in Cilicia at the time of Alexander's death. Cf. Badian 1961, 36ff.; Bosworth 1971b, 125–6; Schachermeyr 1973, 516–19.

Epirus after protracted wrangling with Antipater and devoted herself to undermining his position. Her daughter, Cleopatra, did the same from Macedonia, where she had resumed residence after the death of her husband, Alexander of Epirus.[425] This campaign of denigration by his womenfolk may have caused Alexander more irritation than concern, but it will have helped tip the balance against Antipater. The execution of his Lyncestian son-in-law had already caused tensions, and the failure to send the Macedonian reinforcements Alexander had demanded must have soured relations further. Nothing had resulted from the recruiting party Alexander had sent from Nautaca in the winter of 328/7 and now he probably felt that the only way to get his men was to order Antipater to bring them in person.

Antipater did not respond immediately. Instead he sent his eldest son, Cassander, to court (Plut. *Al.* 74.2), no doubt to explain his situation and to argue that the delicate situation in Greece (see below, pp. 225ff.) precluded his weakening the domestic army of Macedon. The mission was not an unqualified success, to put it mildly. Alexander found Cassander antipathetic and treated him with a brutal ferocity which had a life-long effect.[426] His attitude to the whole family of Antipater seems hostile. The news of the regent's replacement had encouraged embassies of complaint, which the king seems, if anything, to have encouraged, and it was widely believed that he was in deep disgrace. So much so that when Alexander died, it was immediately rumoured that he had him poisoned – and the Athenians ironically voted honours for his son Iolaus, Alexander's cupbearer and supposed assassin.[427] The rumours are wild and of course unverifiable, but the fact that they were made is eloquent testimony of the insecurity of Antipater's position. For the moment he may have won a stay of execution. The sources at least record no further instructions to vacate Macedonia, and Craterus had enough business in Cilicia to keep him (and his men) active until the end of the reign. There is no suggestion that his delay there was not officially approved. But Antipater's prospects were not bright and the time would inevitably come when he must make the choice between following the king's instructions and remaining in Macedonia, a rebel against the royal authority. Which way he would have gone we cannot possibly say, but it is disconcerting to read that he carried out secret negotiations with the Aetolians, Alexander's most uncompromising enemies on Greek soil.[428] At best his actions were ambiguous, and his detractors would make the worst of them.

Back at Opis Alexander was ready to move again. The needs of his huge entourage would have been a severe drain on the resources of Mesopotamia,

---

[425] Arr. VII.12.5–7; Diod. XVII.118.1; Plut. *Al.* 39.7; *Mor.* 180E (Olympias); Plut. *Al.* 68.4–5 (Cleopatra). Hammond 1980b, 473–5, argues that the two women shared an official *prostasia* ratified by Alexander.

[426] Plut. *Al.* 73.2–6. Cf. Bendinelli 1965. On Cassander's hostility to Alexander's memory see Errington 1976, 146–52; *contra* Goukowsky 1978–81, 1.105–11.

[427] [Plut.] *Mor.* 849 F. For the other evidence see Bosworth 1971b, 113–16.

[428] Plut. *Al.* 49.14–15. Cf. Badian 1961, 36–7; Bosworth 1977b; Mendels 1984, 137–40.

and it was a necessity as much as a pleasure to take his court from the stifling plainland to the Zagros uplands, where he would spend the autumn at Ecbatana, the traditional summer capital of the Persian kings (Strabo 523–4). He was in no hurry and there were frequent recreational halts, including a visit to Bagistane (Bisutun). There the army enjoyed the amenities of rich gardens and awesome scenery in that famous sanctuary, which may already have been associated with his ancestor Heracles,[429] before moving up the valley of the Gamasiab to the Nesaean fields,[430] the pasture of the royal horses of the Achaemenid court. Once again the reality proved inferior to expectations. Instead of the reputed number of 150,000 less than 50,000 were found in pasture; the majority were said to have fallen victim to brigands (Arr. VII.13.1; Diod. XVII.110.6). The last six years with civil war and usurpation in Media may well have encouraged the Cossaeans of the Zagros to make inroads on the Nesaean horses, which would have been attractive breeding stock. For the moment Alexander ignored the depredations, treated his men to a month's relaxation in the Nesaean plain, and moved on to Ecbatana, which he reached after seven days' march.

His arrival was the occasion for prolonged celebrations. The march itself had been a relaxed affair with repeated carousing en route; and Atropates, the satrap of Media, had had ample notice of his arrival at the capital and could make extravagant preparations for entertaining his king – his future and even his life might depend upon it. At the same time there was the inevitable agglomerate of visitors, ambassadors and entertainers, and it was most probably here that Alexander received the news that Harpalus had been given refuge in Athens (see below, p. 225). The result was an upswell of hostility against the city, which reached its climax at a sacrifice to Dionysus.[431] Atropates entertained the entire army, and the assembled ambassadors outdid each other in offering crowns and honorific decrees to the king. The culmination was a promise by the distinguished courtier, Gorgus of Iasus, to provide panoplies and siege engines on a gigantic scale for the forthcoming blockade of Athens. Fortunately the situation was soon alleviated by Harpalus' arrest and escape from Athens. War did not materialise, but tensions were at their highest in the autumn of 324. They had their release in the symposium. The sacrifice was followed by several days of athletic and scenic games, accompanied by heavy drinking sessions among the Companions. In the course of the celebrations Hephaestion had fallen ill and, though under medical treatment, he suffered a sudden decline and died on the seventh day of his illness.[432]

---

[429] Diod. XVII.110.5; cf. Bernard 1980b.
[430] Cf. Herzfeld 1968, 15–24.
[431] Ephippus, *FGrH* 126 F 5 (Athen. 538A–B). The value of the fragment has been contested (cf. Jacoby, *FGrH* IID.437–8; Pearson 1960, 64–5; Errington 1975a, 54–5), but the details are circumstantial and credible (except possibly the immense value of Gorgus' crown) and the personages involved are otherwise attested. Cf. Heisserer 1980, 169–93.
[432] Arr. VII.14.1; Plut. *Al.* 72.2; Diod. XVII.110.7–8.

The death came as a profound shock. It is difficult to assess the importance of Hephaestion at court but it seems that he was closest to the king, emotionally and in policy, of all the staff. He had enthusiastically abetted the adoption of Persian ceremonial, in sharp contrast to Craterus, and as chiliarch he was second only to Alexander in the court hierarchy. Since 330 he had commanded the first hipparchy of the Companions and he was one of the most senior bodyguards. All sources stress the closeness of his personal relationship, but he was not indispensable at court; in the last years he was repeatedly used to command secondary army columns and was on occasion away from Alexander for months on end. But there is no doubt that he enjoyed Alexander's particular affection and incurred the jealousy of other senior members of the hierarchy. His clashes with Craterus were legendary, and there had been repeated quarrels with Eumenes, the last reconciled only a few weeks before his death.[433] Suspicions of foul play were probably rife. The king executed Hephaestion's unfortunate physician, and his senior officers – notably Eumenes – were careful to honour their dead colleague in the most extravagant terms. There seems little doubt that there was a heavy atmosphere of distrust and suspicion around the king in those days. But Alexander's main reaction was hysterical grief, recalling Achilles' mourning for Patroclus. The details were perhaps exaggerated, as Arrian claims (VII.14.2–3), to commend his love of his friend or to reprobate the undignified self-indulgence of his grief, but there was general agreement that it was extreme. He kept three days' fast over the corpse, proclaimed a period of empire-wide mourning and, with the approval of an oracle from Ammon, he institutionalised a heroic cult for his friend (see below, p. 288). The body itself was conveyed to Babylon by Perdiccas, his successor in the chiliarchy. There Alexander projected an immense funerary monument. According to Diodorus it was to be a vast brick cube a stade square and over 200 feet high, its base surrounded by the gilded prows of quinqueremes and its walls decorated with five successive friezes.[434] The edifice was never completed, perhaps never even formally begun, but 10,000 talents were earmarked for it and craftsmen assembled from the whole civilised world. These plans were made public after Alexander's death when Perdiccas referred them to the Macedonian army (to be quashed)[435] and are certainly historical, parallel on a larger scale to the funerary games for which Alexander amassed 3,000 competitors, to celebrate not Hephaestion's but his own obsequies (cf. Arr. VII.14.10).

The enormity of the funeral plans is wholly consistent with the other attested plans of Alexander at this period. The projects which Perdiccas had the army reject at Babylon included the building of a tomb for Philip on the model of the Great Pyramid, and there were six grandiose temples, each to be

---

[433] Cf. Berve 1926, 2 nos. 317, 357, 446.
[434] Diod. XVII.115.1–5; Plut. Al. 72.5; Arr. VII.14.8; Justin XII.12.12. Cf. Wüst 1959.
[435] Diod. XVIII.4.2ff. Cf. Badian 1968 with full discussion of earlier literature; some doubts are evinced by Hornblower 1981, 94–6.

built at a cost of 1,500 talents, as well as an unsurpassable sanctuary of Athene at Ilium. These architectural extravaganzas match the grandiose scheme of conquest in the west and are the physical expression of the state of mind which led him on the political level to issue regal edicts to the Greek world in its entirety and in the religious sphere to parade as a god manifest. Alexander, like Arrian (VII.30.2), was aware that he was a man like no other man. His conquests had set him beyond any conqueror in history (so he had repeatedly and self-consciously demonstrated), and the material monuments he left behind him were to eclipse the past and deter emulation. Even his grief went beyond the normal modes of conduct.

The autumn had turned to winter before Alexander's first outburst of mourning ended. Now he turned to campaigning, and Plutarch (*Al.* 72.4) claims that he was deliberately seeking solace in war. That is an over-simplification. The chosen target was the Cossaeans of the Zagros, the descendants of the Cassites of Babylonian times, who now occupied the mountain territory bordering on Media. In particular they dominated the secondary, direct route between Ecbatana and Susa, the road which today passes through Dezful and Korramabad towards Nahavand and Hamadan.[436] Their society was tribal and pastoral, and from time to time they made raids on the agrarian communities that bordered on their territory. In general, however, their relative independence had been tolerated by the Achaemenid regime, and the Persian kings had made regular payments to them when they moved directly through the mountains between Ecbatana and Babylon (Strabo 524 = Nearchus, *FGrH* 133 F 1g). Alexander may have received the same request for passage money that he received from the Uxians (see above, p. 89), and in all probability he considered the Cossaeans responsible for the depletion of the Nesaean horses. That, and his general intolerance of independence, was sufficient for him to launch a winter campaign, dividing his army into columns and starving the mountaineers out of their fastnesses. After forty days he received the submission of some Cossaean tribes at least and installed 'cities', military settlements to control insurgency (Diod. XVII.111.6). The rural work-force was provided by impressed Cossaeans, transformed from pastoralists to tillers of the soil. Nearchus saw this as an extension of civilisation,[437] but the beneficiaries will hardly have been so enthused. The conquest was certainly transient. Nothing more is heard of Alexander's foundations, and, when Antigonus took an army from Susa to Ecbatana in the summer of 317, he found the Cossaeans independent and extremely hostile (Diod. XIX.19.3–8). Alexander may have intimidated the people for the moment, but there was little attempt or intention to pacify the region completely.

Early in 323 the court began its progress back to Babylon. As it reached the plain, embassies began to flock in from most quarters of the western world. Delegations are recorded by Arrian from Epidaurus in Greece and from the

---

[436] Diod. XIX.19.2–8. Cf. Briant 1982a, 57ff.
[437] Arr. *Ind.* 40.8; cf. Briant 1982a, 100–12.

Libyans, Bruttians, Lucanians and Etruscans from the west.[438] Further
delegations were waiting at Babylon, and the last months of the reign were to
see a continuous stream of embassies. The most impressive audience was
given on his first return to Babylon, when Alexander heard a mass of
representations from mainland Greece and received embassies from Carthage
and communities of the west as far afield as Spain. There were also approaches
from the northern Balkans, from the European Scyths and the Illyrian and
Thracian peoples.[439] All had good reason to solicit the king's favour. The
plans of western conquest had been more than a year in gestation, ample time
for rumours to penetrate the entire Mediterranean coast, and most of the
delegations named had real grounds for trepidation. Carthage was the first
overt target of western conquest (see above, p. 67). The Bruttians and
Lucanians had been the chief adversaries of Alexander of Epirus[440] and could
reasonably expect reprisals from his nephew. The Etruscans were less openly
threatened, but there had been protests, in Athens particularly, against their
depredations on navigation in the Adriatic (see below, p. 207), and Alexander
himself is said to have taken notice (Strabo 232). In the north conditions were
chaotic after the disastrous débâcle of Zopyrion, Alexander's general in
Thrace, who had botched an invasion of Scythian territory and after penetra-
ting as far as the river Borysthenes was soundly defeated, his army annihilated
(c. 326 B.C.).[441] In the aftermath of the disaster there was a Thracian uprising,
and the Odrysian prince, Seuthes, managed to maintain his independence
beyond Alexander's lifetime.[442] Any or all of the Balkan communities had an
interest in presenting their own version of affairs and diverting onto other
heads the just anger of the king. Similarly the cities of Greece were
preoccupied with the problems of implementing the Exiles' Decree (see
below, p. 224) and there were embassies of thanksgiving or protest, according
to the interests of the ambassadors, until the end of the reign. We are not
informed what rulings Alexander made. According to Diodorus
(XVII.113.3–4) he arranged the embassies in categories, hearing first delegates
on sacred business, then those who had brought gifts, those who had disputes
with their neighbours, those who were on private missions, and finally those
who were appealing against the return of the exiles. The highest priority was
naturally given to the Panhellenic centres, including the sanctuary of Ammon,
which Alexander ranked second after Olympia. Next came the delegates who
offered submission in the form of presents or acceptance of his regal rulings.
Those with objections were placed firmly at the base of the hierarchy.
Alexander would accept fresh subjects with magnanimity and return gift for

---

[438] Arr. VII.15.4–6 (cf. 14.6).
[439] Arr. VII.19.1–2; Diod. XVII.113.1–2. Cf. Jaschinski 1981, 122ff.; Brunt 1976–83, 2.495–9;
contra Tarn 1948, 2.374ff.
[440] Cf. E. Pais, Storia dell' Italia antica 2.272–3; Berve 1926, 2 no. 38.
[441] Justin XII.2.16–17; Curt. x.1.44; cf. Berve 1926, 2 no. 340; Ziegler, RE x.763–4.
[442] Curt. x.1.45; Diod. XVIII.14.2; cf. Michailov 1961.

gift, but his projects would not change and the war in the west was inescapable.

An intriguing but historically unimportant question is posed by Arrian, who cites the late writers Aristus and Asclepiades for a tradition that Alexander received an embassy from Rome and prophesied the future greatness of the city. He adds that the episode was omitted by Ptolemy and Aristobulus, which has predisposed many modern scholars to judge it unhistorical. Certainly in the late version in which it is cited by Arrian the story is written in the full knowledge that Rome became a world power, and it is embellished with implausible and anachronistic details.[443] But that was not the case with every tradition of the embassy. Cleitarchus mentioned the bare fact that an embassy was sent (*legationem tantum ad Alexandrum missam*)[444] and there is no suggestion that he considered it a particularly noteworthy event. What is more, he may not have recorded it in the context of the reception of Babylon. If the Romans did send a delegation to Alexander, it could have arrived at any time before his death. Cleitarchus would have noted it casually in a part of his narrative not excerpted by Diodorus or Justin/ Trogus (as one of many minor delegations), and neither Ptolemy nor Aristobulus considered it worth special mention. The Romans had as much reason to approach Alexander as any people in Italy. They were embroiled in the opening hostilities of the Second Samnite War and it was prudent to gain the good will of the conqueror of the east, who was shortly to impinge on the western Mediterranean. Possibly they too had a defence to make, if Alexander had already voiced complaints about the piratical activities of the people of Antium, under Roman sway in Latium (Strabo 232). There is no historical difficulty in their having sent an embassy, a minor affair which had little impact at court. In later years it became the raw material of romance, when Aristus and Asclepiades gave Alexander an inspired vision of the future world power, but Cleitarchus wrote before 300 B.C. without the benefit of hindsight and had no propaganda to spread. If he noted the presence of a Roman embassy, it is likely to be an authentic record: he had no motive for invention. In that case the Romans did make an overture to Alexander. It was a moment pregnant with symbolism, which neither side appreciated. For Alexander the embassy was trivial, for the Romans less so, but any advantage or disadvantage that accrued from the meeting was rapidly cancelled by the king's death.

Alexander's death was apparently forecast in Babylon. The details are obscure, but it is agreed that the native astrologers sent word to him, warning against entering Babylon. Various motives are suggested. According to Diodorus (XVII.112.2–6) they claimed that destiny could be averted if he rebuilt the temple complex of Esagila and bypassed the city, whereas one of Arrian's sources (Ptolemy?) claims that there was chicanery: the Babylonian

---

[443] Arr. VII.15.5–6. Cf. Tarn 1948, 2.21–6; Pearson 1960, 232–4; *contra* Sordi 1964; Schacher-meyr 1970, 218–23; Weippert 1972, 1–10.

[444] Pliny, *NH* III.57 = *FGrH* 137 F 31. Cf. Hamilton 1961; Badian 1965c.

priesthood wished to forestall the reconstruction of Esagila and continue to enjoy the revenues which would otherwise be devoted to the upkeep of the temple (VII.17.1–4). Whatever truth underlies these traditions, it seems clear that Alexander took some notice of the warning. Aristobulus (*FGrH* 139 F 54) stated that he avoided a western approach to the city, and, complying with the advice of the priests, he took a detour to the north and followed the Euphrates towards the eastern suburbs. When the approach proved impassable because of marshland, he was forced to make a more orthodox entry, against the warnings of his religious advisers. Whether there was friction between the king and the Babylonian priesthood we cannot say, but their sombre prophecy seems designed to keep Alexander away from the city. They may, as Arrian suggests, have feared regal interference and some infringement of their prerogatives, but that would occur whether or not the king was physically present in Babylon. Another ground of apprehension, not mentioned in the sources, was the construction of the monstrosity that was to support the pyre of Hephaestion, which would overtop and eclipse the temples of the native gods and require the demolition of a significant part of the city wall. The priests might well wish to prevent Alexander coming in person to devote his prodigious energies to the task. If they could persuade him to bypass the city and give first priority to the rebuilding of Esagila (as Diodorus implies), the monument might be indefinitely delayed. Later their delaying action would inevitably be attributed to corruption.

In Babylon the king gave his celebrated audience to the embassies from the west and set to work clearing the ground for his rebuilding of Esagila (and also for Hephaestion's monument). His major preoccupation, as always, was military. The first fleet for his Arabian expedition was almost ready.[445] Nearchus had already arrived with the remnants of his command, sailing up the Euphrates from the Persian Gulf, and the first consignment of warships from the Levant had been floated south from Thapsacus, after being conveyed in segments from the Mediterranean coast. The contingent was small, forty-seven vessels in all, but it was to be vastly supplemented by further products of the Mediterranean shipyards and the cedar groves of Babylonia were ravaged to construct an additional fleet. To provide the necessary facilities a massive harbour was dredged at Babylon with facilities for more than 1,000 warships, and a recruiting agent, Miccalus of Clazomenae, was sent to the Phoenician coast with a fund of 500 talents to procure crews. The first object was Arabia. The reconnoitring expeditions sent out by Alexander had penetrated as far as the Musandam peninsula, and the islands of Icarus (Falaika) and Tylus (Bahrain)[446] in particular were reported fertile and promising for settlement. The legendary abundance of spices in Arabia was

---

[445] What follows is based primarily on Aristobulus (*FGrH* 139 F 55–6) as reported by Arrian VII.19.3–22.5 and Strabo 741. For Alexander's western plans see above, p. 152.

[446] Arr. VII.20.3–8; cf. Högemann 1985, 80ff. For the later Seleucid settlement on Falaika see Jeppesen 1960; Cohen 1978, 42–4, Roueché and Sherwin-White 1985.

also an attraction (Arr. VII.20.2), and Alexander planned not merely to conquer the southern littoral of the Persian gulf but to establish permanent settlements there. A pretext for invasion was ready to hand in that the Arabs had sent no embassy nor paid any act of homage to him. In this they were unique in the area. Aristobulus also had a whimsical story that the Arabs worshipped two gods alone, Uranus and Dionysus, and that Alexander considered himself worthy to be a third, if he conquered them and gave them their traditional independence.[447] Strange though it is, the story comes from a contemporary and it has some corroboration. When Antiochus III visited the Arabian city of Gerrha, he was asked not to revoke what was given them by the gods, namely eternal peace and freedom (Polyb. XIII.9.4). Peace and freedom were guaranteed by the gods, and Alexander felt that he could make the same guarantee *under his sovereignty*. Once conquered, the Arabs would enjoy peace under his protection and he (or his satrap) would see to the continuance of their free institutions. It was the same assurance given the Lydians in 334 and the Ariaspians in 330. Under Alexander's rule there was (in his eyes) perfect freedom, and he was under no illusions that he could assume the role normally taken by the ancestral gods of the Arabs. Whether he expected worship we cannot say, but he certainly considered himself the equal, if not the superior, of the Arabian deities. He also intended conquest and permanent subjection of the natives.[448] To what extent it is difficult to tell. The island of Tylus (Bahrain), the fertility of which had been extolled by Androsthenes and Archias, was certainly a primary objective, a base for colonisation, as was the great entrepôt of Gerrha on the coast opposite. This was one of the main distribution points for the spice trade with Arabia Felix. Its inhabitants transported their wares on rafts up the Euphrates (Aristobulus, *FGrH* 139 F 59 = Strabo 766) and had the resources in later years to pay Antiochus the royal gift of 1,000 talents of frankincense and 200 of oil of myrrh (Polyb. XIII.9.5). But this was probably the beginning. Arrian (VII.20.2) suggests that Alexander had designs on the spice lands proper and intended to press as far as the Yemen. In that case the invasion would be a protracted affair. The south coast of the Persian Gulf would be annexed and equipped with military bases, and from them the conquest of Arabia Felix would be launched. Even that was only the prelude to the wider plans of western conquest, which were still dominant in Alexander's calculations. On his way to Babylon he had commissioned Heracleides of Argos to build a war fleet to explore the shores of the Caspian, to determine whether it was a gulf of Ocean or an affluent of the Black Sea (Arr. VII.16.1–2). This was more than a mere voyage of discovery, important though that was. If Alexander were ever to accomplish his intention to conquer Pontus and link his empire in the east with the western world (see above, p. 113), he needed detailed geographical and strategic data, and

---

[447] Arr. VII.20.1; Strabo 741. Cf. Högemann 1985, 120–35.
[448] See, however, Tarn 1948, 2.394–5; Andreotti 1957, 147–8; *contra* Schachermeyr 1973, 538–46.

Heracleides' main task was to establish whether there were adequate arteries of naval communication between the Pontus and the far east. It was the same work of reconnaissance as had been done by Archias, Androsthenes and Hieron in the Persian Gulf, but Heracleides' expedition was to be far more substantial, involving a war fleet, and he may have been intended to do more than explore.

While the invasion fleet was massing in Babylon, Alexander overhauled the drainage system of the Euphrates, clearing the mouths of some canals and blocking others, so as to optimise its flow for purposes of navigation. The major activity took place at the mouth of the principal drainage canal, the Pallacotta. This diverted the surplus of water at flood time and dispersed it into lakes and marshes near the coast, which formed the boundary of Arabian territory. At low water the mouth of the canal was blocked by a huge work force of Babylonians under the control of the satrap, but the soft alluvial subsoil made the work exceedingly difficult. Alexander accordingly cut a new mouth for the canal thirty stades upstream, where the ground was rocky and provided a firm base for the seasonal dam.[449] For the moment it was high water, and he sailed down the Pallacotta towards the Arabian lakes, where he established the last of his Alexandrias, its Greek population provided by his mercenary forces. In the future invasion it would provide a base for the invading army, comparable to Alexandria Charax at the mouth of the Tigris. Alexander himself retraced his voyage up the Pallacotta, ensuring that its mouth would be dammed when the flood waters of the Euphrates ebbed. The Arabian marshes would then be partially drained and vulnerable to an invasion by land (Aristobulus, *FGrH* 139 F 56 = Strabo 741), while the Euphrates itself retained ample water to carry his fleet.

At Babylon the gathering of forces was nearly complete. The fleet was ready, its morale high, and there were spectacular naval manœuvres on the Euphrates (Arr. VII.23.5). The army was swelled by mercenary forces led from Asia Minor by the satraps of Lydia and Caria, but the most impressive contingent was provided by Peucestas, who had levied a force of 20,000 Persian infantry, including Cossaean and Tapurian mountaineers. These native troops were incorporated in the Macedonian phalanx, complete with their traditional weapons, the bow and javelin, which could not be more incompatible with the Macedonian *sarisae*. Macedonians provided the first three ranks and the rear rank and in the centre of each vertical file were twelve Persians.[450] They were to provide the numbers to give momentum to the three ranks of *sarisae* at the front and they allowed Alexander to eke out his slender reserves of Macedonian veterans. The new phalanx was a far cry from the body that had crossed the Hellespont in 334, but their adversaries were lightly armed Arabs, hardly a match in pitched combat for any trained heavy infantry. Until the reinforcements from Macedon arrived with Antipater they

---

[449] Arr. VII.21.2–7; Strabo 740–1; cf. Högemann 1985, 145–9.
[450] Arr. VII.23.3–4; cf. Bosworth 1980b, 18–19.

would take the brunt of the fighting alongside the Macedonian-trained *Epigoni*. The new army was never put to the test. Alexander's final illness supervened. Towards the end of May his official embassy returned from the Siwah, giving Ammon's seal of approval for the hero cult of Hephaestion (see below, p. 288). The news was greeted with jubilation.[451] Regular sacrifices were followed by festivities, food and drink being allotted to the army by companies. The king himself drank late into the night with his friends and was invited to a further carouse by Medeius of Larisa. This was a more intimate celebration with twenty guests present, and the drinking was prodigious, the stuff of which legends were made. It was soon alleged that Alexander drank himself to death or, worse, was poisoned through the sinister machinations of the sons of Antipater. The climax, it was claimed, was an exchange of toasts in which the king drained a bumper of undiluted wine, twelve pints in capacity.[452] That led to a dramatic collapse accompanied (the vulgate tradition states) by a violent spasm of pain, as though he had been struck by a violent blow.[453] Death supervened rapidly, as his doctors were incapable of handling the illness. This tradition is slanted to emphasise the features of the illness compatible with poisoning and its origins date to the immediate aftermath of Alexander's death. Then the Athenians voted honours for Antipater's son, Iolaus, the supposed assassin ([Plut.] *Mor.* 849 F), and the contemporary Onesicritus may have spoken openly of poisoning (*FGrH* 134 F 37). These allegations come from contemporary rumour and were disseminated by persons hostile to Antipater, notably the Queen Mother, Olympias, who was to desecrate Iolaus' tomb when she occupied Macedonia in 317 B.C., taking revenge for her son's death (Diod. XIX.11.8). That is eloquent evidence of the insecurity of Antipater's position at the end of the reign, but beyond the fact that he had an interest in Alexander's death it proves nothing. Given the suddenness of the king's demise, rumour would inevitably run rife.

There is a much less sensational version, quoted by Arrian (from Ptolemy?) and Plutarch from the 'Royal Diary'.[454] This document gave a selective day-by-day narrative of the king's actions, going back at least ten months, to the month of Dios 324, and its compilation is attributed to the chief secretary, Eumenes of Cardia, and a certain Diodotus of Erythrae (of whom nothing is known). The entries for each day were relatively brief, giving a bare summary of the king's public and private actions with a distinct emphasis on the royal symposia and their after-effects, and the last ten days of Alexander's life are recorded in sketchy outline. The banquet with Medeius took place on the eighteenth of the Macedonian month of Daesios (end of May 323). When it ended Alexander had already developed a fever and spent the night in the

451 Arr. VII.24.4. Cf. Plut. *Al.* 72.3, 75.3.
452 Ephippus, *FGrH* 126 F 3; 'Nicobule', *FGrH* 127 F 1–2.
453 Ephippus, *FGrH* 126 F 3; Diod. XVII.117.1–3; Justin XII.13.7–10; *Metz Epit.* 99; Plut. *Al.* 75.5; Arr. VII.27.2. Cf. Merkelbach 1977, 164ff.; Bosworth 1971b, 113–16.
454 Arr. VII.25.1–26.3; Plut. *Al.* 76. These and other fragments are printed by Jacoby, *FGrH* 117.

bathing chamber. After a day of attempted convalescence he resumed his normal activities with the fever still upon him, sacrificing each morning and holding repeated conferences with his senior officers in preparation for the Arabian expedition. By 24 Daesios the fever had intensified dangerously. The king was now bedridden and his senior commanders held vigil overnight. The following day his voice failed and he lay desperately ill in the palace of Nebuchadnezzar. Eventually (26 Daesios) the rank and file, convinced that he was dead, forced their way into the bedchamber and filed past their king, who was mute but still conscious. He finally lapsed into a coma and died towards evening on 28 Daesios (10 June 323).[455] The record is vivid but its authenticity has been questioned.[456] There are discrepancies, some of them serious, in the versions quoted by Plutarch and Arrian, and the common tradition has one apparent glaring anachronism: seven senior officers are said to have enquired about Alexander by incubation in the sanctuary of Sarapis. Now the Hellenistic deity Sarapis is generally acknowledged to be a creation of the reign of Ptolemy I,[457] and there can have been no temple in Babylon during Alexander's reign. Either the information is fiction, retrojecting the healing cult of Sarapis to an earlier generation, or there is a complex piece of religious syncretism – a Babylonian god was later identified as the Hellenic Sarapis (in which case our versions of the Diary have been edited in the course of transmission) or there actually was a shrine in Babylon devoted to the underworld god of Memphis, Oserapis, the prototype of the Ptolemaic Sarapis.[458] A solution is not easy, and, even if the Diary were vindicated as a contemporary compilation by Eumenes, that would not guarantee the total reliability of the document. Given that there were rumours of poisoning, it was natural that Eumenes, who was a guest at the fatal banquet, edited an account which made the death seem due to illness, possibly exacerbated by drink. In this version Alexander is not stricken in the middle of his cups but succumbs to a fever which only gradually incapacitates him. Until the very end court business proceeded almost as normal. The details given (if Eumenes was the ultimate author) were presumably accurate but they were details carefully selected to exclude suspicions of foul play.[459] In that case the record is too partial for any diagnosis of the illness to be attempted. We can rule out the violent and rapid demise described in the vulgate tradition, but all that remains is a fever intensifying over ten days and ending in coma. Whether the

[455] Sachs 1955, no. 209; Samuel 1962, 46–7; Lewis 1969.

[456] Pearson 1954–5, 429–39; Samuel 1965; Bosworth 1971b, 117–21; Brunt 1976–83, 1.xxiv–vi. For the older theory that the Diary was an official court journal, compiled by Eumenes as part of his regular duties, see Wilcken 1894; Kaerst, *RE* v.2749ff.; Berve 1926, 1.50–1; Hammond 1983a, 4–11.

[457] Fraser 1967; 1972, 1.246–50; *contra* Welles 1972.

[458] For various solutions see Lévy 1913; Wilcken 1922–37, 1.79ff.; Bosworth 1971b, 119–21; Goukowsky 1978–81, 1.199–200.

[459] See Wilcken 1967, 236: 'the journals of these last days, which were drawn up later, probably to refute by an official document the lie that he was poisoned'.

disease was malaria[460] or some other tropical ailment will never be known. It may well have been assisted by the indubitable debilitation of Alexander's constitution after his chest wound at the Malli town and the continual epic carouses of his court, and the progress of the illness could have been artificially and maliciously accelerated. Under the circumstances foul play was bound to be alleged, but the evidence, then as now, is too scanty for any allegation to be sustained.

[460] Cf. Schachermeyr 1973, 561; Engels 1978b; Hammond 1980a, 323 n. 116. For suggestions of strychnine poisoning see Milns 1968, 255–7; Green 1974, 476–7.

# 3

# Epilogue: the shape of things to come

Alexander's death led inevitably to the dismemberment of his empire. There was no immediate successor, and from the outset the marshals at Babylon had no intention of empowering a genuine king. If we may believe Curtius and Justin, their first plan was to await the birth of the child conceived by Rhoxane.[1] Nothing guaranteed a male issue, and it was patent that the ultimate monarch would be a figurehead. The regency would be everything. This settlement with its unborn king was immediately denounced as preposterous. Incited by the phalanx commander Meleager, the infantry mutinied and pressed the claims of Arrhidaeus, Alexander's mentally deficient half-brother. The result was a compromise. Arrhidaeus was proclaimed king, assuming the regnal name of Philip (III), and a few months later Rhoxane's child, fortunately a son, joined him in the kingship, named Alexander (IV), after his father. It was a dual kingship, as contemporary documents show,[2] but this strange pairing of fool and infant was never more than a political expedient. The kings were the puppets of their protectors, first of Perdiccas, who became the effective guardian of the kings at Babylon and then of Antipater, who assumed the guardianship at Triparadeisus (321) and transferred the hapless rulers to Macedonia. The farce ended abruptly late in 317, when Arrhidaeus' wife, Eurydice (a granddaughter of Philip II), challenged the current guardian, Polyperchon, and attempted to enforce regal authority.[3] She and her husband were dead within months, and the ultimate victor of the power struggle in Macedon (Antipater's eldest son, Cassander) interned the infant Alexander with his mother at Amphipolis, pointedly denying them royal privileges. The phantom of royal power remained for a few years. In 311 Cassander was appointed general of Europe 'until the majority of Alexander, son of Rhoxane' (Diod. XIX.105.1). Then the curtain came down. The last of

---

[1] Curt. x.7.8; Justin XIII.2.14. See the full discussion of Errington 1970, 49–53, and, for full bibliography, Seibert 1983, 84–9.

[2] E.g. *OGIS* 4, lines 5–7; *Hesperia* 37 (1968) 222; *MDAI (A)* 72 (1957) 158. See further Habicht 1973.

[3] On these events see Errington 1986, 114–20.

the Argeads was murdered with his mother, and the bodies were concealed on Cassander's orders.[4]

But the process of dissolution was well advanced even before the demise of the kings. The settlement of Babylon had effectively separated Macedon from the eastern empire; Antipater and Craterus were placed over the Balkans in a very obscure division of authority,[5] while Perdiccas commanded the royal forces in Asia. During the civil wars that ensued the separation of Macedon became more and more an established, recognised fact, until Cassander in 316 entrenched himself as the effective ruler. Similar developments occurred elsewhere, particularly in the western empire, where the most able of Alexander's officers were assigned satrapies. Egypt became Ptolemy's undisputed territory after his successful defence of it against Perdiccas' invasion. He regarded the country as 'spear-won'[6] and governed it without reference to any higher authority. The main challenge to separatist ambitions came from Antigonus. The most effective satrap of Asia Minor during Alexander's lifetime, he was appointed general of the royal forces operating against Eumenes and the remnants of the armies of Perdiccas (320). Once appointed, he set his sights on the total control of Asia, blatantly ignoring the directives that came from the royal guardians in 317. His campaign against Eumenes took him as far east as Persia, and he had no hesitation in making and unmaking satraps, deposing Peucestas and Stasander, who owed their appointments to Alexander himself.[7] His ambitions were temporarily confirmed in the peace of 311, when he was ceded the command of 'all Asia' (Diod. XIX.105.1), and in 306 he and his son Demetrius assumed the title and dress of kingship. His rivals (Ptolemy, Cassander, Lysimachus and Seleucus) immediately followed his example.[8] Instead of a single kingdom there were now five. Egypt and Macedon were separate entities as they had traditionally been. The Thracian territories to the Hellespont fell under Lysimachus; and there were two large imperial agglomerates, the lands from the Aegean to the Euphrates under Antigonus and those from the Euphrates to the borders of India under Seleucus. The Hellenistic world had begun to take shape. The ideal of a unified empire was not lost. Antigonus and Demetrius pursued it to the end. But an ideal it remained. The conquests of Alexander were effectively divided into separate power blocks. Their frontiers might change dramatically, as happened after Ipsus and Corupedion, but it was practically impossible for one ruler to dominate the rest.

The world empire was gone – irretrievably. Alexander, however, left

---

[4] Diod. XIX.105.1; Justin IX.2.5; Paus. IX.7.2.

[5] The sources are vague and divergent, and the position of Craterus is particularly difficult to elucidate (for the various suggestions see Seibert 1983, 84ff.). Fortunately there is little doubt that Macedon was effectively separated from the rest of the empire. Antipater's victory in 321 (and Craterus' death) ensured that the division was permanent.

[6] Diod. XVIII.39.5, 43.1; XIX.105.4; XX.76.7. Cf. Hornblower 1981, 51.

[7] See particularly Diod. XIX.48.1–5.

[8] Diod. XX.53.2–4; Plut. Demetr. 18 (see, in brief, Austin 1981, 65–7; Seibert 1983, 136–40).

behind an ideal of monarchy which was seductive and persistent. Immediately after his death (if not before) his generals imitated his mannerisms and dress. As early as 322 Leonnatus moulded his physical appearance to match that of Alexander. He had a contingent of royal Nesaean horses and his own *agema* of Companions.[9] Alexander's characteristic blend of the *kausia* (the Macedonian hat) and the diadem became virtually a badge of royalty, while the pomp and ceremonial of the court in his latter days inspired subsequent dynasts to emulate his conspicuous waste. His relations with the gods were also imitated. Seleucus claimed Apollo as his heavenly father and maintained that his kingship had oracular sanction (from Branchidae).[10] On a less lofty sphere the Lagids of Egypt claimed the same divine lineage as the Argead house, Ptolemy tracing his origins back to Heracles and his wife, Arsinoe, to Dionysus.[11] Deification of the living ruler was now established. As early as 311 B.C. Antigonus was honoured at Scepsis with the full trappings of altar, cult statue, sacred precincts and an annual festival (*OGIS* 6), and four years later both he and his son received a veritable cornucopia of cult honours at the hands of the Athenians. The reigning king was indeed a god among men, and, like Alexander's, his power was autocratic, with no practical constraints upon his freedom of action. It became almost a philosophical commonplace that as monarch he was *nomos empsychos*, law incarnate. Autocracy, as we have seen, was characteristic of Macedonian kingship long before Alexander, but the conquest of Persia and the adoption of oriental court protocol added a new dimension. There was scarcely a parallel for the Alexander of 324 who calmly ordered the restoration of exiles throughout the Greek world, regardless of existing laws and conventions, whether national or international. Alexander had introduced a new style of government, a new concept of regal grandeur for the successor kings to emulate.

He left little else. His unfulfilled ambitions of western conquest were formally annulled by the Macedonian army at Babylon. The dead king's *hypomnemata* were read out by Perdiccas and rejected by the troops as impossibly extravagant. That ended plans of external conquest. Later dynasts such as Pyrrhus might have dreamed of effecting them,[12] but in practice the first necessity was to consolidate the territory within the empire. Several of the satraps at Babylon needed to fight for the commands they were given. Lysimachus found himself in a bitter struggle with the resurgent Odrysian kingdom of Seuthes, and Eumenes required the intervention of Perdiccas and the grand army before he could establish himself in Cappadocia (322). The ensuing civil wars and the fragmentation of the empire meant that aspirations were more limited and were directed against rival dynasts rather than external

---

[9] A vivid description in Arr. *Succ.* F 12 (Roos) = 'Suda' s.v. Λεόννατος.
[10] Günther 1971, 66–73; Hadley 1974, 58.
[11] Satyrus, *FGrH* 631 F 1 (full genealogy); *OGIS* 54, lines 1–5.
[12] Plut. *Pyrrh.* 14; cf. Polyb. v.101.8–10. Austin 1986, 456, rightly emphasises the necessity for Hellenistic kings to acquire territory. The ambitions were doubtless great but the possibilities for realising them were strictly limited.

peoples. Ptolemy might include Cyrenaica in his greater Egypt and extend his frontier south below Elephantine, but that was more than matched by Seleucus' renunciation of the far eastern lands. The Indus satrapies had probably been conquered by Chandragupta by the time Seleucus established himself at Babylon in 312 (Justin xv.4.22), and shortly before Ipsus Seleucus recognised the new regime by ceding the territory east of Arachosia in return for 500 elephants.[13] Many of Alexander's foundations (including the famous Alexandria in Caucaso) came under Mauryan rule, and Seleucid control contracted to the west of the Iranian plateau.[14] Further conquest was impractical. The matrix of empire was laid down by Alexander, and the struggle for supremacy was internal.

The main casualty of the process of fragmentation was Macedon itself. Alexander's prodigious demands for his national troops had exhausted the reserves of infantry. The strains were obvious by the time of his death, when Antipater had difficulties mobilising an army to combat the alliance of the insurgent Greek states. The reason, we are told, was the debilitating effect of the reinforcements sent to Asia.[15] Few of Alexander's men returned. The majority remained in Asia, fuelling the armies of the contending dynasts (and a more terrifyingly professional military machine can never have existed). The manpower of Macedon necessarily declined, and the decline was accelerated by migration to the new centres of power in Asia and Egypt. By the end of the fourth century the forces at Cassander's disposal were a fraction of those bequeathed by Philip in 336.[16] Macedon was no longer the colossus bestriding the Greek world. Even when Cassander was secure in power, he had to face repeated challenges from Antigonus and Ptolemy, who embroiled themselves in the politics of the Greek city states. It was not, as has often been said, the end of Greek independence. The clash of the dynasts had an effect similar to that of the rivalry between Athens and Sparta during the Peloponnesian War. Each contender favoured the political establishment that suited his interests. Like his father Antipater (and Philip II), Cassander favoured oligarchy and the tight restriction of political rights. That allowed the Antigonids to champion the cause of democracy and autonomy. The political factions in each city allied themselves with the rival monarchs, exactly as they had with the hegemonial city states of the past. In some ways the Ptolemies and Seleucids took over the role of Persia and Egypt in the earlier fourth century. They supplied employment for exiles, both as mercenaries (or military settlers) and, at a higher level, as friends and advisers. Demetrius of Phalerum enjoyed a somewhat chequered exile in Egypt after he fell from power in Athens. More significantly Callias of Sphettus, acting as a mercenary com-

---

[13] Strabo 724; App. *Syr.* 55.282; cf. Seibert 1983, 145–7.
[14] In the north-eastern satrapies, however, the Seleucids maintained some control until the middle of the third century B.C.
[15] For full argument see Bosworth 1986.
[16] The forces mustered to counter Demetrius' invasion in 302 numbered 29,000 foot and 2,000 horse (Diod. xx.110.4; cf. Bosworth 1986, 10).

mander for Ptolemy I, was able to take his forces from the island of Andros to support the revolt of the Athenian *demos* against the garrison of Demetrius (287 B.C.), and he subsequently represented Athenian interests with great success at the Lagid court.[17] Later the two Athenian statesmen Chremonides and Glaucon found refuge and support with Ptolemy II and continued to promote their city's interest at Alexandria.[18] Macedon remained a constant threat to Greek autonomy but it never regained the total dominance Philip had exerted after Chaeronea.

Thanks to Alexander, the Balkans had only secondary importance. The political focus necessarily changed. In part this was a financial consequence of Alexander's conquests. The accumulated resources of the Persian empire had been dispersed among the treasuries of the east, the most significant reserves at Babylon and in Cilicia; and they were disbursed first by the satraps appointed at Babylon and then by the monarchs who came to control them. In November 316, even after Eumenes had passed through Cilicia, Antigonus was able to take 10,000 talents from the royal treasury at Cyinda (the annual revenue of the satrapy, which he annexed for himself, came to 11,000 talents).[19] Egypt had always been wealthy; and under Ptolemy II the annual revenues of the monarchy are said to have totalled 14,800 talents, the reserves in the treasury a staggering (surely apocryphal) 740,000 talents.[20] The Seleucid revenues may not have matched that figure, but they were by any calculation formidable. Ptolemy III is alleged to have acquired a booty of 40,000 talents from a single war against Seleucid Syria, and just one of the treasuries he annexed (in Cilicia) contained 1,500 talents.[21] This financial underpinning allowed the dynasts in the east to attract a multitude of military settlers to populate the civic foundations of Seleucid Syria and Mesopotamia and to provide the nucleus of the Ptolemaic armies. Indigent or ambitious men would tend to move eastwards where employment could be expected and fortune was a realistic aspiration.

The process of transition was gradual. At first the European lands benefited from the influx of wealth from Alexander's conquests. Vast accumulations of private riches are attested, and there were grotesque displays of conspicuous wealth. At a regal level we need look no further than Demetrius' grandiose naval preparations of 288 B.C., when the keels of no less than 500 ships were laid in the shipyards of Greece, including 'fifteens' and 'sixteens' of a size never before witnessed.[22] At a less exalted level we have an eyewitness report from the same period of a prodigious banquet given in Macedonia by a certain Caranus, who clearly deployed the riches amassed two generations before in a

[17] Cf. Shear 1978, with modifications by Osborne 1979 and Habicht 1979, 45–67. See also Austin 1981, 78–83.
[18] Teles p. 23 (Hense²); Cf. Étienne and Piérart 1975, 56–8.
[19] Diod. XIX.56.5.
[20] Porphyry, *FGrH* 260 F 42; App. *Prooem.* 10.40.
[21] Porphyry, *FGrH* 260 F 43; cf. *FGrH* 160 F 1, col. II, Austin 1986, 465.
[22] Plut. *Demetr.* 43.4–5; cf. Casson 1971, 138–40.

vulgar and sensational orgy of gastronomic indulgence.[23] But there was no fresh accrual of wealth. After Alexander, Macedon did not have the strength and opportunity for new wars of annexation, and there was no booty from abroad to swell the domestic revenues. The decline was slow but inevitable, thanks to the great shift in focus which Alexander's reign produced. From one perspective he had discharged the functions of kingship unsurpassably. He had acquired territory and secured booty to an unprecedented degree. On the other hand he had created a new kingdom and saw himself as the heir of Darius as much as the heir of Philip. By the end of his reign the capitals of his empire were the capitals of the Great King – Babylon, Susa and Ecbatana, and the spoils of conquest were concentrated at Babylon rather than Pella. It was a personal dynasty on a vast scale. Alexander ruled the world as his father had ruled Macedon, concentrating power in his own hands and delegating wealth and office to his Companions. In nationality the Companions remained overwhelmingly Hellenic. The few Persians admitted to that select body were as much the king's men as the Greeks attracted to the court of Philip. As for the Macedonian commons, they had lost whatever importance they ever had by the time of Alexander's death. The 'mutiny' at Opis had ended in the total humiliation of the Macedonian rank and file. Subsequently the majority of the veterans were demobilised, and those who remained were blended with eastern troops. The Epigoni from the north-eastern satrapies were equipped and trained in Macedonian style, and the native Macedonian phalanx was deliberately filled out with Persian infantry who retained their traditional weapons. Nothing showed more clearly that Alexander's subjects, Macedonian and non-Macedonian, stood on the same level. By this time Alexander's empire was supranational. It did not depend on his legitimacy in Macedon, rather upon the degree to which he could enforce his wishes. That was practically unlimited. His financial resources were unmatched and his armies, no longer predominantly Macedonian, could effectively deter resistance. Whatever sanctions had traditionally modified the behaviour of Macedonian kings, they were no longer applicable.

The model of Alexander's last years inevitably affected his Successors. Although some of the monarchies established had regional bases of power, notably in Egypt, their character was firmly dynastic, with few bonds of common culture between ruler and ruled. The king exercised power through his army, which in turn was financed by the resources of his kingdom. His territory provided the economic basis for his regime, but he was in no sense responsible to his subjects. His 'friends' shared the benefits of kingship, but whatever power they exercised was delegated and revocable. Only in Macedon proper did anything like a national monarchy survive. There Cassander

---

[23] Athen. 128C–139D. The source, Hippolochus, was writing in the lifetime of Theophrastus (before 288) but apparently in the second generation after Alexander's conquests (Athen. 129A).

tended to style himself 'king of the Macedonians',[24] ostentatiously distancing himself from his fellow monarchs, who ruled heterogeneous populations with (at best) a small military élite of Macedonian origins. The new kingdoms were military creations, their strength dependent on the personality of the ruler and the quality of the court he was able to attract to himself. Their legitimacy rested on conquest, their continuity on an effective army, adequately financed. In all these aspects Alexander was the great exemplar, the symbol for all ages of absolute monarchy.

The abiding importance of Alexander lies more in the field of moral and philosophical debate than in practical politics. In the first generation after his conquests his name was invoked as justification for empire. The territories dismembered by his successors were acquired by his conquests, and the satraps and princes directly appointed by him had a moral entitlement to office which was difficult to challenge.[25] At a different level the troops who had fought with Alexander enjoyed a reputation for invincibility which made them a prime acquisition in the years after his death. With them at least Alexander's memory remained evergreen; Eumenes was able to control the troublesome Silver Shields by symbolically establishing the dead king as their spiritual commander. All meetings of his commanders were held before an empty throne bearing the royal insignia and the decisions taken were deemed to be the orders of Alexander.[26] The device was extended in 317 when Eumenes reached Susa and needed to assert himself against a squabbling coterie of rival satraps. All the commanders opposing Antigonus met in committee before the empty throne (Diod. XIX.15.3–4). But that was an admitted sophistry, to produce a unity of command where there was in fact none; and what was evoked by Eumenes was not any concrete recollection of the dead king, rather a symbol of unified political power. A symbol Alexander remained, most notably in Egypt, where his embalmed corpse lay in state at Alexandria in a special mausoleum (the *Sema*) which also contained the sarcophagi of the Ptolemaic kings. The dead Alexander was now the talisman of the Ptolemaic house. It was an ironic outcome. Ptolemy's separatist ambitions had done much to destroy the unity of the empire of the living Alexander. Now his body and name were being used to underwrite a regime whose very existence would have been anathema to him. In the same way Seleucus claimed that his kingship was spiritually endorsed by Alexander. His coins from 305 onwards depict the deceased king with an elephant scalp head-dress[27] at exactly the same time as Seleucus formally ceded the eastern satrapies so painfully acquired by Alexander. From the territorial renunciation he gained the 500 Indian elephants which brought him victory at Ipsus and destroyed any hope

---

24 Aymard 1967, 86, 103. Note the qualifications of Errington 1974, 23–5.
25 Cf. Arr. *Succ.* F 1.36 (Roos). Seleucus, whose command was *not* ratified by Alexander, sought legitimacy in a dream (Diod. XIX. 90.4).
26 Diod. XVIII.60.4–61.3; Plut. *Eum.* 13.8; Polyaenus IV.8.2; cf. Curt. x.6.13–15, with Errington 1976, 140–1.
27 For the dating see Hadley 1974, 52–4.

of the reunification of Alexander's empire. The king's name and image were invoked as his conquests were renounced and dismembered.

The debate over legitimacy lasted a mere generation. After that Alexander was a symbol and nothing else. For subsequent ages he typified the world conqueror, and his territorial acquisitions were a standing inspiration and challenge to successive dynasts. Our evidence is strongest for the Roman period. Pompey, whose very name (Magnus) evoked the Macedonian conqueror, notoriously modelled himself upon Alexander from his boyhood, adopted Alexander's mannerisms and patently saw himself recreating his conquests in the east. The same applied to Trajan, who sacrificed to Alexander in Babylon and, in conscious imitation, sailed down the Euphrates to the ocean, reporting in his dispatches that he had gone further than the Macedonian king. With Caracalla imitation became a mania, to the extent that he recreated a phalanx of Alexander, entirely Macedonian in composition and equipped with the authentic armament of the period. By this time Alexander was a favourite theme of the rhetorical schools. His ambitions, now more legend than history, were debated by aspiring orators, who would advise or dissuade the great king, envisaged on the point of crossing the ocean to conquer new worlds. The trivial bombast set on record by the elder Seneca[28] reflects three centuries of literary, philosophical and rhetorical simplification. Alexander had become a stock figure of popular literature, an example to be quoted endlessly for praise or blame. That unfortunately is his abiding fate. His achievements in his lifetime were soon forgotten and the world shaped by his conquests had few tangible memorials of him. What remained was and is a *folie de grandeur*. Every aspiring general at some stage must ask himself '*Alexander potuit, ego non potero?*' The human cost is all too often forgotten, but it should be set on record. Millions might justifiably lament the glamour and mystique with which Alexander's campaign endued the dirty business of imperial annexation. *Non utile mundo / editus exemplum, terras tot posse sub uno / esse viro* – Lucan's epigram may be exaggerated and one-sided, but with reference to Alexander's posthumous reputation it is only too true.

[28] Sen. *Suas.* 1; *Contr.* vii.7.19. *Suas.* 4 deals with the problem whether or not to enter Babylon in the face of adverse portents.

# II

## THEMATIC STUDIES

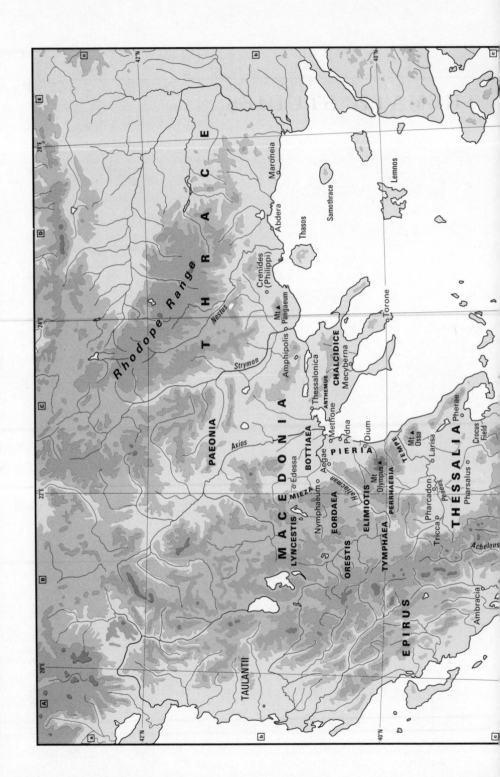

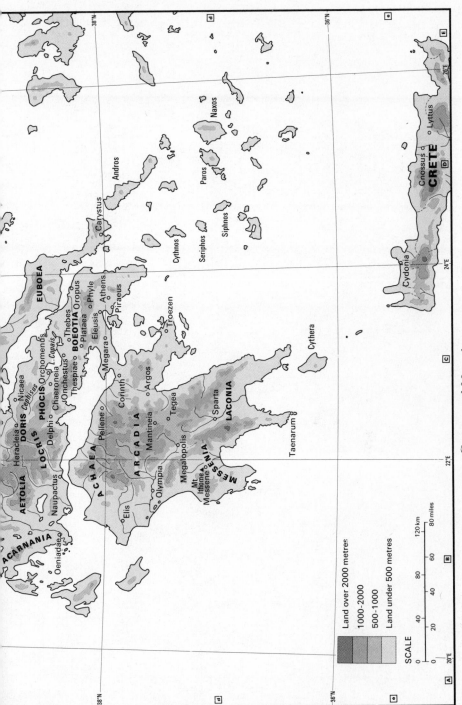

*11. Greece and Macedon.*

# A

# Mainland Greece in Alexander's reign

## 1    Alexander and the Corinthian League

The battle of Chaeronea marked an epoch for all ages. With the dead was buried the freedom of Greece. So Lycurgus was to lament in 330 B.C., and for all the rhetoric it is not too great an exaggeration (*Leocr.* 50). The crushing military defeat was compounded by a political settlement which gave Philip *carte blanche* to intervene wherever and whenever he pleased. The states of southern Greece, most of them under sympathetic governments, had formed individual alliances with him, and the constitutive meeting at Corinth had welded them together in a common peace. All the parties agreed to remain at peace with each other, to maintain the constitutions in force at the time the peace was established and to campaign against violations of the peace when called upon by the council and its *hegemon*. All this was deceptively bland. As all Greeks knew, the history of multilateral agreements over the last century had been a history of exploitation by the dominant power, whether Sparta or Thebes. A peace treaty might guarantee autonomy for all Greeks, but the most powerful state would impose its own concept of autonomy while ignoring the most blatant violations in its own sphere of interest. The Spartans, spurred on by Agesilaus, had insisted that the autonomy of the cities of Boeotia involved the dissolution of their federal government, but they had totally ignored their own subjection of Messenia. A decade or so later the Thebans became the champions of Messenian autonomy but took it as axiomatic that there was a single indissoluble Boeotian state – the existence of the federal constitution was not negotiable (cf. Xen. *Hell.* VII.1.27; Diod. XV.70.2). Autonomy, as Pericles had observed (Thuc. 1.144.2), was largely a question of definition; and it was not hard to see how Philip would define it. Governments such as the Theban oligarchy, which he himself had imposed, could expect to be preserved and to have the sanctions of the League imposed if they themselves were attacked. Other regimes would have been less confident. It was not necessarily in Philip's interest to preserve them, and, if they were undermined, there was no guarantee that the council would give a sympathetic hearing. There is clear evidence of anxiety at Athens immediately before Philip's death. The law proposed by Eucrates in the ninth prytany of 337/6 prohibits all attempts to subvert the democracy and establish tyranny.[1] It specifically forbids the council of the Areopagus to hold sessions after the democracy has fallen. Whatever the political undercurrents behind the legislation, it reflects serious disquiet and the possibility of constitutional change. The danger that seems envisaged is government by a tyrant or oligarchical junta with the support of the council of ex-magistrates – not unlike the oligarchic council of 300 which Philip imposed upon Thebes. Certainly the Athenian legislators of 336 had no expectations that the democracy would be protected by the common peace. It seems rather to have been framed in an atmosphere of crisis and insecurity.

Philip's assassination came only a year after the establishment of the League of Corinth, and there is no evidence how he intended it to operate. It cannot have been widely popular, for the news of his death caused profound unrest throughout southern Greece. At Athens there was predictable jubilation. Embassies were sent to exhort other cities to support the cause of freedom, and there were even secret overtures to Attalus in Asia (Diod. xvii.3.2; Plut. *Dem.* 22.2) – both acts flagrant breaches of the common peace. There were voices of moderation. Phocion in particular pointed out that the Macedonian army had lost only one man by Philip's death. The *demos*, however, was ready to be swayed by the rhetoric of Demosthenes, who was confident that the young madman Alexander would never stir beyond the confines of Macedon. Elsewhere the Thebans voted to expel the Macedonian garrison, while in the Peloponnese there was agitation at Argos, at Elis and in the Arcadian League. It was probably at this juncture that the Messenians expelled the sons of Philiades, who headed the oligarchic regime which Philip had supported. Alexander later restored them to power, enforcing the terms of the common peace ([Dem.] xvii.4, 7), but it required his intervention to maintain his partisans in a city which might have been supposed the most automatic of Macedonian allies (cf. Polyb. xviii.14.5–7). In western Greece there was also trouble. The Aetolians voted to restore exiles to Acarnania – a contravention of the common peace compounded by the fact that they were once more operating as a united federal state despite Philip's dissolution of their *koinon*.[2] In Ambracia the Macedonian garrison was expelled and democracy introduced (Diod. xvii.3.3), again a violation of the peace. This general movement was eloquent testimony of disaffection with Macedonian hegemony; and quick action was necessary if the political unrest was not to extend and deepen into military resistance.

[1] Meritt 1952, 355–9, no. 5 = *SEG* xii.87. The legislation has been interpreted as an attack on Demosthenes (cf. Sealey 1967, 183–5); but there is no reason to doubt that there was real fear of subversion when the measures were passed (cf. Ostwald 1955, 119–28; Gehrke 1976, 66–7; but see Will 1983, 28–30).

[2] For this reconstruction, based on the undoctored text of Theopompus, *FGrH* 115 F 235, see Bosworth 1977b. There seems no other explanation of the virulent and sustained Aetolian hostility to Macedon.

From the outset Alexander acted decisively and with moderation, no doubt with the advice of his veteran diplomat Antipater. He convened the Thessalian League, wooing it with promises (unfortunately not specified) and stirring reminders of their common Heraclid ancestry. Consequently he was voted his father's position as *archon* of the League and also received their endorsement as *hegemon* of the common peace, which was now re-enacted in his name.[3] The same thing happened in central Greece, where he convened the Amphictyonic council at Anthela and had its members (obviously those who could be summoned to the Gates at short notice) repeat the Thessalian vote. Continuing into Boeotia he cowed the Thebans and produced a change of heart at Athens. With no immediate prospect of allies against Macedon the *demos* could only make terms, renewing the alliance in his name and showering honours upon him. Meanwhile it voted to evacuate the countryside, as had been done after Chaeronea, and prepared for the worst. These worries proved unfounded. After Demosthenes discreetly deserted the official embassy on the slopes of Cithaeron his fellow delegates were graciously received by the young king. Peace and alliance were accordingly negotiated.

At Corinth came the final act of this first drama. The *synedrion* was assembled, perhaps only those delegates whose cities had not yet recognised him, and Alexander was confirmed in the office which his father had created – leader of the Greeks in the war against Persia. Both Arrian and Diodorus emphasise that the vote primarily concerned the war in Asia, and there can be no doubt that the *synedrion* of Corinth both policed the common peace and passed legislation for the offensive against Persia.[4] Although it is often denied, the Corinthian League was an alliance. It comprised states which were each bound to Macedon by bilateral treaties; and it was perfectly natural that they should create a general alliance under the leadership of the Macedonian king, acting as the spiritual successors of the Hellenic League of 480 B.C. As a council of allies the delegates passed general decrees for the conduct of the war. Just as the Hellenic League had forbidden medism, so the Corinthian *synedrion* issued decrees prohibiting collaboration with Persia, particularly in the form of mercenary service (Arr. 1.16.6; III.23.8). Such general enactments were largely cosmetic, for once the war was carried into Asia the *synedrion* would have no control over it. Power was in fact vested in

---

[3] Diod. XVII.4.1 mentions only the voting of hegemony in Greece, a vote repeated at the Amphictyony and in Corinth (4.2, 9). Justin XI.3.2 refers only to the federal magistracy of Thessaly. For various attempts to reconcile the discrepancy see Bosworth 1980a, 50. I assume that the authors have selected different aspects of a single complex transaction, as occurs in their reports of the foundation meeting at Corinth in 338/7.

[4] Arr. 1.1.2; Diod. XVII.4.9. The character of the Corinthian League has caused endless debate (for earlier bibliography see Seibert 1972a, 76–7). Some have argued that the common peace was central and that there was no alliance as such; the Persian War was a kind of informal vote, taken at Corinth because it was a convenient forum (see, most recently, Hammond and Griffith 1979, 2.628–31). Other scholars have accepted that there was both a peace and an alliance, but, following Ulrich Wilcken (1917), they have tended to argue for distinct constitutive acts, first the establishment of the peace and then the declaration of war against Persia. The view expounded in the text is more fully documented in Bosworth 1980a, 46–9.

Alexander, the *hegemon*,[5] who could represent himself as the elected leader of voluntary allies in a crusade of vengeance (Arr. II.14.4; cf. Curt. IV.1.13). The corollary of alliance was peace. Once more the delegates at Corinth might be said to follow in the footsteps of the members of the Hellenic League, who had sealed their alliance with the reconciliation of all existing hostilities (Hdt. VII.145.1). As *hegemon* of the League Alexander naturally had a dual function, to supervise the operation of the common peace and to lead the allied forces against Persia. Quite properly the compact is described retrospectively as *the* alliance and *the* peace by Arrian (III.24.5), denoting not two separate covenants but two indissoluble facets of the single settlement.[6]

The allies had obligations under both heads. As participants in the war in Asia they had to contribute forces to the army of invasion. The Athenians had already been assessed for ships and cavalry in Philip's reign (Plut. *Phoc.* 16.4) and the demand was renewed in 336 (cf. Diod. XVII.22.5). We hear much more about the common peace, thanks to a fiery speech in the Demosthenic corpus (XVII), which the ancient commentators assigned, probably correctly, to Hypereides. This oration, probably delivered in 331, indicts the Macedonians for repeated abuses of the peace treaty and cites a number of its clauses. This evidence is corroborated by the extensive inscription documenting the League which Antigonus and Demetrius established in 302, basing their regulations on the model of Philip and Alexander (Moretti, *ISE* no. 44; Schmitt, *Staatsverträge* no. 446). It is clear that the major provisions in the common peace of 338/7 were repeated. Freedom and autonomy were guaranteed; constitutions were to be left as they were at the signing of the peace, and there was to be no internal subversion. There was a total prohibition on executions and exiles contrary to existing laws and on revolutionary measures such as redistribution of land, cancellation of debts and freeing of slaves. No city was to support exiles in an attack upon their home government ([Dem.] XVII.15–16). If there were violations the joint sanctions of the League could be invoked. Under Philip's settlement participation was mandatory in all expeditions voted by the *synedrion* (Tod, *GHI* no. 177, lines 19–22), and the same was true under Alexander ([Dem.] XVII.19). But the council was more than the recipient of complaints. It could if necessary take the initiative. Hypereides speaks of general policing of the peace by the council and 'by those

[5] For the terminology see Tod, *GHI* no. 177, line 22; Arr. II.14.4, VII.9.5. Diodorus twice writes of the Macedonian king being elected στρατηγὸς αὐτοκράτωρ for the war against Persia (XVI.89.3, XVII.4.9, so too the Oxyrhynchus Chronicle, *FGrH* 255 (5 *fin.*)), but his language is notoriously fluid and the term is probably his own. It is grossly improbable that there was one term to describe the king's functions in Greece and another his leadership of the war in Asia. In 302 Demetrius' title for the war against Cassander was apparently *hegemon* (Plut. *Demetr.* 25.2), and he like Alexander both presided over the common peace and commanded the common war.

[6] It would be perverse to lay too much stress on the wording of Arrian: Schehl's view (1932, 139) that the repetition of the definite article is proof of two temporally distinct treaties of peace and alliance goes much too far (cf. Hammond and Griffith 1979, 2.628–9). But I do not think that Arrian would have referred to either peace or alliance unless he had found something similar in his source.

placed over the common defence'.[7] There is no reference to the *hegemon*; instead we find a vaguely defined group of officials. This reflects the situation in 336, when the expedition to Asia was imminent. The *hegemon* himself would not be present in person to conduct League operations. The treaty therefore allows for deputies and its vagueness of terminology is probably deliberate, to leave Alexander free choice. In fact the executive officer in Alexander's absence was to be Antipater, but the garrison commanders may also have been given official status, to deputise for Antipater if he were detained in Macedon or to convene the *synedrion* rapidly in case of a local emergency.

The scope for initiatives was clearly large, given the structure and regulation of the League. If a city's autonomy was violated, all were bound to take military action – but only if such action were voted in the *synedrion*. The majority vote could always be directed in whichever way the executive head of the League decided; and the pressures were all the more effective if, as in the League of Antigonus and Demetrius, delegates were immune from any reckoning in their home cities (Moretti, *ISE* no. 44, lines 75–6). What is more, the Macedonian president had the opportunity of arraigning before the council any state which he considered to be violating the peace, whereas a single member city would have to present its complaints through its delegates and could not rely upon a sympathetic hearing. Once an expedition was voted, it was likely to be effective. The forces to be supplied by each city were prescribed in advance. A tantalisingly fragmentary stone from Athens records details of the military arrangements (Tod, *GHI* no. 183 = Heisserer 1980, 3–26); it seems to cover the provisioning of the forces and the rates of pay, but the details elude exegesis. The document does, however, illustrate the care with which the military obligations were formulated. There were probably sanctions in case of default, heavy fines (the League of Antigonus and Demetrius had a sliding scale ranging from half a mina *per diem* for each cavalryman to ten drachmae for light infantry) or in extreme cases military intervention. These regulations guaranteed a substantial force, though not necessarily a whole-hearted one.

It would be rash to dismiss the League as simply an instrument of repression. It could perform a useful function as an international court of arbitration, defusing disputes between neighbours before they led to war. There is an epigraphic record of a minor settlement between Melos and Cimolus over the possession of three islets (Tod, *GHI* no. 179). The *synedrion* passed a decree delegating the arbitration to the city of Argos, which eventually ruled in favour of Cimolus. We do not know whether the principals brought the matter before the council or whether it intervened on its own initiative, but the results appear to have been beneficial. Unfortunately

---

[7] The general tenor of this description is confirmed by the regulations of Antigonus and Demetrius, which are slightly more specific, referring to 'the general left by the kings in charge of the common peace' (lines 68–9, 72).

matters were less clear-cut when the interests of the ruling power were involved. One simply cannot expect a representative body of Macedonian allies, presided over by Macedonian officials, to have given rulings that damaged Macedon. Nor would it be realistic to expect League action if violations of the peace came from the Macedonian side. It was one thing to have sanctions provided in the treaty, quite another to apply them uniformly and impartially.

Alexander's use of the League is perhaps best documented by his rulings during the Aegean War (see above, p. 52). The islands of the Western Aegean had mostly been governed by restricted oligarchies ever since their defection from Athens in the Social War. Those oligarchies, abusively described as tyrannies in the Athenian sources, had associated themselves with Philip towards the end of his reign and had become members of the Corinthian League. They were not unlike the regimes supported by Philip in Greece proper, strictly limited governments which depended on Macedonian support. We have detailed evidence for Chios and Lesbos. In the small city of Eresus in Lesbos there had been several oligarchic juntas.[8] Some time, probably before 340, three brothers (Apollodorus, Hermon and Heraeus) had exercised power until driven into exile and replaced by another faction led by Agonippus and Eurysilaus. It was this latter faction which allied itself with Philip and dedicated altars to Zeus Philippios in commemoration of the compact (see below, p. 28). At the constitutive meeting at Corinth it was duly confirmed in power. Similarly the Chian oligarchy had responded to Philip's overtures in 340 (Front. *Strat.* 1.4.13a; cf. Hammond and Griffith 1979), and it was probably a foundation member of the League. So far the Macedonian king had operated with the existing oligarchies. There is no suggestion that Philip encouraged or instituted democratic regimes. The change came in 334/3 during the island war. Then, for the first time in decades, the Persians had a substantial naval presence in the Aegean and the Macedonians were in no position to protect their supporters in the islands. As a result there were many defections. Chios was surrendered to Memnon early in 333 and was maintained as a Persian base for nearly two years, while at Eresus the Persian forces seem to have been invited into the city by the junta, which is alleged to have collaborated in various atrocities. The governments sanctioned by the League of Corinth had medised, albeit under pressure. When their cities were recaptured in the course of 332 there was no question of the preservation of the government. Alexander had been creating democracies

---

[8] This construction is based on the famous dossier preserved on two stones from Eresus (*IG* XII.2.526 = Tod, *GHI* no. 191 = Heisserer 1980, 27–78). Other schemata have been proposed. The traditional view (Pistorius 1913, 60–7; Berve 1926, 2 nos. 19,235) is that *Philip* established a democracy and expelled the first group of tyrants around 343, to be followed by Agonippus and Eurysilaus, who seized power in 336/5. Heisserer has argued for a later expulsion of the first group, by Philip's generals in 336. Memnon subsequently captured Lesbos (in 335!) and established the second tyranny. None of these reconstructions takes into account the fact that the existing oligarchy at Eresus would have been perfectly acceptable to Philip. It was the type of regime that had his unqualified support elsewhere.

in Asia Minor to serve as bulwarks against the Persians, who (like Philip) had favoured restrictive oligarchies. The new island constitutions were accordingly democratic. At Eresus Alexander sent the two oligarchic leaders for trial by the newly sovereign *demos*, which predictably executed them and exiled their families in perpetuity. The descendants of the previous junta, untainted by medism, now approached Alexander suing for their restoration. The king once more referred the matter to the *demos*, which set up a court in compliance with his instructions and voted to confirm the sentence of exile. Alexander was dealing directly with the *demos* of Eresus, giving instructions by letter, and there is no suggestion anywhere in the lengthy dossier that the Corinthian *synedrion* played any part in the transactions. The rulings are reasonable enough, but they read like the decisions of an absolute monarch, not the *hegemon* of a league of allied states. There is some justification in a contemporary reproach that the tyrants of Antissa and Eresus were underwritten by the common peace and should have had their regime preserved, like that of the sons of Philiades ([Dem.] xvii.7). At least the *synedrion* should have had some say in the treatment of its delinquent members.

At Chios the situation is even more interesting, for a stone survives almost complete, recording Alexander's settlement of the island.[9] Once again the king writes as a despot, imposing the return of exiles, the establishment of a democratic constitution and the appointment of a committee of lawgivers who were to rewrite the laws so as to remove any obstacle to the democracy. The king himself is to scrutinise the new legislation. So far there is no reference to the League *synedrion*. Alexander acts independently, prescribing a constitutional change and the return of exiles (whose exile had previously been sanctioned by the common peace); and it is clear that the democratic constitution is a total innovation. It is only when he refers to the punishment of the medising oligarchs that the *synedrion* appears. Those who left Chios before the capture, expelled in the abortive democratic uprising before the Macedonian fleet arrived, were subjected to the general decrees already voted by the League; all member cities had sworn to exile medisers from their territory and deliver them to justice if captured, and Alexander applied the sentence to Chios – fugitive oligarchs were exiled from all cities subscribing to the peace. Those who were actually arrested were to be taken to Corinth and tried before the *synedrion*. Here the council is seen as an instrument for punishment, enforcing penal decrees it had previously issued. It has no apparent say in the constitutional settlement of an allied state. Even the trials of the delinquents were ultimately waived, for the captured Chian oligarchs were brought to Memphis in the spring of 331 and exiled to Elephantine (Arr. iii.2.7). I can only assume that the *synedrion* held a preliminary meeting and decided to refer the final judgement to Alexander, exactly as was to happen with the Spartans in 330 (see below, p. 203). News of the decision was relayed

[9] Tod, *GHI* no. 192 = Heisserer 1980, 79–95.

to the Macedonian admiral Hegelochus, who took his prisoners on with him to Egypt.

As far as we can tell, the *synedrion* played no part in the regulation of the Aegean islands. Alexander acted autocratically and issued orders without reference to any other authority. To some degree he could echo Hypereides' apology in 338, that the Macedonian arms had cast a shadow over the city's laws (Plut. *Mor.* 849A). The war in the islands needed immediate decisions and could not be left to the debating chamber at Corinth. His decisions moreover were justifiable. Men who had violated the allied decrees against medism could not invoke the common peace to maintain their regime. None the less it remains true that Alexander made wide-ranging constitutional changes which violated the letter, if not the spirit, of the Corinthian League and made them without reference (even for confirmation) to the allied *synedrion*. It is not surprising to find other technical violations in the sources. The most glaring case was at democratic Pellene, where Chaeron, one of the most successful wrestlers of his day, established himself as tyrant with the help of Corrhagus, the Macedonian general in the Peloponnese.[10] As a result there were mass exiles and distributions of land to slaves. It was a total breach of virtually every clause in the common peace, yet there was no attempt to enforce the sanctions, presumably because the issue was never raised in the *synedrion*. Sanctions could only operate if there was a will to enforce them.

In the autumn of 336 propaganda was still to the fore. The states of Greece reaffirmed the war of vengeance with the young king as their leader and re-enacted the common peace with its emphasis that all allies were free, autonomous and at peace. Alexander returned to Macedon and in the following spring he launched his Triballian campaign. His second crisis in Greece followed. As the campaign in the north continued and no word of its progress reached the south, the rumour circulated that he had been killed. In the Athenian assembly Demosthenes produced an eyewitness of his death, and speculation was rife over the whole of southern Greece. At Thebes there was insurrection. A group of exiles wishing to repeat the glorious revolution of 379 entered the city by night, murdered two members of the Macedonian garrison who were surprised outside the Cadmeia and pressed for revolution in the Assembly (Arr. 1.7.1–2). The Thebans rose to the appeal and laid siege to the Cadmeia. They abolished the oligarchic government imposed by Philip. It was as a democracy that they passed legis' ....un to resist Alexander, the sovereign assembly ratifying a formal *probouleuma* by the leaders of the revolt, who met in council (Diod. XVII.9.1). These actions had challenged every aspect of the common peace: an existing constitution had been subverted by exiles and the city was openly at war with Macedon. Elsewhere there was considerable agitation. The Arcadian League went so far as to send

---

[10] [Dem.] XVII.10; Paus. VII.27.7; Athen. 509B; *Acad. philosoph. index Herculanensis* (ed. Mekler) pp. 28–9. Cf. Berve 1926, 2 no. 818.

an expeditionary force to the Isthmus, where it remained to await events, assisting neither Thebes nor Macedon (Din. 1.18–21). At Elis there was a minor revolution. Alexander's sympathisers were expelled and presumably the character of the regime altered (Arr. 1.10.1). The major debate was at Athens, where Demosthenes and Lycurgus all but produced the body of Alexander and urged support for Thebes. The *demos* accordingly voted assistance but sent no forces. Persian gold was now at work. Darius III had come to the Persian throne in 336 and, his position once secured, he was ready and willing to send money to sympathisers in Greece. There are various exaggerated statements about the sums received by Demosthenes (Aesch. III.239; Din. 1.10, 18), but there is no doubt that Persian funds did come into his hands. Alexander is said to have found documentary proof of it at Sardes (Plut. *Dem.* 20.5). The Thebans accordingly had ample funds made over to them and they were enabled to arm their entire citizen body (Diod. XVII.8.5). For Alexander the situation was deteriorating. The alliance of Chaeronea was almost reforged and the whole fabric of the Corinthian League was in danger.

Alexander's lightning march south saved the day. Thebes was under siege before the Athenians knew of his presence south of Thermopylae, and there was no question of a united defence. The Arcadian army left the Isthmus and Thebes was isolated. Even so its citizens remained unrepentant and countered propaganda with propaganda. When Alexander invoked the common peace, they responded with an appeal to all mankind to join with the Thebans and the Persian king in freeing the Greeks and destroying the tyrant of Greece (Diod. XVII.9.5). Every syllable was a calculated insult. Alexander was in theory the leader of a free and autonomous alliance pursuing the mission of vengeance against Persia. In Theban eyes he was a tyrant and oppressor, and the Persian king was the natural guarantor of Greek liberty. In their appeal to the Arcadians they had stressed the impossibility of autonomy under a resident Macedonian garrison (Din. 1.19–20), and they now represented themselves as the champions of the age-old struggle for liberty (Plut. *Al.* 11.7–8). There was certainly no compromise. The Thebans held out to the end, and the city was captured with dreadful carnage. The traditional enemies of Thebes, men from Phocis, Thespiae, Plataea and Orchomenus, joined enthusiastically with the Macedonians in the slaughter, in which more than 6,000 perished. The fate of the rest was decided at a council of allies. Whether this was regarded as an irregular meeting of the Corinthian League is very dubious. Diodorus (XVII.14.1) talks of a gathering of delegates (*synedroi*) of the Greeks, but it is very unlikely that any of the regular delegates at Corinth could have attached themselves to the whirlwind campaign. Arrian (1.9.9; so Justin XI.3.8) must be correct that the Thebans' fate was discussed by an *ad hoc* council of allies present with Alexander, the very men who had helped in the massacre. It was not technically a League decision but the rough justice of the victors. Interestingly enough the debate over the sentence did not focus upon breaches of the common peace. Instead the old story of Theban medism during Xerxes' invasion was rehearsed yet again, and the judges recalled the oath of the Hellenic coalition to punish the city (Justin XI.3.9–10). The verdict could therefore be represented as an act of piety, and it was draconian. The survivors, some 30,000 in all, were enslaved, the city was destroyed except for the fortress on the Cadmeia and her territory was divided among her neighbours. The verdict was not Alexander's but it was the verdict he wished to be passed. The Greek world now had a shocking example of the consequences of resistance. One of the leading cities of the Greek world had been destroyed in a single day, as though by visitation of the gods. So Aeschines lamented in 330 (III.133), and the litany of shock and sorrow was to be repeated through the centuries. There was a ground swell of sympathy for the victims. Despite the prohibition against giving succour to refugees (Diod. XVII.14.3) they were received into neighbouring cities, notably Athens and Acraephnium (Paus. IX.23.5); and nearly twenty years later, when Cassander proclaimed the restoration of Thebes, there was enthusiastic support from as far afield as Italy and Sicily (Diod. XIX.54.2).

The immediate reaction was panic. At Elis the Macedonian sympathisers were precipitately recalled from exile and the Arcadians condemned to death the statesmen who had advocated assistance to Thebes. Even the Aetolians came to heel, and each tribe sent a separate embassy to solicit pardon, so demonstrating the (temporary) renunciation of their federal polity (Arr. I.10.2). The trepidation ran highest at Athens. At the news of the destruction of Thebes (brought by eyewitnesses of the event) the Athenians abandoned the celebration of the Great Mysteries, evacuated Attica yet again and appealed for emergency contributions of money. As in 336 they sent an embassy to Alexander, again headed by Demades, but this time their reception was cooler. Alexander threw away the honorary decree which congratulated him on his safe return from the Illyrians and his punishment of Thebes and he turned his back on the delegates. His response to their overtures was to demand the surrender of the eight statesmen and generals who were most involved in the movement against Macedon. The names are variously recorded in the ancient sources, but they definitely included Demosthenes and Lycurgus as well as Polyeuctus of Sphettus and the distinguished general Charidemus.[11] They were to be tried by the *synedrion* (Aesch. III.161). Their support of the Theban exiles had been a clear breach of the common peace and it was to be punished as such. But Athens herself was safe, preserved by her glorious past. Alexander had invoked the decrees of the Hellenic alliance against Thebes and he could hardly now take drastic action against the city which had dared and suffered most during the Persian

---

[11] For analysis of the variant traditions see Bosworth 1980a, 92–5. It seems clear that the authentic list is preserved by Plut. *Dem.* 23.4. Other lists (Arr. I.10.4; Plut. *Phoc.*17.2; 'Suda' s.v. Ἀντίπατρος) have interpolations, notably Hypereides and Chares who were added as prominent anti-Macedonian figures.

Wars, least of all when he was about to assume the mantle of Athens and take revenge for her injuries.

It remained to be seen whether the Athenians would show penitence in deed as well as word. Alexander's demand provoked an impassioned debate. The veteran general Phocion argued that there was no choice but to submit; it was sufficient that Greece weep for Thebes, and the statesmen named (who fortunately did not include himself) should offer their lives for their city. On the other side necessity, as always, stimulated Demosthenes' invention, and he was able to inveigh eloquently against the dangers of appeasement (cf. Aristobulus, *FGrH* 139 F 3). Popular opinion was against submission, and Demades steered through a compromise motion, offering to punish the men under Athenian law if they deserved punishment (Diod. XVII.15.4). It is possible that Alexander or his advisers had privately suggested a face-saving formula. At all events the second embassy proved successful. Alexander insisted on the exile of Charidemus, who promptly took service at the Persian court, but took no action against the remaining seven. The example of Thebes had been enough. The Athenians were forced back into the fold of loyal allies and performed their symmachical obligations. Alexander could now launch the invasion of Asia, avenging Xerxes' sack of Athens, and his first victory dedication was a gift of 300 panoplies to Athene (Arr. 1.16.7; Plut. *Al.* 16.17). The city and its goddess were the figureheads of his crusade.

Alexander's actions in 335 tightened his grip on the Greek world. One of the bastions of resistance to Macedon had been destroyed and his enemies in southern Greece had been thoroughly cowed. It was a very reluctant submission, to be sure; and he could be confident that any setbacks would be exploited against him in future years, for he would be remembered with hatred and bitterness. But there were two continuing guarantees of Greek quiescence. The first was the mechanism of the common peace, in particular the supervisory role of the *synedrion* and its Macedonian executive, who could in theory prevent any internal subversion. Secondly, when Alexander crossed the Hellespont in 334, he had with him 7,000 infantry and 600 cavalry from his Greek allies. Some of these no doubt were troops their home cities were glad to be rid of, like the Athenian cavalry sent with Thibron in 400 B.C. (Xen. *Hell.* III.1.4), but the force will have included men who were genuinely valued at home and made effective hostages. The Athenians who exerted themselves repeatedly to repatriate the mercenaries captured at the Granicus will certainly not have forgotten their citizens serving in Asia. Alexander could be reasonably sanguine that no major rising would occur while he was engaged overseas. His confidence was based on a settlement which was based ultimately on military repression, and from the very beginning Macedonian suzerainty was a mockery of any concept of Greek autonomy.

## 11     Agis III of Sparta and the war for Megalopolis

After 335 such resistance as there was to Macedonian supremacy focused around Sparta. At the time of Philip's death the city had been at a very low ebb, demoralised by the death, far away in Italy, of the veteran king Archidamus. There was as yet little to expect from his eldest son and successor, Agis, who had acted as regent during his father's absence but was relatively inexperienced. His Agiad colleague, Cleomenes II, was the archetypal nonentity: nothing whatsoever is recorded of his reign of sixty years and ten months (370–309). There could be no resistance in late 338 when Philip invaded Laconia and annexed Spartan border territories (see above, p. 13). But, if there was no resistance, neither was there acquiescence. The Spartans held themselves proudly aloof from the Corinthian League and would have no part in the war of revenge. After Philip's death they gave no assistance to the disaffected states of the Peloponnese but once again refused to participate in the war against Persia, claiming that the hegemony of Greece was traditionally theirs (Arr. 1.1.2; cf. Plut. *Mor.* 240A–B). They had never yet compromised and submitted to the supremacy of another power and they were not to begin now. Then again there was no question of their adhering to a common peace which guaranteed Messenian autonomy. Sparta's territorial claims were naked, unconditional and incompatible with the autonomy clause of the peace – at least as it would be interpreted by the Macedonian king and the vast majority of the delegates at Corinth. She remained outside the League, much to the chagrin of Alexander, who had clearly relished the prospect of including under his banner the champions of the great Persian War. His displeasure was to be voiced in the first dedication of the war, the spoils of 'Alexander and the Greeks apart from the Spartans' (Arr. 1.16.7; Plut. *Al.* 16.17). But there were no reprisals. Sparta was too weak as yet to enforce her territorial ambitions and Alexander had far more pressing tasks than coercing her into reluctant conformity with the rest of Greece.

As the campaign in Asia Minor progressed and the Persian counter-offensive in the Aegean gained ground, the opportunities for repairing the past seemed more promising. At the height of the Persian successes, after the fall of the Aegean islands and the recapture of Miletus and Halicarnassus, the Spartans sent an ambassador, Euthycles, to the Persian court. He was arrested by Alexander after Issus along with Athenian and Theban delegates.[12] The Thebans were probably soliciting support for a government in exile, while the Athenians were angling for further subsidies to fuel revolt in Greece, if, as was

---

[12] Arr. 11.15.2–5. Curt. 111.13–15 lists four Spartan ambassadors, not including Euthycles, a delegation which Arrian (111.24.4) places at a much later stage, in summer 330. The source problems are complex (cf. Bosworth 1980a, 233–4). It seems best to assume two sets of embassies, an exploratory mission by Euthycles in 333 and a more numerous and high-powered delegation sent out after the beginning of hostilities in 331. The second, more prestigious, embassy was retrojected by Curtius and displaced the more modest overtures of Euthycles.

confidently expected, Alexander was crushed in Cilicia (Aesch. III.164). They cannot have made many specific undertakings, for Alexander released them out of consideration for their city and because of personal ties with the Athenian Iphicrates. Euthycles, however, remained under arrest, for his city was considered openly hostile. The Spartans had probably committed themselves to war in support of the Persian cause. King Agis revealed his plans shortly before the battle of Issus, when he sailed to the Persian base at Siphnos to confer with Pharnabazus and Autophradates in the hope of military and financial support for war in the Peloponnese (Arr. II.13.4). The news of Issus now arrived like a bolt from the blue and with it disappeared any chance of substantial Persian support. The Persian commanders withdrew to the coast of Asia Minor to secure their holdings before the spring offensive, and Agis was left with the relatively paltry sum of thirty talents and a mere ten triremes. These he dispatched to his brother Agesilaus, who was establishing the famous military depot at Taenarum, at the southern extremity of Laconia, and instructed him to cross over to Crete 'to settle the situation there'.

Crete was well chosen as a theatre of operations. It was still a backwater of the Greek world and almost certainly played no part in the Corinthian League. Philip had not intervened there and seems to have had no allies in the island. But the Cretan cities were plagued by internecine war. The people of Cnossus had enlisted Phalaecus and his mercenaries after their débâcle in Phocis and used them in local wars against Lyttus and Cydonia (Diod. XVI.62.2–63.3). Those hostilities had been protracted and inconclusive; almost certainly they were what Aristotle meant by the mercenary war which had revealed the weakness of the Cretan laws (*Pol.* 1272b20–2). The confusion persisted into the reign of Alexander, and Spartan intervention promised rich rewards. They will have operated from Lyttus, which claimed to be a colony of Sparta (Arist. *Pol.* 1271b27–8; Ephorus, *FGrH* 70 F 149) and had summoned King Archidamus to its defence immediately before his Italian expedition (Diod. XVI.62.4). Most probably they gave assistance against Cnossus, exploiting for their own purposes the endemic hatred between the two cities which was to continue intermittently for the next century. This was an operation outside the scope of the common peace. The Cretan cities, not being parties to the common peace, could hardly invoke its sanctions, while the Spartans could amass mercenary forces from their traditional allies and unofficially prepare a haven for the Persian fleet. Early in 332 they were joined by refugees from Darius' army at Issus, Greek mercenaries who had crossed to Cyprus and then transferred to Crete. 8,000 of them apparently attached themselves to the Spartan army (Curt. IV.1.39; Diod. XVII.48.2). Over the summer of 332 they operated successfully in the island. Antipater did send limited help to the cities hostile to Sparta but it was not effectual. The remnants of the Persian fleet regrouped in Crete and together with Agis' mercenary army they were able to control the greater part of the island (Curt. IV.8.15; Diod. XVII.48.2). Now members of the Eurypontid royal house were openly at war in Crete and they had come to blows with at least some Macedonian forces. But the action was far away and still an annexe of the wider Persian war. The Spartans might be reprobated as traitors but as yet they were not at war in the Peloponnese or attacking any city directly allied to Macedon.

When news of the Spartan successes reached Alexander, he was already in Phoenicia, poised for the final campaign against Darius. By comparison Crete was a very minor theatre of operations and the forces he could divert there were very limited. Amphoterus, fresh from his successes in the Aegean, was sent off with a naval squadron, to be reinforced by 100 warships from Alexander's Phoenician and Cypriot subjects, who would paradoxically be fighting their former comrades-in-arms. This mission is reported both by Arrian and by Curtius, with somewhat different emphases. Arrian suggests that the objective was the Peloponnese, but he still views the mission in the context of the Persian war. Curtius states explicitly that Amphoterus was sent to liberate Crete and to clean up piracy.[13] These notices are not inconsistent. Our authors, as so often, stress different aspects of a complex transaction. Amphoterus was to tackle the problem of Crete and also give support in the Peloponnese, particularly to Sparta's traditional enemies. It looks as though Alexander was avoiding an overt declaration of war against Sparta, whose glorious history was a serious embarrassment to him. Instead he intensified operations on Crete, giving massive support to any city which still held out against the Spartan attack, and at the same time planned to strengthen the Macedonian allies in the Peloponnese who were in danger of subversion (Elis was particularly volatile at this time). The effect he hoped for was to prevent war in the Peloponnese while destroying the remnants of the Persian fleet in Crete. Sparta would be isolated and forced into line with the rest of the Greek world.

Amphoterus left Phoenicia and was soon overtaken by events. He may have begun operations in Crete (though no source states it), but he was unable to prevent war in the Peloponnese, which broke out in the summer of 331.[14] It was a season particularly propitious for Spartan ambitions. Over the winter of 332/1 Alexander's officers had been actively recruiting in Macedon (see above, p. 68) and towards the end of spring 331 a massive army column more than 15,000 strong began its long march to Mesopotamia. Of those forces 6,000

[13] Arr. III.6.3; Curt. IV.8.15. The view in the text is (with some modifications) that expounded by Bosworth 1975; 1980a, 279. For a different interpretation see Atkinson 1980, 484–5.

[14] The chronology is hotly disputed. The older view, which is in essence accepted here, dates the conclusion of the war to the spring of 330. It has recently been advocated by Cawkwell 1969, 170–3, and Bosworth 1975. Niese, however, argued that Sparta's defeat took place in autumn 331, and his arguments were expanded by Badian 1967, 190–2 (see, however, Badian 1985, 446–7). This latter view has been more widely accepted in recent years (for bibliography see Will 1983, 76–7). The main piece of evidence in its favour is Curtius' statement (VI.1.21) that the war was over before Alexander won the battle of Gaugamela. If that is true, it is difficult to believe that Alexander had not heard the news when he sent Menes from Susa in December 331 with massive funds for the war against Sparta (Arr. III.16.10; see, however, Atkinson 1980, 484). I cannot claim certainty for the chronology of my narrative, but it allows events to take place in logical succession without awkward gaps.

were native Macedonian infantry and 4,000 mercenary infantry had been levied from the Peloponnese. These were men who in other circumstances might have been used against Sparta, and their departure strengthened Agis' military position. At roughly the same time Antipater was distracted by a revolt in Thrace. This is one of the most mysterious episodes in the entire period, unfortunately recorded by Diodorus alone. Memnon, the general in Thrace, is said to have collaborated with his subjects in defection from Alexander and forced Antipater to take his entire army from Macedon (Diod. xvii.62.4–6). The story is doubly puzzling, for this same Memnon is later reported leading Thracian reinforcements to India (Curt. ix.3.21) and there is no suggestion that he was in any way suspect or out of favour. He may have been able to rehabilitate himself after the revolt, but it is perhaps more likely that Diodorus garbled his material. The truth may be that Memnon had stirred up a Thracian revolt which he could not cope with and invoked Antipater's help.[15] Whatever the cause of the revolt, it was serious and it fully engaged Antipater's depleted forces. That was the trigger for war in the Peloponnese. The Spartan government declared itself for liberty and sent embassies around Greece soliciting support. At the same time, if not before, Agis withdrew his mercenary army from Crete and began operations in the Peloponnese. A Macedonian general, Corrhagus (conceivably the garrison commander at Corinth), was defeated and allies accrued to the Spartan cause. The oligarchic regime at Elis had been unstable ever since it was imposed by Philip; the party exiled in 343 made one abortive attempt to return during Philip's lifetime[16] and for a short time in 335 they did manage to oust their Macedonian-backed opponents. When war was declared at Sparta (if not before) there was a change of government and Elis joined the Spartan alliance. The Achaean League with the single exception of Pellene also committed itself to Sparta, as did the Arcadian cities, all but Megalopolis. The surprise here is Tegea, which had received Spartan border territories after Chaeronea yet joined the Spartan alliance in 331. There may have been internal revolution and a change of government, but the city was in any case so close to Sparta that it would have been a counsel of prudence to accept the Spartan overtures and thereby stave off an invasion that was otherwise inevitable. The joint forces of the alliance were formidable, 20,000 infantry and 2,000 cavalry, their nucleus the battle-hardened mercenaries from Asia; and while Antipater was engaged by the emergency in the north they could expect to dominate the Peloponnese.

---

[15] Many other interpretations are possible: cf. Berve 1926, 2 no. 499 and Badian 1967, 179–80. Badian suggests that Memnon was in league with Agis, which is a possibility but, if true, makes his rehabilitation even more problematical. He also identifies him with the relative of Memnon of Rhodes who was honoured at Athens late in 327 (Tod, *GHI* no. 199). That is most unlikely. Memnon is not the most common name, but it does occur in at least two Athenian families at this period (Davies 1971, 399–400; *IG* ii².500, lines 9–10) and is fairly well attested in the Hellenistic period. It is perfectly credible as a Macedonian name.

[16] Diod. xvi.63.4: Elean exiles were supported by the remnants of Phalaecus' mercenaries, some considerable time after the departure of King Archidamus for Italy. They can only be the

Much depended on the reaction at Athens. The city was inevitably the main target of Spartan diplomacy and received a number of embassies in the course of the crisis. There was a prolonged and acrimonious debate. On the one hand there was a strong current of sympathy for Sparta. The bellicose mood of the *demos* is reflected in the blunt speech on the treaty with Alexander ([Dem.] XVII), which was probably delivered in 331/0[17] and culminates in a rousing appeal to go to war with the Macedonians, the arch-enemies of Greek autonomy. But there was also a negative reaction, notably from Demosthenes.[18] The speech he made, as it is derisively quoted by Aeschines (III.166), is sibylline in its obscurity, and we cannot reconstruct the tenor of his argument. He certainly built up an atmosphere of suspicion, hinting darkly at concealed threats and subversion at home, and he advised taking a waiting position. Demosthenes had never been a friend of Sparta. Early in his career, in 353/2, he had urged the *demos* to help Megalopolis, claiming that it was in Athens' interests that Sparta remained weak. If Megalopolis fell, Messenia was in peril, and a Sparta which acquired Messenia would once again threaten the liberty of Greece (Dem. XVI.19–22). The situation was not dissimilar late in 331. After his defeat of Corrhagus Agis immediately laid siege to Megalopolis, and it looked as though he was bent upon its destruction. The removal of that bastion of the north-west would open the way into Messenia, and the Spartans could then subjugate their old helots under the pretext of Greek autonomy. They were attacking Macedonian allies in the name of liberty, but the ultimate aim was to bring the territory back into the Spartan fold. Demosthenes might well have felt disinclined to assist Sparta's hegemonial ambitions at Athens' expense and the expense of the Athenian citizens still serving with Alexander. Accordingly the Athenians gave only verbal encouragement during the crisis; the *demos* was held in restraint by self-interest and political calculation. As late as February 330 there was public agitation to send out triremes in support of the movement, but it was quashed by Demades, who pointed out the cost and threatened to draw upon the theoric fund to finance the operation (Plut. *Mor.* 818E–F). Eubulus had used similar arguments in 346 with equal success (Dem. XIX.291). The Athenians conserved their funds, and, as they had done in 335, refrained from any positive action.

The delay was fatal. Antipater was able to come to terms with the rebels in Thrace, whose reckoning could be deferred (Diod. XVII.63.1). Then, probably in the early spring of 330, he moved southwards, accumulating forces as he went. The army amassed was vast, 40,000 strong. Its Macedonian nucleus

laconising faction who were expelled at the instigation of Philip in 343 (Dem. XIX.260; Paus. IV.28.4–6).

17 For this dating see Cawkwell 1961; for other suggestions Will 1982; 1983, 67–70.

18 He may have shown some enthusiasm at the opening of hostilities (Plut. *Dem.* 10.1; cf. Burke 1977, 336); if so, he was soon disappointed. But the text of Plutarch is very vague and rhetorical and it may well be erroneous; nothing is said about Demosthenes' well attested opposition to military intervention and it may be Plutarch's guess that he supported the movement.

will have been small after the depredations of Amyntas' recruiting. Numbers were presumably swelled by levies from the northern barbarians, and Macedonian allies fielded both mercenaries and citizen troops. The allies are not specified, but they will have included the Thessalians and the peoples of central Greece as well as the Peloponnesian states hostile to Sparta. The total far outstripped the forces at Agis' disposal, and the Spartan king was in a most unenviable position. His army was still pinned down in the siege of Megalopolis, unable to storm it or starve it into submission, and he remained in the locality awaiting Antipater. The final act in the drama took place near the city, in hilly terrain; Agis had probably fallen back to the south and was defending the road into Laconia. If we can trust Curtius' partial and rhetorical account of the battle, it was a hard-fought engagement with constant movement. The plain land where the bulk of the fighting took place was limited and only allowed a fraction of the forces to engage (Curt. VI.1.10). Agis had obviously chosen his ground with skill and was able to neutralise the superior numbers on the Macedonian side. The Spartan phalanx had one of its finest hours and fought the Macedonians to a standstill. Paradoxically it was Antipater's line which lacked cohesion (Curt. VI.1.6), further evidence that his phalangites were not of the highest calibre. Agis himself fought with heroism but was wounded in the early stages and carried from the battle. His men fought to exhaustion but were ultimately driven to retreat (Antipater's greater reserves told in time). The wounded king was overtaken in the rout and defended himself to the very end, his courage not unworthy of Leonidas. Antipater remained master of the field on which were 5,300 enemy dead, including a large number of Spartiates whose loss was a mortal blow to their city.

The single victory was sufficient. With Sparta crippled the insurgent states could only make overtures to Antipater and sue for the best possible terms. The regent referred the matter to the *synedrion* of the Corinthian League; naturally so, for the main victim of the war, Megalopolis, was an ally of Macedon and signatory to the common peace. There followed a lengthy debate at Corinth, after which Sparta's allies were punished. The Achaeans and Eleans were to pay an indemnity of 120 talents to Megalopolis, while the Tegeans, who had probably acted under compulsion, were pardoned, except for the faction responsible for the revolt (Curt. VI.1.20). The Spartans were in a different category, prime instigators of the war but non-members of the League. The *synedrion* accordingly reserved the decision on their fate for Alexander and permitted them to send a delegation to plead their cause in Asia. Antipater also demanded fifty hostages, an imposition which the Spartans strenuously resisted. The ephor Eteocles offered 100 old men and women in place of the boys requested by Antipater, averring that death was preferable to such submission (Plut. *Mor.* 235B). His opinion, however, was not universal and the Spartans surrendered their hostages, to be referred to Alexander. When Aeschines delivered his speech against Ctesiphon in the late summer of 330 they were about to begin their journey, and the orator waxes eloquent over their misery and their precarious position subject to the caprice of Alexander (Aesch. III.133).[19] These forebodings were probably unjustified by the event. There is no record of Alexander making any judgement which penalised Sparta. The surrender of the hostages and the battle losses may have been adjudged sufficient penalty. Sparta may have been forced into alliance and membership of the League, but even that is dubious. By the time the Spartan ambassadors and hostages reached Alexander he will have been north of the Hindu Kush, embroiled in the Sogdian revolt, and the problems of Greece were very far from pressing concerns, certainly not a Sparta which had been militarily crushed and had lost a considerable part of her citizen population. She could be left to her decline, a living fossil in a changing world, obsessed by the mythology of her past and stubbornly cherishing hegemonic ambitions which she lacked the capacity to achieve.

Sparta now had no choice but to remain at peace and repair the ravages of war. There could be no further risk to the declining citizen body. All Spartiates were needed, and, not surprisingly, the sanctions traditionally imposed upon the survivors of Spartan defeats were suspended, as they had been after Leuctra (Plut. *Ages.* 30). The laws of Lycurgus slept again, and only one bold spirit, the Agiad prince Acrotatus, spoke in favour of the penal tradition, an act of courage which made him a marked man (Diod. XIX.70.4–6). But Agis' successor, his youngest brother Eudamidas, apparently made no attempt to disturb the *status quo* (Paus. III.10.5), and the veteran Cleomenes continued his life of inactivity. Under their rule Sparta played no part in the Lamian War and the coalition was the weaker for her absence. All Agis' efforts had been abortive, and their ultimate result was to strengthen the Macedonian hold on Greece. Greater support from Athens might have altered the picture, but the fatal error was undoubtedly the stubborn siege of Megalopolis. That rendered impossible any defence of the Peloponnese against Antipater and simultaneously raised the spectre of old-fashioned Spartan imperialism. Most states still saw the rule of Macedon as a pleasanter alternative.

III     Athens under the administration of Lycurgus

In many respects Athens achieved the height of her material prosperity during the reign of Alexander. From the battle of Chaeronea to the outbreak of the Lamian War she enjoyed fifteen years of unbroken peace, never having to face more than the passing threat of invasion. The years of peace brought

---

[19] For discussion of the sources see McQueen 1978, 53–6. McQueen involves himself in unnecessary difficulties by his belief that Agis was defeated in 331 and he is forced to reject the evidence of the contemporary Aeschines. If the battle was fought in spring 330, three or four months elapsed before the speeches on the crown, not too long a time for the debates at Corinth and for Spartan opinion to be reconciled to the surrender of hostages. The hostages will have journeyed to Alexander's court in the company of the ambassadors. There is no formal conflict between the sources.

unprecedented financial gains. Athens' revenues rose from the 400 talents attested in 346 B.C. to a staggering 1,200 talents *per annum*. The revenues generated impressive programmes of military and civil expenditure, and there was an intensity of building that had not been seen for a century. At the heart of this activity was the Eteobutad aristocrat, Lycurgus son of Lycophron, who administered Athenian finances directly or indirectly for twelve continuous years. The office he held is unfortunately not clearly defined. The sources describe him simply as in charge of the administration,[20] but from descriptions of his achievements, in particular the honorary decree passed by Stratocles in 307 B.C., it is apparent that he controlled all the Athenian public finances. The theoric fund would have been an important element in his administration. It was still perhaps the largest receptacle of public funds, but its functions seem to have been restricted by the legislation of Hegemon, which was enacted soon after Demosthenes' service as theoric commissioner (337/6) and may well have been aimed at Demosthenes himself.[21] Aeschines (III.25) suggests that the theoric administration was relatively limited by 330. The wide-ranging competence which it had enjoyed in the time of Eubulus was gone, and at least one of the officials whose functions it had absorbed (the *antigrapheus*) reappears in a public document of 335/4 (*IG* II².1700, line 217). Perhaps the theoric commissioners now dealt only with the festival distributions, the primary function which gave them their title, and the more general administration was placed in the hands of the financial superintendent. Certainly the arsenal and the new dockyards which had been begun by the theoric commissioners were completed by Lycurgus, and he is credited with the supervisory role that was formerly exercised by the *theorikon*. It is a reasonable assumption that the legislation which established the financial administration of Lycurgus was a corollary of Hegemon's limitation of the theoric commission. Public confidence in Lycurgus was such that the *demos* was prepared to invest him with a general oversight of the financial machinery of Athens, just as it was willing to allow the theoric commission to expand its functions under the presidency of Eubulus. There were some legal safeguards. At some stage, perhaps when the office was established, a statutory limit was imposed, preventing it being held for more than five years

[20] Diod. XVI.88.1; Hyper. F 118 Sauppe; [Plut.] *Mor.* 841B–C, 852B; Dion. Hal. *Din.* 11, p. 316. The decree of Stratocles survives in part (*IG* II².457 = *SIG*³ 326); an expanded and partly elaborated version is given in the pseudo-Plutarchan *Lives of the Ten Orators* (*Mor.* 851F–852E).

[21] Hegemon was an opponent of Demosthenes (Dem. XVIII.285). For the possible link between Hegemon's law and the establishment of Lycurgus' position, see Cawkwell 1963, 54–5; Rhodes 1972, 107–8; 1981, 515–17. The more traditional dating of Lycurgus' period of office is 338–326, beginning before Hegemon's law; cf. Berve 1926, 2 no. 477; Mitchel 1970, 12; Will 1983, 22–3, 78ff. The argument, however, is based on the assumption that the quadrennial cycles of office ([Plut.] *Mor.* 841C) ran from one celebration of the Great Panathenaea to the next (cf. Arist. *Ath. Pol.* 43.1), but the evidence is at best inconclusive (cf. Rhodes 1972, 236–7). Lycurgus' death probably fell in the archon year 325/4 and he was certainly in office on his death-bed ([Plut.] *Mor.* 842E–F; cf. Davies 1971, 35); it looks as though his third term of office had not yet expired. D. M. Lewis' (unpublished) dating of 336–324 should be preferred.

continuously,[22] and Lycurgus was forced to put forward a proxy from time to time, while retaining the actual administration in his own hands. The details of this arrangement are most obscure. It is uncertain whether there was one or more of these proxies and whether they held office for a single year or for a four-year term. One name only is known. Xenocles of Sphettus is attested as financial administrator during this period,[23] and he certainly acted as a figurehead for Lycurgus, managing the revenues as he directed.

The nature of the financial supervision is a mystery. The major financial officials of the *demos*, the treasurer of the stratiotic fund and the theoric commissioners, continued to exercise their functions and to collect and disburse money as before. Lycurgus presumably reviewed the revenues as a totality and divided them up among the various financial organs of the state. He is said to have provided new sources of revenue (Hyper. F 118 Sauppe) but that was probably done by *psephismata* ratified by the *demos*. Lycurgus' financial office made him the appropriate man to make such proposals but he had no *ex officio* legislative powers. Such powers as he had were in directing the flow of public money, and it is clear that it was Lycurgus who decided how the surplus from the general administration should be directed, whether to public works, distributions to the people or to armaments. The smooth operation of the system depended on co-operation between the various officials, and we have a striking example of it in Lycurgus' provisions for new processional vessels and golden *Nikai* ([Plut.] *Mor.* 841D, 852B). Lycurgus himself made the proposals but they were implemented by the proper official, the treasurer of the stratiotic fund, who made payments to the treasurers of Athena over the archon year 334/3. Now the treasurer of the stratiotic fund was none other than Demades of Paeania[24] whose advocacy of peace in 335 had brought him into conflict with Lycurgus, and Lycurgus had contested the honours voted him. None the less Demades was able to work effectively with Lycurgus the following year, demonstrating that the sharpest political clashes did not preclude co-operation in other areas.

The funds that passed through Lycurgus' hands were colossal. Estimates in antiquity ranged from 14,000 to 18,900 talents, and it is hardly an exaggeration that the annual revenues amounted to 1,200 talents. This huge increase must have been largely generated from commerce. This is no indication that domestic taxation, levies on land and property, were in any way increased, and the *eisphora*, the emergency levy upon the capital of the rich, was not invoked during this time of peace. It was the indirect taxation, harbour taxes and sales taxes, not to mention the leasing of mining concessions, which swelled the exchequer. If the commerce passing through Athens increased, so did the public revenues accruing from it. Since commerce at Athens was largely in the

---

[22] [Plut.] *Mor.* 841C. For the interpretation see Markianos 1969, who argues (unconvincingly) that no such legislation was passed; Lycurgus saw the possibility and forestalled it.

[23] Meritt 1960, 2–4, no. 3.

[24] *IG* II².1493. For the dating and certain restoration of Demades' name see Mitchel 1962.

hands of non-citizens, it was a necessary corollary to encourage metics and foreign traders, who would generate income and, in the case of metics, pay additional levies, the twelve-drachma *metoikion* and the *eisphora* allocated to the arsenal and dockyards. It is not surprising to find Lycurgus protecting the interests of resident aliens, repressing unpleasant officiousness on the part of fiscal authorities ([Plut.] *Mor.* 842B) and proposing legislation to grant merchants of Citium the right to acquire land for a temple of Aphrodite (Tod, *GHI* no. 189: a similar grant had been made to Egyptians for a temple of Isis). Aliens who assisted Athens by importing essential commodities were conspicuously honoured by the *demos*, notably Heracleides of Salamis who received a gold crown and *isoteleia* for his services during the great famine. In his case the *demos* went so far as to send an embassy to Dionysius of Heracleia, demanding compensation for the arrest of Heracleides' vessel and confiscation of his sails and insisting that there be no further interference to trade with Athens (*IG* II².360 = *SIG*³ 304). This diplomatic initiative to protect trade had its military counterpart. Lycurgus was eager to repress piracy, and, following a decree he passed in 335/4, Diotimus was sent out on a mission of protection (*IG* II².1623, lines 276–308). This policy was continued. In 325/4, after complaints of Etruscan piracy, the *demos* voted to establish a colony on the Adriatic coast, led by the Philaid aristocrat Miltiades with a modest naval contingent. The objectives of the expedition are spelled out in detail (Tod. *GHI* no. 200, lines 217ff.), and the first is to secure for the *demos* its own commerce. Few state enterprises in antiquity have an economic motive so clearly defined. Revenues and the commerce that guaranteed them were of paramount importance in Lycurgan Athens.

The exploitation of the silver mines, which Xenophon (*Poroi* 4) had seen as the chief means of augmenting state income, continued and was carefully policed. A certain Diphilus was condemned to death for speculating on the sale of pit-props, and his confiscated estate, which amounted to 160 talents, was distributed among the *demos*.²⁵ The episode is doubly important. It amply demonstrates Lycurgus' scrupulous concern to protect public property, but it also highlights a more sinister aspect of Athenian public finance. The city's revenues could be appreciably swelled by the sale of the effects of condemned men, and in times of financial straits visible wealth could be a positive inducement to prosecution. Lycurgus himself had a high reputation as a prosecutor, noted for his highly moral tone and his passion in denunciation. His pen, it was said, was dipped in death rather than ink. His integrity is not challenged in the ancient literature, but one may suspect that the wealth of the defendant was an additional stimulus to prosecution. This factor helps explain the prosecution of Leocrates so long after his alleged offence (see

²⁵ [Plut.] *Mor.* 843D. Compare, however, the case of Epicrates, where the *demos* voted for acquittal despite the lure of 300 talents offered by the prosecutor. But the trial had scared lessees and cut back the exploitation of the mines. The defence presumably emphasised that acquittal was in the long-term interests of the city (cf. Hyper. *Eux.* 35–6).

below, p. 215). The desertion of Attica in her hour of need certainly enraged Lycurgus; he had prosecuted Lycophron before the Areopagus for a similar offence (*Leocr.* 52; F 15–17). But that had been in the heat of the emergency of 338. Leocrates' indictment was nearly eight years later, and he had been resident in Athens for at least a year before he was brought to trial. It may have been a temporary need for funds which stirred his indignation into legal action. Leocrates was wealthy and, if condemned, would add his estate to the exchequer. Even more disturbing is the case of Euxenippus of Lamptrae, who was impeached for misreporting a dream he had experienced in the temple of Amphiaraus. We have only Hypereides' speech for the defence, but it is clear that the accusation was tendentious, insinuating Macedonian sympathies and irrelevantly harping on the defendant's wealth (Hyper. *Eux.* 19–20, 32). There were political overtones to the case. The accuser, Polyeuctus of Sphettus, had been thwarted by Euxenippus and was retaliating. But he was supported in his accusation by Lycurgus himself, who may have attached himself to the case for financial as well as religious motives. It is clear that the case was trivial and an abuse of the impeachment procedure, which should have been reserved for the most serious offences against the state. And, if Hypereides is stating his facts correctly (*Eux.* 1–3), the abuse was far from unique

The spending of the revenues is easier to document than their collection. A considerable amount of the expenditure went to improving Athens' military preparedness. The decree of Stratocles commends Lycurgus for stockpiling weapons on the Acropolis and maintaining 400 triremes in battle readiness ([Plut.] *Mor.* 852c). The latter statement is confirmed by the inventories of the naval curators which give a total of 392 triremes in 330/29 (*IG* II².1627, line 266). It is not the total that is impressive (Athens could boast 349 triremes in 353/2, after the Social War) but the fact that they were ready for action. Rebuilding was consistent, and the Athenian trierarchs had their eyes on developments in the eastern Mediterranean, where the heavier quadrireme and quinquereme were supplanting the trireme as the basic warship. Accordingly the Athenians strengthened the 'fours' in their navy; from eighteen in 330/29 they rose to fifty in 325/4 (with two 'fives' in addition),[26] while the triremes were reduced from 392 to 360. The total strength remained 410, but the proportion of newer and heavier vessels was increasing. At the same time the new naval installations, the arsenal and dockyards, were resumed after the interruption of the war of 340/39 and completed under Lycurgus' administration. The fleet was now superbly equipped but it was short on experience. The squadrons recorded on service by the naval catalogues are small. At the end of the archon year 330/29, for instance, only seventeen ships were outside the Piraeus. The largest action known for the period was the vote of 100 triremes

[26] *IG* II².1629, line 811. For the correct reading see Ashton 1979 and, for the fleet figures in general Ashton 1977, 3–7. The evidence for the construction of *tetrereis* is given by Schmitt 1974.

to release the grain fleet intercepted at Tenedos, and even that squadron probably did not need to sail, let alone fight ([Dem.] xvii.20). The state's revenues were not dissipated on costly military operations but directed to maintaining the armaments necessary in a future emergency. In theory the logic was impeccable but when the Athenian navy faced grim practical reality in the Lamian War the result was catastrophic defeat. They no longer had the experience and expertise in naval warfare to match the Macedonian admirals, who could call upon all the resources of the eastern Mediterranean.

Parallel to the refurbishing of the navy was the reorganisation of the *ephebeia*. In the earlier part of the century young men had served on a voluntary basis for two years after their reception into the citizen body (Aesch. ii.167). Some time after Chaeronea, perhaps in 336/5, an Epicrates moved legislation to make such service compulsory.[27] All Athenians, *thetes* probably included, were now committed to two years' military training. They were maintained in common messes, subsidised by the state to the tune of four obols a day and issued with weapons at public expense, a privilege formerly reserved for the sons of the fallen. Their officials were elective, one supervisor (*sophronistes*) from each tribe and a superintendent (*kosmetes*) selected from the entire citizen body. There were also more specialised instructors, who gave training in weaponry, both heavy and light, and in catapult technique. The first year of training was spent in forts at Piraeus, this basic instruction culminating in a ceremonial display before the entire *demos* in the orchestra of the theatre of Dionysus (Arist. *Ath. Pol.* 42.4). There followed a year of frontier service, in the garrisons of the Attic countryside (particularly in the northern marches, at Eleusis, Phyle and Rhamnus). The ephebic legislation was clearly intended to produce a more efficient citizen army. It was also geared to inculcate a feeling of tribal brotherhood, with the ephebes separated into tribal units and living on Spartan lines in communal messes, under the eye of their *sophronistes*. At the same time there was some degree of patriotic indoctrination. The traditional ephebic oath, framed in deliberately archaic language, pledged them to the defence of the laws and sanctuaries of Attica (Tod, *GHI* no. 204), and the ephebic corps appeared as a matter of course in the religious festivals; they are attested competing collectively in the torch race as early as 333/2 (Reinmuth no. 6). The result of the training was in theory an effective citizen army, well armed and trained and deeply motivated to defend Athens. It was certainly a considerable expense. If the tribal catalogues are an accurate guide, the number of ephebes was around 500 a year, and the maintenance of the corps and its officers will have consumed well

---

[27] The long series of ephebic dedications begins in 334/3 (cf. Reinmuth 1971) and there are some fifteen attested over the next ten years. There is no earlier evidence for the state-controlled *ephebeia*; Reinmuth no. 1 is now dissociated from the archonship of Nicophemus (Mitchel 1975). The number of ephebes in each tribe ranges from *c.* 44 (Reinmuth no. 9) to 62 (Reinmuth no. 15). This suggests a total corps between 500 and 600 strong, some 3% of the total citizen population of 21,000 – a figure consonant with the proportion of eighteen-year-olds in better attested populations (cf. Ruschenbusch 1979).

over forty talents. The provision of arms would have been a major recurrent expense.

The national festivals of Athens also attracted public revenues. One of Lycurgus' most celebrated achievements was the completion of the Panathenaic stadium, and for its construction he elicited donations from far outside Athens. An extant decree attests his moving honours for Eudemus of Plataea for his provision of 1,000 carts and draught animals (Tod, *GHI* no. 198). The policy of raising private subsidies, which had been successful in the emergency fortification programme after Chaeronea, was now extended outside the city, and prominent aliens were invited to become benefactors of the Athenian state. The care devoted to the permanent housing of the festival was applied to all its details. There is legislation providing for the regular purchase of sacrificial animals and other accoutrements out of funds created by the leasing of state land called *Nea*, allegedly 'the first instance of earmarking a specific source of revenue for a specific purpose'.[28] The Panathenaea was to be truly worthy of the city. In the same way the Athenian administration paid conspicuous attention to the newly acquired territory of Oropus. Under the supervision of the Athenian antiquarian Phanodemus laws were passed establishing a quadrennial festival for the local hero Amphiaraus, with the provision of regular funds and improvements to the temple to do honour to the occasion (*IG* vii.4253 = *SIG*³ 287). The first celebration was duly held in 329/8 with a solemn procession and athletic and equestrian competitions. Ten commissioners were elected by the *demos*, including Phanodemus, Lycurgus, Demades and Niceratus, a descendant of the great Nicias (*IG* vii.4254 = *SIG*³ 298). The local cult of Oropus was now absorbed into the religious calendar of Athens, and the religious integration completed the political annexation of the area. Once again the political enemies of 335, Lycurgus and Demades, appear side by side, as they do in the list of *hieropoioi* sent to represent their city at Delphi in 326/5.[29] Lycurgus' religious expenditures were evidently not controversial, and all could co-operate in the honours offered to the gods.

The *demos* as a whole benefited from all these measures, not least the festival programme in which it participated as audience and recipient of festival largesse. The theoric fund, the so-called cement of democracy, continued to flourish, and the funds it disbursed were substantial. Demades is said to have promised half a mina to each citizen for the festival of the Choae in early 330 (Plut. *Mor.* 818E), a sum which looks suspiciously high but is matched by Lycurgus' distribution after the condemnation of Diphilus. Extravagant largesse may have been the rule in this period of financial buoyancy, and, if its ultimate aim was to discourage dreams of empire and military involvement abroad, it was amply justified. Athens stayed clear of war for fifteen years, and her military capacity increased as a result. The visible

[28] *IG* ii².334 with Lewis 1959.
[29] *SIG*³ 296–7; cf. D. M. Lewis, *ABSA* 50 (1955) 34.

benefit of the policy came from the succession of public works devoted to the
comfort and edification of the *demos*.[30] The younger population was provided
with the wrestling school and gymnasium in the Lyceum. For the mature
citizen body civic amenities were greatly improved. The theatre of Dionysus
was rebuilt and extended, and a programme of construction began on the
Pnyx, with two large stoas built above the auditorium. In the *agora* the new
council chamber had a porch added and a *propylon* was attached to the south
side of the council complex, while the lawcourts were given more impressive
accommodation with the erection of the cloister-like building known as the
Square Peristyle. All the main institutional buildings of the assembly, the
council and the dicasteries were expanded and beautified in the Lycurgan
programme. At the same time the temple of Apollo Patroos was rebuilt in the
*agora*, commemorating the common ancestry of the Ionian people and Athens
as their common origin (cf. Arist. *Ath. Pol.* F 1). An element of patriotism was
always to be found in the Lycurgan programme and it would be a mistake to
think that it was not genuine or widely felt. It would be still more erroneous to
hold to the once fashionable view that the Lycurgan largesse sapped the
political and military morale of the Athenian people. On the contrary. Once
Alexander's death was known, the *demos* rose to the call of liberty and, for all
the scepticism of Diodorus (xviii.10.1–2), who reflects the oligarchic con-
tempt of his Macedonian source Hieronymus, the Athenians rose to the
sacrifices war demanded of them in an effort not unworthy of their greatest
days.

Lycurgus had his enemies. He was forced to defend his accounts
repeatedly, not least upon his death-bed ([Plut.] *Mor.* 842F); and shortly after
his death his sons were accused of collective responsibility for embezzlement,
condemned and imprisoned. It was a miserably vindictive affair, and its
grounds were purely personal. Lycurgus' principal assailant, Menesaechmus,
had suffered an indictment for impiety at Lycurgus' hands ([Plut.] *Mor.*
843D; *P. Ber.* 11748) and cherished a bitter grudge. But he was also Lycurgus'
successor as financial administrator of Athens (Dion. Hal. *Din.* 11, p. 316)
and continued his general policies. In fact it is hard to see how there could be
any objection in principle to Lycurgus' administration, with its priorities
firmly centred on military preparedness and the civic adornment of Athens.
Nothing is more misleading than the conventional picture of Lycurgan
Athens, polarised between pro- and anti-Macedonian factions. This is based
ultimately on the wild allegations of forensic speeches, in which accusations of
collaboration with foreign powers are a regular stock-in-trade. If one takes
seriously the peroration of Demosthenes' *De corona* (and many have), it
becomes necessary to believe that there was a large group of people actively
devoted to the subversion of the Athenian state and the maintenance of
Macedonian supremacy. In fact the only Athenians to take the Macedonian
side when war came in 323 were Pytheas and Callimedon (Plut. *Dem.* 27.2).

[30] See the full catalogue in Will 1983, 79–93.

Of these Pytheas had hitherto been notorious for his populist stance (Dem. *Ep.* III.29) and had opposed a request for ships for the Macedonian fleet (Plut. *Phoc.* 21.1). His defection came after he had been imprisoned as a state debtor, and there is no suggestion that the case for which he was fined was brought because of pro-Macedonian activities. His treachery seems to have been a surprise. It would be fair to say that there was general regret and chagrin at Athens' loss of hegemony and general support for a programme of military readiness. Where there was disagreement was over the necessity to accept the *status quo*. On one side of the spectrum was the veteran Phocion, who appears to have had a realistic appreciation of Macedonian military strength and argued consistently for inactivity and non-provocation. Even in the flood tide of the Lamian War he opposed what he saw as the rash militancy of Leosthenes, but that did not prevent the *demos* electing him general for both years of the war (admittedly in Attica); and his lack of enthusiasm for the general issue did not impair his military efficiency (Plut. *Phoc.* 25). On the other hand it is hard to find any politician consistently in favour of war. Hypereides had been active during the campaign of Chaeronea and was to be one of the prime instigators of the Lamian War. If he was the author of the speech on the treaty with Alexander, he was uncompromising in his demand for war in 331/0. But there is no indication of opposition at the opening of Alexander's reign, and it is significant that he was not one of the statesmen demanded in 335. On the other hand, as we have seen, Demosthenes was bellicose in 336 and 335 but lukewarm to Agis' War, and his actions in the Harpalus affair brought him close to that man of peace, his fellow demesman Demades (see below, p. 219). Foreign affairs in Athens evoked a complicated mosaic of attitudes and emotions, and few men could or would steer a consistent political course.

There were of course contacts with Macedon. Individual Athenians had personal relations with individual Macedonians. The ties of guest friendship and *proxenia* were as close as they ever had been, and the constant interchange of embassies between Athens and the royal court gave ample scope for establishing profitable relationships. Before the death of Philip Demades had moved official decrees conferring citizenship and *proxenia* upon prominent Macedonians, including Alcimachus and Antipater himself (Tod, *GHI* nos. 180–1; Hyper. F 77). Harpalus had strong connections with the family of Phocion and had himself acquired citizenship. Even Demosthenes thought it worthwhile to send his favourite Aristion to court in order to win over Hephaestion (Aesch. III.162; cf. Berve 1926, 2 no. 120). Such ties were largely informal but they were very important. They allowed certain Athenians to gain access to the king's ear and helped mitigate his treatment of the city, while Macedonian guest-friends might recommend counsels of prudence to their Athenian counterparts. It is hard to believe that Phocion's political caution was not influenced by his contacts at the Macedonian court and his friendly relations with the king. Indeed these friendly relations were probably

the main basis for charges of political corruption (cf. Hyper. *Eux.* 22). But
once the city was at war the ties were immediately broken. Nothing shows this
better than the actions of Demades, who was undoubtedly a friend of
Antipater and exploited his friendship in the city's interest in 322. None the
less at the height of the Lamian War he was prepared to write to Perdiccas,
urging him to invade Europe and attack his friend (Diod. xviii.48.2) – a
manœuvre reminiscent of the wooing of Attalus in 336.

There was little disloyalty at Athens, but it should not be thought that there
was total unanimity when war broke out. Diodorus for all his hostile bias must
be correct when he says that there was pressure from the propertied classes to
remain at peace (xviii.10.1). His observations bear a remarkable resemblance
to the equally unsympathetic analysis of Athenian opinion made by the
Oxyrhynchus historian (6.3). In both 396 and 322 the rich were a restraining
influence, reluctant to shoulder the financial burdens of war. These men will
have included the elderly friends of Phocion, prominent in the oligarchy of
322 and collectively condemned in 318 (Plut. *Phoc.* 35.5). Little is known of
them except that Pythocles and Hegemon were associated with Aeschines'
attacks on Demosthenes and Hegemon passed the legislation restricting the
powers of the theoric commissioners. Enmity to Demosthenes, despite
Demosthenes' protestations, did not amount to a pro-Macedonian stance. All
we can be reasonably sure of is that they were monied (Thudippus and
Pythocles belonged to families whose wealth is well attested) and were
reluctant to jeopardise their property. But this reluctance, as we have seen
with Phocion, did not exclude sterling service once the war was voted, and
Thudippus at least saw active service as a trierarch in 323/2 (*IG* ii². 1631, lines
470, 592, 600).

The political tensions of the period were well voiced in the affair of the
Crown. In the summer of 330 B.C. Aeschines revived the indictment of
Ctesiphon which he had first lodged in 337/6, alleging that Ctesiphon's decree
to crown Demosthenes for his service as commissioner of fortifications
(*teichopoios*) was illegal. Six years after the formal notice of indictment the
case was finally heard, certainly at the instigation of Aeschines (Demosthenes
would hardly have glossed over the fact if he had taken the initiative). He was
probably attempting to capitalise on the sympathy which was widely felt for
the defeated Spartans and consequent disenchantment with Athens' lukewarm part in the affair. Accordingly he used the prosecution of Ctesiphon as a
vehicle to indict Demosthenes' entire political career. The technical grounds
for the prosecution were largely irrelevant and it was fortunate for Ctesiphon
that they were, for no amount of sophistical pleading could obscure the fact
that the decree had proposed crowning Demosthenes before he submitted his
accounts and was for that reason alone illegal. It was the content of
Ctesiphon's proposal that formed the basis of Aeschines' indictment. Demosthenes was to be crowned because he had 'continued to say and do what was
best for the *demos*' (Aesch. iii.49–50). On the contrary, claimed Aeschines,

Demosthenes' policies had been consistently ruinous for the city; he had brought on the disaster of Chaeronea, was responsible for the destruction of Thebes and had ignored the golden opportunity of Agis' War. The speech ends with a highly artificial and emotive indictment of Demosthenes' medism; his acceptance of Persian money is an affront to the men of Marathon and Salamis.

This was a challenge Demosthenes could not ignore and he sprang to the defence of Ctesiphon. His speech is one of the monuments of European literature and its rousing appeal to patriotism has inspired generations of statesmen. But it is not only supreme as an example of patriotic rhetoric; it is also a brilliantly clever example of forensic art. Demosthenes' defence is centred exclusively upon his forging of the great alliance of 338, which he presents as a shining example of heroic achievement. He personally upheld the banner of liberty, championing its cause against a host of corrupt time-servers at home. If the resistance to Philip failed it was not his fault, and he skilfully turns the defence into a counter-indictment of Aeschines' life and policies. Unlike his rival he was motivated by loyalty to the *demos* and against all his attacks he steered the alliance to near success. He was responsible for the war being fought 700 stades from Athens, for Euboea providing a bulwark against piracy, and, most importantly, ensuring that the city remained unconquered and received generous terms from Philip (Dem. XVIII.229–31). All this is largely true, but it only answers a fraction of the indictment. Demosthenes totally ignores the complex events of the past six years and his reactions to Agis and the Theban revolt. To defend himself on this ground would have required a totally different emotional tone. He would need to stress the necessity for compromise, for careful choice of the correct moment for military action, whereas the concentration on the campaign of Chaeronea allows him to present his policies as unconditional opposition to Macedonian tyranny. Even if the issue had been foreknown, the city should still have followed the same course. If she had flinched from the struggle and preferred inglorious security to the call of honour, she would have betrayed her entire history. That was what Athens had done in 331/0, but Demosthenes does not allow the contemporary context to impinge. He keeps to the reign of Philip, now almost a semi-legendary past, and paints a picture of heroic aspiration and glorious failure, thanks to a 'Dolchstoss' by Aeschines and his friends.

Demosthenes was triumphantly successful in his exploitation of the contemporary feelings of frustrated patriotism. Aeschines failed to win one-fifth of the votes and retired in chagrin to Rhodes. Both men had tried to manipulate the current sentiments, but Demosthenes had deliberately steered the jurors' minds from the painful present and indulged their sentimental views of the recent past. This was clearly the direction his audience wished to take. For the moment they were forced to accept Macedonian hegemony, but they could pride themselves on their resistance in the past and could look forward to its resumption in the indefinite future. The present reality was a

Macedon militarily supreme in Europe and Asia. The *demos* might live with
the situation and accept political compromises but it preferred not to be
reminded of the fact. Demosthenes utilised those feelings for his forensic
purposes, as had Lycurgus a few months before, when he impeached
Leocrates for leaving the city in panic at the news of Chaeronea. Like
Demosthenes he had a technically weak case and he is unable to refer to any
specific law forbidding Leocrates' actions; he can only cite the extraordinary
and questionable police action by the Areopagus (*Leocr.* 52–4). Instead of
appealing to the laws Lycurgus contrasts the behaviour of Leocrates with the
heroic examples of the Athenian past, citing indiscriminately the ephebic
oath, the *Erechtheus* of Euripides and the elegies of that notable Athenian,
Tyrtaeus. Again there is the blend of the remote and recent past. Lycurgus'
speech culminates in an invocation of the dead of Chaeronea, for whom
Leocrates is a living affront. Would they absolve the man who betrayed the
graves they lie in? The technique is specious, almost mendacious, yet it nearly
succeeded. Leocrates evaded condemnation by a single vote (Aesch. III.252).
The patriotic feeling of Lycurgan Athens was intense and carefully fostered.
As we have seen, it was some consolation for the relative impotence of the
present, but it was also preparation for the future, the psychological counterpart of the armament programme. Athenian morale during the Lamian War
was the ultimate justification of the programme of Lycurgus.

IV     **Athens and the advent of Harpalus**

In 324 B.C. the political stability of Lycurgan Athens was severely tested by
the advent of Harpalus, son of Machatas, formerly Alexander's friend and
treasurer but now a refugee. Harpalus had taken flight from Babylon at the
news of the executions in Carmania (see above, p. 149). With a substantial
mercenary army of 6,000 men and an even more impressive treasury of 5,000
talents (Diod. XVII.108.6) he moved west, probably to the Cilician coast
where he had installed his Athenian mistress, Glycera, in the palace at Tarsus
(Theopompus, *FGrH* 115 F 254). For the moment he was secure. No satrap
would have the resources to offer a military challenge; the edict to disband
their mercenary armies had seen to that. But Harpalus could not remain in
Asia indefinitely. Alexander was moving inexorably north, to Susa and then
into Mesopotamia, and an army could be deployed against him at any time.
After the sailing season began, in the spring of 324, he manned a flotilla of
thirty ships and voyaged west to the Greek mainland. His first destination was
inevitably Athens, the city which had provided his mistresses and given him
honorary citizenship; and in the light of Alexander's decision to support the
restoration of the Samian exiles a wealthy and powerful refugee might expect a
warm welcome there. It may well have been Alexander's first promulgation of
the Exiles' Decree which spurred him to take himself and his resources to
mainland Greece to capitalise on the inevitable resistance there. The chron-

ology of these events is desperately difficult, but Hypereides appears to say that Harpalus suddenly arrived on the scene when the Greek world was agog at the approach of Nicanor and the news of the mandates he brought.[31] It was probably in May 324 that Harpalus first appeared off the coast of Sunium, applying for asylum in Athens.

At first there was uncompromising resistance. Harpalus was denied admission to Athens. No doubt the Athenian refusal was due to their fear of Alexander's reactions if they sheltered what amounted to an insurgent army (cf. Curt. x.2.2). There may also have been a deep-seated suspicion of Harpalus himself. Might he not be tempted to ingratiate himself with his king by occupying the Piraeus, so frustrating any Athenian attempt to defend Samos? At all events the politicians who had waxed hysterical over the entry of a single Macedonian trireme ([Dem.] xvii.27–8) would look askance at thirty warships crammed with battle-hardened mercenaries. The Piraeus remained closed, and Harpalus had no choice but to transfer his forces to the great mercenary base at Taenarum, where they joined the thousands already concentrated there under the command of Leosthenes (see above, p. 149). He then returned to Athens with three ships and an ample supply of money. This time he was admitted by Philocles, the general in charge of Munychia and the docks,[32] the very man who had excluded the larger force (Din. iii.1–5). The refugee now entered the city. Alexander might well view it as a provocation but it was hardly an act of war. Many people will have felt that Athens owed a debt of gratitude to Harpalus, not least Phocion's son-in-law Charicles who had supervised the building of his memorial to Pythionice (Plut. *Phoc.* 22). Others shared Hypereides' view that the friendly reception of Harpalus would encourage other dissidents in Alexander's empire to transfer their funds and forces to Greece (Hyper. *Dem.* col. 19). On the other hand there was strong resistance, notably from Demosthenes, who insisted that the admission of Harpalus might be seized upon as a pretext for a general war against Athens (Plut. *Dem.* 25.3). But Harpalus' money was soon at work and bribes were certainly taken. Demosthenes himself is alleged to have received the massive sum of twenty talents, and he dropped his opposition to Harpalus' presence in the city. The fugitive could remain for the time being, until Alexander's reactions were known.

A decision ultimately had to be made. In due course the news of Harpalus' reception percolated to Macedon and Asia Minor. Antipater and Olympias both demanded his extradition, perhaps by letter (Diod. xvii.108.7). At the

---

[31] Hyper. *Dem.* col. 18. There is a lacuna in the papyrus and Harpalus' name has to be supplied; but there is no other context which can plausibly be suggested for the fragment. This passage indicates that Harpalus arrived in Greece not too long before the Olympic Games. On the other hand he had been admitted to Athens while Philocles was still general in the Piraeus, in the archon year 325/4 (see below, Appendix B). If the year was intercalary (cf. W. B. Dinsmoor, *The Archons of Athens in the Hellenistic Age* (Cambridge, Mass., 1931) 372, 429), as is generally accepted, Harpalus was in Athens before July 21.

[32] See Appendix B (pp. 293–4).

same time Philoxenus, the satrap of Caria, sent agents to Athens with a formal demand for the surrender of the fugitive. The day of decision had been postponed, perhaps for weeks,[33] but something now had to happen. Once again Demosthenes was the principal actor. He opposed the surrender of Harpalus on brilliantly specious grounds. The credentials of Philoxenus' ambassadors were impugned: they were not sent by Alexander himself and might lose the captive, in which case the city might be adjudged an accomplice to conspiracy (Hyper. *Dem.* col. 8). Harpalus could only be surrendered to agents directly responsible to the king. In the mean time he was to be kept in custody ([Plut.] *Mor.* 846B), and his monies (which he declared to amount to 700 talents) were lodged on the Acropolis the following day. In theory the Athenians were impeccably scrupulous in their stewardship of the refugee and his money. In practice their options were open, and, if war over Samos became inevitable, Harpalus and his men could still be enlisted as allies. With luck it would be months before Alexander's emissaries finally arrived.

Harpalus had been some weeks in Athens before his arrest. He had arrived in the city before the end of the civil year 325/4 B.C., but by the time he was taken into custody the next archon year had begun and the Olympic Games were close at hand. Accordingly Demosthenes led the official delegation to Olympia and in the course of the festival he had discussions with Nicanor. Those discussions involved the status of Samos (see below, p. 221), but Demosthenes will also have sounded out Nicanor's impressions of Alexander's attitude to Harpalus. Perhaps it was suggested that the king did not want the embarrassment of extraditing and condemning his old friend. At all events Harpalus was allowed to escape custody. His guard was reduced and finally disbanded (Hyper. *Dem.* col. 12) and he left the city. Harpalus' story was soon over. He collected his forces from Taenarum and began operations as a *condottiere* in Crete. There he was murdered by his lieutenant Thibron, no later than October 324, and his mercenary army was retained by exiles from Cyrenaica.[34] It ceased to be a factor in Greek affairs. Meanwhile at Athens Harpalus' escape had provoked an outcry, which increased in volume when an inventory of the monies on the Acropolis revealed that only 350 talents remained of the purported 700. This is perhaps the murkiest episode of the whole dark affair. Some aspects of it, however, are reasonably clear. There is no suggestion in any source that money was taken from the Acropolis itself.

---

[33] For Philoxenus' embassy see Hyper. *Dem.* col. 8; Paus. II.23.4; Plut. *Mor.* 531A. Hypereides has often been interpreted as correlating Harpalus' arrival in Athens with that of Philoxenus' agents. The context, however, is very vague. Hypereides gives only the roughest of chronological indications, when Harpalus had come to Athens and Philoxenus' delegation was being received by the *demos*. There is no necessary indication that the two events were simultaneous (ἅμα should probably be referred to the immediate context of the assembly: Philoxenus' men were brought before the assembly *together with* Harpalus). One would have thought that an embassy requesting extradition could not be sent out before there was accurate knowledge of the fugitive's whereabouts, and the news of his reception at Athens would have taken time to reach Caria.

[34] For the chronology see below, Appendix A (pp. 291–2).

What is emphasised is the discrepancy between what Harpalus was alleged to have brought into Attica and what was actually found on the Acropolis. The residue was automatically assumed to have been dissipated in bribes (Hyper. *Dem.* col. 7). Until Harpalus disappeared the money was not subjected to close scrutiny. But his escape led naturally to allegations that he had bribed his way out, and the treasure was then examined minutely. The discovery of the discrepancy led to outbursts of fury from all colours of the political spectrum. Some argued that Alexander's money had been embezzled and that the *demos* would face reprisals when the royal agents came to collect it (Din. 1.68, 89). Others like Hypereides argued that the city was robbed of vital resources for the inevitable war with Alexander. At the centre of the furore was Demosthenes, who had taken the leading role throughout the affair; Hypereides indeed dubbed him 'the arbiter of all our affairs' (*Dem.* col. 12). The charges increased in virulence. Not only had he accepted twenty talents but he had accepted them to undermine the constitution and the laws (Hyper. *Dem.* col. 2). Faced with insinuations of treason Demosthenes was forced to defend himself. In the assembly he moved a decree that the Areopagus should conduct an enquiry and report to the *demos* anyone who had received money brought into the country by Harpalus. At the same time he made a strong statement of his own innocence (Hyper. *Dem.* col. 2; Din. 1.61). Unfortunately his case was far from strong. He could not deny that he had received money from Harpalus but claimed that he had taken it as a loan to the theoric fund and used it in the interests of the *demos* (Hyper. *Dem.* col. 13). There may have been some truth in this. Loans from private individuals had been freely used during Lycurgus' financial administration to cope with extraordinary expenses ([Plut.] *Mor.* 852B; cf. *SIG*³ 298.29). Demosthenes may have deployed Harpalus' funds on state business, possibly in the form of preliminary payments to Leosthenes at Taenarum. If so, his disbursements were necessarily secret, like the later payment of fifty talents made by the *boule* (Diod. xvii.111.3), and there was no official record of them. Under those circumstances who could distinguish between a loan and a bribe? Demosthenes was vulnerable and did what he could to defer the reckoning. He had used the Areopagus before to conduct enquiries in his interest (Dem. xviii.132; Din. 1.62–3), and it may be assumed that the council was well stacked with his supporters and would not rush to indict him.

He was not disappointed. The Areopagus began its report, probably in September, and it took six months to publish its findings (Din. 1.45), even though there was continuous public pressure for a statement (Hyper. *Dem.* col. 5). The reasons for the delay are obscure, but it seems certain that Harpalus and his money soon ceased to be a burning issue. Alexander did not claim his treasure or his ships, and there was no sign of the war that was threatened when Athens first admitted Harpalus. Demosthenes' general policy of moderation and avoidance of overt conflict might have been thought to hold some prospect of success. But the bribery scandal was kept alive by interested parties and allegations continued. During the early months of 323 (probably at the Lenaea in late January) the comedian Timocles satirised some of the leading politicians in his *Delos*, writing in happy ignorance of the Areopagus' ultimate findings. Hypereides, who was never implicated, is associated with Demosthenes, as are Moerocles, Demon and Callisthenes, men never elsewhere associated with the scandal (Ath. 341E–342A). What is more, the tone of the comedy is bantering, almost tolerant; there is nothing to suggest an atmosphere of white-hot popular fury. The emotions of the *demos* were no longer deeply stirred, but the charges of bribery were not forgotten. Finally, around March 323, the Areopagus made its report, submitting a list of names with the total amount each was supposed to have received. Demosthenes headed the list with twenty talents; Demades was alleged to have received 6,000 staters (probably silver),[35] and several others were named, including Charicles (Phocion's son-in-law) and Philocles (who had admitted Harpalus into Athens). The *demos* then set up a court of 1,500 jurors, and ten accusers were allocated to each defendant. The only names given are those of Demosthenes' accusers ([Plut.] *Mor.* 846C), an apparently heterogeneous bunch including both Hypereides and Pytheas, men whose policies were to be diametrically opposite at the start of the Lamian War. Obviously the trials united Demosthenes' opponents, whatever their political persuasions, and they combined their efforts to undermine him. Whether the Areopagus had been forced to a declaration by external events we cannot say. It is notable that the men most inculpated, Demosthenes and Demades, had both been instrumental in moving divine honours for Alexander (see below p. 288), and their actions may have lost them popularity. But though the issue is raised by both Hypereides and Deinarchus it is not pressed and there is no indication that popular emotions were still inflamed. More probably Alexander had made some ruling against Athenian claims to Samos. Negotiations were continuously in progress and at any stage bad news from court might exasperate the *demos* and undermine the popularity of the proponents of moderation.

The trials were not spectacular. Some of the speeches which Deinarchus wrote for the prosecution have survived, remarkably lacklustre efforts, as have fragments of Hypereides' oration against Demosthenes. Both writers presuppose a good deal of public indifference to the charges of bribery and harp upon the enormity of the offence and the dangers of acquitting men of proven venality. They had reason to do so. Demosthenes and Demades were convicted, as apparently was Philocles (Dem. *Ep.* III.32), but the penalties inflicted were relatively light. Far from the death penalty which Demosthenes had called upon his head when he launched the Areopagus' investigation or even the tenfold restitution which the law provided, the court imposed a fine of fifty talents, two and a half times the amount of the alleged bribe. The

[35] Deinarchus (1.89) speaks of 6,000 *gold* staters, which is almost certainly forensic exaggeration (cf. Badian 1961, 35 n. 146).

amount of Demades' fine is not recorded, but it was presumably in his means to pay it, for he was active in the city at the time of Alexander's death. Demosthenes, however, could not or would not pay and was imprisoned in default. After a few days he was allowed to escape in a manner ironically reminiscent of Harpalus, and until Alexander's death he lived miserably in exile, first at Troezen and then at Aegina. He was the main victim of the Harpalus affair which he had manipulated so skilfully in its earlier phases. Harpalus had entered and escaped from the city without provoking hostilities with Alexander. The nucleus of his treasure remained on the Acropolis as an emergency fund, which was immediately put to use at the outbreak of the Lamian War (Diod. xviii.9.4), and his warships were used in the Athenian Navy. Athens had admittedly lost the opportunity of allying herself with Harpalus and launching a general war in Greece, but in the summer of 324 such a war would have been fatal to Athens and to any city foolish enough to join her. Only a Hypereides would lament that failure. As it was, war was deferred and the Athenians could continue their rearguard diplomatic action in defence of Samos until the end of the reign.

## v    The Exiles' Decree and its effects

At the Olympic Games of 324 B.C. (which probably culminated at the full moon of 4 August)[36] Alexander pronounced the restoration of exiles throughout the Greek world. His letter, delivered by Nicanor of Stagira, was read out by the victorious herald to a vast and expectant audience comprising more than 20,000 exiles who had gathered for the occasion (Diod. xviii.8.3–5). It was a grand gesture and had wide repercussions, almost causing open war with Athens, whose interests on Samos were threatened, and inflicting grave disruption upon thousands of communities, who were forced to receive back and compensate families long estranged, some of them second- and third-generation expatriates. In addition it breached one of the fundamental tenets of the Corinthian League, which prohibited the return of exiles, at least when backed by force ([Dem.] xvii.16). More seriously, Alexander was acting in blatant violation of Greek autonomy in issuing a general command which struck at the economic and political stability of every city, great and small. The sources give no hint of debate in the Corinthian *synedrion* or of any sort of diplomatic consultation. Instead they speak of a unilateral declaration by Alexander, delivered by letter. As quoted by Diodorus (who here excerpts the contemporary Hieronymus of Cardia), it

---

[36] The dating was proposed by Sealey 1960, who endorsed Beloch's general theory that Olympic festivals alternated between the full moons of July and August. The central date, the Olympics of 480 B.C., still remains controversial (Labarbe's synchronism with the heliacal rising of Sirius was challenged on all points by C. Hignett, *Xerxes' Invasion of Greece* (Oxford, 1963) 449). Sacks 1976 argues that there was not total regularity in the calculation of the Olympic cycle and is prepared to go no further than the limits of late July and late September. If that is correct, we cannot exclude an alternative date of 3 September for the Olympia of 324 B.C..

was a brief communiqué disclaiming responsibility for the exiles, guarantee-ing return to all but those guilty of sacrilege, and revealing that Antipater had instructions to coerce any city which was uncooperative. That is the language of autocracy. Alexander was conferring a general benefaction and nothing was to impede it, least of all the laws of the individual city states. Philip at least had not issued general edicts; he had intervened politically, by direct and indirect methods, and ensured that most regimes were responsive to his wishes. By 324 Alexander had transcended such procedures. Now the Greeks of the mainland were treated as his subjects, the recipients of direct commands. He was prepared to listen to representations, to modify his general edict to accommo-date the problems of particular cities, but there was to be no questioning his powers to organise the Greek world as he thought fit. His monarchy was now universal, and there were to be no areas of exemption and privilege.

The Decree was probably formulated over a period of months. It was promulgated at Olympia but conceived in Mesopotamia. Both Curtius and Diodorus associate it with the dismissal of the veterans from Opis in the summer of 324;[37] and, if Arrian recorded it (and his sources will hardly have omitted an event so ideally suited to propaganda), it fell in the great lacuna, where he covered the events of summer 324, between Opis and Ecbatana. Nicanor at any rate was despatched to Greece in May at the latest, to allow him ample travelling time before the Olympics, and from that moment (if not before) the nature of his mission was public knowledge. As he travelled west, there was increasing public debate and, in some quarters, consternation. In Asia Alexander had probably made a formal announcement before the army. We know that the specific ruling to return Samos to the Samians was openly announced 'in the camp' before an audience of Greeks (*SIG*³ 312.12–14),[38] and the wider ordinance must have been publicised in a similar way. The decree for the restoration of the exiles, the sole subject of the Olympic announcement, was only one of the orders conveyed by Nicanor. He had more specific instructions concerning two problem areas. The Aetolians had their occupancy of the Acarnanian city of Oeniadae threatened, and the Athenian cleruchies on Samos were to be withdrawn, so that the native Samian populace, in exile since 365, could be restored to its homeland. These rulings were not promulgated at Olympia, but they had been forshadowed in earlier pronouncements by Alexander and negotiations were already afoot. Sig-nificantly it was Demosthenes who led the official Athenian delegation to Olympia, and he used the occasion to open discussions with Nicanor (Din. 1.81–2), who was clearly both messenger and ambassador. As well as the specific rulings concerning Oeniadae and Samos there were mysterious instruc-tions which dealt with the federal assemblies of the Achaean and Arcadian

---

[37] Diod. xvii.109. 1–2; Curt. x.2.4–8. The sources based on Hieronymus are less precise: 'a short time before his death' (Diod. xviii.8.2), 'on his return from India' (Justin xiii.5.1).

[38] Errington 1975a, 53–5 argues that the ruling on Samos was first made at Babylon in spring 323, well after the Olympic Games. It is an implausibly late date for a decision which concerned such an important group of exiles (cf. Heisserer 1980, 183–9; Ashton 1983, 62–3).

Leagues. The text of Hypereides (the only source for this) is sadly fragmentary, and it remains very dubious what Alexander intended to do with these communities.[39] But it is more than a possibility that he planned to abolish the federal assemblies altogether, so destroying their legislative machinery. Nicanor brought more than a single letter; he was commissioned with a whole package of regulations designed to reorganise the political structure of Greece.

These regulations were hardly conceived overnight. Alexander had probably been mulling over the affairs of Greece ever since his return from the east. His motives, as always, are difficult to disentangle. Diodorus (XVIII.8.2) gives two reasons for the Exiles' Decree – Alexander's desire for glory and his wish to have partisans in every city as a counter against revolution and defection. This information comes from Hieronymus and it is intrinsically credible. The popularity of the move was obvious enough. There were exiles in plenty at the royal court who agitated constantly for their restoration. If they were not themselves prominent courtiers, there were often powerful friends who could give support. There is epigraphical evidence for the efforts of Gorgus of Iasus in support of the dispossessed Samians; he constantly made representations for them at court, and, when the king announced their restoration, he offered him a crown in recognition and sent concrete assistance to the Samian refugees in Iasus (*SIG*³ 312). Exiles at court were not the only petitioners. There was a constant influx of embassies from communities in exile, soliciting Alexander's help. The exiles of Heracleia Pontica will have been typical. After Alexander became master of the Persian Empire they sent embassies directly to him, requesting their restoration and the imposition of a democratic regime. The result was that Dionysius, the tyrant of Heracleia, was forced to mount a desperate rearguard action, threatened with military intervention by Alexander, and only survived by grace of the patronage of Alexander's sister Cleopatra (Memnon, *FGrH* 434 F 1 (4.1)). Similar representations by exiles may also have been responsible for the imposition of democracy upon Amisus, also in the Pontic area (App. *Mithr.* 83.374). Alexander was well aware of the misfortunes of exiles and avid for the glory of a general restoration. The passion to display magnanimity was always a driving force with him, and his letter to Olympia underscores it; he is not responsible for the exiles' condition but he will assume responsibility for their restoration. It was his royal

[39] Hyper. *Dem.* col. 18. The papyrus refers to κοινοὶ σύλλογοι of the Achaeans and Arcadians and breaks off abruptly. Traces of a few letters of the following line are preserved, and Blass thought he could read [καὶ B]οι[ω]τῶ[ν], a suggestion which has been generally accepted. Aymard 1937, 7–10, however, observed that the Boeotians, impeccably loyal to Alexander, are very unnatural associates of the Achaeans and Arcadians. This gave rise to Colin's colourless and uninformative [καὶ τ]οι[ού]τω[ν]. In fact the traces are so ambiguous (the reading of every letter may be contested) that virtually any supplement is possible, and it is supererogatory to posit a third federal state. It is best to stay with the Achaeans and Arcadians, who present no historical difficulty. Aymard also rejected the traditional interpretation of the passage, arguing that it refers to a request by Alexander that his divinity be recognised by the League assemblies. That is most improbable; why should two states only be singled out for such a demand? Badian 1961, 31 n. 105, is more orthodox and convincing, admitting 'some restriction or punishment, perhaps later remitted as the result of embassies'.

benefaction, and a benefaction not to be refused. Behind the diplomacy of Nicanor was the coercive power of the armies of Antipater, and Alexander's letter made it clear that it would be used.

The reverse of the coin was the political advantage accruing from the return of the exiles. Diodorus stresses Alexander's wish to have his own partisans to counteract revolution in the cities, and the Heracleian exiles provided a model case study. If they were restored, their city became a democracy under a regime which owed its existence to himself. Elsewhere changes would be less dramatic but none the less significant. Families which had spent generations in exile would return to reclaim a portion of their own and, almost by definition, they would be hostile to the existing regimes. At Tegea for instance the exiles of several generations returned together. Some had been away long enough for their previous wives and daughters to marry or remarry and produce offspring who were later exiled in their turn (Tod, *GHI* no. 202.48–57). Those restored in 324 would have included the survivors and descendants of the families exiled during the democratic revolution of the 360s, when the Arcadian League was founded. There were exiles of equally long standing elsewhere, notably the Samians, who had been refugees since 365. Such long-term expatriates would necessarily be out of touch with their home cities and the only real guarantor of their interests was the man who had restored them. Their gratitude and loyalty were therefore dependable. But there were also more recent exiles, many of whom opposed Macedon before the establishment of the Corinthian League and had been expelled during the constitutional rearrangements of 338/7. Alexander was to some degree subverting the policies of his father, and it is not difficult to see why he did so. The governments supported by Philip, particularly those in the Peloponnese, had not been reliable in the recent past. The states which gave material assistance to Agis included the Achaean League, the Arcadian League except Megalopolis, and Elis (Aesch. III.165). Of these Tegea had been awarded Spartan border land after Chaeronea and Elis had co-operated with Philip since 343. The only Achaean city to remain loyal in 331 (Pellene) had a tyrant imposed by Alexander, not a government sanctioned by his father. The Exiles' Decree accordingly struck at the guarantees of political stability which were the foundation of the Corinthian League. Tens of thousands of exiles would return *en masse*, and the home governments would have their hands too full with domestic problems to plan or support any military uprising. In that context the subsidiary instructions relating to the Achaean and Arcadian Leagues make excellent sense. Both had been involved in the war of 331/0, and the Arcadians had sent an army to monitor events at Thebes in 335 (Din. 1.18–20). It might have seemed prudent to set limits on the common assemblies and prevent collective votes which might commit a whole federation against Macedon. Philip had operated in much the same way against the Aetolians when he divided the *koinon* into its constituent tribes. Now his son was apparently planning to fragment and weaken the two federal states in the

Peloponnese which had offered most opposition during his reign. The Decree, then, was Alexander's considered response to the problem of Greek resistance. It was deliberately disruptive, aiming to increase the tensions in Greek city states while at the same time augmenting Alexander's own partisans in each community.

The amnesty though general was not unrestricted. Alexander's letter to Olympia specifically excluded those guilty of sacrilege, and Diodorus (XVII.109.2) extends the exclusion to murderers. Now it is very unlikely that individuals exiled as a result of Alexander's own actions or policies were restored. The letter disclaims responsibility for the exiles' fate, and that is not hypocrisy. Alexander did not consider the people he had exiled as covered by the Decree; he was restoring those persons expelled before his accession and by actions other than his own. The largest group of his victims, the Thebans, had no city to return to. Their territory was divided into cleruchies, farmed by other Boeotians (Diod. XVIII.11.3–4), and there was no suggestion of changing the situation before Cassander invaded Boeotia in 316 (cf. Diod. XIX.53.2). Other exiles could easily be excluded. Given the murderous nature of Greek factional conflict, few exiled families could clear themselves of political homicide, if Alexander wished the charge pressed. Accusations of sacrilege were also difficult to evade. The Ephesian oligarchs for example were alleged to have profaned the temple of Artemis (Arr. 1.17.11). Similarly the Eresian tyrants apparently burned and looted temples (Tod, *GHI* no. 192.5–12); there was no question of their families returning during Alexander's reign and, when the exiles appealed to Philip III for restoration, the sentence was reconfirmed. Most of the people exiled for collaboration with the Persians or with Agis will have fallen within the ambit of the exclusion clause. So at least Philip and Polyperchon seem to have thought. Their famous *diagramma* of 319 B.C. re-enacted the Exiles' Decree, granting return to persons subsequently exiled and with the same exclusions for blood guilt and sacrilege. The upper limit, however, was not the Olympic Games of 324 but Alexander's crossing into Asia ten years before (Diod. XVIII.56.4). By implication the exiles of Alexander's reign were excluded from the amnesty of 324. The families restored at that time were the victims of political conflict before his accession and all the more likely to be grateful for the benefaction. Alexander's own opponents remained in limbo.

Not surprisingly the news of the Decree triggered off a flurry of diplomatic activity. Early in 323 Alexander received a number of embassies which protested against the return of the cities' exiles (Diod. XVII.113.3), and for the rest of his life there was doubtless a continuous stream of representations, as the general terms of the Decree were modified to the conditions of the individual cities. Modifications there certainly were. At Tegea the regulations finally inscribed on stone followed a royal rescript making corrections to meet the city's specific objections (Tod, *GHI* no. 202.2–4). Those objections largely concerned property, and from them we can to some degree trace the amount of disruption caused by the Decree (even though the number of the restored exiles and their financial status is completely unknown). Exiles were to regain part of their property (paternal property or maternal, in the case of women with no surviving male blood relatives), and they were guaranteed a house at the controlled price of two *minae* per room.[40] Disputes were to be heard in the first instance outside the city, probably in Mantineia; Tegean courts only operated if suits were not filed within sixty days of return. The stipulation of outside jurisdiction was probably Alexander's and it was prudent. Tegean courts were not likely to look with favour on residents being dispossessed of property acquired maybe generations ago. The return of the exiles inevitably meant hardship and loss, particularly in the propertied classes, and it must have been bitterly resented. There was no general refusal, for no city and no regime wished to face reprisals from the world conqueror. Like Dionysius in Heracleia they could only stave off the evil day by diplomacy.

The Athenians were the supreme diplomats, and they managed to retain control of Samos until the end of the reign. But it was a close-run thing and they came to the brink of outright war. The crisis came when Harpalus reached Athens (see above, p. 216) in the midsummer of 324. Athens' objections to the loss of Samos were already well known to Alexander, and the arrival of a notorious defector off the coast of Sunium naturally appeared prearranged and a prelude to war (Curt. x.2.1–2). It was when the news reached Ecbatana that Gorgus of Iasus made his famous offer of 10,000 panoplies and catapults for the siege of Athens (Ephippus, *FGrH* 126 F 5; cf. Justin xiii.5.7). Alexander was seriously planning a campaign and war was imminent. Fortunately there were strong forces at work in Athens to prevent open conflict. The key issue was the retention of the Samian cleruchies and it was not to be prejudiced by Harpalus, however great a debt the city owed him. Demosthenes, initially at least, urged the *demos* not to involve the city in a major war for an unjust and unnecessary cause (Plut. *Dem.* 25.3), an argument reminiscent of the peroration of the *De pace*, delivered over twenty years before (Dem. v 24–5). Within a matter of weeks from his admission to Athens Harpalus was under guard on the Acropolis awaiting extradition, and in due course he slipped from custody. The Athenians were spared the humiliation of surrendering their suppliant and fellow-citizen, and the *casus belli* was removed. Harpalus had gone; only his money remained. For the moment Athens was reprieved, but preparations for war continued secretly. Leosthenes, the mercenary commander at Taenarum,[41] was retained with his men for the service of Athens after secret negotiations with the *boule* and he held his forces in readiness for action (Diod. xviii.9.2; xvii.111.3). At the

---

[40] This is the persuasive suggestion of Klaffenbach, briefly proposed in *DLZ* 69 (1948) 503 and largely ignored. The orthodox explanation that each *house* was sold at two *minae* or valued at two *minae* as compensation (Heisserer 1980, 213–14) is much less attractive.

[41] See Appendix B (pp. 293–4).

same time he acted as intermediary between Athens and Aetolia, laying the diplomatic groundwork for the formal alliance which was concluded immediately after Alexander's death was known. These negotiations were strictly unofficial, but they were provocative and Antipater cannot have been unaware of them (cf. Diod. xviii.9.2). Fortunately Antipater himself was insecure. He was shortly to be replaced as regent by Craterus and was to lead an army of fresh recruits to Babylon. The last thing he desired was a major conflagration in Greece to distract his attention and drain his reserves of manpower. He therefore tolerated the seditious negotiations in the south and even made overtures on his own behalf to the Aetolians (Plut. *Al.* 49.14–15).

The Athenians had domestic worries caused by the Decree. Exiles from the city expected their immediate restoration, and by the time of the trial of Demosthenes they had gathered as a group in Megara. They were regarded as a threat to the constitution. Communications with them were prohibited and subject to prosecution. Demosthenes himself began (and later dropped) impeachment proceedings against his enemy Callimedon on the grounds that he was intriguing with the exiles to subvert the democracy (Din. 1.94, cf. 58); and given Callimedon's later record of collaboration with Macedon the charge may not have been unfounded. There was also trouble at Samos, where the exiled Samians apparently made an abortive attempt to return. This episode, only recently revealed by Samian decrees of the restoration,[42] was dramatic. A group of exiles had gathered at Anaea, on the slopes of Mt Mycale facing the island. At some time they crossed the strait into Samos and actually engaged in conflict with the Athenian cleruchs.[43] The attempt was a failure. The insurgents were captured by the Athenian general delegated to Samos and were shipped to Athens where the *demos* condemned them to death. While in prison awaiting execution they were ransomed by a sympathiser, Antileon of Chalcis, who transported them to safety in his home city and was later honoured for his action by the restored Samians. These events are difficult to date, but clearly they did not occur after the battle of Crannon (322) when Athens was at the mercy of Antipater. It is also improbable that Antileon, whose city was a belligerent against Athens in the Lamian War, was able to intervene so decisively in an enemy city while hostilities lasted. In my opinion the episode is best placed in the last months of Alexander's reign. A group of exiles anticipated the king's final ruling on Samos and exposed themselves to Athenian reprisals. They were accordingly condemned to death, but the Athenians were reluctant to carry out the sentence. It was better to ransom them to a friendly neutral for propaganda purposes. They had advertised that they would defend what they considered to be their just claims, but they

---

[42] Habicht 1957, 156–69, nos. 1–2. Habicht himself was inclined to date the events immediately before Perdiccas' final decision in favour of Samos (early 321), while Errington 1975a, 55, suggests that the Samian exiles crossed from Anaea in the late spring or early summer of 323. Rosen 1978, 26, goes further and dates the events to the last weeks of Alexander's reign.

[43] For this interpretation and the restoration περὶ τὸμ π[όλεμον τὸμ] πρὸς τοὺς κληρού[χους] in Habicht 1957, no. 2, lines 8–10 see Badian 1976b.

stopped short of inflicting a penalty which their enemies would execrate as an atrocity. It remained to be seen which way Alexander would finally decide, whether he would recognise the Athenian claims in some measure or view their resistance as a deliberate affront to his authority. What was not now in doubt was that the Athenians would fight to preserve their hold on Samos.

The other state directly threatened by the Decree was the Aetolian League. The Aetolians were far more openly at loggerheads with Alexander than were the Athenians. They had clearly revoked Philip's settlement and reconstituted their federal polity. They had also occupied the Acarnanian town of Oeniadae and expelled its inhabitants, an action which made them liable to the collective sanctions of the Corinthian League to which the Acarnanians were signatories. They would ultimately face reprisals and Alexander had already promised punishment in the most explicit terms.[44] For the moment they were preserved by their remoteness and the fact that the major actors in the drama had more pressing concerns. But there was necessarily a reckoning to be faced, and the Aetolians were the automatic allies of any state which resisted Macedon. They were still too insignificant to be the focus of a general rising and could only hope that others, above all the Athenians, would make the first move.

There is no evidence for the reaction elsewhere. Presumably the majority behaved like Tegea, first protesting and pleading special circumstances and then allowing their exiles to return under fixed conditions. But there must have been widespread discontent, and resentment of the Exiles' Decree was probably a major cause of the defections from Macedon in the early months of the Lamian War. The Thessalians in particular reversed thirty years of loyalty to the Argead house when they changed sides *en masse* during the autumn of 323 (Diod. XVIII.11.1, 3). They had recently been faced with the return of families exiled during the long years of conflict between the Thessalian League and the tyrants of Pherae. The beneficiaries of that conflict had been Philip's partisans, the nobles who dominated the great cities of Larisa and Pharsalus – men like Daochus, Cineas and Thrasydaeus, whom Demosthenes (XVIII.295) stigmatised as traitors; and significantly it was Pharsalus, the city most favoured at the end of Philip's reign, whose cavalry was the élite of the Thessalians with Alexander, that formed the centre of Thessalian resistance during the Lamian War. In Pharsalus at least the restoration of the exiles of Philip's reign will have made many (certainly the most important) citizens feel defrauded and it is not surprising that they reacted violently.

Alexander was not given time for his policies to work. He died only ten months after the Decree was promulgated at Olympia, too short a time for the exiles to be returned, re-established and entrenched as his loyal supporters. The destabilisation he planned never eventuated. It is clear, however, that the Exiles' Decree amounted to a repudiation of the policies and partisans of Philip. The settlement imposed after Chaeronea had been no safeguard

[44] Diod. XVIII.8.6: Plut. *Al.* 49.15; cf. Mendels 1984, 129–49.

against armed resistance to Macedon, and the regimes sanctioned by Philip had been of equivocal loyalty. Alexander accordingly reversed his policy and struck against the whole fabric of the Corinthian League, whose keystone was the maintenance of existing governments and the enforcement of sentences of exile. His new supporters were to be the old dispossessed, and there was now not even lip service to the concept of autonomy. Alexander simply imposed his will by fiat. He might subsequently be swayed by diplomacy but the final decision was his alone. It was absolute rule by royal command, the polar opposite of the façade of consensus which Philip had attempted to create. At all events, when Alexander died, the regents at Babylon considered it prudent to send a circular letter to the cities announcing the restoration of 'the peace and the constitutions which Philip had established' (Diod. xviii.56.2). It was a proclamation for propaganda purposes, to gain popularity, and was a reaction against the despotism of Alexander's last months. By comparison even the militarily enforced peace and the political inertia of the Corinthian League was a welcome change.

# B

# Alexander and his empire

## 1 Satrapal government

When he invaded Asia, Alexander was literally on new ground. There were no precedents for the administration of the territory he annexed, no system inherited from his father. From the beginning he acted not merely as a conqueror but as the proper heir of the Achaemenids. His first gesture, if one may believe the vulgate tradition (Diod. XVII.17.2; Justin XI.5.10), was to make a spear-cast into Asia and claim the land as 'spear-won'.[1] There is no reason to dismiss the story as apocryphal, and it is to some degree corroborated by Alexander's first administrative acts, which were simply to place his own men over the existing satrapies, preserving the Persian hierarchy of command. In Hellespontine Phrygia he appointed as satrap Calas son of Harpalus, one of the commanders of the expeditionary force of 336, and he ordered the level of tribute to remain unchanged (Arr. 1.17.1). The territory was still subject under precisely the same conditions as under the Persian administration; the ruler was merely Macedonian and not Persian, as was his governor, who retained the Persian title of office (*SIG*³ 302).

The centre of Persian rule in Asia Minor was Sardes, its impregnable acropolis both fortress and treasury. From earliest times, it seems, this citadel had been occupied by a garrison commander directly appointed by the king, and its garrison was quite separate from the mercenary army maintained by the satrap. The Lydian administration may indeed have been the inspiration for Xenophon's formalised picture of Persian government with its rigid distinction between satrapal and fortress commanders (Xen. *Cyrop*. VIII.6.1–13; *Oec*. 4.5–7). Alexander continued the system. As satrap of Lydia (including the Ionian coast) he appointed Asander son of Philotas with a rudimentary army of cavalry and light-armed foot. The citadel had a separate high-ranking commander and an independent homogeneous garrison, the allied contingent from Argos (Arr. 1.17.7–8).

A somewhat different arrangement obtained in Caria. Here the civil

---

[1] Schmitthenner 1968, 32–8; see, however, Badian 1965b, 166 n. 1.

government was placed in the hands of the Hecatomnid princess Ada, who had ruled the satrapy for four years (from 344/3) before being displaced by her brother. Thoroughly alienated from the previous regime, she had retired to her formidable fortress at Alinda and she surrendered her person and lands to Alexander as he entered Caria.[2] She also adopted him as her son, which no doubt increased his legitimacy in the eyes of the local populace. In due course she received the entire satrapy of Caria, but her competence cannot have extended outside the civil administration. The military side of government was in the hands of a Macedonian general, Ptolemy, who commanded a large mercenary army, infantry and cavalry, some 3,200 strong (Arr. 1.23.6). Once more there was a weak Persian precedent. A year or two before, Ada's brother Pixodarus had submitted himself to the mercy of the Persian king and applied for a Persian governor to share his rule and marry his daughter. For a brief period before Pixodarus died there had been a joint command in Caria, but it was the Persian Orontobates who had the title of satrap (Strabo 657). Ada, however, had the titular government under Alexander, and Ptolemy may have been technically her subordinate, as was the case in Lydia in 322, when Perdiccas placed the Macedonian military commander directly under Alexander's sister Cleopatra, whom he installed as satrap (Arr. *Succ.* F 25.2 Roos). Whatever the theory, Ptolemy acted as a free agent during the Aegean War and fought in co-operation with Asander, the satrap of Lydia (Arr. 11.5.7). Like the Persian commanders before them they were not confined within the geographical boundaries of their provinces but took their forces wherever there was a military need for them.

These early appointments were military. Alexander installed men who would defend and secure their territory against the Persian counter-offensive. The civil administration was less important and could be delegated to subordinates or vested in a native ruler like Ada. Alexander to some extent followed Persian precedent but he was not hidebound by it, as he showed in his settlement of Lycia. The communities there had maintained a local independence under their native princes for the first part of the century, but they had gradually come under the sway of the Hecatomnid dynasty of Caria. By 337 Lycia had become part of the satrapy of Pixodarus, who placed two Greek-named lieutenants over it and imposed a supervisor (*epimeletes*) upon the important city of Xanthus. Pixodarus ruled directly, requiring even details of cult practice (the introduction of the Carian cult of *Basileus Kaunios*) to be referred back for ratification – in Greek, Lycian and Aramaic.[3] Alexander could easily have continued the joint satrapy of Caria and Lycia, but instead the Lycian communities were joined with their Pamphylian neighbours under the control of Alexander's friend Nearchus of Crete. Given the earlier history of the reign, Hecatomnid rule will not have been popular, and its removal was

[2] Arr. 1.23.7–8. Cf. Bosworth 1980a, 152–3; Hornblower 1982, 45–51.
[3] Metzger et al. 1974, 82–149. For the correct date see Badian 1977a; Hornblower 1982, 47–9. For Pixodarus' relations with Phaselis see Hornblower 1982, 122–3, 367 (M. 10).

almost certainly one of the requests made of Alexander during his passage of Lycia (Arr. 1.24.4–5). It cost nothing to liberate the area from its former masters, but the result was not the restitution of local independence. Alexander created an entirely new satrapy, placing the coastline between Telmissus and Side in the hands of a single commander with military oversight of the whole area. It was an arrangement made for the duration of the Persian War. After Nearchus was recalled to court in 330/29 there is no record of a replacement; and both Lycia and Pamphylia had been annexed to the satrapy of Antigonus by the end of the reign. The rearrangement comes most naturally after Nearchus' retirement, when Asia Minor was no longer threatened by naval action. The territory could be placed in the hands of the satrap of Greater Phrygia, operating from his capital of Celaenae immediately to the north. Alexander was prepared to create and take away satrapal jurisdiction as it suited the current military situation.

In the summer of 333 every calculation was overshadowed by the forthcoming clash with Darius. Antigonus was left at Celaenae as satrap of Phrygia with a modest force of 1,500 mercenaries (Arr. 1.29.3). The king himself moved rapidly eastwards, making only the most perfunctory settlement of the interior of Asia Minor. The Paphlagonians, who offered prompt submission, were simply put under the control of the satrap of Hellespontine Phrygia, not an easy assignment, for they were remote from the capital of Dascylium, separated from it by the territories of the wild and intractable Bithynians. Not surprisingly they revoked their submission once Alexander's back was turned and co-operated in the Persian-led resistance after Issus (Curt. IV.5.13). The settlement of Cappadocia was a similar story. This territory had been divided into two satrapies during the convulsions of the fourth-century revolts. The northern Pontic district was under the control of a native dynast, Ariarathes, and it was not affected by Alexander, whose line of march ran considerably to the south.[4] It was the southern satrapy, whose ruler had fallen at the Granicus (Arr. 1.16.3), which surrendered to Alexander. The government was immediately entrusted to a native Cappadocian, Sabictas, while the king moved rapidly to the Cilician Gates without apparently leaving a holding force of any description; he was reserving his men for the imminent encounter with Darius. In the aftermath of Issus, Sabictas was lost without trace during the Persian counter-offensive in Anatolia. Antigonus conducted hostilities on the Macedonian side and won three victories, but Cappadocia seems to have remained a no-man's-land. The royal road between Sardes and the Cilician Gates must have been controlled by Antigonus, who is known to have operated in Lycaonia (Curt. IV.5.13), but his writ may not have run far to the north. At all events the whole of Cappadocia, together with Paphlagonia, was included in Eumenes' satrapy in 323, which comprised territory never pacified in Alexander's reign and marked out to be regained by military force.

By contrast 332 was a year of consolidation. The rich, strategically vital,

4 Cf. Bosworth 1980a, 188–9; Hornblower 1981, 240–4.

satrapy of Cilicia was placed under a royal bodyguard, Balacrus son of Nicanor, who was both satrap and general (Diod. XVIII.22.1). He also supervised the finances, continuing the satrapal silver coinage of Cilicia in his own name,[5] and he may have been primarily responsible for the payment of the army during the long siege of Tyre. Cilicia was a coherent geographical entity, relatively compact and with clear-cut frontiers. All the functions of government could be placed in the hands of one man. Syria by contrast was far more complex, a vast swathe of territory from the Euphrates to the Egyptian border, including communities of every imaginable complexion, from the city states of Phoenicia to the hieratic government of Judaea. Here Alexander's arrangements were variable and complex. Shortly after Issus he placed Menon son of Cerdimmas in charge of the newly acquired territory in north Syria, with a modest holding force of mercenary cavalry.[6] The centre of his authority was probably the Amik plain, later to be dominated by the Seleucid tetrapolis, and his competence will have extended south to the borders of Phoenicia. He would clear the area of Persian refugees and keep it pacified while Alexander moved south.

The conqueror now passed through Phoenicia and received the surrender of its city states one by one. The local kings were retained in office, Gerostratus at Aradus and Enylus at Byblus. At Sidon the reigning king, Straton II, was deposed because of his friendship with Darius and replaced by Abdalonymus, a member of a collateral branch of the royal house. These monarchs, like their Greek and semitic counterparts in Cyprus, retained quasi-independence under the suzerainty of Alexander, but their autonomous coinage ceased.[7] The Phoenician mints now struck Alexander's regal currency (see below, p. 244), keeping only the city monogram as identification. As usual there was an exception. Tyre, which resisted Alexander for seven months, had its population enslaved and replaced from its perioecic peoples, under the supervision of a Macedonian garrison (Curt. IV.5.9). Phoenicia as a whole had no Macedonian governor. While Alexander was at Tyre it was unnecessary, and after his departure Philotas, the garrison commander at Tyre, may have had a general supervisory role.

The interior is more problematical. After Issus Parmenion had operated inland, dealing with the areas east of the Libanus massif, Damascus and the south. The local rulers were coerced into submission. At the opening of the siege of Tyre Alexander received the homage of Sanballat III, the hereditary ruler of Samaria, and confirmed him in his office (Jos. AJ XI.321–2). But he also appointed a Macedonian military commander over Coele Syria, to deal with any tasks of pacification left over by Parmenion (Curt. IV.5.9). This officer's functions were strictly military and contrast with those of Menon in the more settled north. Syria was still in the process of conquest and at the end

[5] Von Aulock 1964.
[6] Bosworth 1974, 46–53; Atkinson 1980, 370–1.
[7] Bellinger 1963, 49–53.

of 332 it formed an administrative mosaic, local native rulers side by side with Macedonian commanders still actively engaged in the military work of occupation. Just before Alexander entered Egypt Sanballat died in Samaria (Jos. *AJ* XI.325), and there was turmoil among his subjects. Andromachus, the Macedonian military commander, was captured by Samaritan insurgents early in 331 and burnt alive. Alexander's response was to transfer Menon from the north and replace him there by Arimmas, perhaps one of his subordinates. There was a brief campaign of reprisal, which has left its traces in the gruesome remains at the Wadi Daliyeh,[8] and Alexander returned to Tyre to prepare for the final campaign against Darius. Menon remained military commander in the south, and a new official was appointed in Phoenicia; Coeranus of Beroea, one of Alexander's treasurers, was placed over the fiscal system of Phoenicia (see below, p. 242). There was still no satrap of Phoenicia, but the garrison commander at Tyre would provide the military counterweight to Coeranus' fiscal position. Together they would be amply competent to convince any recalcitrant city king of the error of his ways.

Alexander's final administrative act in Syria was to replace Arimmas, whose preparations for the army's march to the Euphrates had been less than satisfactory (Arr. III.6.8). His successor was Asclepiodorus son of Eunicus. Syria was for the moment controlled by two Macedonian commanders in the north and south, with local rulers in Phoenicia coexisting with Macedonian military and fiscal officials. This situation lasted less than a year. At the end of 331 Alexander sent to the coast a certain Menes, who was to act as *hyparch* of Cilicia, Syria and Phoenicia. At the same time the incumbent commanders were withdrawn. Asclepiodorus brought mercenary troops to Bactra in the winter of 329/8 together with a man whose name is corrupt in the tradition but who is termed satrap of Syria (Arr. IV.7.2). It is most economical to assume that both the former satraps were recalled to court with reinforcements for the army. In their place Menes, a bodyguard of high standing, was given a major military post, co-ordinating the coastline between Cilicia and the Egyptian border. We cannot tell whether he operated in conjunction with other governors or held a single vast command: the evidence is simply too vague and defective.[9] But Syria did not remain divided. At the time of the Babylon settlement (June 323) it was governed as a single entity and Cilicia was a separate satrapy. Western Anatolia provides the most useful analogy. During the confusion of the Aegean War Lycia and Pamphylia formed a separate satrapy under Nearchus, but once peace obtained it was unified with Phrygia under the overall control of Antigonus. The exigencies of war had demanded smaller commands which could be combined later, when the mercenary armies which had sustained the fighting were channelled back to the central command, still led by their former satraps.

[8] Cross 1963; 1966.
[9] Bosworth 1974, 53–9; Brunt 1976–83, 1.278–9. For other views see Leuze 1935, 436ff.; Tarn 1948, 2.176–8.

Egypt presented less of a problem. Alexander had been peacefully admitted with the collusion of the Persian satrap, and the populace welcomed him as a liberator. There was every reason to pay lip service at least to the nationalistic aspirations of the Egyptians. Accordingly two natives, Doloaspis and Petisis, were entrusted with the civil administration of Egypt, now divided again into its immemorially old twin kingdoms. Arrian (III.5.2) gives them the title of *nomarch*, which indicates that they were to perform at a national level the functions of the humbler governors of the forty-two nomes, the administrative subdivisions of the country. But the appointments seem to have been window-dressing. When Petisis refused his commission Doloaspis received the entire administration – its functions cannot have been too onerous. In effect there was a plethora of Macedonian officials. The garrison centres of Pelusium and Memphis had Macedonian commanders, as did the two armies of Upper and Lower Egypt and the thirty-strong fleet of triremes. The resident mercenary forces, enlisted military settlers of the Saitan and Persian periods, were retained under the command of an immigrant Greek, Lycidas the Aetolian, but Alexander delegated one of his Companions to act as secretary. There were also two mysterious overseers (*episkopoi*), whose functions are not clearly defined by Arrian (III.5.3); they may have been additional inspectors of the resident mercenaries, but it is more probable that they were the civil counterparts of the generals, reviewing the administration of Egypt and supervising the native nomarch.[10] Superficially the division of competence is not unlike that in Caria, but the appointed officials are far more numerous, and the single Egyptian seems wholly swamped by the Macedonians. As yet there is no satrap attested. Alexander seems to have shrunk from giving a single man control of the whole of the old kingdom (whose inhabitants might well have resented the retention of the Persian title).

The most interesting figure in the Egyptian administration was Cleomenes, an immigrant Greek from Naucratis. He was first appointed to the Arabian command, centred at Heroopolis and involving the supervision of the desert regions east of the Delta (the regions to the west had a separate commander, Apollonius son of Charinus). But he was also placed in charge of the entire fiscal system of Egypt; the nomarchs of the forty-two subdivisions were instructed to collect the local tribute as they had done under Persian rule and to pay it into Cleomenes' hands (Arr. III.5.4). This gave him enormous real power throughout Egypt. As the recipient of tribute he naturally controlled public expenditure, in particular the payment of royal garrisons and armies. He was also instructed to supervise the building of Alexandria ([Arist.] *Oec.* 1352a29; Arr. VII.23.7). On the other hand his work entailed the direct supervision of the nomarchs, and, whether formally authorised or not, he imposed directives upon them. During the great famine of the 320s B.C. he regulated the export of grain from the nomes. The nomarchs had their export

[10] So Bosworth 1974, 55 n. 2; 1980a, 276. For the other view see Ehrenberg 1965, 437; Pearson 1960, 61–2; Atkinson 1980, 365.

quotas severely restricted and subjected to a heavy duty, which returned automatically to Cleomenes with the taxation payments ([Arist.] *Oec.* 1352a17–23). At the same time he speculated on his own behalf, using the administrative surplus to buy up grain at attractive rates from the local growers and then reselling it at the colossal price of 32 drachmae per measure, a triple profit. He had cornered the market and he exploited it for his own gain – and that of the exchequer. The results were seen in the grandiose buildings of Alexandria, and its founder was more than gratified. A famous letter, cited by Arrian (vii.23.7–8), instructs Cleomenes to erect *heroa* for Hephaestion and gives an assurance that none of his delicts, past or future, will be punished if the construction is sufficiently impressive. The letter is likely to be genuine,[11] perhaps quoted by Ptolemy to justify his execution of Cleomenes; and it sheds considerable light on Alexander's attitude to government. Exploitation and peculation were permissible, even commendable, provided that sufficient profit accrued to the government. Cleomenes himself was duly recognised as satrap of Egypt. From the beginning he was the principal administrator of the province and in his management of its finances he acted *de facto* as satrap, presumably with the co-operation of the Macedonian military authorities. Finally, no later than Alexander's return from India, he was formally invested with the satrapy. He had proved his worth and could never present a threat to the royal authority.[12]

After Gaugamela Alexander's administrative policy took a new turn. For the next year he selected satraps from the defeated Persian nobility. The first of these new appointments was at Babylon late in 331. Mazaeus, satrap of Cilicia and Syria from the early years of Artaxerzes III, presided over the surrender of the city to Alexander and was promptly appointed satrap of Babylonia. He probably had a Babylonian wife (his sons have distinctively Babylonian names) and was as acceptable to the populace as any Persian could be. Alexander seems to have had no qualms about his loyalty, and, whatever happened, the native Babylonians would be unlikely to side in revolt with a member of the Persian aristocracy. Once again the military establishment was placed under a Companion, Apollodorus of Amphipolis (Arr. iii.16.4, vii.18.1), and the formidable citadel of Babylon was held by Agathon of Pydna with a Macedonian garrison 700 strong (Diod. xvii.64.5). Mazaeus will have had the civil administration of Babylonia, a burdensome enough task in itself, and he was the theoretical head of the satrapy, with some influence over the coinage. The satrapal issues he had struck in Syria were continued in Babylonia, the first strikings bearing his own name.[13] How far he controlled the coinage is unknown, but on the economic side his activities were severely circumscribed by the appointment of a separate official to collect the tribute of the satrapy and they would have been limited still more when Harpalus made

11 So Hamilton 1953, 157; Vogt 1971, *contra* Tarn 1948, 2.303–6; Seibert 1972b.
12 Badian 1966, 58–9.
13 Bellinger 1963, 60–8; Badian 1965b, 171; Bosworth, 1980a, 315.

Babylon the centre of his administration. Real power, as elsewhere, was in the hands of the Macedonian military commanders.

The pattern continued at Susa, where the incumbent satrap Abulites was confirmed in office alongside a Macedonian garrison commander and a general for the holding army (Curt. v.2.16–17; Arr. III.16.9). Even in Persis, the heartland of the old Achaemenid empire, he appointed a Persian satrap, Phrasaortes, but there was an unusually strong holding force of Macedonians (Curt. v.6.11). Media is a particularly interesting case. Alexander skirted the province at breakneck speed during his pursuit of Darius, leaving a large contingent of phalanx infantry to transport the vast treasure from Persepolis to the northern capital of Ecbatana. Parmenion was at the head of the operation and subsequently remained at Ecbatana along with four senior commanders of mercenary and Thracian infantry. For the moment the senior treasurer, Harpalus, was attached to them. It was a concentration of military strength unparalleled in Asia and the satrap was inevitably overshadowed. That satrap was once more a Persian, this time a dissident, Oxydates, who had been discovered under sentence of death at Susa (Curt. vi.2.11; Arr. III.20.3). Despite his credentials he lasted a relatively short time. He showed conspicuous lack of enthusiasm during Bessus' counter-offensive in 329 and was replaced by the original satrap, Atropates, who surrendered to Alexander only after the death of his royal master (Arr. iv.18.3). Having offered submission he could be restored to his previous satrapy, where he remained until the end of the reign, enjoying the king's favour while the Macedonian military commanders were executed. He also seems to have had a military competence. It was he who suppressed the nationalistic insurrection of Baryaxes in 324 (Arr. vi.29.3), showing loyalty to his new king against his own people while his Macedonian colleagues were removed as unreliable.

A similar train of events is attested in Parthyaea, the strategic crossroads of eastern Iran. There Alexander's first satrap was Amminapes, who had been an exile at the court of Philip and, subsequently restored to favour, helped surrender Egypt to Alexander. He could be expected to be loyal but he had no local connections and was unable to control his satrapy when Bessus instigated revolt. The previous satrap, Phrataphernes, surrendered in the wake of the murder of Darius and was reinstated in his former satrapy by the early months of 329 (Arr. III.28.2). Once in office he defended Parthyaea against Brazanes, whom Bessus had nominated satrap, and preserved the territory for Alexander. When he reported his success, in the winter of 328/7, he was given another commission, to arrest Autophradates, satrap of the neighbouring peoples of the Elburz mountains, and to annex his satrapy. This assignment was no doubt congenial and it was successfully executed (Curt. x.1.39). Like Atropates, Phrataphernes could be relied upon to defend his satrapy, which he probably considered as much his as Alexander's, and he would crush any local attempt to usurp his position as ruthlessly as would Alexander himself.

The key factor was loyalty. Atropates and Phrataphernes behaved faultlessly in this respect, but not every Iranian satrap proved so impeccable. Satibarzanes was confirmed in Areia, but no sooner was Alexander's back turned than he transferred his allegiance to Bessus, who had adopted the royal name Artaxerxes, massacred the small Macedonian force left with him and waged a guerilla war against Alexander and his lieutenants which lasted nearly a year. He clearly preferred a king of his own race to the Macedonian conqueror. His successor, Arsaces, was hardly more successful, arrested on Alexander's orders after a few months in office and replaced as satrap by a Companion, Stasanor of Cypriot Soli.[14] This time the appointment was successful. Stasanor proved energetic and effective, and in 327 he was rewarded with the extension of his satrapy southwards to the lakelands of Sistan (ancient Drangiana). He replaced the previous native satrap, Arsames.[15] Drangiana itself had previously been united with Arachosia, the vital corridor of the Helmand river, and the joint satrapy was ruled by the regicide Barsaentes. In the military emergency of 329, with the northern route to Bactra in enemy hands, Alexander considered it prudent to divide the commands, leaving a Persian in charge of the lakelands of Sistan and appointing a Companion, Menon, to police the vital highway through the Hindu Kush (Arr. III.28.1; Curt. VII.3.5).

The next area of importance was the north-east marchland of Bactria and Sogdiana, the home satrapy of Bessus. Here Alexander began by repeating the pattern he had established in 330, appointing the Persian noble Artabazus as satrap of Bactria (Arr. III.29.2). The territory had been won with surprising ease, and Alexander felt that he could leave it under a Persian, with Macedonian commanders in the major citadels to assist or hinder him as circumstances dictated. Artabazus was one of the most distinguished surviving members of the Persian aristocracy, a grandson of Artaxerxes II with a lineage worthy of a satrapy usually reserved for princes of the blood royal;[16] on the other hand his connections were with Hellespontine Phrygia, on the opposite frontier of the empire, and he had no ancestral ties with Bactria. He was also an enemy of Bessus and could be expected to resist him. Alexander was not disappointed in Artabazus' loyalty, but for once his military calculations were astray. In the summer of 329 the whole area from the river Iaxartes to the Hindu Kush rose in insurrection (see above, pp. 110ff.), and it took nearly two years of grim warfare to contain the revolt. It was only too clearly revealed that the satrapy presented one of the most intractable military problems of the empire, and in the late summer of 328 Artabazus abdicated his command, giving the diplomatic excuse of old age (he was hardly sixty). In his place Alexander first appointed one of his most senior generals, Cleitus the Black (Curt. VIII.1.19–21) and then (after the fatal banquet at Maracanda) Amyntas son of Nicolaus. The army left in the satrapy was commensurate

[14] Cf. Berve 1926, 2 nos. 146, 697, 719; Bosworth 1981, 19–22.
[15] Curt. VIII.3.17; cf. Bosworth 1981, 22–3.
[16] Berve 1926, 2 no. 152; Brunt 1975.

with its importance: 10,000 infantry and 3,500 cavalry, the largest defence force in the empire (Arr. IV.22.3). There was also a network of military colonies with a governing élite of Graeco-Macedonians (see below, p. 248). At the same time the native military population was reduced by the levies Alexander imposed for his Indian campaigns and for his new corps of Epigoni.[17] Bactria and Sogdiana had been changed by Alexander more profoundly than any other sector of the empire. The balance of population had been affected by war, massacre and military settlement, and Alexander was able to leave a European ruling class many tens of thousands strong, the nucleus which developed into the Indo-Greek empire a century later. The powerful Iranian barons of the satrapy retained their domains for the most part; there is specific evidence for Chorienes, who was confirmed in his hyparchy of Paraetacae. But the actual government was firmly in Macedonian hands. Alexander was prepared to marry a Bactrian princess to make his rule more palatable, and the senior officers he left in the satrapy apparently followed suit, demonstrating that a new ruling class had emerged.[18] In this satrapy the Persians were directly subordinate and there was no question of a division of powers.

When Alexander moved eastwards in the summer of 327 he entered territory which lay outside the Persian empire and was governed by a multitude of native princes, often at loggerheads with each other.[19] Here Alexander made little attempt to interfere with existing governments. Princes (termed hyparchs by Arrian) had their regimes confirmed if they surrendered; otherwise, they were deposed and replaced by more compliant rulers. At first there was a conscious policy to promote expatriate Indians: in Peucelaotis Sangaeus was placed in office after returning from exile at the court of Taxiles (Arr. IV.22.8), and Sisicottus, who was given the great citadel of Aornus, had spent many years in Bactria, giving loyal service first to Bessus and then to Alexander (Arr. IV.30.4). Alexander also left a large number of garrison troops, inevitable because of the stubborn resistance offered during his march into India. A Macedonian satrap, Nicanor, exercised overall supervision of the territory between Parapamisadae and the Indus, but his functions were military, to continue the pacification of the area. The civil administration must have remained in the hands of the native rulers. Beyond the Indus Alexander was promptly acknowledged by Taxiles, the most powerful Indian prince in the region. Fresh to the throne, he had sent an embassy to Sogdiana, inviting the conqueror to help him against his recalcitrant neighbours. He offered his submission and material assistance as soon as Alexander crossed the borders of Parapamisadae (Arr. IV.22.6). He was duly confirmed in his dominions but under Macedonian control. He had renounced suzerainty and

[17] Arr. V.11.3, 12.2, VII.6.3. Cf. Bosworth 1980b, 15–18.
[18] Metz Epit. 31; Diod. XVII, index λ; cf. Bosworth 1980b, 11.
[19] See particularly Niese 1893, 1.500–9; Berve 1926, 1.268–73; Badian 1965b, 180; Bosworth 1983.

Alexander imposed his own royal authority, represented by a Macedonian satrap, Philip son of Machatas; and he took the precaution of leaving a garrison in Taxila (Arr. v.8.3). There was also a regular tribute (Arr. vi.14.2). Taxiles had some degree of local autonomy, but it was exercised at the pleasure of Alexander and his satrap.

The Hydaspes became the effective border of the empire. Beyond it Porus was allowed to retain his kingdom, which Alexander carefully expanded, placing neighbouring peoples under his sway until he controlled all the territory between the Hydaspes and the Hyphasis, proverbially rich lands comprising (according to the most conservative figure) seven tribes and 2,000 cities (Arr. vi.2.1; v.29.2). Here Porus was plenipotentiary, holding power without Macedonian troops or a Macedonian satrap. Alexander was sufficiently impressed by his courage and ability to install him as vassal ruler of his advance frontier territory. West of the Hydaspes the Macedonian presence was more obtrusive. Philip had been forced to intervene in Assacene in conjunction with the Iranian satrap of Parapamisadae after the Macedonian Nicanor had fallen in action against insurgents, who were still reluctant to accept Alexander's rule (Arr. v.20.7). His own territory was extended south to include the troublesome Malli and ultimately covered the whole course of the Indus as far as its confluence with the Acesines (Arr. vi.14.3, 15.2). His satrapal forces were very considerable. He had the entire Thracian contingent remaining in the army and additional infantry for garrison work – eloquent testimony of the unsettled nature of his command. South of the confluence another satrap, Peithon son of Agenor, held sway as far as the Ocean, and he was operating in the vicinity of Patala when Alexander left for the west.

The division did not last long. When he reached Gedrosia late in 325, Alexander received the news that Philip had been assassinated by some native mercenaries in his service (his Thracians were insufficient for all the military calls upon him). For the moment the northern satrapy was left under Taxiles and Philip's Macedonian lieutenant Eudamus (Arr. vi.27.2; Curt. x.1.20–21). Alexander intended to send another satrap but he apparently changed his mind. At the time of his death Taxiles was still ruler of the northern satrapy, while Peithon had been transferred to the north-west, to the Cophen valley. Porus' territory was further extended. In 321 it reached as far south as Patala and the Ocean, and it is implied that the extension was made under Alexander (Arr. *Succ.* F 1.36). It looks as though Alexander was unwilling to pay the military price of governing the entire course of the Indus through Macedonian satraps. Instead he enlarged the vassal kingdom of Porus, leaving him to keep control of the troublesome peoples of the south.[20] The Macedonian military forces were then transferred with their commander to patrol the vital highway between the Indus and Parapamisadae, which had never been properly pacified. In the valley of the Indus Taxiles was paramount prince in the north, ruling with the help of the European army of

[20] For this interpretation see Berve, *RE* XIX.219; *contra* Tarn 1948, 2.310–13.

occupation, and beyond the Hydaspes, to the east and south, Porus ruled independently, theoretically subject to Alexander but only bound by his verbal allegiance. It was a vast buffer zone from the foothills of the Himalayas to the Indian Ocean, where even Porus' writ was probably unenforceable outside his ancestral domains. Macedonian rule had contracted to the north-west, the narrow corridor through the Khyber Pass directly governed by a Macedonian satrap and a bridgehead in the Punjab under a native prince. The conquest of India, for all its paper victories, proved only that the country could not be held down without an unacceptable expenditure of manpower.

The final developments came after Alexander returned to the west and launched his purge of delinquent satraps over the winter of 325/4. The majority of victims were Iranians: Astaspes in Carmania, Orxines in Persis, Abulites and Oxathres in Susiana and Paraetacene.[21] They were charged with incompetence and misgovernment, but there was certainly more to Alexander's actions than repression of extortion. The example of Cleomenes in Egypt shows that exploitation of the subject people could be excused and even licensed if the exploitation had positive returns. It is more important that there were nationalistic uprisings in central Iran. A pretender had emerged in Media and assumed the upright tiara of royalty (Arr. vi.29.3), and Craterus had arrested a number of rebels in his passage of Arachosia and Drangiana (Arr. vi.27.3; Curt. ix.10.19). There was also the problem of insubordination. When Alexander was absent in India, communications with him were virtually severed and there was a natural temptation for satraps to act as independent despots. Nothing shows the situation better than the affair of Orxines, general of the Persian levy at Gaugamela and a noble of royal lineage. While Alexander was in India he had usurped the satrapy, taking advantage of an interregnum caused by the death of Phrasaortes. He had never been confirmed by Alexander, nor indeed had he communicated with him (Arr. vi.29.2). He submitted readily enough as the king approached Persis, but he was soon accused of complicity in the profanation of Cyrus' tomb and promptly executed. The usurpation of power could not be forgiven, even if it was not punished as such. There were similar actions elsewhere. In Carmania Astaspes was accused of plotting revolution while Alexander was in India (Curt. ix.10.21), and Abulites and his son may also belong to this category: Arrian (vii.4.2) implies that their misbehaviour was encouraged by a belief that Alexander would never return.

The king may have been alerted to the problems of satrapal insubordination as early as 325, when Tyriespis was accused of misgovernment in Parapamisadae, deposed from office and executed (Arr. vi.15.3; Curt. ix.8.9). His successor was Alexander's own father-in-law, Oxyartes, whose loyalty under the circumstances was unimpeachable. Alexander had taken drastic action against insubordination in the east and continued the process in the west as he found further evidence of the flouting of his authority. As a result Iranian

[21] Documentation in Badian 1961, 17; see, however, Higgins 1980, 140–52.

satraps virtually disappeared. The only survivors apart from Oxyartes were Atropates in Media and Phrataphernes in Parthyaea, both of whom proved their loyalty by arresting insurgents and delivering them to justice. Their successors were Macedonian. In Persis it was Peucestas who took over the satrapy, with Alexander's active encouragement to learn Persian and assimilate himself to the *mores* of the country; and in Carmania Tlepolemus had had years of experience as military supervisor in Parthyaea, closely associated with Phrataphernes. They were hand-picked to govern efficiently and loyally, and their potential for causing trouble, already small, was further reduced by the general edict to disband all satrapal armies (Diod. XVII.111.1).

The only punitive action against Macedonian commanders is the execution of the generals in Media. Cleander and Sitalces (and probably Agathon) were put on trial when they met Alexander in Carmania, accused of sacrilege and oppression by their subjects, and they were promptly sentenced to death. Heracon was reprieved for the moment but condemned shortly afterwards for similar outrages in Susa (his military competence had evidently extended far outside the satrapy in which he was installed). The whole affair is a mystery.[22] Arrian (VI.27.4) and Curtius (X.1.1–9) agree that there was misgovernment, but the officers in Media hardly had a monopoly on that. Insubordination was again an important factor. The culprits had behaved as quasi-independent monarchs, as though they were responsible to nobody (cf. Curt. X.1.7). At the same time their execution was popular with the army. They had been deeply involved in the assassination of Parmenion and were now expiating their guilt. They were now discarded, while the Iranian satrap of Media, whose loyalty had been signally displayed against his fellow-countrymen, retained his office with distinction. As usual Alexander's acts were determined by relatively short-term considerations. It is difficult to see any permanent policy beyond his primary requirements that the satrapies once conquered should remain peaceful with the minimum expense of manpower and that his kingship should be universally and unconditionally acknowledged.

II **Financial administration**

In general Alexander accepted the Achaemenid fiscal system as he found it. Under his rule the satraps were largely responsible for the collection of tribute as they had been before. They used the receipts to pay for their current expenditures and conveyed the surplus (if any) to central repositories. The collection will have remained in the hands of local officials, as is specifically attested in Egypt, where the forty-two nomarchs continued to raise tribute locally and paid it into the hands of the central authority (Arr. III.5.5). Alexander himself was not greatly concerned with the regular payments of tribute. He relied on periodical influxes of bullion to finance the expenses of his campaigns and drew prodigally upon the accumulated reserves he dis-

22 Cf. Badian 1961, 20–5; Bosworth 1971b, 124.

covered at Sardes, Damascus, Susa and, above all, Persepolis. Ultimately no less than 180,000 talents were concentrated at Ecbatana,[23] a truly colossal sum which freed him from any budgetary constraints. The provinces' surpluses were not vital to him, and he may well have been content to allow them to be consumed by the satraps, almost all of whom were intermittently plagued by war and rebellion and had standing armies to maintain and pay.

In most cases the satrap was at the head of the fiscal organisation; but we occasionally hear of separate officials with responsibility for the tribute of the larger satrapies. In Lydia a Greek, Nicias, was placed over 'the assessment and the collection of tribute' (Arr. 1.17.7).[24] He is not listed as a subordinate of the satrap, but on the other hand he was not given a separate military establishment and would inevitably be dependent upon the satrap if there was resistance to his fiscal activities. It was a logical appointment given the complexity and diversity of the Lydian satrapy and the fact that the satrap Asander would soon be fully engaged in the Aegean War. The intricate business of policing the fiscal obligations of the Lydian communities, whether barbarian settlers on royal land or Hellenic cities, was best left to a separate official. The same was the case with the rich central satrapy of Babylonia, which also had a separate official to manage its taxation, Asclepiodorus son of Philon (Arr. III.16.4), and once more the financial complexity of the province justified the additional appointment. Other key areas also had financial supervisors. The tribute of the Phoenician cities was placed under the Macedonian, Coeranus of Beroea; and, as we have seen, Cleomenes' control of the tribute of both Lower and Upper Egypt made him inevitably the most influential man in the satrapy. There is a possible parallel in the appointment of Philoxenus in south-western Asia Minor. He was given the commission to collect tribute 'this side of the Taurus' (Arr. III.6.4), an appallingly vague description but at least consistent with the management of tribute over several satrapies of Asia Minor. In 331 the commanders in Phrygia and Caria in particular had been fully extended by the wars of the past two years and can have had little time to devote to the fiscal administration of their commands. There would also be a significant amount of post-war reorganisation, and it made sense to delegate a single official to co-ordinate the finances of the most hard-pressed satrapies. If so, Philoxenus' wide competence made him one of the most influential men in the sub-continent, and it is not surprising to find that he succeeded old Princess Ada as satrap of Caria.[25] His wide-ranging powers made him a natural person to assume the satrapal functions until he was confirmed by Alexander.

The financial heartland of the empire comprised the royal capitals: Babylon, Susa, Ecbatana and Persepolis. Here were the accumulated reserves

[23] Strabo 731; cf. Diod. XVII.80.3; Justin XII.1.3. The figures in the sources are hard to reduce to a coherent scheme; cf. Bellinger 1963, 68–70; Bosworth 1980a, 330.

[24] Bosworth, 1980a, 130; *contra* Griffith 1964, 25–30; Wirth 1972.

[25] Arr. VII.23.1, 24.1; [Arist.] *Oec.* 1351b36. See Bosworth 1980a, 281–2, *contra* Berve 1926, 2 nos. 793–4; Badian 1966, 56–60.

of the Persian empire, which Alexander had originally intended to concentrate in the citadel of Ecbatana under his principal treasurer, Harpalus son of Machatas (Arr. III.19.7). During the summer of 330 Harpalus was detached from court and for the next five years he acted as the central treasurer of the empire. The focus of his administration seems to have been at Babylon, where he installed his Athenian mistress, Pythionice; but his influence went as far afield as Tarsus and Rhosus on the Levantine coast, and he was accused by his enemy Theopompus of behaving like a king in his own right (*FGrH* 115 F 253–4). His competence extended over the central provinces of the empire and involved more than mere finance – 7,000 mercenaries who joined Alexander in India are said to have been sent by him (Curt. IX.3.21). Thanks to the dearth of evidence we cannot define the limits of his authority or assess how far his *de facto* power was approved by the king, but, whether or not there was royal approval for it, his actual power was immense. He remained the controller of the royal treasure, with unparalleled funds at his disposal, and at the same time he was a long-standing friend of the king and a member of the old princely house of Elimiotis. It would have been a brave man who challenged him directly. Diodorus (XVII.108.4) describes him as a satrap, and, even if technically incorrect, the term is not improper. There is little doubt that his successor, Antimenes of Rhodes, had effective powers of command. His ingenious insurance scheme for the slaves of the royal army involved direct instructions to satraps either to recover escapees or to reimburse their value; and he had no hesitation in reviving an obsolete Babylonian tithe on imports to raise money from the distinguished ambassadors who visited the capital during Alexander's last year ([Arist.] *Oec.* 1352b28–32, 1353a2–4). Unlike Harpalus, Antimenes was relatively undistinguished, but he retained Harpalus' financial oversight of the central satrapies. It would seem that it was not the extent of Harpalus' authority that Alexander found objectionable but the royal airs he had assumed. Like the military commanders in Media he had acted as though his king would never return (Diod. XVII.108.4), and rather than suffer their fate he defected to Europe with a mercenary army and 5,000 talents from the royal treasury, as much as could be taken at speed by his modest convoy. His very distinction had contributed to his downfall and Alexander ensured that the mistake would not be repeated. His successor inherited his powers, but he could only exercise them with the king's support and under his mandate. Antimenes could never become an independent pawn in the game.

There is no evidence for any specific financial administration for the territories east of the Zagros. Here Alexander encountered an economy that was non-monetary, and tribute doubtless continued as payments in kind, reckoned in terms of produce, livestock and bullion. The Uxian tribute of horses, draught animals and sheep (Arr. III.17.6) may have been typical of the impositions laid upon pastoral peoples;[26] and agricultural communities will

---

[26] Briant 1982a, 57ff.

have dispensed portions of their produce, to be largely consumed in the satrapy of origin in the form of rations to royal officials.[27] Such perishable commodities cannot have been transported far afield, particularly in the unstable period after Alexander's conquest, and the eastern satrapies probably remained separate economic entities, the business of tribute collection devolving, as it always had, upon the satrap.

The permanent memorial of Alexander's finances is his coinage. After his accession he began issues in his own name from the royal mints of Pella and Amphipolis. The famous tetradrachms with the head of Heracles and the seated Zeus (the king's ancestor and putative father) went side by side with the gold staters with the head of Athene and a winged Nike, commemorating the patron goddess of the war of revenge and his own aspirations of victory. At first the issues came exclusively from the Macedonian mints,[28] but in the immediate aftermath of Issus emissions of royal coinage began at mints all over the Levantine coast, first Tarsus and then the Syrian and Phoenician mints of Myriandrus, Byblus and Sidon. In some cases the local coinage ceased. At Sidon for instance the double shekels struck before Alexander's arrival continued in circulation, but from 332 onwards[29] the city produced Alexander tetradrachms with the city's monogram ($\Sigma I$) the only concession to local autonomy. The pattern was repeated in Cyprus. There the city kings discontinued their own issues (there is a ten-year hiatus in the dated gold coinage of Pumiathon of Citium) and acted as local producers of the royal currency. It was not a voluntary act, as is shown by the temporary resurgence of local Cypriot issues after Alexander's death; Nicocles of Paphos discreetly foreshadowed the move by advertising his name in almost invisible letters on the lion's mane of Heracles.[30] Undoubtedly Alexander's primary intentions were political, to produce an empire-wide coinage declaring his universal monarchy. Expressions of local autonomy were discouraged, but as usual there is no set pattern. Local issues did continue, in Cilicia and most notably in Babylonia. What is more, the strikings of Balacrus in Cilicia at first bore the satrap's name in full, following the precedent of the satrapal issues under Persian administration. They were later struck with the simple initial, as Balacrus was brought into line with his Phoenician neighbours.[31] The same happened at Babylon, where the famous lion 'staters' first bore the name of the satrap Mazaeus but after four issues appeared without legend. Whether or not the inscribed issues were struck after Alexander's arrival (see above, p. 235), the ultimate effect of his intervention was to make the local coinage anonymous. It continued to be minted in profusion – double shekels in Cilicia, lion

[27] Lewis 1977, 4ff.; Hornblower 1982, 155–6.
[28] For the dating problems see Bellinger 1963, 3–13 and the recent debate between Orestes H. Zervos 1982 and M. J. Price 1982. There are some very pertinent points in Martin 1985, 122–31.
[29] Cf. Newell 1916; Merker 1964; Mørkholm 1978, 136–8.
[30] Cf. Mørkholm 1978; *contra* Gesche 1974.
[31] Von Aulock 1964.

staters in Babylon together with issues of gold darics. There must have been a substantial local market for it, but it remains a mystery what that market comprised. Alexander's coinage, however, was predominant, a universal currency that was uniquely and explicitly his.

The minting of coins was peculiarly a royal function. The contemporary Aristotelian *Oeconomica* (1345b20ff.) sets aside coinage as the first division of the royal economy, which is explicitly distinguished from satrapal administration. None the less Alexander himself cannot have had much to do with the production of coins, particularly in the period 330–324, when he was in the east, far separated from his mints, which did not exist east of the Zagros.[32] It must have been the royal treasurer, Harpalus, who supervised the minting in the heart of the empire. His last attested residences, Tarsus and Babylon, were minting centres, and the vast hoard of bullion from Susa and Persepolis was in his keeping. Its distribution and conversion into currency was naturally his responsibility. In Phoenicia Coeranus may have had similar duties. The king's contribution was to supply the demand; he required coinage even in India and he was evidently well supplied with it (Plut. *Al.* 59.5; Curt. VIII.12.16). How that supply was maintained is yet another unanswered question. The one attested convoy from Harpalus did not apparently bring coin (Curt. IX.3.21; cf. Diod. XVII.95.4), and one would think that the transport of money across the Iranian plateau would have been a very difficult and costly business. The fact remains that for most of his reign Alexander was far away from his mints, particularly Amphipolis, which produced most of his coinage during the first years of the campaign, and his effect upon the production was indirect. His own supervision was necessarily minimal and his treasurers, notably Harpalus, were largely free agents. The power they enjoyed was commensurate with the funds they disbursed, and they must have been some of the most powerful figures of the empire. It is most unfortunate that so little direct evidence survives to elucidate their role.

III    **The new foundations**

Alexander's reputation as a founder of cities is unsurpassed. In a famous passage Plutarch (*Mor.* 328E) accredits him with seventy cities founded among barbarian peoples, which brought civilisation and culture to the brutish recesses of Asia. It is a brilliant outburst of Hellenic chauvinism but is totally divorced from reality. The city foundations were a necessary corollary of conquest, providing a permanent alien garrison force in unquiet territory, and, like the *coloniae* in the Roman world, they were conceived as *propugnacula imperii*.

Alexander's activity in this field began early, in 340 B.C., when he suppressed a rising among the Maedi of the upper Strymon valley and

[32] Bellinger 1963, 70–7.

introduced new settlers in their main centre of population.[33] This action was modelled on Philip's procedure in Thrace, where the local population was held in check by immigrants from the world of southern Greece, who were established in rich and strategic sites such as Philippopolis (Plovdiv). Among the Maedi also there was to be a garrison site, cleared of its old native inhabitants and resettled with a heterogeneous immigrant population. This was explicitly a garrison centre, named after the young prince (Alexandropolis on the analogy of Philippopolis) either by grace of his father or by his own fiat after he came to the throne. Alexandropolis was his first foundation and his last for nearly ten years. Nothing comparable is attested during the early part of the campaign in Asia. The Alexandrias later recorded in Asia Minor and the near east, in particular Alexandria by Latmus (Alinda?) and Alexandria by Issus, are most likely to be posthumous foundations by the Successors,[34] as is known to have been the case with Alexandria Troas, refounded by Lysimachus upon an earlier synoecism of Antigonus (Strabo 593). Something like refoundation took place after the sieges of Tyre and Gaza. Both cities were repopulated from native perioeci who remained under the supervision of a Macedonian garrison,[35] and they served as regional control centres in the same way as Philip's Thracian settlements. But the European garrison soldiers were not regarded as permanent settlers and the cities were still distinctively semitic communities.

The first new foundation of the reign was probably Alexandria in Egypt. Here Alexander established a wholly new city on the site of an Egyptian harbour installation at Rhacotis[36] and personally laid out its ground plan with the help of the famous architect Deinocrates of Rhodes. This was to be a fundamentally Greek foundation, as Alexander foreshadowed with his personal selection of an *agora* and temple sites for predominantly Hellenic gods (Arr. III.1.5). From the beginning the native Egyptian population formed a non-privileged sub-class, attached to the new foundation by synoecism from other centres, notably Canopus.[37] As far as we can see, there was no detachment of troops from Alexander's army. The Greek settlers there will have been attracted from the homeland and their number was swelled by Hellenic residents in Egypt and Cyrenaica.[38] The lack of a distinctively military component suggests that the primary motive for the foundation was not military. Instead the sources stress the magnificence of its site, on the isthmus between the Mediterranean and Lake Mareotis, saliently placed for commerce with the hinterland, blessed with a uniquely salubrious climate and enjoying rich agricultural surroundings. The new city added a secure harbour

---

[33] Plut. *Al*.9.1. Cf. Hammond and Griffith 1979, 2.557–9, *contra* Tarn 1948, 2.248–9; Hamilton 1969, 23.

[34] Cf. Errington 1976, 162–8; Hornblower 1982, 314.

[35] Arr. II.27.7 (Gaza); Curt. IV.5.9 (Tyre). Cf. Bosworth 1980a, 256–60.

[36] Fraser 1972, 1.5–7, 2.4–10; Cavenaile 1972; Jähne 1981, 68–72.

[37] Curt. IV.8.5; [Arist.] *Oec.* 1352a29ff.; cf. Athen. 1.33D.

[38] Fraser 1972, 1.63–5.

to the inhospitable coastline of Egypt and the gateway to the satrapy now became a Greek stronghold. Perhaps some of the initiative for the foundation came from the resident Greeks of Egypt. It is unlikely that Alexander hit on the site in the casual manner that the sources suggest, on a boat trip around Mareotis (Arr. III.1.5; Curt. IV.8.1–2); and he was probably advised by local Greeks eager for the establishment of a favoured new city in which they would have the dominant role. Alexander himself had strong personal motives to found an Alexandria which would surpass his father's Philippi, and he seems to have taken a strong personal interest in its development (Arr. VII.23.7) such as is not attested for any of the eastern settlements. His desire for glory, in this case to be honoured in perpetuity as founder, may have been the fundamental factor. The site's potential for commerce, which no doubt loomed large in the minds of his advisers, was a very secondary consideration for him.

The next instances of city foundations come in 330, when Alexander was campaigning in central Iran. The trigger was Bessus' self-proclamation as Artaxerxes V and the consequent wave of insurrection throughout the eastern satrapies. The first to be settled was probably Alexandria in Areia (modern Herat),[39] founded in the aftermath of Satibarzanes' rebellion. There followed Alexandria in Arachosia (Kandahar?),[40] perhaps established in the first months of 329 during Alexander's march up the Helmand valley. These were new foundations, balancing the old native centres at Artacoana in Areia and the former Arachosian capital, and were introduced as new garrison points in the conquered territory. Our only explicit evidence concerns Alexandria in Caucaso (Begram) at the confluence of the Gorband and the Panjshir in the central Hindu Kush. Here Alexander established a city with a nucleus of 3,000 Graeco-Macedonian settlers, soldiers no longer fit for service and volunteers from the mercenaries, together with 7,000 of the local population. This blend will recur repeatedly: a Greek centre, comprising, in part at least, impressed veterans and a pool of indigenous peoples to work the rural hinterland. If the European element was to work effectively as a garrison, it needed sufficient agricultural labour to enable it to continue its military function. Alexander was later to enlarge the colony, adding further discharged soldiers and more native people from the surrounding territory (Arr. IV.22.5). The site was now a formidable bastion of empire. It was sited at the crossroads of the Hindu Kush, with a European population several thousand strong and a far more numerous rural population providing the surplus to keep them under arms.

The most explicit evidence comes from Sogdiana. Here Alexander decided to establish a new foundation on the river Iaxartes as a defence point to repel nomad incursions and also, one suspects, to match the great fortress established by Cyrus some 40 km to the east.[41] While he was still surveying the site, revolt broke out over the whole of Bactria and Sogdiana. Alexander responded

---

[39] Tscherikower 1927, 102; Bosworth 1980a, 356–7.
[40] Fisher 1967, 132ff.; Fraser 1979–80.
[41] Arr. IV.1.3. For Cyrupolis see Arr. IV.2.2; Curt. VII.6.6, with Benveniste 1943–5.

with massacre and mass enslavement, destroying the main centres of resistance, including Cyrupolis. There accrued a large number of slaves, whom
Alexander 'liberated' to provide the rural populace for the new foundation and
settled alongside a core of Greek mercenaries and discharged Macedonian
veterans.[42] Alexander set the whole army to work at the task of primary
construction and he allegedly completed the circle of walls within seventeen
days (Curt. VII.6.25–6; Justin XII.5.12). This foundation, Alexandria Eschate
(modern Leninabad), was to be the model for settlement during the next
years, as the local revolts persisted. In 328 Alexander established a network of
six cities north of the Oxus, sited on elevated positions and at moderate
distances apart. A short time later they were supplemented by native prisoners
of war, captured during the siege of the rock of Ariamazes and allotted to the
new foundations as agrarian serfs.[43] Once more the new cities were in essence
garrison points, their livelihood secured by transplanted members of the
native population. Their nucleus, according to Curtius Rufus (VII.10.15), was
an important local centre which he terms Margania. The land was already
under cultivation and only needed to be appropriated by the conquerors. The
process is nicely illustrated by the French excavations around Ai-Khanum,
probably the site of Alexandria on the Oxus. Here the new city was established
in the plain of the river Kokcha, which was already irrigated by a network of
canals, the main arterial conduit (the Rud-i Sharavan) already complete. The
new settlers extended the existing network but it is clear that they found the
area flourishing, under intensive cultivation.[44] The city proper was a Greek
implant, complete with gymnasium and theatre, where the Greek population
lived exclusively, only the acropolis (it seems) showing traces of an earlier
Achaemenid settlement.[45] Nothing could show more vividly that the new
foundation was parasitic upon the rural population, which was forced to
support a superimposed Greek enclave.

We have no indication how many cities were established in Bactria and
Sogdiana, but they were clearly numerous and when combined with the
garrisons in the native citadels and the satrapal army of occupation they
amounted to a concentration of European settlers unparalleled elsewhere in
the empire. Alexander had decimated, disrupted and transplanted the native
population and added a new alien force of very considerable numbers. The
pattern was repeated on a smaller scale in India. In the Cophen valley there
was at least one new foundation: the native centre of Arigaeum was repopulated with the normal blend of veterans and locals (Arr. IV.24.7), and the
major strongholds were occupied with garrisons. Alexander's major work of
city foundation was in the Indus plain. Twin cities, Nicaea and Bucephala,

[42] Curt. VII.6.27; Justin XII.5.12; *contra* Arr. IV.4.1. Cf. Briant 1982b, 244–7.
[43] Curt. VII.10.15, 11.29; Arr. IV.16.3. For the identification of these sites see Bosworth 1981,
    23–9; they have nothing to do with any foundation in the province of Margiana (Merv), as is
    usually assumed (cf. Tscherikower 1927, 105; Berve 1926, 1.294; Tarn 1948, 2.234–5).
[44] Cf. Bernard 1974, 281–7; 1975, 195–7; Gardin 1980, 498–501.
[45] Bernard, *Fouilles d'Aï-Khanoum* 69ff.; 1980a, 435ff.

were established on opposite sides of the Hydaspes, theoretically in commemoration of his victories but in practice frontier defences of empire after the
eastern regions had been ceded to Porus (see above, p. 134). There was also a
major foundation further south, which Alexander planned as a naval base, at
the great confluence of the Indus and the Acesines.[46] In Sind a similar process
began. Alexander fortified some of the major centres in the Indus delta and
ordered his officers to resettle them with a new population. The principal
native city, Patala, was evacuated in the face of his advance, and the
population had to be tempted back by promises of security of tenure.[47]
Alexander needed the native producers to keep his army provisioned and in
this case was willing to give guarantees securing their interest. That meant
that Patala itself could not be refounded with a Greek population. Even so a
garrison occupied the citadel, and the new installations for the fleet may have
amounted to a new city in its own right. That was probably the *Xylinepolis*
('wooden city') which Pliny states was Nearchus' point of departure for his
ocean voyage.[48] But the foundations in southern India were still at a
rudimentary stage when Alexander left the region, and they probably did not
survive Peithon's transfer to the north-west (see above, p. 239). The cities
which survived the reign were in the northern Punjab, in the territory of
Taxiles.

Alexander continued to found cities as he returned west. In the territory of
the Oreitae, immediately west of the Indus delta, he selected the largest native
village, Rhambaceia, which he re-established as an Alexandria, leaving
Leonnatus to complete its settlement with a population drawn in part from
Arachosia to the north.[49] The local tribesmen were dispossessed, and the new
foundation was understandably a major grievance, stiffening their resistance
to the Macedonian occupation. Back in Mesopotamia he founded a new city at
the confluence of the Eulaeus and the Tigris, another Alexandria later to be
known as Spasinou Charax. Here, once again, Alexander based his settlement
on a large native community, Durine. It was broken up and its inhabitants
were attributed to the new city. Once more the soldiers incapable of further
service were left as its nucleus, in a special quarter named Pellaeum after the
Macedonian capital (Pliny, *NH* vi.138). Apart from Alexandria in Egypt that
seems to have been the invariable pattern in Alexander's new foundations. For
the local inhabitants they were an undeniable hardship, introducing an alien
privileged class to be supported by the existing resources of the territory. For
the settlers themselves the outlook was not much rosier. They were resented
immigrants in hostile territory, thousands of kilometres away from the centres
of Hellenic culture and enjoying all the discomforts of pioneer life. Most were

---

[46] Arr. vi.15.2, 4 (a double report of the same foundation – cf. Bosworth 1976b, 130–2); Diod.
xvii.102.4; Curt. ix.8.8.

[47] Arr. vi.17.5–6; cf. Briant 1982a, 250–2.

[48] Pliny, *NH* vi.96 = *FGrH* 134 f 28 (Patala is not mentioned by name either by Strabo or by
Arrian in their digests of Nearchus).

[49] Arr. vi.21.5, 22.3; cf. Pliny, *NH* vi.97; Curt. ix.10.7; Diod. xvii.104.8. Cf. Hamilton 1972.

reluctant colonists, held in place by fear of Alexander. A false report of his death, soon contradicted, sent 3,000 of them on the long march back to the Mediterranean.[50] When the end actually came, more than 20,000 of them banded together and made for the coast 'out of longing for the Greek manner of life' (Diod. XVIII.7.1). It took a vicious massacre by Macedonian troops sent from Babylon to convince them that their residence was permanent, and the new cities remained. But they were not an enticing prospect, and transplantation to the eastern satrapies was the final sanction of Alexander's Successors (Diod. XVIII.25.5). The ultimate result of Alexander's activity was the huge Seleucid programme of city foundations and the partial hellenisation of the near east, but he can hardly have foreseen the development. His own foundations were for military purposes and imposed reluctant settlers upon still more reluctant hosts. Plutarch interpreted it as a work of civilisation, tempering barbarism with an influx of higher culture. Contemporaries might have been excused for thinking that the barbarism had come from the west.

IV    **The Greeks of Asia Minor**

The Greek cities of Asia Minor were an anomaly within the administrative structure. On the one hand their liberation was an avowed objective of the war with Persia (Diod. XVI.91.1; XVII.24.1), and they could not reasonably be given the same treatment as Alexander's barbarian subjects. But they were also strategic pawns in a war zone, and they could not be left wholly to their own devices, if there was a possibility that they would side with the Persians or submit to occupation by them. They were also subject to the fortunes of war. If they resisted their liberators or harboured a Persian garrison, even involuntarily, they were liable to the usual sanctions if their city was taken by storm. That emerges clearly from the fate of the little Aeolic community of Gryneium, which was stormed by Parmenion in 335 and suffered enslavement (Diod. XVII.7.9). It was the treatment meted out to Thebes that same year and, like Thebes, Gryneium was tainted by medism. It was one of the fiefs granted to Gongylus of Eretria, Pausanias' colleague in treason, and may still have been ruled by his descendants.[51] Parmenion's drastic treatment may have been in part retribution for the past. One may contrast the case of Miletus, taken by storm in 334. The citizens surrendered at the very last second, falling before the king as suppliants after their walls were breached, and they were not only spared but granted liberty (Arr. 1.19.6; Diod. XVII.22.4–5). Liberty in this instance will have been little more than dispensation from slavery, but the Milesians were at least left in possession of their property and territory. The city enslaved by Darius in 494 could not suffer the same fate at the hands

[50] Curt. IX.7.1–11; Diod. XVII.99.5 (somewhat garbled).

[51] De Ste Croix 1972, 39; Lewis 1977, 54. The family of Damaratus, domiciled around Pergamum and intermarried with the Gongylids, certainly survived in Mysia until the reign of Lysimachus (SIG³ 381, 584 with Homolle, BCH 20 (1896) 510–12); one of its members married Pythias, daughter of Aristotle (Sext. Emp. Adv. math. 1.258).

of the avenger of Persian sacrilege. At Halicarnassus, however, the city proper was partially destroyed,[52] and, though the civilian population was spared from slaughter, it was certainly reduced to penury and perhaps redistributed among the other communities of the peninsula.

In practice the promise of liberation could mean very little. Once the Persians were expelled, their subjects were by definition liberated, even the miserable Halicarnassians or the native Lydians, who were free to pay tribute and obey a Macedonian satrap (Arr. 1.17.4, 7). On the other hand, given his impulsion to magnanimity, Alexander will certainly have wished to give all the concessions to freedom that were compatible with military efficiency – and his own sovereignty. But the latter qualification is important. Liberated they might be, but the Greeks of Asia Minor were in conquered territory and Alexander did not renounce the rights of victory. Consequently all settlements with Greek cities were imposed by the king. It was he who determined governments, decided tributary status and dispensed autonomy as his personal gift. There is never any suggestion of a bilateral treaty of alliance or even of friendship. He dictated the terms he pleased as despot and victor, and the process was wholly unilateral. Formal treaties seem to have been reserved for peoples outside the empire proper, such as the 'European Scyths' and the Chorasmians (Arr. IV.15.2–4) or the Greek communities of Cyrene (Diod. XVII.49.3; Curt. IV.7.9). Within the empire diplomacy was conducted on a basis of inequality, as the people of the Greek city of Phaselis discovered when they sent an embassy to Alexander and sued for his friendship (winter 334/3). Alexander's blunt response was to demand the city's surrender to the officers he sent (Arr. 1.24.5–6). We are not informed what settlement followed, but it was clearly the personal decision of the king. Whatever the Phaselites thought their embassy represented, he took it as a gesture of submission.

The conditions of conquest allowed for great variation in the treatment of individual cities. Ilium, secured by its ancestral ties to the Molossian royal house, could bask in Alexander's favour, endowed with new public buildings and adjudged free and immune from tribute (Strabo 593). On the other hand Zeleia, which served as the Persian base before the Granicus, had to face charges of medism and was fortunate to escape penalties (Arr. 1.17.2). At Ephesus the situation was complex.[53] The city was in the grip of party unrest. It had been 'liberated' in Philip's reign, probably in the wake of Parmenion's first offensive in summer 336, but it subsequently fell into the hands of Memnon, who was invited in by the faction of Syrphax and his family. The result was mass exile of the Macedonian sympathisers and a tight oligarchic government. On Alexander's approach its mercenary garrison withdrew and the king restored his exiled supporters. The principal oligarchs were lynched by the people, until Alexander insisted upon an amnesty, and their government was replaced by a democracy. The conqueror had imposed his will and

[52] Bosworth 1980a, 151; Hornblower 1982, 102–3.
[53] Arr. 1.17.10–12. On these events see Badian 1966, 47; Heisserer 1980, 58–9.

the Ephesian populace co-operated enthusiastically. Syrphax may have been genuinely unpopular, but it was a prudential move to show their loyalty by extreme action against his supposed crimes, until the king indicated the acceptable limits of vengeance. Ephesus was left with a democracy, but a democracy dominated by Macedonian partisans. It was also materially better off. Alexander had waived any claim to the tribute previously paid to the Persian administration and diverted it to the city's great temple of Artemis. Nothing is said about military occupation of the city, but in the summer of 334 it is almost inconceivable that such a strategic position could be left without a garrison in the face of the Persian fleet, now rapidly approaching.

From Ephesus Alexander sent out a senior officer, Alcimachus son of Agathocles, to operate in the areas of Aeolis and Ionia which were still under Persian occupation, instructing him to replace oligarchies with democracies, restore autonomy and remit the tribute imposed by the Persians (Arr. 1.18.2). This was in part a response to the military situation, a gesture to win over the cities of the northern seaboard (particularly, one may suspect, Cyme and the peninsula of Erythrae) which would otherwise be occupied by the Persian fleet. Remission of tribute was an obvious way to attract support, as was the promise of autonomy. The establishment of democracy was also a political necessity. The prevailing oligarchies were far from popular. In particular the coast between Atarneus and Assus, previously the principality of Hermeias, had fallen into Persian hands as recently as 342, and the governors imposed by Mentor of Rhodes (cf. [Arist.] *Oec.* 1351a32–8; Diod. xvi.52.6–7) will have been particularly unwelcome. There will have been little local objection to democracy. What the promise of autonomy meant is harder to fathom. Arrian speaks only of *restoration* of the particular laws of each city, implying that there had been a period of usurpation under Persian rule in which the proper rule of law had been disregarded. Most probably he is thinking in terms of legislation enacting democracy, which Alexander regarded or claimed to regard as the original constitution of the Asiatic Greeks. At Amisus on the Pontic coast he imposed democracy by edict and claimed that it was the city's ancestral polity (App. *Mithr.* 8.24, 83.374); in the same way democracy could be represented as the natural government for Ionian cities whose common ancestress was Athens. The new legislation and the new governments could then be represented as a restoration of the past. The cities were intended to be autonomous, and Erythrae and Colophon, both in Alcimachus' sphere of operations, were later to boast of the freedom conferred upon them by Alexander and Antigonus. The Erythraeans speak explicitly of autonomy and freedom from tribute.[54] But in both contexts the cities are petitioning for benefactions from later rulers, and it was in their interest to make the most of Alexander's settlement. In the wartime situation of 334 their autonomy was necessarily qualified, not least by the imposition of protective garrisons, which could be denounced by hostile critics as violation of autonomy (cf. Diod.

[54] *OGIS* 223, line 22 (Erythrae); *AJP* 56 (1925) 361 (Colophon).

xx.19.3) but which Alexander might represent as the bulwark of their newly won freedom.

From Miletus Alexander moved south through Caria, wooing the population by his generosity. The Greek cities on his route to Halicarnassus were treated like their brothers in Ionia, receiving autonomy and freedom from tribute (Diod. XVII.24.1). At Iasus democracy had apparently survived, even under Hecatomnid rule (*SIG*³ 169; Hornblower 1982, 112ff.). It was confirmed by Alexander. The *demos* is attested receiving some disputed territory (the 'little sea') at his hands, thanks to the intercession of two of its magnates, the brothers Gorgus and Minnion, who had acquired the king's ear and favour and clearly controlled the fortunes of democratic Iasus (Tod, *GHI* no. 190 = Heisserer 1980, 173). We cannot trace how far Alexander intervened in the government of the city or whether he introduced a garrison to ensure that its loyalty persisted. There is precise information for one community only, the city of Priene, recently refounded by the Hecatomnids if not by Alexander himself.[55] There is no literary evidence for the king's presence but the epigraphic record is striking. He gave his patronage to the new temple of Athene Polias which in due course was dedicated in his name. That was only natural. Athene was the tutelary goddess of his crusade, honoured by him at Athens and Ilium, and she enjoyed his largesse at Priene, where the citizens, unlike the Ephesians, had no reservations about inscribing his name as dedicator (see below, p. 290). More important is the fragmentary and defective inscription which records part of his detailed settlement of the city (Tod, *GHI* no. 185 = Heisserer 1980, 146). The rulings were probably made in 334, while Alexander was present in person on the western seaboard,[56] for they affect the status of Priene in the most fundamental way, delineating what parts of its territory should be royal land and what parts autonomous. They do not look like retrospective revisions. First of all citizens of Priene resident in the harbour city of Naulochum are declared free and autonomous, in full possession of any property they own in city or country. They are contrasted with some other non-Prienian group, whose autonomy must have been restricted in some way (the details are lost in a lacuna). Alexander next arrogates as his own certain villages in the hinterland which he declares to be subject to the regular tribute (*phoroi*). These had probably been annexed as royal domains during the Persian administration, and Alexander continued the arrangement, insisting on the previous fiscal obligations. The city of Priene was exempted from *syntaxis*.[57] This expression is not found elsewhere

---

55 For the dating to Alexander's reign see van Berchem 1970, Hornblower 1982, 323–30; for a Hecatomnid date see Heisserer 1980, 157–62, following Hiller von Gaertringen, *Inschr. Priene* xi.

56 Against Badian 1966, 47–8; Heisserer 1980, 161–2. The inscription itself seems late, part of an archive of related documents set up in Lysimachus' reign (Sherwin-White 1985).

57 τῆς δὲ συντάξεως ἀφίημι τὴμ Πριηνέωμ πόλιν. The definite article I take to refer to a generally imposed *syntaxis*, not to a specific levy imposed upon Priene in the past (so Badian 1966, 48). Sherwin-White 1985, 85, argues that the term is a synonym for *phoros*, inserted for stylistic variation.

during Alexander's reign, but it clearly denotes a payment of some kind which was not tribute proper. It has often been compared with the *syntaxis* imposed upon Athens' allies in the second confederacy, the term deliberately chosen as a euphemistic alternative to tribute. The analogy may be correct, but it would be wrong to accuse Alexander of cynical semantic manipulation. The original contributions (*syntaxeis*) of the Athenian confederacy appear to have been irregular levies for specific objectives, not annual imposts;[58] and Alexander's *syntaxis* may have been similar in its intention, a levy imposed upon Greek cities to help meet the current expenses of the campaign. In that case it anticipated the later Seleucid practice where special imposts for particular wars supplemented the regular tribute.[59] Priene was certainly exempted from any financial exaction (tribute was not imposed), but the tone of the inscription suggests that the *syntaxis* was fairly general elsewhere. Other cities might be dispensed from tribute but they could not avoid a contribution to the war of liberation. Priene, however, was immune from any impost, its freedom was guaranteed and its citizens were either given exclusive rights of residence at Naulochum or a privileged position there, ensuring that the Persian fleet would be denied yet another base.[60] Whether or not he imposed a garrison (one is mentioned on the stone but the context is lost), the harbour would be in friendly hands. This was a generous settlement, which the people of Priene recognised as such, proclaiming their autonomy in a regular formula upon the decrees it issued after the liberation, but it was still a settlement dictated and imposed by Alexander. The city could lose its privileges as easily as it had gained them, if the conqueror so decided.

The prime example of a change in status is the case of Aspendus in Pamphylia. The degree of hellenism there has been questioned in recent years, but Alexander certainly regarded the city as Greek. There seems to have been no doubt about the Aeolic origins of the barbarised population of Side (cf. Arr. 1.26.4). The Aspendians, who at least used a dialect which was recognisably Greek,[61] were granted citizen rights at Argos in the latter part of the fourth century, as kinsmen and (probably) colonists, and the people of Cilician Soli who also claimed Argive origins were given privileged access to the assembly.[62] They were certainly regarded as Hellenic communities and Alexander will have treated them as such, as he did the people of Mallus, whose Argive origins inspired his generosity (Arr. II.5.9). In the winter of

---

[58] Accame 1941, 132.

[59] Herrmann 1965, 104; Bosworth 1980a, 166, 281; Giovannini 1983.

[60] The subsequent status of Naulochum is not known. The Argive *thearodokos* inscription of *c*. 330 (*BCH* 90 (1966) 157, 11 line 10) mentions Naulochum rather than Priene as host city; but we must assume that the invitation to the games was given at the harbour and later transmitted to Priene, so that the envoys did not lose time travelling inland. In the same way Notium to the north is listed and not the inland city of Colophon (11 line 7). If anything, the inscription shows Naulochum to be a part of the state of Priene. Had it been totally independent, Priene would presumably have had a separate entry. See now Sherwin-White 1985, 88–9.

[61] Brixhe 1976. See, however, Hornblower 1982, 121.

[62] Stroud 1984, esp. 201–3.

334/3 plenipotentiary ambassadors from Aspendus surrendered the city to Alexander, asking only that no garrison be imposed there. Alexander agreed, but demanded fifty talents' donations towards his army's pay and also the horses which they were breeding as part of their tribute to the Persian king (Arr. 1.26.3). It was a sizeable demand, but Aspendus was notoriously wealthy and could be expected to make a substantial contribution to campaign coffers. The Aspendians, however, thought otherwise. They denied payment and prepared to resist. The sight of the Macedonian army inspired more sober reflection and they offered submission again. This time the king's demands were harsh: annual tribute was to be paid in addition to the immediate levy, now doubled to 100 talents, they were to be subject to the satrap appointed by Alexander and hostages were taken to ensure their compliance (Arr. 1.27.4). The two settlements illustrate the difference between privileged and unprivileged communities. At worst a city might be subject to tribute and supervision by the satrap under the watchful eye of a garrison commander. We have no evidence what was involved in satrapal supervision, but there were presumably regular inspections and the city's ordinances may have been submitted to the satrap for review. There was no question that Aspendus had lost her autonomy but she could still be considered liberated from the barbarian, even if she had shown herself unworthy of Alexander's full liberality. Circumstances could change in the other direction. The people of Soli in Cilicia suffered a vast punitive fine of 200 talents for alleged pro-Persian sympathies (Arr. II.5.5). After the battle of Issus the residue was remitted along with the hostages Alexander had taken from the city (Arr. II.12.2). Now that he had acquired the Persian treasure at Damascus, the fine from Soli had become insignificant and could be cancelled. Alexander's settlements were made with one eye on the military situation, to win allies, punish defectors, raise funds; and his rulings varied with the vicissitudes of war. Apart from the imposition of democracy, which was a necessary reaction against the oligarchies which the Persians had generally encouraged, there is no regularity of treatment, rather a range of benefactions which the king gave or withheld at his pleasure.

It is most unlikely that the Greeks of Asia were incorporated in the Corinthian League. This is an issue which has been endlessly debated with surprising intensity,[63] but argument inevitably founders on the lack of evidence. That silence does have some weight. If the Greek cities had been involved in the League with its symmachical obligations, it is remarkable that there is never any reference to alliance or even to a formal treaty. As we have seen repeatedly, Alexander dealt with them as a victorious despot not as the executive head of an expanding League. The single attestation of *syntaxis* makes no breach in this wall of silence. The terminology may recall the Athenian confederacy but does not imply that Alexander borrowed the institutions of the confederacy. Contributions could be imposed whether or

63 For bibliography see Seibert 1972a, 85–90.

not there was a formal alliance or treaty. On the other hand it is hard to see what advantages would have accrued from their joining the League. The main function of the common peace in Europe was to ensure that there was no rebellion or constitutional change among the participating cities; and it provided a common army and common action against defectors. Ionia and Caria, however, were remote from the League's centre at Corinth, and it would be hard for them to co-operate in military action, harder for League forces to be mobilised against them. But Alexander's satraps and satrapal armies were close at hand to give assistance to hard-pressed regimes and, if necessary, repress disaffection. There was no need for their inclusion in the Corinthian League, even as a quasi-independent Asian annexe. Propaganda might have been a consideration. It would have been an inspiring gesture to combine the liberated with the liberators as joint allies in the war of revenge, but, if such propaganda existed, it has left no traces in the source tradition – and one would have expected Callisthenes at least to have given the theme especial emphasis, an emphasis that cannot have escaped Ptolemy and Aristobulus. Until such time as new evidence appears, it will be best to view the Greek cities as autonomous entities within subject territory, dependent on the continuance of royal favour and without the sanctions or the guarantees of the common peace.

After 333 Alexander was no longer directly involved with the problems of Greek cities in Asia. In his eyes they were now liberated, as he proclaimed after Gaugamela, writing that all tyrannies had been abolished and autonomy now prevailed (Plut. *Al.* 34.2). As he continued east, the Greeks receded into obscurity and there is virtually no record of them. Such evidence as there is concerns the mysterious Philoxenus who was active on the south-west coast of Asia Minor in the latter years of the reign. A Philoxenus was certainly satrap of Caria during this period, holding office until the early months of 323. It remains conjectural whether there was another official, also named Philoxenus, who was active along the coast at Rhodes and Ephesus and is termed 'general of the coastal areas' or 'hyparch of Ionia'.[64] It is most economical to assume a single Philoxenus who began in 331 as fiscal superintendent west of the Taurus (see above, p. 242) and occupied the satrapy of Caria after the death of Ada. In the fluid conditions of 324 he operated outside the technical borders of his satrapy and achieved *de facto* a general oversight of the south-west coast. The attested activities are all compatible with a single individual operating from a base in Caria. Late in 324 Philoxenus intervened at Rhodes to arrest Harpalus' fugitive treasurer (Paus. II.33.4), and he demanded Harpalus' extradition from Athens that same year (see below, p. 217). Both actions could be attributed to an ambitious satrap eager to increase his favour at court. There is no reason to posit any extraordinary

[64] Plut. *Mor.* 333A, 531A, *Al.* 22.1; Polyaenus VI.49. For a single Philoxenus see Bosworth 1980a, 281–2; for two individuals see Berve 1926, 2 nos. 793–4; Leuze 1935, 435–8; Bengtson 1937; Badian 1966, 56–60.

command. The same applies to his intervention at Ephesus, again (it seems) in
324.[65] There a certain Hegesias is said to have been tyrant. Whether that
implies the overthrow of the democracy is uncertain. Hegesias may simply
have been the dominant personality of Ephesus, a political boss who could
impose his will on the city's democratic institutions. He was murdered by
three brothers whose arrest Philoxenus demanded. When his demand was
ignored, he introduced a garrison, seized the culprits and sent them ignominiously to the central prison at Sardes. It was a violation of sovereignty, as
Perdiccas tacitly admitted when he sent Diodorus (the only brother remaining
in custody at Alexander's death) to be tried by the laws of Ephesus.
Philoxenus had had no scruples about military intervention. A Macedonian
sympathiser had been murdered on the borders of his satrapy and he moved to
inflict condign punishment. The culprits were ultimately intended to be
referred to Alexander for punishment but were temporarily held at Sardes, the
strongest fortress of Asia Minor which did double duty as a place of
confinement for the whole coast (Plut. *Phoc.* 18.4–5; Ael. *VH* 1.25). This is
unlikely to have been an isolated incident. When Alexander turned his back on
the Aegean coast in 334, he had left the area in the grip of a Persian
counter-offensive. His satraps were left to a desperate struggle against
superior enemy forces, and there were two years of bitter fighting before the
coast was pacified. Miletus will hardly have been the only city to suffer
reconquest (Curt. IV.1.37, 5.13); the war required any number of interventions in cities that were technically autonomous. Satraps may have felt
themselves entitled to impose their wills upon the Greek cities, even through
military coercion, and, once accustomed to intervene, they will have found it
hard to desist when times were more settled. *Necessitate armorum excusata
etiam in pace mansere.*

Alexander himself seems to have made little distinction in his last years
between Greeks of Europe or Asia, or even between Greeks and barbarians.
The Exiles' Decree was a blatant infringement of autonomy, enforced by royal
edict upon all Hellenes (see below, pp. 220ff.). More perturbing still is a
circumstantial anecdote doubly reported by Plutarch (*Phoc.* 18.5) and Aelian
(*VH* 1.25). One of Craterus' instructions in the summer of 324 was to offer
Phocion the choice between four cities in Asia to exploit as his personal fief
(the relationship envisaged seems not unlike Chares' occupation of Sigeium
earlier in the century). The communities listed are a mixed bunch, too
obscure to have been readily invented, and the impeccably Hellenic Cius rubs
shoulders with Mylasa, a Carian but hellenised settlement. If the story is true
(and it cannot be disproved),[66] Alexander treated all communities in Asia
Minor as his personal property, conferring them as benefactions upon

---

[65] Polyaenus VI.49. Tarn 1948, 2.174–5, dismissed the story on *a priori* grounds without tackling
the circumstantial detail; Badian 1966, 56–7, 64, rightly rejects his argument.
[66] Rejected by Tarn (1948, 2.222–7; so Gehrke 1976, 145 n. 79) again on wholly inadequate
grounds; see, however, Hornblower 1982, 68 n. 116; Heisserer 1980, 177.

favoured individuals. Autonomy had been his gift, and he was prepared to revoke it. For most Greek cities the liberation seems to have been genuine. The cults established throughout Asia Minor were largely expressions of gratitude, voted at the king's suggestion no doubt but popular and enduring (see below, p. 289). Even so, the cities' position was precarious. No declaration of autonomy guaranteed against coercion or physical intervention if it suited the interest of the king or his satraps. The Greeks of Asia were certainly privileged subjects, but subjects in the last analysis they remained.

# C

# Alexander and the army

## 1     The invasion army of 334 B.C.

In the spring of 334 Alexander's army was assembled at Amphipolis and a smaller expeditionary force was already operating in Asia Minor. The total number of troops is difficult to estimate because of the diversity of figures given in the sources, ranging from a maximum of 43,000 foot and 5,500 horse to a minimum of 30,000 foot and 4,000 horse.[1] Some of the discrepancy may be explained by some authorities including the advance force in their total and others omitting it; but the inconsistencies run deep and cannot all be resolved on that hypothesis. Fortunately the size and composition of the Macedonian contingents is not seriously in doubt. Alexander took with him 12,000 infantry and left the same number with Antipater, his regent in Macedonia (Diod. XVII.17.4, 5). There was also a body of Macedonians already serving in Asia (Diod. XVII.7.10), several thousands strong. After Alexander crossed the Hellespont the total of his Macedonian infantry was around 15,000. The majority were brigaded in six phalanx divisions (which Arrian usually terms *taxeis*) and had the collective title of Foot Companions (*pezhetairoi*). Three of these divisions at least were recruited from the old principalities of Upper Macedonia and are termed *asthetairoi*, a most mysterious appellation which has yet to be explained satisfactorily.[2] The other *taxeis* do not apparently bear any distinctive nomenclature, but they may well have been recruited on a similar regional basis (cf. Arr. III.16.11). The other major component of the Macedonian infantry was the corps of hypaspists. This force had evolved from the old bodyguard of the Macedonian kings and its nucleus, the *agema*, still acted as Alexander's guard when he fought on foot. The rest of the hypaspists were organised in chiliarchies (units of 1,000), perhaps three in number. They were an élite, selected for their skill and physique and equally expert at phalanx work in pitched battle and in rapid skirmishing with light infantry and

[1] Berve 1926, 1.177–8; Brunt 1963, 32–6; Bosworth 1980a, 98–9.
[2] Bosworth 1973, 1980a, 251–3; Milns 1976, 97–101; Hammond and Griffith 1979, 2.709–13. On the possibility of a cavalry unit named *asthippoi* see Hammond 1978a, Milns 1981.

cavalry support. In the major battles they stood alongside the *taxeis* in the phalanx, and there is no doubt that their armament was the same.[3] It was their general calibre that was superior.

The equipment of the Macedonian infantryman was a blend of hoplite and peltast armament. The main offensive weapon was the *sarisa*, a huge pike up to six metres long with a leaf-shaped blade and a butt spike, both about 50 cm in length.[4] Its total weight would have been nearly 7 kg. As a result the weapon could only be manipulated with two hands, which allowed only a small button-shaped shield, slung around the neck to protect the left shoulder.[5] There were subsidiary weapons, a more orthodox short spear and a slashing sword, but they were of very secondary importance in pitched battle. The *sarisa* was primary and not intended to be used in isolation: the story of the single combat between Corrhagus and Dioxippus is a vivid illustration of how vulnerable the lone infantryman could be when isolated from the rest of the phalanx.[6] The defensive armour was relatively sparse.[7] There are no contemporary descriptions of it, but the Roman emperor Caracalla, who carried Alexander-imitation to absurd lengths, created an allegedly authentic Macedonian phalanx, armed with the three offensive weapons (*sarisa*, spear and sword) together with a helmet of ox-hide, a triply strengthened linen corselet and tall boots (Dio LXXVIII.7.1–2). Greaves are also attested (Polyaenus IV.2.10) and are not improbable. The light body armour was logical enough. It was the line of *sarisae* that gave the primary protection, making the phalanx infantry practically invulnerable except to missile attack, and it was superfluous to equip them with heavy body armour. As it was, if they temporarily dispensed with the *sarisae*, they had a mobility which matched that of the light infantry.

The phalanx was organised in basic units of sixteen (originally ten, as their technical name *dekas* shows) which were combined in larger groupings called *lochoi*. In its primary formation it seems that the phalanx was sixteen deep, the *dekades* deployed side by side with the more expert and highly paid men to the front. In an actual engagement only the first three or four ranks used their *sarisae* in couched position; the rest kept their weapons vertical and used their body weight to increase the momentum of the front line.[8] There was a good deal of variation possible. The *dekades* could be doubled to deepen the phalanx to thirty-two ranks or halved to reduce it to eight; and the change of front could be gradual, as happened before Issus, when the Macedonian line, originally thirty-two deep, was gradually expanded as the plain opened out. As gaps appeared in the front lines, files were continuously transferred from the

---

[3] Tarn 1948, 2.153–4; Hamilton 1955, 218–19; Milns 1971, 186–8; Ellis 1975; Hammond and Griffith 1979, 2.414–18.
[4] Andronikos 1970; Markle 1977, 323–6; 1980.
[5] Asclep. *Tact.*. 5; cf. Markle 1982, 92–4.
[6] Diod. XVII.100.2–8; Curt. IX.7.16–22; Ael. *VH* X.22.
[7] Moretti, *ISE* no. 114, B1; cf. Griffith 1956–7; Markle 1977, 327–8.
[8] Polyb. XVIII.29.2–30.4; Ael. *Tact.* 14.6; Arr. *Tact.* 12.11.

rear until the phalanx depth was finally contracted to eight.[9] The most impressive performance recorded was the display Alexander organised for the Illyrians in 335. Then he massed the phalanx 120 deep and carried out a number of changes of front, turning the direction of march and the thrust of the *sarisae* to left and to right. Finally he drew back the entire front line to create a wedge-shaped apex on the left (Arr. 1.6.1–3). These manœuvres were carried out in silence, and the parade ground discipline was obviously immaculate. The training was geared to produce a flexible, unbroken mass of infantry. In the period after Alexander the integrity of the phalanx became a fetish: breaks in the line were fatal and commanders could not conceive taking their men over broken ground or across watercourses.[10] Alexander's men were more versatile. They *were* led in line over highly difficult terrain at Issus and fought the engagement across a river; and their line *was* broken both at Issus and at Gaugamela without catastrophe resulting.[11] The middle-rank men could obviously deal to some degree with breaches at the front, in a way that was impossible later, when the *sarisa* was eight metres or more long. Not every action will have required the full weaponry. It is most unlikely, for instance, that the infantry involved in the final pursuit of Darius carried the heavy *sarisa* (Arr. III.21.2–7); they presumably marched with spears alone. But it seems clear that the *sarisa* was their basic weapon. It was used by the Macedonian guards at court, in situations where it was cumbersome and inappropriate (Arr. IV.8.8–9); and we are explicitly informed that when the Macedonian infantry crossed the Danube in 335 they took their *sarisae* with them (Arr. 1.4.1). The individual phalangite, then, was essentially a part of a corporate mass, intensively trained to a very specialised form of fighting and enjoying a cohesiveness and weight of offensive armament that was unmatched in the contemporary world.

The counterpart of the phalanx infantry was the Macedonian cavalry, collectively termed the Companions (*hetairoi*). At the Hellespont they were 1,800 strong and divided into eight squadrons (*ilai*), one of which, the *ile basilike*, defended the king when he fought on horseback.[12] This Royal Squadron formed an élite, probably comprising most of the courtiers, those of the Companions proper who had no specific command. Otherwise they were recruited on a regional basis. Those squadrons whose origins are recorded came from the Thraceward districts where Philip had established military settlers: Bottiaea, Amphipolis, Apollonia, Anthemus.[13] The one exception is a mysterious 'Leugaean *ile*' (Arr. II.9.3), which may be a much older unit created before the institution of territorial recruitment. The Upper Macedonian cavalry (Arr. 1.2.5) were another regional group, but there is no direct evidence that they were taken on campaign in Asia. They may have been part

[9] Polyb. XII.19.5–6 = Callisthenes, *FGrH* 124 F 35; Arr. II.8.2; Curt. III.9.12.
[10] Polyb. XII.22.4–6; cf. Markle 1978, 493–5 (somewhat exaggerated).
[11] Arr. II.10.5; III.14.4–5.
[12] Arr. III.11.8; Diod. XVII.57.1; cf. Hammond and Griffith 1979, 2.411–14.
[13] Arr. 1.2.5, 12.7, II.9.3; cf. Berve 1926, 1.105.

of the 1,500 cavalry left with the home army under Antipater (Diod. XVII.17.5), but it is much more likely that Alexander took troops from all sectors of his kingdom into Asia, leaving a proportion from each recruiting area. At first there is no record of any subdivision of the *ilai*; each squadron apparently fought as a unit under its local commander. Their armament was simple, a thrusting lance of cornel wood with a reserve supply of javelins and perhaps a cavalry shield, together with a minimum of body armour, including the Macedonian helmet, the broad-brimmed *kausia*. In pitched battles the cavalry was Alexander's main striking force. Time and time again it was a cavalry charge, usually in wedge formation,[14] that exploited the vital breach in the enemy line. Unfortunately the numbers in each squadron are very much a matter of guesswork. The royal guard may have totalled 300 by the end of the reign (see below, p. 269), but there is no indication of its strength at the time of the Hellespont crossing. More seriously, we do not know whether Diodorus' figure of 1,800 covers the Companions alone or includes other units of Macedonian cavalry.

The matter is complicated by the problem of the *prodromoi*. These troops were a division of cavalry regularly associated with the Companions and the Paeonian light horse; and, as their name implies, they were used on reconnaissance missions. But they are also termed *sarisa*-bearers (*sarisophoroi*);[15] and it is clear that they operated in the vanguard of the assault at the Granicus armed with the cavalry *sarisa*, which by all indications was equal in length to the infantry weapon.[16] They were divided into *ilai* like the Companions, and there were at least four of them (Arr. 1.12.7). The use of *sarisae* in battle, together with the fact that they are habitually mentioned by Arrian without any ethnic qualification, suggests that they were native Macedonians, organised separately from the Companions proper but to be included in Diodorus' total of 1,800 Macedonian cavalry.[17] They seem to have fulfilled a dual function, advance scouting (clearly without the *sarisa*) and anti-cavalry fighting in open order. The *sarisa*, which projected murderously before and behind the horse, could not be used in close formation without mortal danger to one's own troops. Cavalry using it would need to be widely spaced or to be massed in single extended lines, in which case they would provide an effective counter to frontal assaults by more lightly armed opponents (cf. Arr. IV.4.6). Although there is evidence, notably in the Alexander Mosaic, that the Companions might use the *sarisa* on occasion, it is

[14] Ael. *Tact.* 18.6; Arr. *Tact.* 16.6–7; cf. Rahe 1981; against Markle 1977, 338–9.

[15] The equation is explicit: Arr. 1.14.1 and 6; III.12.3 with Curt. IV.5.13.

[16] Markle 1977, 333–9; 1982, 105–6.

[17] Diod. XVII.17.4 has a note Θρᾶκες δὲ πρόδρομοι καὶ Παίονες ἐννακόσιοι, which has been taken to imply that the *prodromoi* were Thracians (Tarn 1948, 2.157) or emended to dissociate the Thracians from the *prodromoi* (cf. Milns 1966a). Neither is necessary; *prodromoi* could be used as a generic term for light cavalry and applied to Thracians and Paeonians (Arr. III.8.1) as well as the Macedonian *sarisophoroi*. But, if the *sarisophoroi* were Macedonian, as seems almost certain (Berve 1926, 1.129; Brunt 1963, 27–8), they should be listed by Diodorus with the main body of Macedonian cavalry, not separated and associated with the cavalry of the north.

evident that the weapon could not be used profitably in the wedge-shaped assault formation. The principal weapon of the Companions must have been the shorter thrusting lance, and their training was designed for intensive attacks in close formation and dense column, contrasting with the *prodromoi* who were intended to operate in more open conditions. Both were Macedonian in extraction, but we have no means of assessing their relative numbers, and the total of *ilai* in the *prodromoi* remains unknown.

The indispensable complement of the Macedonian forces was the light infantry. Some of these units may indeed have come from Macedon proper, but there is little explicit evidence. Arrian occasionally mentions divisions (*taxeis*) of light-armed troops, but he rarely gives an indication of their national origins and never designates any of them as Macedonian. On the other hand he does appear to include Thracians and Agrianians among the *taxeis* of javelin-men.[18] The only known group of light troops which may have consisted of Macedonians is the contingent of javelin-men commanded by Balacrus; it is listed without ethnic in Arrian's description of the line at Gaugamela, which specifies the national origins of the other units.[19] If there were Macedonian light-armed they were clearly not numerous. As we have seen, the phalanx soldiers had a relatively light defensive equipment, and few Macedonians can have been excluded from service in it on grounds of poverty. Alexander would have been well advised to concentrate his native infantry in the phalanx, relying on his neighbours in the north to supply the light infantry. By and large that was what happened. The most important of Alexander's light-armed troops were the Agrianian mountaineers, a relatively small body of javelin-men from the upper Strymon. They are attested some fifty times in Arrian alone, used on almost every occasion which called for rapid movement on difficult terrain. From the time of the Danubian campaign they were employed with the hypaspists and selected phalanx infantry for particularly arduous marches, and in the formal battles they formed part of a defensive screen in advance of the main line. Their usual associates were the archers. Once again there may well have been a corps of Macedonian archers (Arr. III.12.2) but its numbers were small. Otherwise the archers largely comprised Cretans, and two attested commanders of the contingent were Cretans by birth.[20] The archers were evidently a specialist body, recruited outside Macedon, but with the Agrianians they were used alongside the Macedonian troops whenever skirmishing tactics were called for. The Thracians were occasionally used in the same role (Arr. I.28.4), but the archers and Agrianians are far more frequently attested, and Diodorus (XVII.17.4) lists them as a composite body, 1,000 strong at the Hellespont. That was a minimum figure. Alexander had deployed twice that number in the north

---

[18] Cf. Arr. I.27.8 with I.28.4; VI.8.7.
[19] Arr. III.12.3, 13.5; cf. IV.4.6; Berve 1926, 1.131; Hammond and Griffith 1979, 2.430.
[20] Arr. II.9.3; Diod. XVII.57.4; Curt. IV.13.31. The commanders are Eurybotas (Arr. I.8.4) and Ombrion (III.5.6). For the Macedonian archers see Arr. III.12.2 with Bosworth 1980a, 302.

(Arr. 1.6.6), and once the campaign in Asia began they were swelled by reinforcements. By the middle years of the reign there were at least 1,000 Agrianians,[21] and the archers were brigaded in chiliarchies (Arr. IV.24.10). They had proved themselves key units and were systematically expanded.

The rest of the army consisted of allied troops and mercenaries. Of these the most important contingent by far was the Thessalian cavalry, probably equal in numbers to the Macedonian cavalry and almost equal in calibre. Like the Companions they were divided into *ilai*, of which the Pharsalian contingent was the most prestigious and numerous (Arr. III.11.10), and they performed much the same functions as the Companions themselves, protecting the left wing of the phalanx in the first three major battles. The structure of command seems to have been parallel to that of the Macedonian cavalry, with regionally based *ilai*, but at the head was a Macedonian commander. The rest of the allied cavalry, predominantly from central Greece and the Peloponnese, was much less important and effective, fewer in number and less prominent in action. Like the Thessalians they were divided into *ilai* (Tod, *GHI* no. 197.3) under the command of a Macedonian officer. The infantry from the allied Greek states is more problematic. They formed a contingent numerically strong, 7,000 of them crossing the Hellespont in 334, and they were predominantly heavy-armed hoplites. But once in Asia they are mainly notable for their absence. There is no explicit record of them in any of the major battles. At Gaugamela we may infer that they provided most of the men for the reserve phalanx (Arr. III.12.1), but in the other engagements there is no room for them. They are only mentioned as participants in subsidiary campaigns, usually under Parmenion's command (in the Troad, at the Amanid Gates, in Phrygia and in the march on Persis),[22] and they never appear in the entourage of Alexander. One contingent, that of Argos, was detached for garrison duty in Sardes (Arr. 1.17.8) but that is the only case recorded (the allied cavalry, however, formed the original garrison of Upper Syria). Part of the reason for the neglect must have been the heterogeneous nature of the allied infantry, drawn as it was from a plethora of different cities and virtually impossible for its Macedonian commander to organise as a single unit. There was also the question of loyalty. Alexander might well have been reluctant to rely on men recently vanquished at Chaeronea to face the Hellenic mercenaries in Persian service. It was too much kin against kin, and his Greek allies naturally had less stomach for the task than his native Macedonians.

The other major infantry group was the 7,000-strong contingent of Thracians, Triballians and Illyrians. These troops are, if anything, more elusive than the Hellenic infantry. The Triballians are never mentioned in the campaign narrative and the Illyrians only rate a passing reference in Curtius' account of Gaugamela (IV.13.31), where they are associated with the mercenary infantry. The Thracians are a little more prominent. Under the Odrysian

---

[21] Arr. IV.25.6; cf. Curt. V.3.6.
[22] Arr. 1.17.8; 1.24.3, II.5.1; III.18.1.

prince Sitalces they were active before and during the battle of Issus, and at Sagalassus and Gaugamela they performed exactly the same function on the left of the line as the Agrianians on the right (Arr. 1.28.4, III.12.4). It may be only chance that we hear nothing more of them in action, but their subsequent history suggests that Alexander did not find them in any way indispensable. A large proportion was left behind in 330 to man the satrapal armies of Media and Parthyaea (Arr. III.19.7; v.20.7). A few returned to the main army in 326/5, but the entire contingent of Thracians was soon discarded, left in the unenviable role of garrison army in northern India (Arr. VI.15.2). The evidence, such as it is, suggests that they were not normally employed as front-line troops but used on secondary missions or in positions where weight of numbers rather than expertise was important. It was they who formed the occupying force on the island of Lade with 4,000 other non-Macedonians, denying access to the Persian fleet (Arr. 1.18.5), and they were also consigned to road-building in Pamphylia (Arr. 1.26.1). It looks as though Alexander had no interest in repatriating any of them, and the main *raison d'être* of his Thracian contingent may have been simply to be out of Thrace. Their absence meant that the territory was easier to control. The same considerations applied even more forcefully to the Illyrians and Triballians.

The Thracian cavalry comes in the same category. These troops were placed alongside the Greek allied cavalry at the Granicus and Gaugamela, but their employment was very sporadic and they were assigned to the Median garrison together with the infantry. A further contingent of Thracian cavalry which reached India late in 326 (Curt. IX.3.21) was certainly left with the satrapal army of northern India. The other cavalry body from the north, the Paeonians, had a more distinguished career. They are associated with the *prodromoi* and were in the vanguard of fighting at the Granicus and Gaugamela; and they were lightly enough equipped to be termed scouts in their own right (Arr. III.8.1). But they are not mentioned in any narrative after 331, and there is no record of their being detached to any garrison force. Their numbers must have been small (with the Thracian cavalry they only amounted to 900), and they could easily have been amalgamated with other units (see below, p. 271).

Finally Alexander, like his father, made extensive use of mercenaries. Only 5,000 are recorded at the Hellespont, but there were certainly many thousands already active in the expeditionary force in Asia Minor, including the whole of the mercenary cavalry.[23] One distinct group, the 'old mercenaries', were grouped together under the command of the Macedonian Cleander.[24] Otherwise they seem to have been divided up as the occasion demanded. The mercenary cavalry at Gaugamela were divided into two groups, under

---

[23] The total force in Asia numbered over 10,000 (Polyaenus v.44.4), a proportion of which was Macedonian (Diod. XVII.7.10). The majority were doubtless mercenaries, as was clearly the case with the cavalry (Diodorus lists no mercenary cavalry with the army at the Hellespont).

[24] Arr. III.12.2; cf. Griffith 1935, 17, 29–30.

Menidas and Andromachus, again both Macedonians, and the division of command persisted for some time (Arr. III.25.4). That is the only organisation of any permanence that can be traced. In general the mercenaries seem to have been organised on a far more fluid basis than the rest of the army. Their numbers constantly fluctuated, as new units were recruited and mercenaries already in service were detached to man the satrapal armies or, in the latter years of the reign, to provide settlers for the new foundations in the east. They were probably the most dispensable part of the army, in terms of front-line fighting. In the major battles they were kept in reserve, except for the cavalry which played an important part at Gaugamela; and, like the infantry of the Corinthian League, they tended to fall under the command of Parmenion, to be used in secondary expeditions. In later years the forces sent out to deal with Satibarzanes in Areia and Spitamenes in Sogdiana were almost exclusively composed of mercenaries (cf. Curt. VII.3.2; Arr. IV.3.7). Indeed outside the immediate entourage of Alexander the fighting troops throughout the Empire tended to be mercenaries. At first the need to pay them regularly and the fact that the Great King was a competing paymaster will have kept numbers down. Apart from the 300 mercenaries taken in from the garrison at Miletus (Arr. 1.19.6) there are only attested 4,000 raised in the Peloponnese by Cleander and 400 cavalry sent to Memphis by Antipater. This is admittedly a partial record, but it contrasts vividly with the situation after 331, when Alexander's funds were practically limitless. Then there was a vast and continuous influx; nearly 60,000 recruits are listed in the extant sources and many more may have been unrecorded.

## II    Evolution and reorganisation: 333–323 B.C.

It was the Macedonian nucleus, perhaps 15,000 infantry out of an original force numbering more than 40,000, which was overwhelmingly important, the main striking force in the army and the sheet anchor for all the major battles. On the cavalry side the Macedonians were less dominant, at least balanced by the Thessalians, but they were still far more frequently used by Alexander than any other cavalry units. In numerical terms his army was huge, surpassing the total number of combatants at Nemea in 394, but the vital Macedonian complement was a relatively small part of it. In practice all Alexander's victories, except perhaps Gaugamela, were won with a fraction of the forces at his disposal. Accordingly the first years of the campaign saw a planned increase in the size of the Macedonian core of the army, as Alexander prepared to meet the full levy of the Persian empire. Our sources record an impressive number of reinforcements from Macedon between 333 and 330. At Gordium 3,000 Macedonian infantry and 500 cavalry, Macedonian and Thessalian, arrived to swell his forces (Arr. 1.29.4); and just before he entered Cilicia later that summer an additional 5,000 infantry and 800 cavalry arrived from Macedonia.[25] This influx expanded the original phalanx by half, and it may not represent the entire total. Curtius indicates that other forces had arrived or were on their way by the time Issus was fought (III.1.24; 7.8). By the end of 333 the Macedonian component of the army reached its highest strength hitherto. Numbers will have fallen the following year as the sieges of Tyre and Gaza took their toll, and at the end of 322 one of the phalanx commanders, Amyntas son of Andromenes, was sent on an urgent recruiting mission to Macedon across the wintry seas of the Mediterranean.[26] Before the summer of 331 he had amassed a force of 15,000, an army in itself, including 6,000 Macedonian infantry and 500 cavalry.[27] That is the last that is heard of specifically Macedonian reinforcements. Though there is ample record of new arrivals later, no contingent includes native Macedonians; the troops which came from Antipater were Thracians, Illyrians or mercenaries. Alexander himself sent for replacements from Macedon in 327 (Arr. IV.18.3), but there was apparently no response, and in 324, when he demobilised the 10,000 veterans from Opis, he insisted that Antipater bring prime recruits from Macedon to take their place.[28] But Antipater never left Macedon and the reinforcements never arrived. The country was already drained of fighting men by the levies already sent (Diod. XVIII.12.2), and the home army could not be weakened further. As it was, Antipater had trouble enough raising an army in 331/0 and still more at the outbreak of the Lamian War, when he was very seriously embarrassed. In effect the Macedonians who were in the army in 330 had no reinforcement until the end of the reign. Even so their numbers are impressive. At Opis in the summer of 324 10,000 Macedonians were demobilised and a strong contingent remained, a minimum of 8,000 at the time of Alexander's death.[29]

The crucial period in terms of reinforcements was 333–331 B.C. Even on the basis of the defective reports that have come down to us it is clear that both the Macedonian infantry and cavalry were doubled, and the increase was in all probability much greater. It is unlikely that the mortality rate was less than 50%, given the constant fighting and the rigour of the physical conditions encountered. In that case the number of Macedonian troops taken from the homeland totalled well over 30,000. The actual operational numbers reached a peak late in 333 and then again at the end of 331, and they declined throughout the rest of the reign. The effect of the additional numbers is hard to trace. They did not result in any major change in organisation. As far as we can tell, the incoming reinforcements were divided up among the existing units according to their regional origins. The phalanx battalions accordingly remained six in number between the Granicus and Gaugamela, even though the complement of each battalion was greatly increased. Even the massive

[25] Polyb. XII.19.2; cf. Brunt 1963, 37; Bosworth 1975, 42–3; Milns 1976, 106.
[26] Diod. XVII.49.1; Curt. IV.6.30 (cf. VII.1.37–40).
[27] Diod. XVII.65.1; Curt. V.1.40–2; cf. Arr. III.16.10.
[28] Arr. VII.12.4; Justin XII.12.9.
[29] Cf. Brunt 1963, 19. For other estimates see Schachermeyr 1973, 491; Milns 1976, 112.

reinforcements brought by Amyntas were simply included in the existing units according to nationality. It is only at the time of the invasion of India that there is evidence for a seventh battalion of the phalanx, and the evidence for that is at best circumstantial: seven commanders appear to be named simultaneously at the head of phalanx *taxeis*.[30] The reasons for such a change are totally opaque. One of the battalions may have become disproportionately large through reinforcements and irregular losses and so became divided into two commands. That is, however, speculation. We do not know the reason, and there is no indication when the change took place or for how long it lasted.

There was some reorganisation at the end of 331 when Amyntas' Macedonian reinforcements arrived. Alexander divided the existing cavalry *ilai* into two *lochoi* and appointed new sub-commanders, promoted by merit and not by regional affiliation.[31] It was a break with tradition, and the king must have had strong reasons for his action. In all probability it was a first step towards breaking the ties between the original commanders and their men. There was now an intermediate level of command in which the officers had no necessary connection with their men but owed their appointment solely to royal favour. A similar development may well have taken place in the organisation of the hypaspists. The details are sadly garbled by Curtius (v.2.2–5),[32] but it seems that another command was introduced in the hierarchy, the new officers again achieving preferment solely through military merit. From this time onwards the hypaspist corps had both chiliarchies and pentakosiarchies, units of 1,000 and 500, and there was a new category of officers of relatively humble status.

After 330 the entire Macedonian cavalry appears to have been reorganised. The basic unit was now not the *ile* but a new formation named 'hipparchy'. These new units are first recorded in the Ptolemaic part of Arrian's narrative during the spring of 329,[33] and from then onwards 'hipparchy' is the almost invariable nomenclature of the cavalry units. When we hear of *ilai*, they appear as subdivisions, each hipparchy comprising a minimum of two *ilai* (Arr. VI.21.3–4, 27.6). The Royal *ile* also disappears as a title and is replaced by the term *agema*; Alexander's cavalry and infantry guards now had the same nomenclature. Unfortunately there is no list of hipparchies and commanders comparable to the list of *ilai* at Gaugamela, and we can only infer their numbers from random hints in the campaign narrative. It looks as though there were eight hipparchies in addition to the *agema* throughout the Indian campaign,[34] but whether there was a constant number from the beginning is an insoluble problem. Ptolemy at least had three hipparchies of Companions

---

[30] Arr. IV.22.7 (Gorgias, Cleitus, Meleager); IV.24.1 (Coenus, Attalus); IV.25.6 (Coenus, Polyperchon); IV.27.1 (Alcetas). Cf. Milns 1966; Bosworth 1973, 247, 249.

[31] Arr. III.16.11; cf. Diod. XVII.65.3.

[32] Arr. VII.25.6; Plut. *Al.* 76.6. Cf. Bosworth 1980a, 148–9; Milns 1971, 189–92.

[33] Arr. III.29.7. There is an earlier anachronistic reference at Arr. 1.24.3. Diodorus XVII.57.1 describes the *ilai* at Gaugamela as hipparchies – a clear instance of substitution of the later term.

[34] Brunt 1963, 29; Bosworth 1980a, 375–6.

for his pursuit of Bessus, and that was clearly only a fraction of the total force. It is not unlikely that there were eight hipparchies as early as 329.

The other main change at this period is the apparent disappearance of the *prodromoi*. The unit is not attested in action under that title after the death of Darius. There is one fleeting reference to *sarisophoroi* in 329, when they were still apparently grouped in *ilai* (Arr. IV.4.6). They may not as yet have been divided into hipparchies, but the mercenary cavalry had been so organised and *a fortiori* one would expect the Macedonian troops to have undergone the same transformation. It may be that *ile* is already being used in its later technical sense and the *sarisophoroi* in 329 were mobilised in sub-groups against their Saca enemies. At all events it is their last appearance, and it is a reasonable assumption that they were amalgamated with the Companion cavalry and organised with the hipparchies. Each hipparchy for instance may have had a subdivision of *sarisophoroi*. They would have added to its versatility when away from base, and the sub-units could be detached for special service during an emergency such as the crossing of the Iaxartes.

The relative strength of the hipparchies is unknown. There is some slight evidence from the period of the Successors that the number in the *agema* was 300.[35] As regards the rest of the Companions there is only Arrian's figure of 1,700 for the troops embarked at the start of the Indus voyage (Arr. VI.14.4), but there is no indication that they were the whole contingent. Perdiccas at least was away on other business (Arr. VI.15.1) and he may not have been the only absentee.[36] All we have is a minimum figure and it is surprisingly high, almost as large as the entire body of Macedonian cavalry at the Hellespont. Reinforcements had been numerous until 331/0, but the attrition rate will have been high. If the Companions numbered a minimum of 1,700 in 326, there is every reason to believe that they had absorbed the *prodromoi*.

The causes of the reorganisation are not recorded, but they were presumably important. Technical terms, especially traditional ones, are not changed simply for novelty's sake. The execution of Philotas was certainly related in some way to the move. After his death Alexander refused to appoint a new commander for the entire cavalry body but divided the Companions between Cleitus, the veteran commander of the Royal *ile*, and Hephaestion, his closest personal friend.[37] The division was made for reasons of security (Arr. III.27.4), and it may have been part of a more general reorganisation of the cavalry, to lessen the ties of personal loyalty. Almost a year before, he had introduced sub-units (*lochoi*) with commanders chosen by merit. There is

---

[35] Diod. XIX.28.3, 29.5 (*agemata* of Eumenes and Antigonus in 317).

[36] According to Arrian (*Ind.* 19.2) the hypaspists, archers and Companion cavalry amounted to 8,000 in 325, but it is not clear how the groups are to be divided. Elsewhere (VI.2.2) he states that only the *agema* of cavalry was embarked on that occasion.

[37] Arr. III.27.4. Arrian calls these commanders ἱππάρχαι, but that does not imply that there were only two hipparchies. He uses the term ἱππάρχης in a very fluid way and can apply it to minor officers (cf. VII.11.6) as well as to commanders-in-chief (1.25.2); it is not a technical term in the same sense as ἱππαρχία.

other slight evidence for experimentation: his turning force at the Persian Gates included a *tetrarchia* of cavalry (Arr. III.18.5), a unit recorded neither before nor later. Alexander may have been consciously changing the balance of the cavalry, striking at the regional ties of the *ilai* and aiming at a more homogeneous force. There may also have been logistical considerations. The *ilai* may have become unbalanced in size, owing to disproportionate losses in battle and random accretions through reinforcements, which are not likely to have been divided with mathematical equality between the recruiting areas. Some levelling off may have been necessary. At all events the old *ilai* went, as did their commanders: only Demetrius son of Althaemenes is known to have continued with a hipparchy.[38] In their place were the new composite units, whose commanders were the élite of Alexander's court.

No such reorganisation is attested for the phalanx infantry. The division between hypaspists and phalanx battalions persisted until the end of the reign, and, except for the addition of a seventh battalion, there is no evidence for any major change. There is one minor innovation of nomenclature. Just before he entered India Alexander is said to have introduced silver shields in his army and coined the title *argyraspides* (Justin XII.7.5). This new term was reserved for the hypaspists and was apparently in vogue by the end of the reign;[39] but it only came into its own after his death. Then Alexander's hypaspists maintained their corporate identity and insisted on the title of *argyraspides*, which distinguished them from the various corps of hypaspists formed by the Successors.[40] In Alexander's lifetime, when there was no competition, 'hypaspist' seems to have been the term generally used. The unit maintained its élite status throughout the reign, and it was presumably supplemented from the rest of the phalanx to keep its complement relatively stable. After Alexander's death it was still 3,000 strong, its members all battle-hardened veterans of his campaigns. In 317 B.C. every man of them is said to have been over sixty, a statement which is no doubt exaggerated but which derived from the contemporary and eyewitness, Hieronymus of Cardia.[41] The hypaspists contained the most expert of the infantry throughout the reign and there must have been a constant transfer of picked men from the phalanx battalions, which suffered as a result. After the demobilisation of the 10,000 veterans at Opis the nucleus of phalanx troops, including hypaspists, fell below 10,000 and by the end of the reign Alexander was forced to supplement it with Iranian infantry (Arr. VII.23.3–4). Only four men in each file of sixteen were Macedonians, stationed to the front and the rear; the mass of the formation was now Persians, armed with bows and missile javelins. The mixed phalanx that emerged was designed for frontal attack only and had none of the flexibility that characterised the infantry manœuvres at the beginning of the

[38] Arr. III.11.8; IV.16.3: cf. Berve 1926, 2 no. 256.
[39] Arr. VII.11.3: it appears anachronistically in the vulgate accounts of Gaugamela (Diod. XVII.57.2; Curt. IV.13.27).
[40] Anson 1981; *contra* Lock 1977b.
[41] Diod. XIX.41.2 (cf. 30.6); Plut. *Eum.* 16.7–8; cf. Hornblower 1981, 190–3.

reign. It was an improvisation to make the most of a dearth of *sarisa*-trained phalangites and a superabundance of untrained Iranians. This relatively small number of Macedonian infantry in 323 goes a long way towards explaining their rapid capitulation to the cavalry in the conflict after Alexander's death. The vast differential between the two bodies at the beginning of the reign had been greatly reduced.

III     **The use of oriental troops**

The turning-point in the evolution of Alexander's army appears to have been the year 330. Until then the Macedonian component was progressively reinforced, reaching peaks before Issus and after the arrival of Amyntas' great contingent late in 331. Alexander then thought it safe to divest himself of non-Macedonian troops. The forces from the Corinthian League, infantry and cavalry, were demobilised from Ecbatana in the spring of 330;[42] even the Thessalian cavalry who re-enlisted were dismissed at the Oxus less than a year later (Arr. III.29.5). Alexander now relied on the Macedonian nucleus for front-line work and the mercenaries for support functions. The latter were important and were recruited in increasing numbers (see above, p. 266); but they were probably reallocated almost as soon as they arrived. The sources, partial record though they are, list over 36,000 left in satrapal armies or in the new foundations, and there are many settlements attested where the number of mercenaries is not given.[43] The wastage was constant, and Alexander cannot have had a large number with his field army at any given time. With the Hellenic complement of his army reduced and few, if any, reinforcements arriving from Macedonia, the king plunged into three years of guerrilla fighting, first in the Iranian plateau and then in Bactria/Sogdiana. It is not surprising that he was forced to draw upon oriental troops in increasing numbers. The date at which the development began is hard to fix. From late 330 Alexander employed a specialist troop of mounted javelin-men, who are usually assumed to have been Persian in origin. That is possible but nowhere attested; and the new corps was immediately drawn upon to provide a garrison force for Areia (Arr. III.25.2), a role in which no oriental unit is attested, even in the Indian satrapies. It is equally possible that the new unit was composed of European cavalry.[44] The Paeonians, for instance, are not mentioned after Gaugamela, and as light cavalry they could well have formed the nucleus of the specialised unit of javelin-men, which is associated in action with the Agrianians, themselves troops from Paeonia (cf. Arr. IV.26.4, VI.17.4).

The first unambiguous use of oriental troops is in the winter of 328/7. At the end of the campaign in Sogdiana locally levied cavalry were serving alongside the Macedonian forces (Arr. IV.17.3). Alexander took more of them with him

---

[42] Arr. III.19.6–7; Plut. *Al.* 42.5; Diod. XVII.74.3–4; Curt. VI.2.17; cf. Tod, *GHI* no. 197.
[43] For the detailed figures see Berve 1926, 1.146–9; Griffith 1935, 20–3. Cf. Wirth 1984.
[44] Bosworth 1980b, 14–15; *contra* Berve 1926, 1.151; Brunt 1963, 42.

into India, and at the Hydaspes he employed cavalry from Arachosia, Parapamisadae, Bactria, Sogdiana and the Saca territories to the north (Arr. v.11.3, 12.2). They were supplemented by levies from friendly Indian princes until the forces under his command reached the almost fantastic total of 120,000 (Arr. *Ind.* 19.5), only a fraction of which will have been Macedonian. As yet the oriental cavalry fought in separate national units, the one exception being the corps of horse archers, recruited in part at least from the nomad Dahae, who were regularly deployed alongside Macedonian troops. The majority were in the same category as the Illyrian and Thracian contingents in 334, levied as much to reduce the resistance in their homelands as to increase the strength of Alexander's army. They apparently kept their separate identities until the return to the west, when there was some integration with the Macedonian cavalry. According to Arrian one of the Macedonian grievances at Opis was the admission of selected orientals into the Companion cavalry: four hipparchies were formed exclusively from the easterners and there was a fifth which combined Macedonians and Iranians.[45] We should dearly like to know more about the transition, the numbers of Iranians involved and their strength relative to the Macedonians, but Arrian's language is systematically elusive. All we can say is that Alexander gave a certain number of Iranians the coveted title of Companions and brigaded them in hipparchies alongside the Macedonians. Except for the few Iranians in the fifth mixed hipparchy (and the handful of nobles in the *agema*) there was little attempt to integrate the two national groups. Rather Alexander had set two groups of Companions side by side in a very uneasy relationship. In any case the selected Iranians who were admitted to the ranks of the Companions were a small minority of their national contingents, which comprised the great majority of the cavalry present with Alexander in his last years.

The evidence for oriental infantry is less ambiguous. When Alexander left Bactria in 327, he gave orders for 30,000 youths to be recruited and trained in Macedonian arms and discipline. Accordingly the satraps and city commandants in the eastern provinces organised a concerted programme of training, no doubt using the veterans settled in the new foundations as instructors; and early in 324 the new phalanx presented itself at Susa and staged an impressive display before the king himself.[46] There was no attempt to amalgamate this new body with the Macedonian phalanx. It was to be a rival formation, an *antitagma* as Diodorus calls it,[47] to be used as a separate entity. The suggestive name (*Epigoni*) given to these recruits implies that Alexander thought of them as the heirs of his Macedonian phalanx, now almost superannuated. The new unit maintained its integrity while the Macedonian phalanx proper was adulterated by the admixture of Peucestas' levies from

---

[45] Arr. vii.6.4. For this interpretation see Bosworth 1980a, 15–17, 20–1. See also Brunt 1963, 43–5; Griffith 1963, 68–74; Badian 1965a; Hammond 1983b.

[46] Arr. vii.6.1; Plut. *Al.* 71.1; Diod. xvii.108.1–3; Curt. vii.5.1.

[47] xvii.108.3: cf. Briant 1982b, 32–41.

Persis (see above, p. 170). Until such time as reinforcements arrived from the homeland, the Macedonians (with the exception perhaps of the hypaspists) were swamped in a mass of Iranian infantry, indispensable in expertise but numerically weak. On the other hand selected Iranians were now expert in Macedonian techniques and formed a reserve which the king might eventually use as his front-line infantry.

The character of the army had changed irrevocably. The Macedonians no longer enjoyed supremacy over the other units of the army. Not only were they outnumbered but there were contingents of Iranians who had almost equal prestige – the new hipparchies of Companions and the phalanx of Epigoni. The change in the army reflected Alexander's own transition from king of Macedon to king of Asia. His Macedonians were in his eyes no longer a privileged élite but subjects on much the same level as the Iranians. He had served notice at Opis that, if necessary, he would man his army and officer corps from Persians, and his new army was a constant reminder of the fact. Its future moreover was clearly defined. The recruiting grounds had been the eastern satrapies of the empire, but service was to be in the west, in conditions as alien as Bactria had been to the Macedonians. Ultimately they would become deracinated, the only constant being their employer, Alexander. The process would go even further in the next generation. Alexander had deliberately retained the offspring of his Macedonian veterans when he demobilised them, promising to train them in Macedonian style.[48] His ultimate purpose was to weld them into a military force without attachment of race or domicile, loyal to himself alone. The transformation of the Macedonian national army with its regionally based units could not have been more complete.

IV    **The structure of command**

Little is known of the command structure of the army at its lower levels, although there are indications of a complex gradation of ranks. In the phalanx each file or *dekas* had four members of superior status, who were paid accordingly. Apart from the file leader (*dekadarches*) there were two who received double pay (*dimoiritai*) and a third who received pay and a half (Arr. VII.23.3; *Succ.* F 24.2). They served in particularly prominent positions and were paid according to expertise. Above them were the commanders of *lochoi*. Nothing is known of their numbers and we do not have a single name on record, but they were important enough to be included in Alexander's council before Gaugamela (Arr. III.9.6). The hypaspists will have had a similar organisation at file level, but the only intermediate rank between file and chiliarchy appears to have been the *pentakosiarchy*, the commanders of which were relatively obscure.[49] The subdivisions of the Companion cavalry are a

[48] Arr. VII.12.2; Justin XII.4.2–10.
[49] Curt. V.2.5: cf. Berve 1926, 1.127–8; Milns 1971, 192–4; Bosworth 1980a, 149.

similar mystery. The lowest division recorded is the *hekatostys*,[50] which should have had a nominal strength of 100 (though the analogy of the *dekas* in the infantry is a warning against taking the figure too seriously); and from 331/0 there were the larger subdivisions of *lochoi*. Nothing is known of these minor commands, and the only name recorded is that of the 'hipparch' Callines who intervened briefly at Opis (Arr. vii.11.6).

The positions in the hierarchy which mattered most were of course the commands of individual contingents, but even at the higher levels there were differences of rank which are hard to elucidate. Before Issus Alexander summoned to his council the commanders of the infantry, the cavalry ilarchs and the commanders of the allies (Arr. ii.7.3); and there was a similar meeting before the siege of Tyre which included the entire body of *hetairoi* as well as the commanders of specific units (Arr. ii.16.8). These episodes merely give us the totality of the high command, not the gradations of rank within it. It appears, however, that the commanders of the cavalry *ilai* were on a slightly inferior level. Arrian (ii.10.2) associates them with the officers of the infantry *lochoi* and the more prominent mercenary officers, below the officers of highest rank. That fits the rest of the evidence. Though the ilarchs are occasionally mentioned by name in the campaign narrative, they are not of great distinction (except for Cleitus the Black, commander of the Royal *ile*); and they never have independent commissions. The same seems to have been the case with the hypaspist officers: the chiliarchs and pentakosiarchs were on a markedly lower level than the battalion commanders of the phalanx, the generals proper (cf. Arr. vii.25.6). It looks as though the first stratum of command below Parmenion and the king himself comprised the overall commanders of the Companion cavalry and hypaspists (Parmenion's two sons, Philotas and Nicanor) and the six generals of the phalanx *taxeis*. It is they who are attested at the head of multiple contingents in the absence of the king and Parmenion: Philotas, for instance, took the cavalry and three phalanx *taxeis* to counter the Persian fleet at Mt Mycale (Arr. i.19.8) and Craterus and Perdiccas were left in charge of operations at Tyre while Alexander campaigned in the Antilibanus (Curt. iv.3.1). If there was any member of this group who outstripped the others in the early years, it was probably Craterus, who had general command of the infantry on the left at both Issus and Gaugamela and took care of the camp at the Persian Gates while Alexander made his turning march.[51]

A somewhat anomalous position in the hierarchy of command is that of the Royal bodyguards. This group, the inner circle of the *hetairoi*, was the institutionalised relic of the old bodyguard of nobles, and it still provided the king's immediate entourage.[52] Membership was incompatible with any post away from court, and both Balacrus and Menes were replaced as soon as they

[50] Arr. vi.27.6; vii.24.4.
[51] Arr. ii.8.4; Curt. iii.9.8; Arr. iii.11.10; 18.4; Curt. v.4.14.
[52] Berve 1926, 1.25–30; Hammond and Griffith 1979, 2.403.

were assigned to provincial commands.[53] It also seems to have been incompatible with commands in the army. In the early years of the reign there is no known instance of a bodyguard holding a senior commission; and, when Ptolemy son of Seleucus took over command of a phalanx battalion he ceased to hold the title of bodyguard.[54] None the less individual bodyguards are occasionally attested in command of army groups on an *ad hoc* basis; another Ptolemy, also a bodyguard, led a joint force of hypaspists and light-armed during the siege of Halicarnassus (Arr. 1.22.4–7). It would appear that the group as a whole enjoyed the same status as the commanders of the phalanx battalions, but its members had no place of their own in the command structure. The same was true of Parmenion. He had no specific command of his own but was consistently used as Alexander's second-in-command, taking the left in the major battles and the first choice for subsidiary campaigns. As a result he was particularly associated with the allied and mercenary forces (Diodorus XVII.17.3 even gives him a vague general command of the infantry), which usually came under his leadership, but there was no single body of troops permanently attached to him.

Various changes took place in the course of the reign. In particular the cavalry commands became much more important, largely eclipsing the phalanx positions. This was a definite policy decision on Alexander's part. After the execution of Philotas and the assassination of Parmenion Alexander set his face against large single commands and abolished the position which Philotas had enjoyed.[55] The Companions were first divided between Cleitus the Black and Hephaestion, but the individual hipparchies soon became important entities in their own right, and by the time of the invasion of India the hipparchy commanders appear to have been equal in status. Now the more highly favoured of the phalanx taxiarchs were transferred to hipparchies: Perdiccas, Craterus and later Cleitus the White.[56] At the same time the separation of the bodyguard from the command structure was gradually eroded. Perdiccas, who was elevated to the bodyguard in 330, had command of a hipparchy by 327 and Hephaestion similarly combined the two functions. There were possibly other combinations. It is highly probable that Peithon son of Crateuas, a bodyguard by 325, is the Peithon attested in command of a phalanx battalion in 326/5.[57] But the bodyguard was principally associated with the cavalry, and the association grew stronger as the infantry declined in number during Alexander's last years. When Craterus took his contingent of veterans from Opis in 324, he had with him at least three phalanx taxiarchs,

[53] Berve 1926, 2 nos. 200, 507.

[54] Arr. 1.24.1; cf. II.8.4, 10.2, 12.2.

[55] Arr. III.27.4; cf. 1.25.5.

[56] Arr. IV.22.7; V.12.2 (phalanx *taxis*); V.22.6; VI.6.4 (hipparchy). The fact that Cleitus was dismissed from Opis with Craterus (Justin XII.12.8) does not entail that he retained his phalanx command. See, however, Berve 1926, 2 no. 428; Hammond 1980b, 466–7.

[57] Arr. VI.6.1, 7.2–3 (phalanx *taxis*); VI.28.4 (bodyguard). *Pace* Berve 1926, 2 nos. 621, 623, there is no good reason to deny the identity of the phalanx leader with Peithon son of Crateuas. By the end of the reign he may have moved on to a cavalry command (Arr. *Succ.* F 1.2).

including the veteran Polyperchon.[58] Meleager was the only phalanx commander to remain in his post until Alexander's death, and he sustained the infantry mutiny at Babylon almost single-handed. On the other hand the eight commanders who are listed with the cavalry were the most distinguished men remaining at court, and six of them are previously attested as bodyguards.[59] It is a dramatic illustration of how the balance of power had changed. The phalanx commands had not been down-graded but the cavalry had become enormously more important as the cream of the court was assigned commands in it. Above all, when Alexander installed Hephaestion as vizier (chiliarch), he did not associate him with his infantry guard, as seems to have been the case with his Achaemenid predecessors, but left him in charge of his hipparchy, thereafter known as Hephaestion's chiliarchy.[60] The change of emphasis is certain but the reason for it can only be guessed. There is some evidence for increasing disillusionment among the infantry from the time of the murder of Parmenion, culminating in the two mutinies at the Hyphasis and Opis, and it would not be surprising if Alexander had deliberately aimed at increasing the prestige and importance of the cavalry.

The other main development in military organisation is an increasing mobility of command. From late 330, when the guerrilla warfare in eastern Iran broke out, there was an increasing tendency to divide the army between several commands, formed for a specific strategic purpose. At the beginning of 328, for instance, Alexander left four phalanx commanders at Bactra to control the area south of the Oxus and then split the rest of his army into five separate columns commanded by senior officers, three of whom are known bodyguards (Arr. IV.16.1–3). These divisions are quite different from the separate campaigns attested at the beginning of the reign. Then Alexander tended to detach his allied and mercenary troops while retaining the Macedonian forces in their entirety. Now he divided his forces more or less indiscriminately, Macedonians and mercenaries alike. These separate commands were given to a relatively small number of officers: Craterus, Hephaestion, Coenus and Perdiccas tended to be used in the first instance and Ptolemy (son of Lagus), Leonnatus and later Peithon if secondary columns were necessary. On the march into India Hephaestion and Perdiccas were sent ahead to the Indus with a massive force, comprising almost half the Macedonians and all the mercenary foot (Arr. IV.22.7), while Alexander fought an intensive campaign along the Cophen valley, using a multitude of smaller columns put together as the occasion demanded.[61] One of the peculiar features of these missions is the tendency to detach the phalanx commanders from their troops. In the summer of 327 Craterus was left to pacify the territory around the city of Andaca together with the rest of the infantry commanders, even

[58] Justin XII.12.8 (Polyperchon, Gorgias and Antigenes (cf. Arr. V.16.3)).
[59] Arr. *Succ.* F 1.2 (Perdiccas, Leonnatus, Ptolemy, Lysimachus, Aristonous, Peithon).
[60] Arr. VII.14.10; Diod. XVIII.48.4; cf. Schachermeyr 1970, 31–7 (see, however, Lewis 1977, 17–19).
[61] Arr. IV.23.5–24.1; 24.8–10; 27.1, 5–6; 28.7–8; 30.6.

though his force contained at most two *taxeis* (Arr. IV.23.5–24.1); and at the
Hydaspes three phalanx commanders (Meleager, Attalus and Gorgias) were
apparently separated from their *taxeis* and employed on diversionary tactics
with the mercenary infantry and cavalry (Arr. V.12.1). Most notably Coenus,
who commanded a phalanx battalion from 334 to his death late in 326, played a
prominent role at the head of the cavalry at the Hydaspes, and he is even
assigned a hipparchy by Arrian.[62] This latter command was probably
temporary, but it is puzzling, a good illustration of the variability of the senior
posts towards the end of the reign. Not only senior posts were affected. When
Nearchus, the hypaspist chiliarch, was sent off on a reconnaissance mission in
327, his troops were confined to light-armed and his own chiliarchy was
assigned elsewhere, maybe to his colleague Antiochus.[63]

The reasons for this development were to some degree military. The more
multifarious the operations of the army, the more fluid the command structure
became. But there was also a political factor at work. From the time of
Philotas' execution and even before, Alexander was concerned with the
problem of confiding large bodies of troops to a single commander. He
countered it in various ways, interposing new subordinate ranks in the
hierarchy, transferring commands more frequently and detaching senior
officers for special service away from their units. The result he intended was to
make himself the single focus of the army's loyalty. There was to be no
successor to Parmenion. Craterus is the nearest parallel in the scope of his
commands and the devotion he inspired in his men, but even he was not
allowed to be identified with any single group in the army. Although a cavalry
commander, he is only once attested with his own hipparchy (Arr. V.11.3),
and the expeditionary forces he led varied widely in composition, usually
including phalanx battalions but a different selection each time. He had no
monopoly over any sector of the army, nor had any other commander.
Regional ties and personal ties had become much less important. The sole
uniting factor was the person of the king.

[62] Arr. IV.28.8; V.12.2 (phalanx *taxis*); V.16.3 (hipparchy); V.21.1 (phalanx *taxis*).
[63] Arr. IV.30.6: see, however, Badian 1975, 150–1.

# D

# The divinity of Alexander

The reign of Alexander marks a watershed in the development of the ruler cult. After his death divine honours for living monarchs become almost commonplace. Before his time such phenomena are very scantily reported in the sources, and the few attested instances of divine honours for living men have been treated with scepticism by some modern scholars. There can be little doubt that Alexander changed the entire climate of thought, creating a precedent for the worship of a sovereign as god incarnate and prefiguring the cults of the Hellenistic rulers. What is far from clear is the process of evolution in the course of the reign and the extent of Alexander's belief in his own divinity. At one level there is his deep consciousness of his heroic ancestry (as an Argead he took his lineage back to Heracles and ultimately to Dionysus), at another there is his conviction that he was in some sense the son of Zeus, the equal at least of Heracles, and finally there is the conception of himself as a god among men. These categories are fundamentally different and represent different aspects of Greek religious thought, but in Alexander's mind they must have been conflated. His acceptance of one role could lead automatically to another, and the son of Zeus might (after sufficient infusions of flattery) come to view himself as a god in his own right.

Originally there had been a clear distinction between god and man, based on the impassable gulf between mortality and immortality. The gods by definition were ageless and deathless, whereas mortals by definition were neither. Hero cults provided a half-way house. After death mortals of acknowledged virtue and achievement might be honoured by a sacred precinct and blood offerings, but the cult was essentially a cult of the dead and the ritual differed fundamentally from that observed towards the Olympian gods. Before the fourth century B.C. a heroic cult was the most any mortal could expect, and that was largely confined to city founders, such as Battus at Cyrene or Hagnon and Brasidas at Amphipolis (Pind. *Pyth.* v.93–4; Thuc. v.11.1). The heroes were superhuman. They were demigods, even the peers of the gods, but they were only associated with the gods by analogy. The analogy, however, is frequent from the earliest times and it is not confined to heroes. At times the mortal man could be thought to transcend the limits of his mortality. Pindar, who usually is adamant upon the fundamental distinction between mortal and immortal, was prepared to concede that despite the ephemeral character of human life man does in some way approach the immortals by greatness of mind or nature (*Nem*. vi.4–6). Achievement may bring a man close to the divine, as Pindar suggests elsewhere when he describes the supreme felicity of victory in the games in terms reminiscent of the blessed state of the gods (*Pyth*. viii.88–92). For mortals this godlike state is transient, fated to be overtaken by adverse fortune, whereas the gods' felicity is permanent. But what if a man's prosperity were to be constant? Could not a dynast achieve the permanent felicity of a god and exert power comparable to that of the gods in its scope to change men's destinies? Here Pindar is apparently unequivocal. In his earliest ode he states that the highest splendour for a man is to achieve victory himself and see it repeated by his son; the brazen heaven remains inaccessible (*Pyth*. x.22–9). That message was to be repeated for the tyrants of Sicily, but in the later odes there is an interesting tone of warning. Theron of Acragas, who has reached the pillars of Heracles by his success at Olympia, is admonished that what is beyond is inaccessible; he would be a fool to attempt it (*Ol*. iii.43–5). The same sentiments emerge in the brilliant ending of the First Olympian, where Hieron is warned that he can only maintain his position; he may not transcend it (*Ol*. i.113–15). This reiterated warning suggests that there was a temptation for the tyrants to forget the limitations of mortality and to assimilate themselves to the divine, particularly in the heady atmosphere of court flattery. Hieron at any rate had the glory of victory over Carthage and Etruria; he was the founder of Aetna and, as such, the future recipient of a hero cult (Diod. xi.66.4) and, as Pindar emphasised (F 105 Snell), his very name had religious connotations.

Pindar's evidence is particularly important. There is no later genre of literature in which we can trace the same tension between immediate panegyric and traditional religious sanctions. Nevertheless a similar train of thought is apparent in the political philosophy of the fourth century B.C. Aristotle in general accepts the basic division between god and man (*NE* 1123a9–10). but he is prepared to envisage a hypothetical situation of ideal monarchy, in which one man would be so superior to his fellows as to appear a god among men (*Pol*. 1284a10–11, 1332b16–22). This remark cannot be pressed too far, for Aristotle is describing a situation which he does not think a practical possibility, and in any case he is not explicitly describing men as gods. He comes close to it, however, in the *Nicomachean Ethics*, when he delineates the opposite of brutishness as a superhuman excellence like that of gods and heroes and he suggests that the popular saying may be true, that men become gods by a surpassing display of excellence (*NE* 1145a18–27). This popular saying is perhaps best illustrated by Isocrates' description of King Evagoras of Cyprus: he achieved the greatest of felicity without any admixture of adversity, excelling in mind and body, reaching a healthy old age and leaving numerous progeny, all in positions of power. Everything that poets said of men in the past, that they were gods among men or the divine made mortal, is appropriate to him (Isocr. ix.72). In the language of the encomium Isocrates clearly regards it as appropriate to assimilate the ruler to the divine. So evidently does Aristotle, when he defines the various components of honour, grouping together the divine and human: 'sacrifices, memorials in prose and verse, privileges, sanctuaries, front seats, public burial' (*Rhet.* 1361a34–6). When Aristotle talks of sacrifices and sanctuaries, he may be envisaging heroic honours, not the worship of men as gods, but, even so, his language suggests that heroisation was relatively frequent in the Greek world of his day.

It was one thing to describe a ruler as a god among men. It was quite another to offer him actual worship and the physical trappings of a cult. The earliest case of such public acknowledgement is that of Lysander. According to the third-century historian, Duris of Samos, Lysander was honoured as a god by Greek cities after the battle of Aegospotami. He was the first of the Greeks to have altars erected to him and to have sacrifices made to him as a god. The Samians actually renamed their national festival the Lysandreia (Plut. *Lys.* 18.5–6 = *FGrH* 76 f 71). These details have often been challenged, but it is now epigraphically attested that the Lysandreia were celebrated at least four times in the fourth century.[1] There seems no reason to challenge what Duris reported, that Lysander was worshipped as a god. That worship must have been during his lifetime. The alternative of a posthumous cult seems most improbable. It was in his lifetime that Lysander wielded the power of life and death over the cities which honoured him, and it was his temporal power which they attempted to propitiate by sacrifices and offerings. It is possible (though not likely) that the cult was revived later for political reasons, but its origins must lie within Lysander's lifetime. There is no comparable instance of an official cult attested in the next decades, but then no commander enjoyed the colossal power which Lysander had exercised in 405/4 B.C. There may, however, have been local acts of worship on a more modest scale. It is possible (though the sources are not wholly concordant) that Dion was voted heroic honours during his return to Syracuse in 357.[2] More seriously Clearchus, the eccentric tyrant of Heracleia (364–352), is claimed to have disported himself as son of Zeus, naming his son Keraunos; and one tradition notes that he was worshipped and exalted with Olympian honours.[3] If Clearchus had divine pretensions, he was certainly in a position to impose them on his unfortunate subjects.

[1] Habicht 1970, 243–4, dates the Lysandreia to 404, while Badian (1981, 33–8) argues strongly for a posthumous cult, established after 394.

[2] For Dion see Diod. xvi.20.6, perhaps oversimplified. Plut. *Dion* 46.1 claims that the Syracusans hailed him as 'saviour and god' in the heat of the battle, but reveals that there was serious opposition to the honours proposed for him subsequently (*Dion* 48.4–6). The enthusiasm before the battle was diluted later, and even the vote of heroic honours may not have been carried.

[3] 'Suda' s.v. Κλέαρχος, corroborated in various details by Memnon, *FGrH* 434 f 1 (1.1); Justin xvi.5.8–11; Plut. *Mor.* 338B. For other examples see Weinreich 1933, 9–19.

By the time Philip acquired power in Greece there was a climate of thought congenial to the idea that the outstanding ruler was a god among men. There was also some dubious precedent for worship of the living ruler. It is hardly surprising to find a scattering of stories that Philip himself received various honours bordering on the divine. The Ephesians introduced his (secular) statue into the temple of Artemis (Arr. 1.17.11), a gesture that was certainly honorific but not an act of deification (cf. Paus. vi.3.15–16). More significant is the fact, unimpeachably attested, that the people of Eresus in Lesbos erected altars to Zeus Philippios (Tod, *GHI* no. 191.6). The precise meaning of this act cannot be recovered, but it seems certain that Philip was deeply associated in the cult of Zeus, and the sacrifices made to Zeus were also in a sense offered to Philip. Whether that honour was unique to Eresus we cannot say, but it seems prima facie unlikely. Many of the small city states of the islands and mainland may well have taken the opportunity of linking Philip in some way with their city cults. There is even a late and unreliable tradition that the Athenians sanctioned his worship in the sanctuary of Heracles at Cynosarges;[4] at best it refers to the erection of an honorary statue in the precinct, as at Ephesus. At all events Philip conceived a very exalted notion of his own status, and the very last ceremony of his life included a procession in which his statue was associated with the twelve Olympians as their *synthronos* (Diod. xvi.92.5, cf. 95.1). This display would make more sense if it were foreshadowed by a number of specific occasions when Philip was associated with local cults.

There is no evidence for Alexander's early conception of his divine or heroic status. In the early years of the campaign in Asia the emphasis is upon his heroic lineage, his descent from Aeacus and Achilles on his mother's side and from Heracles on his father's. As early as the visit to Ilium (334) he was careful to sacrifice to Priam, an apotropaic act to purge the sacrilege of his ancestor Neoptolemus (Arr. 1.11.8), and his benefactions to the city were justified by his kinship through Andromache (Strabo 594). A year later he was to show similar consideration to the Cilician city of Mallus on the flimsy ground that both he and it derived their origins from Argos (Arr. ii.5.9). This was much more than propaganda. Alexander believed deeply in his heroic forebears and constantly envisaged himself following in their footsteps. He accepted the traditional Greek syncretism, viewing the deities of the near east as local manifestations of the Greek gods. Accordingly his ancestors were never far away. For the people of Tyre this was fatal. Their city god, Melqart, was identified with Heracles, and in defiance of chronology (cf. Hdt. ii.44.4, Arr. ii.16.1) Alexander recognised him as his ancestor (Curt. iv.2.3) and demanded to sacrifice to him. Their refusal led directly to the siege and destruction of the city. Alexander not only recognised his ancestors; he saw himself in competition with them. His journey to Siwah was in part motivated by emulation of Heracles and Perseus, who were said to have visited the oracle

[4] Clem. Al. *Protr.* iv.54.5; cf. Fredricksmeyer 1979a; *contra* Badian 1981, 67–71.

in mythical times. Some years later, in 327/6 B.C., he was to embark on the epic (and unnecessary) siege of Mt Aornus because of the local tradition that Heracles had failed to capture it (Arr. IV.28.2, 30.4; Curt. VIII.11.2). Alexander had a driving obsession to excel and surpass, fulfilling in all respects the injunction of his ancestor Peleus (*Il.* VI.208).

Early in his reign Alexander became convinced that he was more than the distant progeny of Zeus by heroic ancestors and was in some sense the actual son of the god. The sources retail a number of stories according to which Olympias was impregnated by Zeus in some manifestation, as a thunderbolt or a serpent. Eratosthenes reported that the queen herself hinted at a birth secret when Alexander left for Asia (Plut. *Al.* 3.3). The belief in his divine origins seems to have been widespread, enough so for Seleucus I to imitate him and claim that his own mother, Laodice, was visited by Apollo. The stories may well have had an early origin. In Philip's reign they are not likely to have been voiced publicly, particularly in the turbulent last year when Alexander's legitimacy was challenged. The Spartan Damaratus had found to his cost that a non-human father was no guarantee against deposition (Hdt. VI.69.4), and, while there were rivals, it was dangerous for Alexander's birth to be ascribed to anybody other than Philip. After his accession the field for speculation was open and it was possible to argue that Alexander had a dual paternity comparable to that of Heracles – he had an earthly father and a divine father. There is some indication that the idea had taken shape in Alexander's mind before the visit to Siwah. Arrian (III.3.2) states that one of the reasons for the consultation of the oracle was his belief that some of his own origin was due to Ammon, in the same way that the myths related Heracles and Perseus to Zeus. This motif is not found in Callisthenes' original report of the visit (Strabo 814 = *FGrH* F 14), which only mentioned emulation of his ancestors. But there is confirmation in the oracles which Callisthenes claimed were brought to Memphis from Miletus and Erythrae. The Milesian oracles, miraculously issued at Branchidae, related to Alexander's birth by the agency of Zeus; and the utterances of Athenais of Erythrae stressed his *eugeneia*, undoubtedly hinting at divine sonship. These oracles were delivered at Memphis in the early spring of 331. It was too soon for them to be influenced by reports of the actual consultation, and it was probably the news of Alexander's claims to be son of Zeus *before* the journey to Siwah which inspired them to respond with oracles of their own.

Whatever Alexander's attitude before the visit, the consultation of the oracle made a profound and lasting impression upon him. It is evident that he regarded Ammon, the oracular deity of Siwah, as the local Libyan manifestation of Zeus. The equation is explicit from the time of Pindar, and in his contemporary account Callisthenes referred to the deity simply as Zeus. Now, if Alexander viewed the god of Siwah as a manifestation of his divine father, he was most gratifyingly confirmed in his belief by the salutation of the officiating priest. He was greeted publicly as son of Zeus. This key fact, underlined by

Callisthenes, is repeated in almost all the later sources and cannot be dismissed. The consultation proper was in private and details of it were apparently never released. Later sources report a sequence of questions which must be apocryphal but which revolve around recognition of Alexander as son of Zeus.[5] Divine sonship was seen by contemporary and later writers as the central theme of the consultation. There are frequent references to the relationship with Ammon after the visit. Callisthenes represented Alexander in heroic guise on the morning of Gaugamela, praying in Homeric terms to his divine father and supplicating his assistance; an eagle promptly appeared in response (Plut. Al. 33.1–2 = FGrH 124 F 36). By 328 at least the claim to be son of Zeus Ammon was commonplace at court, and it was resented by the older and more conservative of the Macedonian nobility. It is clear that one of Cleitus' many grievances was Alexander's pretension to be son of Zeus Ammon, and his criticisms were later echoed in the gibes of the mutineers at Opis, who urged Alexander to dismiss them and continue the campaign with his father (Arr. VII.8.3). A Cleitus might object, but others were prepared to accept the claims, out of flattery or conviction. Accordingly the prominent Iasian dignitary Gorgus is said to have conferred an enormously extravagant gold crown upon Alexander at Ecbatana (324), proclaiming him son of Ammon. The source, Ephippus of Olynthus, has been thought somewhat disreputable (he was certainly hostile to Alexander), but, even if there is fiction in the report, it is obviously fiction which Ephippus (a contemporary) thought would carry conviction.[6] In fact there is confirmation in Demosthenes' proposal that same year, that Alexander should be son of Zeus or of Poseidon, if he wished (Hyper. Dem. col. 31). The proposal was tinged with irony, but it was certainly made.

Alexander did not officially reject his mortal father. Except for a reference to his 'so-called father' in a letter to Athens, quoted by Plutarch (Al. 28.2) and of dubious authenticity, his public statements were laudatory, and one of the Last Plans unearthed by Perdiccas was to build a tomb for Philip on a par with the pyramids (Diod. XVIII.4.5). Like Heracles, who acknowledged both Amphitryon and Zeus, he could claim both a divine and a human paternity. Yet it seems clear that Alexander came to believe in Zeus Ammon as his actual father and expected the relationship to be recognised publicly. Being the son of a god did not, however, imply divinity, as Alexander, the devotee of Homer, knew well. The gods usually engendered mortals in their liaisons with mortal women. But there were exceptions to the rule, and the exceptions significantly concerned the cult figures most closely associated with Alexander. Heracles transcended the barrier between hero and god at a relatively early date. He was worshipped at Marathon from at least the sixth century, and for Pindar he has the equivocal status of hero god (Nem. III.22). He was a hero on earth but went to Olympus where he dwelt in bliss as the

5 Diod. XVII.51.2–4; Curt. IV.7.25–7; Justin XI.11.9–10; Plut. Al. 27.5–8.
6 Ephippus, FGrH 126 F 5. For the background see Heisserer 1980, 169–203.

husband of Hebe and the son-in-law of Hera.[7] Similarly Polydeuces as son of
Zeus had the choice of escaping death and living with the gods in Olympus or
alternating between heaven and Hades with his heroic brother Castor (*Nem.*
x.80–90). The concept of apotheosis had emerged: the hero could acquire
divinity by his achievements and be translated to heaven, avoiding death (cf.
Diod. iv.38.5). There is a persistent tradition that the subject was debated
during the Sogdian campaigns of 328/7. According to Arrian (iv.8.3) the
provocation which led to Cleitus' outburst at Maracanda was comparison
between Alexander and the Dioscuri, and it is the basic theme of the debate on
*proskynesis* as it is reported both by Arrian (iv.10.5–7) and by Curtius
(viii.5.8). That debate is dressed in the language of Roman imperial rhetoric,
but its leitmotiv is firmly anchored in contemporary thought and is multiply
attested. There is no reason to doubt that Alexander's status was the subject of
intense discussion and that some courtiers at least suggested that it was
appropriate to recognise his divinity with divine honours.

Indissolubly interlocked with the debate on divinity is the introduction of
*proskynesis* in the late spring of 327 B.C. *Proskynesis* was the Greek term for
the age-old act of homage performed before the Persian king by his subjects. It
might involve a slight stooping forward and the simultaneous blowing of a
kiss, as is depicted on the Persepolis Treasury relief, or it could be a complete
prostration before the monarch. It was a purely secular act and was found at all
levels of Persian society; a social inferior would prostrate himself before a
person greatly superior in the hierarchy (Hdt. 1.134).[8] In the Greek world,
however, *proskynesis* was a cult act, performed before the gods. It was in
general performed in a standing position, the hands raised towards the
heavens palms forward. Occasionally the worshipper might kneel in suppli-
cation before a deity, above all a deity of healing or deliverance such as
Asclepius, Artemis or Zeus himself, but it is an attitude mostly attested for
women and there are traces of disapproval in the sources; Diogenes in
particular thought it an undignified act of superstition.[9] To what extent did
the Greeks interpret the Persian act of prostration as a cult act? The question
has been endlessly debated, but some issues are clear. Apart from Aeschylus,
who does seem to represent abasement before the king as an act of worship
(*Pers.* 588–9), Greek authors apparently agree that the Persian monarch was
not regarded as divine by his subjects and that *proskynesis* was not an act of
worship. None the less it evoked widespread abhorrence. It was regarded as
intolerably servile, so much so that accepting it was *hybris*, and appropriate
only to the natural slaves of Asia (cf. Aeschyl. *Ag.* 918–20, Eur. *Orest.* 1508).
Aristotle (*Rhet.* 1361a36) classifies it as a specifically barbarian mark of
honour. At the same time there was a feeling that *proskynesis* should not be

---

[7] *Isthm.* iv.61–6; *Nem.* 1.69–72, x.17–18; cf. Shapiro 1983–4.
[8] For *proskynesis* in the Persian court see Bickerman 1963a; Frye 1972.
[9] Diog. Laert. vi.37–8; cf. Theophr. *Char.* 16.5. Full documentation is provided by von Straten
1974.

offered to any mortal man. The Spartan ambassadors to Xerxes were allegedly coerced to prostrate themselves and protested that it was not their custom to do *proskynesis* to any human (Hdt. VII.136.1), and Isocrates (IV.151) excoriates the Persians for performing the act to a mortal. Greeks felt repugnance at several levels. *Proskynesis* (in the sense of abasement) was a violation of their personal dignity; it was an act of total submission, inconsistent with any concept of *eleutheria* (Xen. *Hell.* IV.1.35), and there was also some religious disquiet at offering it to a living man.

Not surprisingly, Alexander's attempt to introduce *proskynesis* provoked resentment and resistance, not only among Macedonian traditionalists. The focus of opposition was provided by Callisthenes of Olynthus. In the sources two episodes are recorded, one an act of non-co-operation at a private ceremony and the other a speech of opposition at a staged public debate. According to the prevailing view both episodes cannot have happened, and scholars have opted for one or the other according to their prejudices.[10] In fact they are not incompatible and both may well have taken place. The first was recorded by the court chamberlain, Chares of Mytilene, who probably observed the scene and at the very least had first-hand descriptions of it.[11] There was a symposium among a few intimates who had allegedly discussed the scenario beforehand. The participants in turn drank a toast, performed *proskynesis* and received a kiss from the king. Callisthenes, however, omitted the *proskynesis*, taking advantage of momentary inattention on Alexander's part, but claimed the kiss. He was frustrated by one of the Companions, Demetrius, who pointed out that he had not conformed. Alexander then declined the kiss and Callisthenes left with the provocative statement that he was only a kiss poorer. This episode is not vitally important. It was a limited experiment which was largely successful. Only Callisthenes refused to do *proskynesis* and even he attempted to be unobtrusive and avoid open opposition. There is no indication that his behaviour on this occasion caused any change of heart in Alexander and no reason for it to have done so. The story is additional to the main drama, an anecdote selected by Plutarch and Arrian as an interesting sidepiece, but it is perfectly credible in itself as a private prelude to the public ceremony of inauguration.

The public ceremony is the occasion of the rhetorical debates we find in Arrian and Curtius, in both cases worked up as display pieces, but the central core is common and reported in Plutarch (*Al.* 54.3). Once more prior arrangements were made. Alexander primed some of his Greek intellectuals as well as Persian and Median dignitaries, so the subject of *proskynesis* was introduced during the conversation at the banquet (Arr. IV.10.5; Curt. VIII.5.9). The occasion was public and ceremonial, clearly designed for the

---

[10] Chares' story is the more popular, accepted by those who wish to relate *proskynesis* wholly to Persian ceremonial (see Balsdon 1950, 379–82; Hamilton 1969, 152–3). Badian 1981, 48–54, has argued for the historicity of the debate tradition, dismissing Chares as apologetic invention, while Goukowsky 1978–81, 1.47–9, distinguishes two separate episodes.

[11] Plut. *Al.* 54.5–6; Arr. IV.12.3–5 (*FGrH* 125 F 14).

formal introduction of a universal act of court protocol. The conversation began, as Alexander had intended, with the subject of *proskynesis* formally mooted by Cleon of Syracuse (Curtius) or the philosopher Anaxarchus (Arrian). Both our principal sources suggest that the overall context was that of divine honours, and emulation of Alexander's ancestors is again a common theme. The king had excelled Heracles and Dionysus in his achievements and fully deserved to be honoured as a god (Arr. IV.10.6–7; Curt. VIII.5.11–12). In both authors the opposition is voiced by Callisthenes. He insists upon a strict division between human and divine honours, claiming that it is impious to give Alexander more than mortal recognition, and he objects specifically to *proskynesis* as an affront to Greek traditions of liberty. The core of the speeches of Callisthenes looks historical; and it is certain that he voiced public opposition, articulating the criticisms which the older Macedonians secretly shared. His speech was received with open approval, which Alexander could not ignore. The banquet then continued. Senior members of the Persian nobility offered *proskynesis* in turn, until a senior Companion burst out laughing at a particularly profound act of abasement. The king erupted in fury, but the damage was done. Callisthenes' public rejection was compounded by open ridicule, and the experiment was dropped, never to be revived. In future *proskynesis* was confined to the king's barbarian subjects, as were his kisses (Arr. VII.11.1, 6).

Callisthenes' behaviour is relatively easy to explain. Some ancient authors indicted him for insincerity. Timaeus in particular pilloried him as a flatterer for his literary apotheosis of Alexander (Polyb. XII.12b.2–3 = *FGrH* 566 F 155), but his criticism was primarily based on Callisthenes' treatment of the Siwah episode. There, as later, Callisthenes represented Alexander as son of Zeus but not as a god proper. He had also described the Pamphylian sea around Mt Climax doing *proskynesis* to Alexander and, implicitly at least, his language had echoed Homer's picture of the sea's homage to Poseidon (*FGrH* 124 F 31). That was understandable. Alexander had just crossed the traditionally recognised southern boundary of Persian Asia Minor, and the barbarian sea naturally performed the appropriate homage before its new lord. Few Greeks or Macedonians would have objected to the barbarian subjects of Alexander performing *proskynesis*, as the captured princesses appear to have done from the outset (Arr. II.12.6; Diod. XVII.37.5). Even the portraiture of Alexander as son of Zeus was venial. Many people, Callisthenes probably included, will have shared Polybius' view that Alexander's nature was indeed superhuman (Polyb. XII.23.5). But actual worship was a totally different matter. Callisthenes may well have felt total repugnance against any act of recognising divinity in a mortal man. It was worse when the recognition involved an act which for centuries had epitomised barbarian servility; Alexander was placing victors and vanquished on the same plane. The combination outraged Callisthenes and he protested publicly.

It is a much deeper mystery why Alexander attempted to introduce a ceremony which he must have known would be hated and resented. I can only assume that he now believed firmly in his godhead, and that the continuous and insidious flattery which elevated him above Heracles and Dionysus had taken firm root. At the same time Persian court ceremonial was becoming more pervasive. In the spring of 327 Alexander had taken his first Iranian wife and he would have received *proskynesis* as a matter of course from his new relations. It might have seemed appropriate to impose the same ritual upon all his subjects, so emphasising the universality of his monarchy. If the act involved implicit recognition of his divinity it was all the more attractive. As it was, he underestimated the resistance and was forced to retract. But he may not have given up his aspirations to be worshipped in some form. *Proskynesis* was doubly abhorrent in Greek eyes, both impious and barbaric, but other ceremonials may have been acceptable.

Unfortunately the evidence now becomes sparse and anecdotal, but at least it is relatively early. Ephippus gave a typically lurid account of court behaviour towards the end of the reign. At banquets Alexander assumed the guise of Ammon with purple robes and ram's horns. At other times he wore the cult dress of Hermes and even of Artemis (*FGrH* 126 F 5). The assumption of the Ammon horns, if nothing else, is historical. They appear on portraits of the king immediately after his death, most notably on the Alexander Sarcophagus (311) and the celebrated tetradrachms of Lysimachus, and they must have been a recognisable feature of his dress. To have assumed divine attributes Alexander must have believed that he shared divinity: not only son of Ammon but in some sense Ammon incarnate. Others were prepared to acquiesce in the portrait and to propagate it. Apelles depicted Alexander with the thunderbolt of Zeus in the celebrated painting for the Artemisium at Ephesus, and he was handsomely rewarded for doing so (Pliny, *NH* xxxv.92). The precedent was certainly set by the king himself when he authorised the decadrachms of Babylon, which depict him in military dress, crowned by victory and unmistakably grasping a thunderbolt in his right hand.[12] But even portraying the king with the attributes of the gods did not imply worship. We need positive evidence for cult acts performed to the king. Ephippus comes close to providing it when he speaks of incense being burned before him and his being attended with reverential silence (*FGrH* 126 F 5). A similar picture emerges from Phylarchus' brilliant description of Alexander's receptions (Ath. 539F = *FGrH* 81 F 4). Alexander was clearly treated with all the reverence due to a god. Arrian somewhat ironically characterises the Greek embassies which honoured him at Babylon as for all the world like sacred envoys sent to a god.[13] They may not have offered actual worship (and Arrian's mode of expression suggests that they did not), but their demeanour was deeply reverential and they treated

[12] Cf. Bellinger 1963, 27; Kaiser 1962; Goukowsky 1978–81, 1.61–4.
[13] Arr. VII.23.2. Cf. Badian 1981, 55–9; *contra* Fredricksmeyer 1979b; Goukowsky 1978–81, 1.185.

Alexander with the awe they would accord a god. The ground for worship was well and truly prepared.

In the last year of his life Alexander seems to have promoted his divinity more explicitly and aggressively. The catalyst was the death of Hephaestion in the autumn of 324. Alexander immediately established a hero cult for his friend and had the institution formally ratified by an oracle from Siwah.[14] At court the cult was naturally *de rigueur*, and Alexander appears to have enforced it (Lucian, *De calumn.* 17). Elsewhere the astute Cleomenes of Naucratis promptly dedicated a Heroon in Alexandria, and even in mainland Greece the cult was formally introduced. Hypereides hints at coercion when he claims that under Macedonian domination the Greeks have been compelled to countenance the neglect of traditional religious practices and the scrupulous maintenance of honours for living men; they have also been compelled to honour their servants as heroes (Hyper. *Epitaph.* 21). This is generalised and rhetorically couched, but Hypereides can be referring to one thing only – worship of Alexander as a god (no other living man is feasible) and the simultaneous cult of his servant (and Grand Vizier) Hephaestion. Compulsion is only associated with the honours of Hephaestion; Hypereides implies that the cult of Alexander existed, was practised to the detriment of traditional religious institutions, but was not formally imposed.

The question of the worship of Alexander was certainly raised at Athens in the months before the trial of Demosthenes (March 323). It remains a hotly debated question whether it was the response to a formal demand for worship or a more spontaneous attempt to win favour with Alexander.[15] The principal narrative sources have no suggestion of any official request, but the text of both Arrian and Curtius is riddled with *lacunae* at this juncture and their silence is not significant. On the other hand the anecdotal tradition of the debates at Athens and Sparta seems to presuppose some sort of request. At the very least it proves that the enactment of divine honours was well known to be something the king greatly desired. It is neither impossible nor improbable that when Alexander sent formal letters requesting (or demanding) a hero cult for Hephaestion he also suggested that recognition of his own divinity would be welcome and appropriate.

However it was conveyed, Alexander's desire for divine honours evoked debate and dissent in Greece. At Athens alone is there any record of the transactions and that is sadly fragmentary. Demades moved a decree enacting divine honours. The precise form of the proposal is lost; the tradition that he

[14] Arr. VII.14.6–7, 23.6; Plut. *Al.* 72.3; Hyper. *Epitaph.* 21. The vulgate tradition (Diod. XVII.115.6; Justin XII.12.12) speaks of worship as a god. That is certainly wrong, and it is possible that there is a confused reflection of the tradition that Alexander requested Ammon's sanction for the deification of Hephaestion but was refused.

[15] The supposed demand for deification was an axiom of German scholarship (cf. Wilcken 1970, 2.391; Schachermeyr 1973, 525–31). Eduard Meyer 1910, 330–2, argued that it was politically motivated, and he influenced many subsequent scholars (e.g. Tarn 1948, 2.370–3; Atkinson 1973, 331–5). For a more sceptical approach see Hogarth 1887; Balsdon 1950, 383–8; Badian 1981, 54–8.

was to be made the thirteenth god is late and unreliable (Ael. *VH* v.12). At some stage in the debate it was proposed to erect a statue (not a cult statue) of 'king Alexander the invincible god' (Hyper. *Dem.* col. 33), and, as we have seen, Demosthenes was prepared to recognise the divine sonship in some form. On the other hand there was considerable opposition, the pious and conservative Lycurgus exclaiming that worshippers of the new god would have to purify themselves after every act of worship ([Plut.] *Mor.* 842D). The tensions were pulling in two directions. The Athenian occupancy of Samos was under threat, thanks to the Exiles' Decree, and Alexander had to be wooed to reverse his decision, but there remained an abhorrence against the worship of any living man, let alone the destroyer of Thebes. Some honours may have been voted in the hope of short-term political gains, but they certainly lapsed at the beginning of the Lamian War, when their proposer Demades was heavily fined and suffered *atimia*. For events at Sparta there is even less information. A certain Damis is accredited with a single apophthegm: 'since Alexander wishes to be a god, let him be a god' (Ael. *VH* 11.19; Plut. *Mor.* 219E). Again we can only speak of a debate; there is no evidence that honours were actually voted at Sparta. But it is important that there was a debate. If Athens and Sparta, cities inveterately hostile to Macedon, could seriously entertain the establishment of cult honours for Alexander, similar motions would have been passed with alacrity in cities which were friendlier or more pliable.

The process can to some extent be traced in Asia Minor and the islands. There are a number of cults attested in the centuries after Alexander's death. Some are as late as the second century A.D. and connected with the idealisation of the king in the Roman Empire. At Thasos, however, Alexander was honoured with a festival in the first generation after his death and Erythrae had a priesthood for 'King Alexander' by 270 B.C.[16] At this time the Ionian *koinon* held a regular annual festival, apparently celebrated on Alexander's birthday, and it provided the model for honours to Antiochus I (*OGIS* 222). Nearly three centuries later the festival was still observed, now in a permanent precinct west of Teos (Strabo 644). These are divine honours and most likely to have originated during Alexander's lifetime, while he was actually exercising power. There is unfortunately no evidence when these cults were voted. They could have come at any time, once Alexander's divine aspirations were widely known, and they need not have been voted simultaneously. It is likely enough that the heroisation of Hephaestion and the encouragement of divine honours for Alexander evoked in Asia Minor the same type of proposals (and possibly the same opposition) as is attested in Athens. There is no trace of such honours in the historical record of the early part of the reign, and the first

16 Salviat 1958, 244–8 (Thasos); *SIG*³ 1014, line 111 (Erythrae). On these cults see Habicht 1970, 17–25, 245–6, explaining them as spontaneous acts of gratitude for the 'liberation' of 334. Unfortunately there are no unambiguous dating criteria, as Badian stresses (1981, 59–63), arguing that the cults of Asia Minor were a gradual development during the last four years of the reign.

attested recognition of Alexander's godhead in Ionia seems to have been in the oracles sent to Memphis in 331. There is an anecdote that the Ephesians rejected Alexander's offerings to the Artemisium on the grounds that it was inappropriate for a god to make dedications to the gods (Artemidorus *ap.* Strabo 641), but the story, even if true, is undated.

In 323 the god died, but his cult continued tenaciously. The fiction soon developed that he like Heracles had been translated to heaven. It emerges in documents soon after his death (*OGIS* 4.5; Diod. xviii.56.2) and presently it became common currency, culminating in the absurd story that he attempted to disappear in the Euphrates and create his own apotheosis. His progress was complete. Beginning as a Heraclid and descendant of heroes, he had become son of Zeus and competitor with the heroes. Finally he had become a god manifest on earth, to be honoured with all the appurtenances of cult. The precedent for the worship of a living man was firmly established, and cults were offered to his Successors with greater frequency and magnificence.

# Appendix A
# Thibron in Cyrenaica

Thibron's activities after the murder of Harpalus are described by Diodorus and Arrian (*Succ.* F 1.16–19 Roos). Both sources give considerable detail, clearly taken from a common original, but concentrate on different aspects of the story. Arrian (or rather his excerptor Photius) is more attracted by the sensational details of his defeat and capture by Ophellas, whereas Diodorus concentrates on the earlier part of the narrative. It is evident from their joint account that the campaigns in Cyrenaica were full of action and took place over a considerable period. Unfortunately they relate the story in a single piece, placed in the general context of the end of the Lamian War; there is no precise chronological fixing. Justin permits a rough dating when he places Ptolemy's acquisition of Cyrene (the ultimate result of Thibron's campaigns) some time before Perdiccas' invasion of Egypt in 321 (XIII.6.20, 8.1). The Parian Marble to some degree confirms, synchronising Ophellas' operations in Cyrene with the fall of Athens, in the archon year 322/1 (*FGrH* 239 B 10: Ptolemy's visit in person (Arr. *Succ.* F 1.19) is dated to the next year, after the death of Perdiccas). The evidence so far is consistent and indicates that the war was over and Thibron dead by the end of 322 B.C.

Ptolemy's intervention in the war came very late. The oligarchic exiles from Cyrene only appealed to him after the democratic revolution which was provoked by the long stress of Thibron's siege operations (Diod. XVIII.21.6). The upshot of their appeal was the expedition of Ophellas, which united the *demos* of Cyrene with Thibron. The war which followed was not a lightning affair. Ophellas had to gain control not only of Cyrene but also of Taucheira, previously in Thibron's hands (Arr. *Succ.* F 1.17; cf. Diod. 20.6). Even before the appeal of the oligarchs there were protracted operations. Thibron's siege of Cyrene and its port was preceded by a major battle for which Cyrene had made lengthy preparations, sending for assistance from as far afield as Carthage (Diod. 21.4). The city had been alarmed by the arrival of mercenaries to reinforce Thibron. He had sent a recruiting mission to Taenarum, where there were still mercenaries in search of a paymaster, and he enlisted 2,500 men there (Diod. 21.1–2). That is important. It is almost inconceivable that there were still unemployed mercenaries after the outbreak of the Lamian War. Leosthenes had enlisted those who were available and used them as the nucleus of his army in central Greece (Diod. 9.2–4); and the Hellenic coalition needed every man it could retain. It is unlikely to the last degree that Thibron's recruiting occurred later than the summer of 323. But the recruiting only took place after Thibron had spent a considerable time campaigning in Cyrenaica. After he arrived in the region there was a good deal of desultory skirmishing. He forced Cyrene into submission with the help of the exiles who had invoked his aid in Crete (Diod. 19.2–4). While he was planning further operations in the Libyan hinterland (Diod. 19.5) there was an internal revolution in Cyrene, confining him to the port while the city maintained its freedom. There followed a period of general warfare in which the cities of Barca and Euesperides assisted Thibron but were attacked by Cyrene. In the course of this war Thibron lost control of the port of Cyrene but stormed Taucheira (Diod. 20.6). The seesaw of fortune continued as his troops were decimated by Libyan natives while foraging and his fleet was almost destroyed at sea (Diod. 20.7). It was only then that Thibron sent his recruiting agents to Taenarum. These events would have covered several months, and it is scarcely possible that Thibron left Crete any later than the autumn of 324. The following scheme gives a rough approximation to the chronology; variations are obviously possible within it but the limits must be correct.

| | |
|---|---|
| October 324 | Thibron sails from Crete to Cyrenaica. |
| | Occupation of Cyrene and possibly Barca (Arr. *Succ.* F 1.16; Diod. 20.3). |
| | Preparation for the Libyan campaign. |
| December 324 | Uprising in Cyrene: Thibron retains the port and makes an abortive attack on the city. |
| Winter/spring 323 | Warfare in the countryside: Thibron relieves Barca and Euesperides but loses the port of Cyrene. |
| March/April 323 | Thibron captures Taucheira but shortly afterwards loses his fleet. |
| May/June 323 | Recruiting at Taenarum. Thibron is meanwhile worsted in Cyrenaica. |
| July 323 | Preparations for war: Cyrene sends for reinforcements to combat the new arrivals. |
| August 323 | Thibron's victory over Cyrene: he lays siege to the port and makes daily attacks on the city. |
| Autumn 323 | Domestic revolution in Cyrene. The oligarchic exiles make overtures to Ptolemy. |
| Spring 322 | Ophellas leads Ptolemaic forces into Cyrenaica. War with Thibron, now allied with the democrats of Cyrene. |
| Summer 322 | Defeat and capture of Thibron. Cyrenaica is annexed by Ptolemy. |

This chronology gives a fixed terminus for Harpalus' stay in Athens. From the city he moved to Taenarum, embarked his forces and sailed to Crete, where he was assassinated. These movements must have taken at least a month (though probably not much longer), and it is virtually impossible that Harpalus left Athens later than mid-September 324.

# Appendix B
# Athens in 324/3 B.C.: some questions of prosopography

In 1918 B. Leonardos published an ephebic dedication from the sanctuary of Amphiaraus at Oropus ('Ἀρχ.'Ἐφ. 1918, 73–100, nos. 95–7. Cf. Reinmuth, 1971, 58–82, no. 18). The stone lists the ephebes of the tribe Leontis together with their *lochagoi* and ends with a number of officials crowned for their services. They include the officers of the *ephebeia* and three generals. Two of the names particularly concern us: Leosthenes, son of Leosthenes, of Cephale was general in charge of the *chora* and Philocles, son of Phormion, of Eroeadae was *kosmetes*. These men were immediately identified with Leosthenes the hero of the Lamian War and with Philocles, the general at Munychia when Harpalus approached Athens, who is known to have held an ephebic office at the time of his trial in 323 (Din. III.15). It was a natural corollary to date the inscription to the archon year 324/3, when Dicaeogenes, attested on the stone as general in Piraeus, is known to have held the generalship, very probably in Piraeus (*IG* II².1631, lines 380–1). Unfortunately the identifications involve severe historical problems. Reinmuth (67–8) denied that Philocles could be the Philocles of the Harpalus affair on the cogent ground that he could hardly be crowned as *kosmetes* if he had been ignominiously voted from office (Din. III.15) and condemned for bribery. To make any sense of it we need to assume that he was restored to office before the end of the archon year, which is a logical possibility but unattested and highly improbable. Jaschinski (1981, 51–4) has gone further and denied the identification of Leosthenes. That is the key point. If Leosthenes is not the general at Taenarum, there is no cogent reason to retain the dating to 324/3.

The main obstacle to the identification is the literary evidence. No source suggests that Leosthenes held any official position at Athens. Diodorus (XVII.111.3) states that the mercenaries at Taenarum elected him their supreme general and implies strongly that he had been a mercenary himself. Similarly, when working from Hieronymus, Diodorus (XVIII.9.2) states that the *boule* communicated with Leosthenes as a private individual, and his secret mission to Aetolia can hardly have been carried out in the role of an Athenian general. It is theoretically possible to argue that the negotiations took place in 325/4, while Leosthenes was still a private individual, and that he was general in 324/3. If so, it was remarkably stupid for the Athenians to have appointed him general in the *chora*, a job which involved home defence and confined the incumbent to Attica (Arist. *Ath. Pol.* 61.1), when it was vital that Leosthenes' connections with the mercenaries were maintained. If he were not at Taenarum in person, other predatory paymasters might poach his troops. In any case Diodorus emphasises the continuity of his residence at Taenarum and makes it clear that he was there with his men when news of Alexander's death reached Athens (XVIII.9.4). This is consistent with the contemporary but highly rhetorical picture of Hypereides (*Epitaph.* 10–11), which suggests that Leosthenes only became commander of his city's forces at the beginning of the Lamian War, after he had acquired his mercenary army. The cumulative weight of evidence tells strongly against Leosthenes having been general at Athens in 324/3. There could well have been two prominent men named Leosthenes. The name is not uncommon: apart from the famous general exiled in 361 for failure at Peparethus there are at least two others known in mid-fourth-century Athens (*PA* 9145, 9146). It would follow that Leosthenes the general at Taenarum held no official position at Athens before the outbreak of the Lamian War. His homonym, Leosthenes of Cephale, was general of the *chora* and trierarch during the Lamian War. He was apparently dead by the summer of 322 (*IG* II².1631, lines 601–2), but there is nothing surprising in two men of the same name dying in an archon year so full of action, particularly at sea. Given this reconstruction, there is ample opportunity for Leosthenes of Cephale to have served as trierarch, whereas on orthodox views presupposing a single Leosthenes 'it is a little difficult to see when in the war his activities would have allowed time' (Davies 1971, 343). Leosthenes of Cephale was probably the son of the general of 361; the father's disgrace may have impoverished his family in Attica (he himself lived comfortably at the Macedonian court) and the son was consequently unable to pay liturgies on a large scale before the crisis of the Lamian War.

There is less necessity to argue that two men named Philocles were associated with the *ephebeia*. It is admittedly most unlikely that the Philocles of the Harpalus affair was crowned *kosmetes* at the end of 324/3, but there is no compelling reason to date the inscription to that year. It is clear that Philocles was popular with the *demos* (Din. III.12) and he may well have held ephebic office in years other than 323 (he was general more than ten times). Similarly, if Dicaeogenes was general in 324/3 and 323/2, he may well have held the office on many previous occasions. The Oropus inscription is best removed from the context of 324/3; and, if Reinmuth (70–2) is correct that it belongs to a festival year, we should probably look to the great celebration of 329/8 (*IG* VII.4254 = *SIG*³ 298). Fortunately the precise date of the stone has no impact on the dating of the Harpalus affair. It seems certain that Philocles was general in Munychia in 325/4; that position was probably held by Dicaeogenes in 324/3 and it was an ephebic office from which Philocles was deposed before his trial (if he had been general (so Jaschinski, 1981, 40–1, following Adams and Berve) Deinarchus would surely have emphasised the fact). In that case Philocles admitted Harpalus to Athens before the end of the archon year 325/4.

# Bibliography

## 1 Ancient sources[1]

The reign of Alexander is sparse in contemporary documents. A mere handful of inscriptions can be dated with reasonable confidence to that period. The slim corpus is conveniently edited by Heisserer, 1980 (see also Tod, *GHI* nos. 183–203). Other inscriptional evidence from earlier or later periods is often relevant. My footnotes refer to the standard compilations. Note particularly L. Moretti, *Inscrizioni Storiche Ellenistiche* (Florence, 1967, 1976), for a collection of more recently discovered stones, and Austin 1981, who provides translations of selected documents. The coinage of the reign is important and complex (see the discussion above, pp. 244ff.), and the material record of sites and routes is often historically pertinent. The bibliography is given in the footnotes where it is relevant to the discussion.

The preponderance of evidence is literary. Most of it comes from the Roman period,[2] three centuries and more after Alexander's death, and it is necessarily derivative. It is particularly difficult to re-create the original sources for the reign, the efflorescence of memoirs and histories published in the first generation after the conquests. What we have is preserved by selective quotation and citation, and all too often it is the sensational and biased details that are cited with the authors' names. The mass of material, that at least which was sober and apparently uncontroversial, was absorbed into the secondary tradition without any acknowledgement of authorship. What explicitly named material exists was collected by Felix Jacoby in his monumental corpus of fragments (*Die Fragmente der griechischen Historiker (FGrH)*, Berlin and Leiden, 1923– ). The texts are assembled in Vol. IIB:618–828 with a brief German

[1] This section cannot claim to be a full coverage. It attempts to acquaint the reader with the range of material available on Alexander both now and in antiquity, and indicates the principal problems of source criticism. For further discussion I must refer to my *Commentary on Arrian* (Bosworth 1980a) and my forthcoming work on historiography (*From Arrian to Alexander: Studies in Historical Methodology*. Oxford, 1988).

[2] Of the five primary sources (see below, p. 300) Diodorus wrote his *Bibliotheca* in the third quarter of the first century B.C., Strabo wrote in the late Augustan period, Curtius at some time in the first century A.D. (the date is perennially disputed (cf. Atkinson 1980, 19–57; H. Bodefeld, *Untersuchungen zur Datierung der Alexandergeschichte des Q. Curtius Rufus*. Düsseldorf, 1982) but the problem is not of importance here), Plutarch and Arrian in the first part of the second century A.D. Pompeius Trogus wrote a world history during Augustus' reign but his work is best known primarily through the brief and perfunctory epitome of Justin, composed in the third century.

commentary in Vol. IID:403–542. A few additional fragments, of little historical value, are compiled in *FGrH* III.B.742–3 and by H. J. Mette, *Lustrum* 21 (1978) 18–20. There is a translation by C. A. Robinson, Jr, *The History of Alexander the Great* I (Providence, R.I., 1953): 30–276 and commentary on individual non-extant works by Pearson 1960 and Pédech 1984. Bibliography on specific authors is provided by Seibert 1972a.

The earliest history as such was the *Deeds of Alexander* by Callisthenes of Olynthus (*FGrH* 124). A relative of Aristotle by marriage, he distinguished himself in the field of history, compiling a list of Pythian victors with the great philosopher and composing a formal monograph on the Sacred War and an encomium to Hermeias of Atarneus. His most famous work before Alexander's reign was the *Hellenica*, a ten-book history which covered the thirty years from the King's Peace to the Phocian occupation of Delphi (356).[3] In 334 he crossed to Asia as official historian of Alexander and until his death in 327 he wrote up the stirring events he witnessed. His work covered events at least to Gaugamela and may have reached the death of Darius in 330, and for the first half of the reign it was clearly an authoritative source, influencing much of the extant tradition. Eulogistic and panegyrical as far as Alexander was concerned (see above, pp. 51, 72), he none the less must have included a great amount of uncontroversial first-hand material, which was later absorbed into the secondary tradition. The dozen identifiable fragments of his work give an inadequate and possibly misleading impression of its contents, but its importance was primary. It was the first formulation of what we may term the court tradition of Alexander's reign.

Other contemporary works are nebulous. Anaximenes of Lampsacus wrote at least two books *On Alexander*, treating events down to 333 and probably further (*FGrH* 72 F 15–17, 29), but practically nothing is known of the scope and content of the work. For further work that is reasonably attested we must look beyond the king's death, which triggered an outpouring of writings by participants in the campaign, a combination of personal memoirs and history proper. The earliest of these works was produced by Alexander's chief helmsman, Onesicritus of Astypalaea, who (perhaps in conscious imitation of Xenophon) wrote a work of uncertain title,[4] again a panegyric of Alexander (*FGrH* 134). It is primarily known through citations in Strabo and Pliny, who drew upon it for descriptions of the natural curiosities of India. Little enough is known of its general character or of its portraiture of Alexander. The most interesting fragments deal with the Indian philosophers and the Utopian kingdom of Musicanus,[5] where the Cynicism of Onesicritus (he was apparently a pupil of Diogenes) comes clearly to the surface. His picture of Alexander would have been interesting but it is irretrievably lost. Our extant citations, maybe influenced unduly by Nearchus, condemn him as a liar and his impact on the extant historical tradition is negligible.

Nearchus of Crete (*FGrH* 133) is much more accessible. His work is partially attested in that it is only cited for its description of India. If it covered the earlier part of the reign, there is no indication of the fact. But the Indian description is exploited by the later authors Arrian and Strabo, and extensive portions of his work, notably the description of the southern Ocean and his account of the hardships of the Gedrosian desert (see above, p. 145), are relatively well attested. His narrative, particularly his account of his ocean voyage, was strongly anecdotal and it is certain that he

[3] Cf. Jacoby, *RE* x.1685–98; Pearson 1960, 26–33; Pédech 1984, 18–40.
[4] Cf. Pearson 1960, 89–92. See also Brown 1949a, 1–2; Strasburger 1982, 1.178–9.
[5] *FGrH* 134 F 17, 24. Cf. Brown 1949a, 24–77.

exaggerated and sensationalised his own achievements, at the same time denigrating Onesicritus, whom he manifestly disliked.[6] But in the course of his narrative he gave precise routine details of individuals, distances and places, and the blend of sober fact and romance is not unlike that detectable in Callisthenes. His work was probably written soon after Alexander's death and may be in part a reaction against Onesicritus.

Somewhat later came the works of Ptolemy (*FGrH* 138) and Aristobulus (*FGrH* 139), which share with Nearchus the distinction of being the primary sources used by Arrian (cf. Bosworth 1980a, 22–32). Both could be said to be 'court histories' in that their view of Alexander is consistently favourable and their works were consistently focused upon the person and headquarters of the king. Otherwise they are very different. Ptolemy covered the entire reign from at least 335 to Alexander's death in Babylon and he apparently gave a narrative which was predominantly military, with a strong and understandably favourable emphasis upon his own achievements. Without doubt he provided Arrian with the military outline of his history, an account which is admirably clear but was shaped to emphasise the successes of Alexander and his Macedonians. It would be helpful to know the date of composition, but no reasonable criterion has yet been discovered and there are wide theoretical limits, between roughly 320 B.C. and Ptolemy's death in 283.[7] As it is, we have no idea of the date or the relative length of the work. It is known overwhelmingly through citations in Arrian and can only be approached through study of Arrian.

We are slightly better served for Aristobulus, who wrote in his old age some time after the battle of Ipsus (301). He served with Alexander in a relatively humble capacity and, like Ptolemy, he gave an account which was partly autobiographical (see above, p. 154). His work was widely quoted by a range of authors, notably Arrian, Strabo, Plutarch and Athenaeus; and occasionally, as in his description of Alexander's activities on the Euphrates (F 55, 56), we have two versions of the same passage and can reconstruct the original to some degree. The weight of citations, as always, concerns curiosities, geographical and botanical, but it is clear that Aristobulus could and did report campaign details soberly and apparently with accuracy. Like Ptolemy he was inclined to eulogise Alexander and his army and there was a streak of conscious apologetic in his work that was excoriated even in antiquity.

The most influential of the earlier historians of Alexander was probably Cleitarchus of Alexandria (*FGrH* 137). His work was substantial, more than twelve books long, and covered the entire reign. It was also relatively early, perhaps written before 310; and, even if Cleitarchus was not a participant in the campaigns, he had access to first-hand reports. He is particularly unfortunate in the named citations of his work, all of which centre on trivial detail or sensational exaggeration, and he has been repeatedly characterised as a dealer in rhetoric and bombast.[8] But Cleitarchus was widely read, particularly in the Roman period, and his work clearly underlies much of the extant material on Alexander. That is particularly true of the so-called 'vulgate tradition'. Large segments of the work of Curtius Rufus and Diodorus Siculus xvii are derived from a common source, and at times the narrative runs parallel, each author giving his own version of the longer original, omitting many details included by the other but presenting the same outline. The same source can be detected in Justin's much later epitome of Pompeius Trogus and in the *Metz Epitome* (a compilation of late antiquity

[6] See particularly Pearson 1960, 131–9; Badian, 1975.
[7] For a survey of possibilities see now Roisman 1984.
[8] See, most recently, Hammond 1983a, 25–7. Contrast Jacoby, *RE* xi.645–8.

covering the campaign between Hyrcania and Southern India). Some of this material, along with much else, is included in Plutarch's *Life of Alexander*. There is a high degree of probability that Cleitarchus is the ultimate source of the common tradition. He is named as one of Diodorus' sources and, more significantly, he is named as the authority for a point of detail in Curtius' Indian narrative (IX.8.15 = *FGrH* 137 F 25), a narrative that is paralleled in Diodorus.[9] Cleitarchus in this instance is proved to be the source of a shared tradition and there is every likelihood that the rest of the parallel narratives are taken from his work. In that case we have a body of material which vastly supplements the scanty corpus of named fragments. What we have is necessarily distorted by the extant vehicles of the tradition, which are either contaminated by rhetoric or abridged to the point of unintelligibility, but there is a formidable secondary corpus which can be set alongside the court tradition of Ptolemy and Aristobulus. The material based on Cleitarchus has a greater emphasis on events outside the Macedonian headquarters and tends to be distinctly less eulogistic of Alexander. There is a clear penchant towards sensation and exaggeration but also factual and relatively sober reporting. The 'vulgate' cannot be neglected, and most of the problems of Alexander scholarship arise from the contradictions and inconsistencies between it and the tradition of Arrian.

Other histories of Alexander are known, such as those by Hegesias of Magnesia (*FGrH* 142) and Aristus of Salamis (*FGrH* 143), but they are late and derivative and had little impact on the extant sources. More important is the great work of Hieronymus of Cardia (*FGrH* 154; cf. Hornblower 1981). This was the most authoritative account of events *after* Alexander. Written by an associate of Eumenes and Antigonus, it dealt with the period from 323 down to the death of Pyrrhus and was the principal source used by Diodorus (XVIII–XX) in his narrative of the period of the Successors. Hieronymus' work was detailed, highly informed and given to political analysis. It also included reference to documents: treaties, edicts and letters. Although not directly relevant to Alexander's reign, it refers back constantly, giving the political context of the events which arose from the king's death. His preface to the Lamian War with the apparent *verbatim* citation of the Exiles' Decree (Diod. XVIII.8.4) is of prime importance, as is the *diagramma* of Philip Arrhidaeus on the return of exiles (Diod. XVIII.55). What survives of Hieronymus substantially enriches the historical tradition of the last two years of Alexander's reign.

There is also a detritus of anecodotal material, mostly preserved in Athenaeus. This derives from pamphlets, usually attributable to the period immediately after Alexander's death, or from personal memoirs. The most impressive remains come from Chares of Mytilene (*FGrH* 125), one of Alexander's court chamberlains. His *Histories of Alexander* drew extensively upon his experiences during the latter years of the reign and (as excerpted by Athenaeus) give rich detail about the great marriage celebrations at Susa (F 4). The extant citations include a good deal of romance, but there may be undue emphasis on that aspect of his work. Plutarch used him as a named source and some of the material adduced is detailed and informative. Other material, cited by Strabo in geographical excursuses, comes from the Thessalian writers, Polycleitus and Medeius of Larisa (*FGrH* 128–9). More emotively slanted details are cited from Ephippus of Olynthus and Nicobule (*FGrH* 126–7), dealing with the circumstances of the deaths of Hephaestion and of Alexander himself. This

[9] Diod. XVII.102.6. Cf. Hamilton 1977, 129–35.

material was certainly tendentious, but the fragments cited are rich in apparent fact. It is part of a tradition of propaganda and speculation which was to be elaborated over the centuries and coalesced in the extant Alexander-Romance and the *Liber de Morte* of the *Metz Epitome*, where, under the overlay of late romance, there is an authentic echo of the original pamphleteering by Perdiccas (cf. Merkelbach 1977, 164–92; 253–83).

Some of the cited material has a documentary perspective. There is some record of the writings of Alexander's professional surveyors, the bematists. Works are attested by Baeton, Diognetus and Amyntas (*FGrH* 119, 120, 122), purporting to give the stages (*stathmoi*) of Alexander's marches. Some precise figures were indeed given of the distances between the various capitals along the route, and there is little doubt that the bematists were one of the principal sources of information for the great Alexandrian geographer, Eratosthenes. But these works were far more than itineraries, with the most colourful and exaggerated information about the native flora and fauna. The bematists were at least participants in the campaign and their works were apparently authentic. Much more dubious are the numerous letters cited in the literary tradition (Pearson 1954–5, 443–50). Some, like the correspondence in the Alexander-Romance, are obviously fictitious. Others are literary elaborations on material preserved in the original sources. The most elaborate example of this genre is the exchange of correspondence between Alexander and Darius after Issus. It is recorded by Arrian and Curtius, who display similarities of content but divergences in detail.[10] In this case variant reports by the original historians are variously reported in the extant authorities, both imposing their own framework on the material. Most letters are reported once only, usually in Plutarch. Many are of quite indeterminate authenticity; others, like the letter condoning Cleomenes' corruption (Arr. VII.23.6–8) or the response to the Athenians on Samos (Plut. *Al.* 28.2), may be correctly transmitted. What is clear is that compilations of purported letters of Alexander were in vogue in the Hellenistic period and there were many spurious letters in circulation. Usually we can go no further than admit that a reported letter is an embroidery on attested facts. Few can be used as evidence without corroboration from other sources.

The most peculiar of the alleged documents is the *Ephemerides*, or *Royal Diaries*, which Arrian and Plutarch cite as a day-by-day account of the king's final illness (*FGrH* 117). It was long believed that this account was an extract from an official diary which gave a coverage of the entire reign and was used as a primary source by Ptolemy. The theory was given wide circulation by Wilcken 1894 and is sometimes repeated in modern accounts of Alexander.[11] But there is no evidence that the *Ephemerides* went beyond the last years of the king's reign, and the details given centre on court routine and symposia. There are also alleged anachronisms which have suggested the possibility of late forgery, and the 'document' is clearly connected with the rumours and speculation which surrounded Alexander's death. The *Ephemerides* probably occupy a peculiar middle ground between fiction and reportage – an account which deliberately selected facts to suggest a specific interpretation (see above, p. 172). A 'document' it probably is, in that it originated in the Macedonian court, but its testimony is not beyond suspicion and more seriously, there is no evidence that a court diary was systematically used by Ptolemy or by any other primary source.

I hope that it is by now apparent that the original tradition of Alexander's reign is only accessible through the distorting filter of the extant sources. That means in

[10] Arr. II.14; Curt. IV.1.7–14. See above, p. 64.

[11] See above, p. 171. I discuss the issue exhaustively in *From Arrian to Alexander*, Ch. 7.

practice six primary authorities: Strabo (particularly books xv–xvii), Curtius Rufus, Diodorus, Plutarch, Arrian and Justin's epitome of Pompeius Trogus. Serious work cannot be done on the original histories before the characteristics and methods of the extant writers are fully appreciated. I have attempted to do that for Arrian in my book *From Arrian to Alexander: Studies in Historical Interpretation*, to which I must refer for detail and further bibliography.

The texts and translations of the extant sources which I consider most helpful are:

| | |
|---|---|
| Arrian | Brunt 1976–83 (Loeb text, based on the standard Teubner edition by A. G. Roos. There is a text and translation of the Alexander history and the *Indike* together with historical annotation and general appendices). For full commentary on Books I–III see Bosworth 1980a, and for Arrian's career and methods one may consult P. A. Stadter, *Arrian of Nicomedia*, Chapel Hill, 1980. |
| Strabo | (The *Geography* of Strabo) ed. and tr. H. S. Jones, 1–8, Cambridge, Mass. (Loeb), 1917–32. |
| Plutarch | (Plutarchus, *Vitae Parallelae*) ed. K. Ziegler, Leipzig (Teubner), 1968, 11.2, pp. 152–253. This is the text used in the standard commentary (Hamilton 1969). |
| | (*Plutarch's Lives*) ed. and tr. B. Perrin, Cambridge, Mass. (Loeb), 1919. The paragraphing differs from the Teubner, which is the standard reference text for most historical work. |
| Curtius Rufus | (Quinte-Curce, *Histoires*) ed. and tr. H. Bardon, I–II, Paris (Budé), 1947–8. |
| | (Quintus Curtius Rufus, *The History of Alexander*) tr. H. Yardley, introd. and notes W. Heckel, Harmondsworth (Penguin), 1984. For full commentary on Books III–IV see Atkinson 1980. |
| Diodorus Siculus | (Diodore de Sicile, *Bibliothèque Historique*) xvii–xviii, ed. P. Goukowsky, Paris (Budé), 1976, 1978. |
| | (Diodorus of Sicily) 8 (xvi. 66–95 and xvii), ed. C. B. Welles, and 9 (xviii–xix.65), ed. R. M. Geer, Cambridge, Mass. (Loeb), 1963, 1967. There are useful general comments in Hornblower 1981. |
| Justin | (*M. Iuniani Iustini, Epitoma Historiarum Philippicarum Pompei Trogi*) ed. O. Seel, Stuttgart (Teubner), 1972. |
| | The only English translation that is at all accessible is the old Bohn's Libraries production (Justin, Cornelius Nepos and Eutropius, tr. J. S. Watson, London 1875). |

## II   Modern authors

The following list gives bibliographical details for all literature mentioned summarily in the text and footnotes. It is a reasonably full compendium of recent work on Alexander but in no way a systematic bibliography of the subject. That is well provided by the two research surveys by Jakob Seibert (1972a, 1983), which are indispensable for the serious student of the period.

Accame, S. (1941) *La lega ateniese nel secolo IV a.c.* Rome

Altheim, F. and Stiehl, R. (1970) *Geschichte Mittelasiens im Altertum*. Berlin

Anderson, J. K. (1970) *Military Theory and Practice in the Age of Xenophon*. Berkeley

Andreotti, R. (1956) 'Per una critica dell' ideologia di Alessandro Magno', *Historia* 5: 257–302

  (1957) 'Die Weltmonarchie Alexanders des Grossen in Überlieferung und geschichtlicher Wirklichkeit', *Saeculum* 8: 120–66

Andronikos, M. (1970) 'Sarissa', *BCH* 94: 91–107

  (1979) 'The finds from the Royal Tombs at Vergina', *PBA* 65: 355–67

  (1980) 'The Royal Tomb at Vergina and the problem of the dead', *AAA* 13: 168–78

Anson, E. M. (1981) 'Alexander's hypaspists and the argyraspids', *Historia* 30: 117–20

Anspach, A. (1903) *De Alexandria Magni expeditione Indica*. Leipzig

Ashton, N. G. (1977) 'The *naumachia* near Amorgos in 322 B.C.', *ABSA* 72: 1–11

  (1979) 'How many *pentereis*?', *GRBS* 20: 327–42

  (1983) 'The Lamian War: a false start', *Antichthon* 17: 47–61

Atkinson, J. E. (1980) *A Commentary on Q. Curtius Rufus' Historiae Alexandri Magni Books 3 & 4* (London Studies in Classical Philology 4). Amsterdam/Uithoorn

Atkinson, K. M. T. (1973) 'Demosthenes, Alexander and Asebeia', *Athenaeum* 51: 310–35

Aulock, H. von (1964) 'Die Prägung des Balakros in Kilikien', *JNG* 14: 79–82

Austin, M. M. (1981) *The Hellenistic World from Alexander to the Roman Conquest*. Cambridge

  (1986) 'Hellenistic kings, war and the economy', *CQ* 36: 450–66

Aymard, A. (1937) 'Un ordre d'Alexandre', *REA* 39: 5–28

  (1967) *Études d'histoire ancienne*. Paris

Badian, E. (1958a) 'The eunuch Bagoas: a study in method', *CQ* 8: 144–57

  (1958b) 'Alexander the Great and the unity of mankind', *Historia* 7: 425–44

  (1960a) 'The death of Parmenio', *TAPA* 91: 324–38

  (1960b) 'The first flight of Harpalus', *Historia* 9: 245–6

  (1961) 'Harpalus', *JHS* 81: 16–43

  (1963) 'The death of Philip II', *Phoenix* 17: 244–50

  (1965a) 'Orientals in Alexander's army', *JHS* 85: 160–1

  (1965b) 'The administration of the empire', *Greece & Rome* 12: 166–82

  (1965c) 'The date of Clitarchus', *PACA* 8: 5–11

  (1966) 'Alexander the Great and the Greeks of Asia', *Ancient Society and Institutions* (studies presented to V. Ehrenberg, Oxford), 37–69

  (1967) 'Agis III', *Hermes* 95: 170–92

  (1968) 'A king's notebooks', *HSCP* 72: 183–204

  (1971) 'Alexander the Great, 1948–67', *CW* 65: 37–83

  (1975) 'Nearchus the Cretan', *YCS* 24: 147–70

  (1976a) 'Some recent interpretations of Alexander', *Entretiens Hardt* 22: 279–311

  (1976b) 'A comma in the history of Samos', *ZPE* 23: 289–94

  (1977a) 'A document of Artaxerxes IV?', *Greece and the Eastern Mediterranean in History and Prehistory* (studies presented to F. Schachermeyr; ed. K. Kinzl, Berlin), 40–50

  (1977b) 'The battle of the Granicus: a new look', *Ancient Macedonia* 2 (Thessaloniki): 271–93

  (1981) 'The deification of Alexander the Great', *Ancient Macedonian Studies in Honor of Charles F. Edson* (ed. H. J. Dell, Thessaloniki), 27–71

(1982) 'Greeks and Macedonians', *Macedonia and Greece in Late Classical and Early Hellenistic Times* (Studies in the History of Art 10, Washington), 33–51

(1985) 'Alexander in Iran', *Cambridge History of Iran* II (ed. I. Gershevitch; Cambridge), 420–501

Bagnall, R. S. (1979) 'The date of the foundation of Alexandria', *AJAH* 4: 46–9

Balsdon, J. P. V. D. (1950) 'The "Divinity" of Alexander', *Historia* 1: 363–88

*Baluchistan District Gazetteer* (1906) Series VII (Makrán), ed. R. Hughes-Buller. Bombay

Bean, G. E. and Cook, J. M. (1955) 'The Halicarnassus Peninsula', *ABSA* 50: 85–171

Bellen, H. (1974) 'Der Rachegedanke in der griechisch-persischen Auseinandersetzung', *Chiron* 4: 43–67

Bellinger, A. R. (1963) *Essays on the Coinage of Alexander the Great* (Numismatic Studies No. 11). New York

Bendinelli, G. (1965) 'Cassandro re di Macedonia nella Vita plutarchea di Alessandro Magno', *RFIC* 93: 150–64

Bengtson, H. (1937) 'Φιλόξενος ὁ Μακεδών', *Philologus* 92: 126–55

Benveniste, E. (1943–5) 'La ville de Cyreschata', *Journal Asiatique* 324: 163–6

van Berchem, D. (1970) 'Alexandre et la restauration de Priène', *MH* 27: 198–205

Bernard, P. (1974) 'Fouilles d'Aï Khanoum. Campagnes de 1972 et 1973', *CRAI* 280–308

(1975) 'Campagne de fouilles 1974 à Aï Khanoum', *CRAI* 167–97

(1980a) 'Campagne de fouilles 1978 à Aï Khanoum', *CRAI* 435–59

(1980b) 'Heracles, les Grottes de Karafto et le sanctuaire de Mont Sambulos en Iran', *Studia Iranica* 9: 301–24

Berve, H. (1926) *Das Alexanderreich auf prosopographischer Grundlage* I–II. Munich (Vol. II, *Prosopographie*, is a catalogue of individuals attested during Alexander's reign. The arrangement is by number, in alphabetical order.)

(1938) 'Die Verschmelzungspolitik Alexanders des Grossen', *Klio* 31: 135–68

(1967) *Die Tyrannis bei den Griechen*. Munich

Bickermann, E. J. (1934) 'Alexandre le Grand et les villes d'Asie', *REG* 47: 346–74

(1940) 'La lettre d'Alexandre le Grand aux bannis grecs', *REA* 42: 25–35

(1963a) 'À propos d'un passage de Chares de Mytilène', *PdP* 18: 241–55

(1963b) 'Sur un passage d'Hypéride', *Athenaeum* 41: 70–83

Bieber, M. (1964) *Alexander the Great in Greek and Roman Art*. Chicago

Bigwood, J. M. (1978) 'Ctesias as historian', *Phoenix* 32: 19–41

Borza, E. N. (1967) 'Alexander and the return from Siwah', *Historia* 16: 369

(1972) 'Fire from heaven: Alexander at Persepolis', *CPh.* 67: 233–45

(1979) 'Some observations on malaria and the ecology of Central Macedonia in antiquity', *AJAH* 4: 102–24

(1981–2) 'The Macedonian Royal Tombs at Vergina: some cautionary notes', *Archaeological News* 10: 73–87; 11: 8–10

(1982) 'The natural resources of early Macedonia', *Philip II, Alexander the Great and the Macedonian Heritage* (ed. W. L. Adams and E. N. Borza, Washington), 1–20

Bosworth, A. B. (1970) 'Aristotle and Callisthenes', *Historia* 19: 407–13

(1971a) 'Philip II and Upper Macedonia', *CQ* 21: 93–105

(1971b) 'The death of Alexander the Great: rumour and propaganda', *CQ* 21: 112–36

(1973) 'ΑΣΘΕΤΑΙΡΟΙ', *CQ* 23: 245–53
(1974) 'The government of Syria under Alexander the Great', *CQ* 24: 46–64
(1975) 'The mission of Amphoterus and the outbreak of Agis' War', *Phoenix* 29: 27–43
(1976a) 'Arrian and the Alexander Vulgate', *Entretiens Hardt* 22: 1–46
(1976b) 'Errors in Arrian', *CQ* 26: 117–39
(1977a) 'Alexander and Ammon', *Greece and the Ancient Mediterranean in History and Prehistory* (Studies presented to Fritz Schachermeyr; ed. K. Kinzl, Berlin), 51–75
(1977b) 'Early relations between Aetolia and Macedon', *AJAH* 1: 164–81
(1978) 'Eumenes, Neoptolemus and *PSI* XII.1284', *GRBS* 19: 227–37
(1980a) *A Historical Commentary on Arrian's History of Alexander I*. Oxford
(1980b) 'Alexander and the Iranians', *JHS* 100: 1–21
(1981) 'A missing year in the history of Alexander the Great', *JHS* 101: 17–39
(1982) 'The location of Alexander's campaign against the Illyrians in 335 B.C.', *Macedonia and Greece in Late Classical and Early Hellenistic Times* (Studies in the History of Art 10, Washington), 75–84
(1983) 'The Indian satrapies under Alexander the Great', *Antichthon* 17: 37–46
(1986) 'Alexander the Great and the decline of Macedon', *JHS* 106: 1–12
(1987) 'Nearchus in Susiana', *Zu Alexander dem Grossen* (Festschrift G. Wirth; ed. W. Will, Amsterdam)
Braunert, H. (1968) 'Staatstheorie und Staatsrecht in Hellenismus', *Saeculum* 19: 47–66
Breloer, B. (1933) *Alexanders Kampf gegen Poros* (Bonner Orientalische Studien 3), Stuttgart
Briant, P. (1973) *Antigone le Borgne; les débuts de sa carrière et les problèmes de l'assemblée macédonienne*. Paris
(1982a) *État et pasteurs au Moyen-Orient ancien*. Cambridge and Paris
(1982b) *Rois, tributs et paysans* (Centre de Recherches d' Histoire Ancienne 43). Paris
Brixhe, Cl. (1976) *Le Dialecte grec de Pamphylie*. Paris
Brown, T. S. (1949a) *Onesicritus: a Study in Hellenistic Historiography*. Berkeley
(1949b) 'Callisthenes and Alexander', *AJP* 70: 225–48
(1967) 'Alexander's book order (Plut. *Alex.* 8)', *Historia* 16: 359–68
Brundage, B. C. (1958) 'Herakles the Levantine', *JNES* 17: 225–36
Brunt, P. A. (1963) 'Alexander's Macedonian cavalry', *JHS* 83: 27–46
(1975) 'Alexander, Barsine and Heracles', *RFIC* 103: 22–34
(1976) 'Anaximenes and King Alexander I of Macedon', *JHS* 96: 151–53
(1976–83) *Arrian: History of Alexander and Indica* (Loeb Classical Library) I–II. Cambridge (Mass.)
Burke, E. M. (1977) '*Contra Leocratem and de Corona*: political collaboration?', *Phoenix* 31: 330–40
Burn, A. R. (1952) 'Notes on Alexander's campaigns 332–330 B.C.', *JHS* 72: 81–91
Carney, E. (1981) 'The death of Cleitus', *GRBS* 22: 149–60
Caroe, O. (1962) *The Pathans*. London
Casson, L. (1971) *Ships and Seamanship in the Ancient World*. Princeton
Cauer, F. (1894) 'Philotas, Kleitos, Kallisthenes', *Jahrbücher für classische Philologie* Suppl. 20: 8–38

Cavenaile, R. (1972) 'Pour une histoire politique et sociale d'Alexandrie – les origines', *AC* 41: 94–112

Cawkwell, G. L. (1961) 'A note on Ps.-Demosthenes 17.20', *Phoenix* 15: 74–8
   (1963) 'Eubulus', *JHS* 83: 47–67
   (1969) 'The crowning of Demosthenes', *CQ* 19: 161–80

Classen, D. J. (1959) 'The Libyan god Ammon in Greece before 331 B.C.', *Historia* 8: 349–55

Cohen, G. M. (1978) *The Seleucid Colonies* (Historia Einzelschr. 30). Wiesbaden

Cook, J. M. (1983) *The Persian Empire*. London

Cross, F. M. (1963) 'The discovery of the Samaria papyri', *BA* 26: 110–21
   (1966) 'Aspects of Samaritan and Jewish history in late Persian and Hellenistic times', *HTR* 52: 201–11

Davies, J. K. (1971) *Athenian Propertied Families 600–300 B.C.* Oxford

Davis, E. W. (1964) 'The Persian battle plan at the Granicus', *James Sprunt Studies in History and Political Sciences* 46: 34–44

Demandt, A. (1972) 'Politische Aspekte in Alexanderbild der Neuzeit', *Archiv für Kulturgeschichte* 54: 325–63

Develin, R. D. (1981) 'The murder of Philip II', *Antichthon* 15: 86–99
   (1985) 'Anaximenes (*FGrHist* 72) F4', *Historia* 34: 493–6

Devine, A. M. (1975) 'Grand tactics at Gaugamela', *Phoenix* 29: 374–85
   (1983) 'ΕΜΒΟΛΟΝ: a study in tactical terminology', *Phoenix* 37: 201–17
   (1984) 'The location of Castabulum and Alexander's route from Mallus to Myriandrus', *Acta Classica* 27: 127–9

Dobesch, G. (1975) 'Alexander der Grosse und der Korinthische Bund', *Grazer Beiträge* 3: 73–149

Droysen, J. G. (1952) *Geschichte des Hellenismus: I Geschichte Alexanders des Grossen*. 2nd ed. Gotha, 1877; 3rd ed. Basel

Dürr, N. (1974) 'Neues aus Babylonien', *Schweizer Münzblätter* 33–6

Eadie, J. W. (1967) 'The development of Roman mailed cavalry', *JRS* 57: 161–73

Edmunds, L. (1971) 'The religiosity of Alexander', *GRBS* 12: 363–91

Egge, R. (1978) *Untersuchungen zur Primärtradition bei Q. Curtius Rufus*. Freiburg

Eggermont, P. H. L. (1970) 'Alexander's campaign in Gandhāra and Ptolemy's list of Indo-Scythian towns', *Orientalia Lovaniensia Periodica* 1: 63–123
   (1975) *Alexander's Campaigns in Sind and Baluchistan* (Orientalia Lovaniensia Analecta 3). Leuven

Ehrenberg, V. (1938) *Alexander and the Greeks*. Oxford
   (1965) *Polis und Imperium*. Zurich

Ellis, J. R. (1971) 'Amyntas Perdikka, Philip II and Alexander the Great', *JHS* 91: 15–24
   (1975) 'Alexander's hypaspists again', *Historia* 24: 617–18
   (1981) 'The assassination of Philip II', *Ancient Macedonian Studies in honor of Charles Edson* (ed. H. J. Dell, Thessaloniki), 99–137

Engels, D. W. (1978a) *Alexander the Great and the Logistics of the Macedonian Army*. Berkeley
   (1978b) 'A note on Alexander's death', *CPh.* 73: 224–8
   (1980) 'Alexander's intelligence system', *CQ* 30: 327–40

Errington, R. M. (1969) 'Bias in Ptolemy's History of Alexander', *CQ* 19: 233–42
   (1970) 'From Babylon to Triparadeisos: 323–320 B.C.', *JHS* 90: 49–77

(1974) 'Macedonian "Royal Style" and its historical significance', *JHS* 94: 20–37

(1975a) 'Samos and the Lamian War', *Chiron* 5: 50–7

(1975b) 'Arybbas the Molossian', *GRBS* 16: 41–50

(1976) 'Alexander in the Hellenistic world', *Entretiens Hardt* 22: 137–79

(1978) 'The nature of the Macedonian state under the monarchy', *Chiron* 8: 77–133

(1986) *Geschichte Makedoniens*. Munich

Étienne, R. and Piérart, M. (1975) 'Un décret du koinon des Hellènes à Platées', *BCH* 99: 51–75

Fakhry, A. (1944) *Siwa Oasis: its History and Antiquities*. Cairo

Farber, J. J. (1979) 'The Cyropaedia and Hellenistic kingship', *AJP* 100: 497–574

Fears, J. R. (1975) 'Pausanias, the assassin of Philip II', *Athenaeum* 53: 111–35

Fischer, K. (1967) 'Zur Lage von Kandahar an Landverbindungen zwischen Iran und Indien', *BJ* 167: 129–232

Foss, C. (1977) 'The battle of the Granicus: a new look', *Ancient Macedonia* 2 (Thessaloniki): 495–502

Foucher, A. (1942) *La Vieille Route de l' Inde de Bactres à Taxile*. Paris

*Fouilles d' Aï Khanoum I* (1973) (Mémoires de la délégation archéologique française en Afghanistan 21). Paris

Fraser, P. M. (1967) 'Current problems concerning the early history of the cult of Sarapis', *Opuscula Atheniensia* 7: 23–45

(1972) *Ptolemaic Alexandria* I–II. Oxford

(1979/80) 'The son of Aristonax at Kandahar', *Afghan Studies* 2: 9–21

Fredricksmeyer, E. A. (1961) 'Alexander, Midas and the oracle at Gordium', *CPh*. 56: 160–8

(1979a) 'Divine Honours for Philip II', *TAPA* 109: 39–61

(1979b) 'Three notes on Alexander's deification', *AJAH* 4: 1–9

(1981) 'On the background of the ruler cult', *Ancient Macedonian Studies in Honor of Charles F. Edson* (ed. H. J. Dell, Thessaloniki), 145–56

Frye, R. N. (1972) 'Gestures of deference to royalty in Ancient Iran', *Iranica Antiqua* 9: 102–7

Gardin, J.-C. (1980) 'L'archéologie du paysage bactrien', *CRAI* 480–501

Gehrke, H. J. (1976) *Phokion* (Zetemata 64). Munich

Gerov, B. (1981) 'Zum Problem der Wohnsitze der Triballen', *Klio* 63: 485–92

Gesche, H. (1974) 'Nikokles von Paphos und Nikokreon von Salamis', *Chiron* 4: 103–25

Giovannini, A. (1983) 'Téos, Antiochos III et Attale Ier', *MH* 40: 178–84

Goukowsky, P. (1969) 'Un lever de soleil sur l'Ida de Troade', *R.Ph.* 43: 249–54

(1972) 'Le roi Poros et son éléphant', *BCH* 96: 473–502

(1976) *Diodore de Sicile XVII* (Budé). Paris

(1978–81) *Essai sur les origines du mythe d'Alexandre* I–II. Nancy

Green, P. (1974) *Alexander of Macedon*. London

(1982) 'The Royal Tombs of Vergina: a historical analysis', *Philip II, Alexander the Great and the Macedonian Heritage* (ed. W. L. Adams and E. N. Borza, Washington) 129–51

Griffith, G. T. (1935) *The Mercenaries of the Hellenistic World*. Cambridge

(1947) 'Alexander's generalship at Gaugamela', *JHS* 67: 77–89

(1956/7) 'Μακεδονικά: notes on the Macedonians of Philip and Alexander', *PCPS* 4: 3–10

(1963) 'A note on the hipparchies of Alexander', *JHS* 83: 68–74

(1964) 'Alexander the Great and an experiment in government', *PCPS* 10: 23–39

(1968) 'The letter of Darius at Arrian 2.14', *PCPS* 14: 33–48

Gullath, B. (1982) *Untersuchungen zur Geschichte Boiotiens in der Zeit Alexanders und der Diadochen*. Frankfurt am Main and Bern

Gunderson, L. L. (1982) 'Quintus Curtius Rufus', *Philip II, Alexander the Great and the Macedonian Heritage* (ed. W. L. Adams and E. N. Borza, Washington), 177–96

Günther, W. (1971) *Das Orakel von Didyma in hellenistischer Zeit* (MDAI(I) Beih. 4). Tübingen

Habicht, Chr. (1957) 'Samische Volksbeschlüsse der hellenistischen Zeit', *MDAI(A)* 72: 152–274

(1970) *Gottmenschentum und griechische Städte* (Zetemata 14). 2nd ed. Munich

(1973) 'Literarische und epigraphische Überlieferung zur Geschichte Alexanders und seiner ersten Nachfolger', *Akten des VI Internationalen Kongresses für Gr. und Lat. Epigraphik* (Vestigia 17, Munich), 367–77

(1975) 'Der Beitrag Spartas zur Restitution von Samos während des Lamischen Krieges', *Chiron* 5: 45–50

(1979) *Untersuchungen zur politischen Geschichte Athens im 3 Jahrhundert v. Chr.* Munich

Hadley, R. A. (1974) 'Royal propaganda of Seleucus I and Lysimachus', *JRS* 94: 50–65

Hamilton, J. R. (1953) 'Alexander and his "so-called" father', *CQ* 3: 151–7

(1955) 'Three passages in Arrian', *CQ* 5: 217–21

(1956) 'The cavalry battle at the Hydaspes', *JHS* 76: 26–31

(1961) 'Cleitarchus and Aristobulus', *Historia* 10: 448–58

(1969) *Plutarch Alexander: a Commentary*. Oxford.

(1971) 'Alexander and the Aral', *CQ* 21: 106–11

(1972) 'Alexander among the Oreitai', *Historia* 21: 603–8

(1973) *Alexander the Great*. London

(1977) 'Cleitarchus and Diodorus 17', *Greece and the Ancient Mediterranean in History and Prehistory* (studies presented to Fritz Schachermeyr; ed. K. Kinzl, Berlin), 126–46

Hammond, N. G. L. (1978a) 'A cavalry unit in the army of Antigonus Monophthalmus', *CQ* 28: 128–35

(1978b) '"Philip's Tomb" in historical context', *GRBS* 19: 331–50

(1980a) *Alexander the Great: King, Commander and Statesman*. Park Ridge, N.J.

(1980b) 'Some passages in Arrian concerning Alexander', *CQ* 30: 455–76

(1980c) 'The battle of the Granicus river', *JHS* 100: 73–88

(1980d) 'The march of Alexander the Great on Thebes in 335 B.C.', Μέγας Ἀλέξανδρος: 2300 χρόνια ἀπὸ τὸν θάνατον τοῦ (Thessaloniki), 171–81

(1982) 'The evidence for the identity of the Royal Tombs at Vergina', *Philip II, Alexander the Great and the Macedonian Heritage* (ed. W. L. Adams and E. N. Borza, Washington), 111–27

(1983a) *Three Historians of Alexander the Great*. Cambridge

(1983b) 'The text and the meaning of Arrian VII.6.2–5', *JHS* 103: 139–44

Hammond, N. G. L. and Griffith, G. T. (1979) *A History of Macedonia* II. Oxford

Hampl, F. (1953) 'Alexanders des Grossen *Hypomnemata* und letzte Pläne', *Studies Presented to D. M. Robinson* II (St Louis), 816–29

(1954) 'Alexander der Grosse und die Beurteilung geschichtlicher Persönlichkeiten', *La Nouvelle Clio* 6: 115–24

Hansman, J. (1967) 'Charax and the Karkheh', *Iranica Antiqua* 7: 21–58

(1968) 'The problems of Qūmis', *JRAS*: 111–39

(1972) 'Elamites, Achaemenians and Anshan', *Iran* 10: 101–25

Hansman, J. F. and Stronach, D. (1970) 'Excavations at Shahr-i Qūmis', *JRAS* 29–62

Hatzopoulos, M. B. (1982a) 'Dates of Philip II's reign', *Philip, Alexander the Great and the Macedonian Heritage* (ed. W. L. Adams and E. N. Borza, Washington), 32–42

(1982b) 'A reconsideration of the Pixodarus Affair', *Macedonia and Greece in Late Classical and Early Hellenistic Times* (Studies in the History of Art 10, Washington), 59–66

Heckel, W. (1975) 'Amyntas son of Andromenes', *GRBS* 16: 393–8

(1977a) 'The conspiracy against Philotas', *Phoenix* 31: 9–21

(1977b) 'The flight of Harpalus and Tauriskos', *CPh.* 72: 133–5

(1979) 'Philip II, Kleopatra and Karanos', *RFIC* 107: 384–93

(1980) 'Alexander at the Persian Gates', *Athenaeum* 58: 168–74

(1981) 'Some speculations on the prosopography of the Alexanderreich', *LCM* 6: 63–9

Heisserer, A. J. (1980) *Alexander the Great and the Greeks of Asia Minor.* Norman, Oklahoma

Hellenkemper, H. (1984) 'Das wiedergefundene Issos', *Aus dem Osten des Alexanderreiches* (ed. J. Ozols and V. Thewalt, Köln) 43–50

Herrmann, P. (1965) 'Antiochos der Grosse und Teos', *Anadolu* 9: 29–160

Herzfeld, E. (1908) 'Pasargadae', *Klio* 8: 20–5

(1968) *The Persian Empire.* Wiesbaden

Higgins, W. E. (1980) 'Aspects of Alexander's imperial administration: some modern methods and views reviewed', *Athenaeum* 58: 129–52

Hogarth, D. G. (1887) 'The deification of Alexander the Great', *EHR* 2: 317–29

Högemann, P. (1985) *Alexander der Grosse und Arabien* (Zetemata 82). Munich

Hornblower, J. (1981) *Hieronymus of Cardia.* Oxford

Hornblower, S. (1982) *Mausolus.* Oxford

Instinsky, H. U. (1949) *Alexander der Grosse am Hellespont.* Godesberg

(1961) 'Alexander, Pindar, Euripides', *Historia* 10: 250–5

Jähne, A. (1981) 'Die 'Αλεξανδρέων χώρα', *Klio* 63: 63–103

Janke, A. (1904) *Auf Alexanders des Grossen Pfaden. Eine Reise durch Kleinasien.* Berlin

(1910) 'Die Schlacht bei Issos', *Klio* 10: 137–77

Jaschinski, S. (1981) *Alexander und Griechenland unter dem Eindruck der Flucht des Harpalos* (Habelts Dissertationsdrucke, Reihe alte Geschichte 14). Bonn

Jeppesen, K. (1960) 'A royal message to Ikaros: the Hellenistic temples of Failakā', *KUML*: 174–87

Jones, T. B. (1935) 'Alexander and the winter of 330/20 B.C.', *CW* 28: 124–5

Jouguet, P. (1940) 'La date Alexandrine de la fondation d' Alexandrie', *REA* 42: 192–7

Judeich, W. (1908) 'Die Schlacht am Granikos', *Klio* 8: 372–97

Kaiser, W. B. (1962) 'Ein Meister der Glyptik aus dem Umkreis Alexanders', *JDAI* 77: 227–39

Kienast, D. (1965) 'Alexander und der Ganges', *Historia* 124: 180–8

308    Bibliography

Kienitz, F. K. (1953) *Die politische Geschichte Ägyptens*. Berlin
Kingsley, B. M. (1986) 'Harpalos in the Megarid and the grain shipments from Cyrene', *ZPE* 66: 165–77
Koenen, L. (1977) *Eine agonistische Inschrift aus Ägypten und frühptolemäische Königsfeste* (Beiträge zur klassischen Philologie 56). Meisenheim am Glan
Kraft, K. (1971) *Der 'rationale' Alexander* (Frankfurter Althistorische Studien 5) Kallmünz
Lambrick, H. T. (1964) *Sind: a General Introduction*. Hyderabad
Lammert, F. (1953) 'Alexanders Verwundung in der Stadt der Maller und die damalige Heilkunde', *Gymnasium* 60: 1–7
Lane Fox, R. (1973) *Alexander the Great*. London
Leuze, O. (1935) *Die Satrapieneinteilung in Syrien und in Zweistromland von 520–320* (Schriften der Königsberger Gelehrten Gesellschaft; Geisteswiss. Kl 11). Halle
Lévy, I. (1913) 'Sérapis', *Revue de l'histoire des réligions* 67: 308–17
Lewis, D. M. (1955) 'Notes on Attic Inscriptions II', *ABSA* 50: 1–36
    (1959) 'Law on the Lesser Panathenaia', *Hesperia* 28: 239–47
    (1969) 'Two days', *CR* 19: 271–2
    (1977) *Sparta and Persia* (Cincinnati Classical Studies 1). Leiden
Lock, R. A. (1977a) 'The Macedonian Army Assembly in the time of Alexander the Great', *CPh.* 72: 91–107
    (1977b) 'The origins of the Argyraspids', *Historia* 26: 373–8
McQueen, E. J. (1978) 'Some notes on the anti-Macedonian movement in the Peloponnese in 331 B.C.', *Historia* 27: 40–64
Markianos, S. S. (1969) 'A note on the administration of Lycurgus', *GRBS* 10: 325–31
Markle, M. M. (1977) 'The Macedonian Sarissa, spear and related armour', *AJA* 81: 323–39
    (1978) 'Use of the Macedonian Sarissa by Philip and Alexander of Macedon', *AJA* 82: 483–97
    (1980) 'Weapons from the cemetery at Vergina and Alexander's army', Μέγας Ἀλέξανδρος: 2300 χρόνια ἀπὸ τὸν θάνατον τοῦ (Thessaloniki) 243–67
    (1982) 'Macedonian arms and tactics under Alexander the Great', *Macedonia and Greece in Late Classical and Early Hellenistic Times* (Studies in the History of Art 10, Washington) 87–111
Marquart, J. (1907) 'Untersuchungen zur Geschichte von Eran', *Philologus* Suppl. 10: 1–258
Marsden, E. W. (1964) *The Campaign of Gaugamela*. Liverpool
    (1969–71) *Greek and Roman Artillery*. I. *Historical Development*. II. *Technical Treatises*. Oxford
    (1977) 'Macedonian military machinery and its designers under Philip and Alexander', *Ancient Macedonia* 2 (Thessaloniki): 211–23
Marshall, J. H. (1951) *Taxila* I–III. Cambridge
Martin, T. R. (1982) 'A phantom fragment of Theopompus and Philip II's first campaign in Thessaly', *HSCP* 86: 55–78
    (1985) *Sovereignty and Coinage in Classical Greece*. Princeton
Martin, V. (1959) 'Un recueil de diatribes cyniques: Pap. Genev. inv. 271', *MH* 16: 77–115
Mehl, A. (1980/81) 'Δορίκτητος χώρα: kritische Bemerkungen zum "Speererwerb"

in Politik und Völkerrecht der hellenistischen Epoche', *Ancient Society* 11/12: 173–212

Mendels, D. (1984) 'Aetolia 331–301: frustration, political power and survival', *Historia* 33: 129–80

Mensching, E. (1963) 'Peripatetiker über Alexander', *Historia* 12: 274–82

Meritt, B. D. (1952) 'Greek inscriptions', *Hesperia* 21: 340–80
  (1960) 'Greek inscriptions', *Hesperia* 29: 1–27

Merkelbach, R. (1977) *Die Quellen der griechischen Alexanderromans* (Zetemata 9). 2nd ed. Munich

Merker, L. (1964) 'Notes on Abdalonymus and the dated coins of Sidon and Ake', *ANSMN* 11: 113–20

Merlan, P. (1950) 'Alexander the Great or Antiphon the Sophist?', *CPh.* 45: 161–6
  (1954) 'Isocrates, Aristotle and Alexander the Great', *Historia* 3: 60–81

Metzger, H., Laroche, E. and Dupont-Sommer, A. (1974) 'La stèle trilingue récemment découverte au Létôon de Xanthos', *CRAI* 82–93, 115–25, 132–49

Meyer, E. (1910) *Kleine Schriften zur Geschichtstheorie und zur wirtschaftlichen und politischen Geschichte des Altertums*. Halle
  (1927) 'Alexander und der Ganges', *Klio* 21: 183–91

Michailov, G. (1961) 'La Thrace au IVe et IIIe siècles avant notre ère', *Athenaeum* 39: 33–44

Mikrogiannakis, E. I. (1969) αἱ μεταξὺ Ἀλεξάνδρου Γ καὶ Δαρείου Γ διπλωματικαὶ ἐπαφαί. Athens

Milns, R. D. (1966a) 'Alexander's Macedonian cavalry and Diodorus XVII.17.4', *JHS* 86: 167–8
  (1966b) 'Alexander's seventh phalanx battalion', *GRBS* 7: 159–66
  (1968) *Alexander the Great*. London
  (1971) 'The hypaspists of Alexander III: some problems', *Historia* 20: 186–95
  (1976) 'The army of Alexander the Great', *Entretiens Hardt* 22: 87–136
  (1981) '"ΑΣΘΙΠΠΟΙ" again', *CQ* 31: 347–54

Mitchel, F. W. (1962) 'Demades of Paeania and *IG* II². 1413/4/5', *TAPA* 95: 213–29
  (1965) 'Athens in the Age of Alexander', *Greece & Rome* 12: 189–204
  (1970) *Lykourgan Athens: 338–322* (lectures in memory of Louise Semple Taft, 2nd series). Cincinnati
  (1975) 'The so-called earliest ephebic inscription', *ZPE* 19: 233–43

Mørkholm, O. (1978) 'The Alexander coinage of Nicocles of Paphos', *Chiron* 8: 135–47

Mughal, M. R. (1967) 'Excavations at Tulamba, West Pakistan', *Pakistan Archaeology* 4: 1–152

Murison, J. A. (1972) 'Darius III and the battle of Issus', *Historia* 21: 399–423

Neubert, M. (1934) 'Alexanders des Grossen Balkanzug', *Petermanns Mitteilungen* 80: 281–9

Newell, E. T. (1916) *The Dated Alexander Coinage of Sidon and Ake*. New Haven

Niese, B. (1893) *Geschichte der griechischen und makedonischen Staaten seit der Schlacht bei Chaeronea*. Gotha

Nodelman, S. A. (1960) 'A preliminary history of Characene', *Berytus* 13: 83–121

Olmstead, H. T. (1948) *A History of the Persian Empire*. Chicago

Osborne, M. J. (1979) 'Kallias, Phaidros and the revolt of Athens in 287 B.C.', *ZPE* 35: 181–94

Ostwald, M. (1955) 'The Athenian legislation against tyranny and subversion', *TAPA* 86: 103–28

Papavastru, J. (1936) *Amphipolis (Klio Beih. 37)*. Leipzig

Papazoglou, F. (1977) *The Central Balkan Tribes in Pre-Roman Times*. Amsterdam

Parke, H. W. (1933) *Greek Mercenary Soldiers*. Oxford

(1967) *The Oracles of Zeus*. Oxford

(1985) 'The massacre of the Branchidae', *JHS* 105: 59–68

Parker, R. A. and Černy, J. (1962) *A Saite Oracle Papyrus from Thebes*. Brown Egyptological Studies 4. Providence, RI

Parsons, P. J. (1979) 'The burial of Philip II', *AJAH* 4: 97–101

Pearson, L. (1954–5) 'The diary and the letters of Alexander the Great', *Historia* 3: 429–39

(1960) *The Lost Histories of Alexander the Great* (Philological Monographs 20). New York

Pédech, P. (1958) 'Deux campagnes d' Antiochus III chez Polybe', *REA* 60: 67–81

(1984) *Historiens compagnons d' Alexandre*. Paris

Picard, G. and C. (1964) 'Hercule et Melqart', *Hommages à J. Bayet* (Collection Latomus 70, Paris) 569–78

Pistorius, H. (1913) *Beiträge zur Geschichte von Lesbos im 4 Jahrh. v. Chr.* Jena

Prag, A. J. N. W., Musgrave, J. H. and Neave, R. A. H. (1984) 'The skull from Tomb II at Vergina: King Philip II of Macedon', *JHS* 104: 60–78

Prestiannini Giallombardo, A. M. (1973–4) 'Aspetti giuridici e problemi cronologici della reggenza di Filippo II di Macedonia', *Helikon* 13/14: 191–209

Price, M. J. (1982) 'Alexander's reform of the Macedonian regal coinage', *NC* 142: 180–90

Radet, G. (1931) *Alexandre le Grand*. Paris

(1932) 'La dernière campagne d' Alexandre contre Darius', *Mélanges Glotz* (Paris) 2: 765–78

(1935) 'Alexandre et Porus: le passage de l' Hydaspe', *REA* 37: 349–56

(1938) 'Explorations Indo-Iraniennes', *REA* 40: 421–32

(1941) 'Les colonies macédoniennes de l' Hydaspe', *REA* 43: 33–40

Rahe, P. A. (1981) 'The annihilation of the Sacred Band at Chaeronea', *AJA* 85: 84–7

Reinmuth, O. (1971) *The Ephebic Inscriptions of the Fourth Century B.C. (Mnemosyne* Suppl. 14). Leiden

Renard, M. and Servais, J. (1955) 'À propos du mariage d' Alexandre et de Roxane', *ACl.* 24: 29–50

Rhodes, P. J. (1972) *The Athenian Boule*. Oxford

(1981) *A Commentary on the Aristotelian Athenaion Politeia*. Oxford.

Ritter, H. W. (1965) *Diadem und Königsherrschaft* (Vestigia 7). Munich

Robert, L. (1962) *Villes d' Asie Mineure*. 2nd ed. Paris

(1975) 'Une nouvelle inscription grecque de Sardes', *CRAI*: 306–30

Robinson, C. A. (1957) 'The extraordinary ideas of Alexander the Great', *AHR* 62: 326–44

Roisman, J. (1984) 'Ptolemy and his rivals in his history of Alexander the Great', *CQ* 34: 373–85

Rosen, K. (1978) 'Der "göttliche" Alexander, Athen und Samos', *Historia* 27: 20–39

Roueché, C. and Sherwin-White, S. (1985) 'Some aspects of the Seleucid Empire: the Greek inscriptions from Falaika, in the Arabian Gulf', *Chiron* 15: 1–39

Rubin, B. (1955) 'Die Entstehung der Kataphraktenreiterei im Lichte der chorezmischen Ausgrabungen', *Historia* 4: 264–83

Rumpf, A. (1962) 'Zum Alexander Mosaik', *MDAI(A)* 77: 229–41

Ruschenbusch, E. (1979) 'Die soziale Herkunft der Epheben um 330', *ZPE* 35: 173–6

Rutz, W. (1965) 'Zur Erzählungskunst des Q. Curtius Rufus', *Hermes* 93: 370–82

Sachs, A. (1977) 'Achaemenid royal names in Babylonian astronomical texts', *AJAH* 2: 129–47

Sachs, A. J. (1955) *Late Babylonian Astronomical and Related Texts*. Rhode Island

Sacks, K. S. (1976) 'Herodotus and the dating of the battle of Thermopylae', *CQ* 26: 232–48

de Ste Croix, G. E. M. (1972) *The Origins of the Peloponnesian War*. London

Salviat, F. (1958) 'Une nouvelle loi Thasienne: institutions judiciaires et fêtes réligieuses à la fin du IVᵉ siècle av. J.C.', *BCH* 82: 193–267

Samuel, A. E. (1962) *Ptolemaic Chronology* (Münchener Beiträge zur Papyrusforschung und Rechtsgeschichte 43). Munich

(1965) 'Alexander's royal journals', *Historia* 14: 1–12

Schachermeyr, F. (1954) 'Die letzte Pläne Alexanders', *JÖAI* 41: 118–40

(1955) 'Alexander und die Ganges-Länder', *Innsbrucker Beiträge zur Kulturgeschichte* 3: 123–35

(1970) *Alexander in Babylon und die Reichsordnung nach seinem Tode* (Sitzb. Vienna 268.3). Vienna

(1973) *Alexander der Grosse: das Problem seiner Persönlichkeit und seines Wirkens* (Sitzb. Vienna 285). Vienna

Schefold, K. (1968) *Der Alexander-Sarkophag*. Berlin

Schehl, F. (1932) 'Zum Korinthischen Bund vom Jahre 338/37 v. Chr.', *JÖAI* 27: 115–45

Schier, T. (1909) 'Zur Lage des Schlachtfeldes von Issos und des Pinaros', *WS* 31: 153–68

Schiwek, H. (1962) 'Der persische Golf als Schiffahrts– und Seehandelsroute', *BJ* 162: 4–97

Schmidt, E. F. (1953–70) *Persepolis* I–III. Chicago

Schmidt, L. (1959) 'Der gordische Knoten und seine Lösung', *Antaios* 1: 305–18

Schmitt, J.-M. (1974) 'Les premières tétrères à Athènes', *REA* 87: 80–90

Schmitthenner, W. (1968) 'Über eine Formveränderung der Monarchie seit Alexander d. Grossen', *Saeculum* 19: 31–46

Schwartz, J. (1948) 'Les conquérants perses et la littérature égyptienne', *BIFAO* 48: 65–80

von Schwarz, F. (1906) *Alexanders des Grossen Feldzüge in Turkestan*. 2nd ed. Stuttgart

Schwarzenberg, E. von (1967) 'Der lysippische Alexander', *BJ* 167: 58–118

(1976) 'The portraiture of Alexander', *Entretiens Hardt* 22: 223–78

Sealey, R. (1960) 'The Olympic festival of 324 B.C.', *CR* 10: 185–6

(1967) *Essays in Greek Politics*. New York

Seibert, J. (1969) *Untersuchungen zur Geschichte Ptolemaios' I* (Münchener Beiträge zur Papyrusforschung und antiken Rechtsgeschichte 56). Munich

(1972a) *Alexander der Grosse* (Erträge der Forschung 10). Darmstadt

(1972b) 'Nochmals zu Kleomenes von Naukratis', *Chiron* 2: 99–102

(1983) *Das Zeitalter der Diadochen* (Erträge der Forschung 185). Darmstadt

(1985) *Die Eroberung des Perserreiches durch Alexander dem Grossen auf kartographischer Grundlage* (Beihefte zum Tübinger Atlas des Vorderen Orients: Reihe B, Nr. 68). Wiesbaden

Seton-Williams, M. V. (1954) 'Cilician Survey', *Anatolian Studies* 4: 121–74

Shapiro, H. A. (1983–4) 'Heros Theos: the death and apotheosis of Heracles', *CW* 77: 7–18

Shear, T. L. (1978) *Kallias of Sphettos and the Revolt of Athens in 286 B.C.* (*Hesperia* Suppl. 17). Princeton

Sherwin-White, S. M. (1985) 'Ancient archives: the Alexander Edict', *JHS* 105: 69–89

Snead, R. E. (1966) *Physical Geography Reconnaissance: Las Bela Coastal Plain, W. Pakistan*. Baton Rouge

Sordi, M. (1965) 'Alessandro e i Romani', *Rend. dell. Ist. Lombardo* (Classe di lett. e sc. mor. e stor.) 99: 445–52.

von Stahl, A. (1924) 'Notes on the march of Alexander the Great from Ecbatana to Hyrcania', *Geogr. J.* 64: 312–29

Standish, J. F. (1970) 'The Caspian Gates', *Greece & Rome* 17: 17–24

Stein, A. (1929) *On Alexander's Track to the Indus*. London

(1931) *An Archaeological Tour in Gedrosia* (Mem. Arch. Survey of India 43). Calcutta

(1932) 'The site of Alexander's passage of the Hydaspes and the battle with Porus', *Geogr. J.* 80: 31–46

(1937) *Archaeological Reconnaissances in North-West India and South-East Iran*. London

(1940) *Old Routes of Western Iran*. London

(1942) 'Notes on Alexander's crossing of the Tigris and the battle of Arbela', *Geogr. J.* 100: 155–64

(1943) 'On Alexander's route into Gedrosia. An archaeological tour in Las Bela', *Geogr. J.* 102: 193–227

Steindorff, G. (1904) *Durch die libysche Wüste zur Amonsoase*. Bielefeld

Strasburger, H. (1982) *Studien zur Alten Geschichte* (ed. W. Schmitthenner and R. Zoepffel). Hildesheim

von Straten, F. T. (1974) 'Did the Greeks kneel before their gods?', *Bulletin Antieke Beschaving* 49: 159–89

Stronach, D. (1978) *Pasargadae*. Oxford

Stroud, R. S. (1984) 'An Argive decree from Nemea concerning Aspendos', *Hesperia* 53: 193–216

Sutton, D. F. (1980) *The Greek Satyr Play* (Beiträge zur klass. Philologie 90). Meisenheim am Glan

Taeger, F. (1951) 'Alexander der grosse und die Anfänge des hellenistischen Herrenkultes', *HZ* 172: 225–44

(1957) *Charisma. Studien zur Geschichte des antiken Herrscherkultes* I. Stuttgart

Tarn, W. W. (1948) *Alexander the Great* I–II. Cambridge

Tibiletti, G. (1954) 'Alessandro e la liberazione delle città d' Asia Minore', *Athenaeum* 32: 3–22

Tolstov, S. P. (1953) *Auf den Spuren der altchoresmischen Kultur*. Berlin

Tomaschek, W. (1890) 'Topographische Erläuterung der Küstenfahrt Nearchs bis zum Euphrat', *Sitzb. Vienna* 121 (9): 31–88

Tronson, A. (1984) 'Satyrus the Peripatetic and the marriages of Philip II', *JHS* 104: 116–26

Tscherikower, V. (1927) *Die hellenistische Städtegründungen von Alexander dem Grossen bis auf die Römerzeit (Philologus* Suppl. 19.1)

Unz, R. K. (1985) 'Alexander's brothers?', *JHS* 105: 171–4

Urban, R. (1981) 'Das Verbot innenpolitischer Umwälzungen durch den Korinthischen Bund (338/37) in antimakedonischer Argumentation', *Historia* 30: 11–21

Vogt, J. (1971) 'Kleomenes von Naukratis: Herr von Ägypten', *Chiron* 1: 153–7

Volkmann, H. (1975) *Endoxos Douleia. Kleine Schriften zur Alten Geschichte* (ed. H. Bellen). Berlin

Wankel, H. (1976) *Demosthenes' Rede für Ktesiphon über den Kranz.* Heidelberg

Weinreich, O. (1933) *Menekrates Zeus und Salmoneus* (Tübinger Beiträge zur Altertumswissenschaft 18). Stuttgart

Weippert, O. (1972) *Alexander-imitatio und römische Politik in republikanischer Zeit.* Augsburg

Welles, C. B. (1930) *Royal Correspondence in the Hellenistic Period.* London
(1962) 'The discovery of Sarapis and the foundation of Alexandria', *Historia* 11: 271–98
(1963) 'The reliability of Ptolemy as an historian', *Miscellanea di studi alessandri in memoria di A. Rostagni* (Turin) 101–16

Welwei, K. W. (1979) 'Der Kampf um das makedonische Lager bei Gaugamela', *Rh. Mus.* 122: 222–8

Wheeler, M. (1962) *Charsadda: a Metropolis of the North-west Frontier.* Oxford
(1968) *Flames over Persepolis.* New York

Wilcken, U. (1894) 'Ὑπομνηματισμοί', *Philologus* 53: 84–126
(1917) 'Beiträge zur Geschichte des Korinthischen Bundes', *Sitzb. Munich*, Abh. 10.
(1922–37) *Urkunden der Ptolemäerzeit.* Berlin
(1967) *Alexander the Great* (with preface, notes and bibliography by E. N. Borza). New York
(1970) *Berliner Akademieschriften zur alten Geschichte und Papyruskunde* (1883–1942). Leipzig

Wilhelmy, H. (1966) 'Der "wandernde" Strom: Studien zur Talgeschichte des Indus', *Erdkunde* 20: 265–76
(1968a) 'Indusdelta und Rann of Kutch', *Erdkunde* 22: 177–91
(1968b) 'Verschollene Städe im Indusdelta', *Geogr. Zeitschrift.* 56: 156–94
(1969) 'Das Urstromtal am Ostrand der Indusebene und das Sarasvati-Problem', *Zeitschrift für Geomorphologie* Suppl. 8: 76–93

Will, W. (1982) 'Zur Datierung der Rede Ps.-Demosthenes XVII', *Rh. Mus.* 125: 202–13
(1983) *Athen und Alexander* (Münchener Beiträge zur Papyrusforschung und Rechtsgeschichte 77). Munich

Wirth, G. (1971) 'Dareios und Alexander', *Chiron* 1: 133–52
(1972) 'Die συντάξεις von Kleinasien 334 v. Chr.', *Chiron* 2: 91–8
(1977) 'Erwägungen zur Chronologie des Jahres 333 v. Chr.', *Helikon* 17: 23–55
(1980–1) 'Zwei Lager bei Gaugamela', *Quaderni Catanesi di Studi Classici e Medievali* 2: 51–100; 3: 5–61
(1984) 'Zu einer Schweigenden Mehrheit. Alexander und die griechischen Söldner', *Aus dem Osten des Alexanderreiches* (ed. J. Ozols and V. Thewalt, Köln) 9–31

(1985) *Studien zur Alexandergeschichte*. Darmstadt

Woodward, A. M. (1962) 'Athens and the oracle of Ammon', *ABSA* 57: 5–13

Worthington, I. (1984) 'The first flight of Harpalus reconsidered', *Greece & Rome* 31: 161–9

Wüst, F. R. (1953–4a) 'Die Rede Alexanders des Grossen in Opis', *Historia* 2: 177–88

(1953–4b) 'Die Meuterei von Opis', *Historia* 2: 418–31

(1959) 'Zu den Hypomnematen Alexanders: das Grabmal Hephaistions', *JÖAI* 44: 147–57

Zervos, O. H. (1982) 'Notes on a book by Gerhard Kleiner', *NC* 142: 166–79

# Index